The Deer Book

Edited by LAMAR UNDERWOOD

Foreword by
JOHN MADSON
Drawings
by AL BARKER

The Amwell Press
CLINTON, NEW JERSEY
1980

Library of Congress Catalog Card Number 80-69536
Published November 1980
Printed in the United States of America.

First edition (limited to 1,000 copies)
Printed November, 1980

Second edition (trade hardbound)
Printed February, 1983

Third edition (trade hardbound)
Printed February, 1984

Fourth edition (trade hardbound)
Printed May, 1986

CONTENTS

FOUR: HUNTERS' TRACKS

FOREWORD

John Madson

IT WAS AT A CONFERENCE for "nature educators" in Minneapolis that the middle-aged teacher asked me: "Deer are such fascinating animals—why is it necessary to hunt them in order to enjoy them?"

I can't remember my reply. It was probably lame enough, for trying to explain deer hunting to a nonhunting schoolmarm is like trying to explain sex to a Chinese eunuch. But it jarred me into thinking instead of just feeling.

An often-used justification for hunting deer is that we're doing the deer a great favor by killing them. This is unacceptable to most non-hunters and it's not hard to understand why. We weaken our position as hunters when we rationalize our hunting as a clinical act of deer population control. I doubt if any man honestly feels he is hunting deer for the deer's own good. The man is hunting deer for *his* own good, and if certain benefits accrue to the herd as a result, so much the better.

Well, I don't think I need to justify my act of hunting to any non-hunting educator, although I may owe her some proof that my hunting does not endanger her interests—or those of the deer. No, I doubt if we hunt deer to benefit the species or their range by trimming the herd. We hunt deer because we want to. So maybe the real question is not why we hunt deer, but rather why we enjoy it.

One of the most common reasons, I suppose, is the *meat reason.* The woods are full of guys who claim to be hunting for prime meat, although I've a hunch this is the standard alibi for busting the first deer that comes along. Still, there are some real meat hunters—men who can judge venison on the hoof, who have the patience and experience to pick and choose, and who take infinite pride in the quality of their venison. There are still some old hands who will pass up a real whangdoodle buck for a plump little yearling—although they are often experienced hunters who've already taken their share of whangdoodle bucks.

This leads us into the *trophy reason.*

Aldo Leopold wrote: "Poets sing and hunters scale the mountains for one and the same reason—to thrill to beauty. Critics write and hunters outwit their game primarily for one and the same reason—to reduce that beauty to possession."

Those trophy antlers on the wall are not only the man's effort to possess beauty, but also to keep something important to him from slipping away and being lost and forgotten. And if the trophy testifies to the world that here is a strong and skillful hunter—well, why deny it? And so the great stag is stalked and taken. And although the hunter may drip with modesty and seem reluctant to speak, it's not hard to wring his story out of him. The hard part is turning him off.

Ten thousand years ago that hunter would have stood by a fire and recounted the great deed to his clan brothers, while the old men nodded their approval and the stripling boys back in the shadows listened in wonder. It hasn't changed much. The trophy hunter, the ethical killer of the great stag or great bear, still commands attention by the fire as he recites his deeds. His peers still salute him; the old men still nod and remember, and young boys dream of tomorrow's hunts.

The days of the great trophies are not past; there are still great stags lurking in cedar swamps and along the ridges even though most of us will never shoot them. Yet, we've all taken deer that held special trophy value for us—and such value isn't always the measure of tine and beam. It may be just a measure of hard, solid hunting in which both you and the deer conducted yourselves well, so that neither was shamed. Trophy hunting has been bitterly condemned of late, but it can be worthy if the hunter is ethical and if he knows the best antlers are grown only in good habitat and then works to support such habitat even if it sometimes means the hunting of antlerless deer.

Companionship is a strong element in deer hunting. For as long as man has hunted, he has done so in organized packs with special taboos, traditions and rituals. There's that, and many other reasons as well.

One is the fact that the deer is the ultimate game in most states, where it is the biggest, wariest and most prized of all wildlife. But more than anything else, the greatest urge of the genuine deer hunter is his search for freedom, and for the genuine personal adventure that's the hallmark of such freedom. Whatever it is that motivates men to hunt is distilled in deer hunting. Such hunting embodies the essence of hunting, for deer embody the essence of quality freedom within quality environments. The genuine deer hunter is probably as free as modern man can be in this technocracy of ours. Free not because he sheds civilized codes and restraints when he goes into the woods, reverting to an animal, but free because he can project himself out of and beyond himself, out of and beyond the ordinary, and be wholly absorbed in a quieter, deeper and older world.

You know how it is. You go into the woods and your presence makes a splash, and the ripples of your arrival spread like circles in water. Long after you have stopped moving, your presence widens in rings through the woods. But after a while this fades and the pool of forest silence is tranquil again, and you are either forgotten or accepted—you are never sure which. Your presence has been absorbed into the pattern of the woods. You have begun to be part of things. This is when the hunting really begins.

You can always feel it when the circles stop widening. You can feel it in the back of your neck and in your gut, and in the awareness of other presences. This is when a man starts to hunt, and he always knows when it happens and when he is beginning to hunt well.

Such things are important to the man; they may be even more important to the boy.

There were those times when I was a kid, hunting and trapping and sometimes spending several days and nights alone in the woods, when I'd have a flash of insight that was usually gone as swiftly as it came—the vaguest feeling of how aboriginal hunters must feel, and what real hunting, pure-quill, honest-to-God *real* hunting, is all about. One strong flash of this to a boy—one swift heady taste of this utter wild freedom and perception—is enough to keep him hunting all his days. Not just for meat or horns, but hunting for that flash of insight again, trying to close the magic circle of man, wilderness and deer.

I don't know where else today a boy can really get this sort of thing. I doubt if team sports or speed or drugs will bring it. No, it's more likely to come when the boy is alone, in some deer swamp or turkey woods—hunting on his own and as free as he may ever be.

And why didn't that occur to me when the teacher asked her question?

Our critics sometimes say: "We could condone hunting if the hunter were hungry. But the modern hunter is not hungry; he simply kills for the joy of killing."

Nonsense. Of course deer hunters are hungry. We all hunt deer because we are hungry. The question is, hungry for what? Meat? Glory? Freedom? Personal proof? I contend that the genuine deer hunter (as opposed to the synthetic deer hunter, which is another case entirely) hunts to satisfy hungers just as sharp as the belly-hunger of Neolithic man. He is not killing for the joy of killing; he is hunting for the joy of living.

And how about "personal proof" as a motive for hunting? Does a man prove himself by killing a deer? Of course not. The mere act of killing a deer proves nothing. It may not even prove that a man can really shoot. If there is any proof of a man in a hunt, it's not whether he has killed a deer but how he has hunted it.

For the best deer hunts are not really contests between man and deer, but between man and nature. The man does not compete with just the deer, but with his own growling belly and freezing feet, with weakness, loneliness, impatience, discouragement, and the growing desire to quit. If a man can overcome these things he has won an important contest with himself. And maybe the prize for winning that contest is a deer—and maybe not. So does a man prove he's *muy hombre* just by killing a deer? I doubt it. But at its best, the hunt can mean that a man has met some ancient tests that still wear true. He has used brain and spirit to rise above ignorance and weakness—and if that isn't proof of something worth having, then fifty thousand generations of hunters have been wrong.

To some people, of course, it proves only that the hunter is a rather dangerous barbarian whose actions clash with civilized values. And there is some truth in this, though not in the sense that our critics mean.

James Fenimore Cooper, who wrote a lot about the woods, was deeply concerned over the tragic clash between wilderness and civilization. He observed that the wilderness had one set of values which should be preserved, while civilization had certain values which might be brought into the wilderness but which usually destroy it. This may be the greatest single challenge to modern America: to preserve the intrinsic values of wildlands while enjoying the benefits of urban culture.

The genuine deer hunter is among the men best equipped to do this, for he has one foot in the woods and the other in town. More than most men, and certainly more than almost all his critics, he understands the value of both places.

It was over a century ago that Cooper lamented the impact of civilization on wilderness. But at the same time, without knowing it, he was writing about the breed of man who would someday cushion that impact—the figure that literary historians have since called "the ideal man in the state of nature," and which James Fenimore Cooper simply called "The Deerslayer."

INTRODUCTION

LONG BEFORE DAYLIGHT, a deer hunter turned his car off a graveled road and eased slowly along a rough lane. He swung into a clearing and killed the motor. The cold air biting sharply at his lungs, he shouldered his pack, picked up his rifle and headed across the field. The frozen ground was easy to walk on. Overhead a thick smudge of clouds hid the stars and any trace of the moon. Food. If strong moonlight had been showing, or if snow covered the ground, the deer would likely move out to feed during the middle of the night and bed down in some thicket before dawn. In the darkness of this night, however, they would probably wait for some trace of dawn before easing out to browse.

At the edge of some high trees, he found the semblance of a path and followed it down through a parklike forest. Eventually, the beam of his flashlight played across a tall oak with a light gash in the trunk. This was the spot. He sat down with his back against the tree, facing down the slope toward the forest and waited for the dawn, his heart pounding with excitement.

He had discovered this spot two weeks before while combing the countryside in search of a perfect place from which to ambush a buck. Here, he had found plenty of deer sign—droppings and tracks—and once during the early morning and again during the late afternoon he had seen nice bucks and several does on the slope beside the fields.

Now he was back on opening morning. His equipment was excellent—warm clothing and good rifle. He was comfortable and had sandwiches and coffee to last the day. All the experts had stressed this style of hunting as being very effective. "Find an area deer use; then sit very still and wait 'em out," they said. Now he was ready. He waited for his chance—and waited—and waited.

I know the details of that hunt well—not only because I was the guy who did the waiting but also because I played the same script over so many times. Things began to improve only after I woke up to the fact that there are more ingredients to venison stew than a few hours' wait on an old deer trail.

This winter, plenty of freezers from New York to California will be stuffed with deer meat collected by lucky ribbon clerks who wouldn't know a deer track from a bear track but who happened to have a buck shoved into their sights by sheer fortune. Everyone draws a good hand sometime. But you can bet your best rifle that more steaks (and the finest trophies) will be toted home by guys who did everything they could to stack the cards against the deer.

They will use many methods. On the rim of a western canyon, a hunter will glass a distant slope, then commence a careful stalk through the low brush. On an old tote road deep in a Michigan pine forest, another hopeful will be walking as though he were stepping on eggs when the brush ahead will suddenly explode as a buck rips from his bed. Good techniques all—under certain conditions.

My own adventures in these styles of hunting, in which one moves around in search of game, have resulted in zero action. The areas I hunt are handy to several eastern and midwestern megalopolises. Only in the deepest mountains have I been able to explore more than a mile or so of country before spotting some other red-coated wanderer. Not wanting to get my name into the newspaper (Underwood . . . suddenly, by 30.30.), I gave up the technique for the less unnerving and, I hoped, more productive method of waiting for the game to come to me.

But I found no immediate reward. Only after compiling a catalog of mistakes did I begin to score with any consistency.

Take the hunt I described at the beginning of this piece. My preparations failed to take into account an absolutely critical factor. As I had walked through the woods that morning, my feeling of solitude had been an illusion. Not too far away, at other spots along the same stretch of woods, car doors were slamming and other hunters were spilling into the forest. Worse yet, many arrived late, at dawn or after, and not all shared my passion for stand hunting. Many hoped to spot bucks by walking through the bottoms and along the ridges.

If you think any self-respecting whitetail is going to commit suicide in this kind of invasion, you have another empty hunt coming. The normal feeding and movement patterns that I had observed during my pre-season scouting (and to which I had geared my hunt by placing my stand close to the fields) were completely disrupted. Any bucks easing from their favorite bedding and hiding haunts would have sneaked deep into the cover by dawn or shortly after.

Although I did not see another hunter from my stand, my suspicions that competitors were working the general area were confirmed by the occasional shot that boomed through the hills and by the clusters of cars I saw parked on nearby lanes and roads as I drove away that evening.

This was typical of many of the locations where I did my hunting. Some areas were actually worse, since the forests were open to roads and lanes on both sides. As the next season approached, I decided to try a new method to cope with the situation.

During my pre-season scouting trips, I again concentrated on finding areas deer were using—but this time went one step further. Instead of being satisfied with the sight of game and the evidence that an area was being heavily frequented, I pushed deeper into the forests to seek out the swamps and thickets where the animals might take cover when spooked. Some hard work went into the project, as I slogged through wet swamps and briar-tangled thickets. But by opening morning I had several good spots to choose from.

I was afield much earlier than usual, a flashlight's beam showing me the way through the tangle of cover. Well before daylight, I was comfortably settled with my back against a tall white pine that overlooked a thicket of low saplings. The entire spot was the only high ground in an alder spot that paralleled the run of a tiny creek.

The first flush of dawn washed thinly over the forest. Birds began to call and dart through the bushes. Overhead, squirrels chattered and jumped across the limbs. Far off an owl called, and a flock of crows began to complain. The air was filled with sound and movement, and I enjoyed a ringside seat at my favorite show in hunting—a new day beginning.

Suddenly, I caught the faint sound of leaves rustling. Half expecting to see a squirrel running on the ground, I peered past the scattered bushes toward the gentle rise that marked the boundary of the creek bottom and beginning of the hardwood timber. At first, nothing. Then magically, almost wraithlike, a buck eased into view, slinking toward the pine thicket behind me. I centered the iron sights on his chest and squeezed. The .257 bucked sharply.

The animal lunged forward in what seemed like a tremendous leap. I worked the bolt furiously, slamming it home as the buck crashed in a heap at the edge of the creek.

The taking of that buck, a delicious four-pointer, was particularly satisfying—not merely because I had scored, but because the event was the culmination of the strategy that I had evolved from my previous failures. I felt I was becoming a *deer hunter*—not just a hopeful who happened to luck into a good shot.

In putting this book together, I've learned that my own deer-hunting experiences, while more or less typical for the average eastern hunter, merely skim the surface of the rich pool of hunting adventure offered by deer hunting in all its forms. The sport is as varied in hunting styles as the terrain which is its setting, and the hunter who does not pause to listen to the observations and experiences of his brethren of the stand and the stalk is automatically limiting his enjoyment.

The gentlemen in the pages ahead know deer and deer hunting, of course, but they also have that precious knack of sharing what they have seen and learned with words that are engaging and fun to read. Whether your deer trails are in a moss-draped swamp or in the wind-blown crags of the high country, here in this book you will make new friends, and what they have to say will become both a part of your own lore and your own memories.

Perhaps deer hunting epitomizes the very soul of hunting in our country because it stirs the ancient ashes of pioneering and the skills needed for survival. I shall leave that one for the sages to ponder. For me, the deer camp and the deer woods are where I want to be because they're a great animal to hunt and eat and because my buddies will be there.

But one week out of fifty-two just isn't enough for me. I look to good books to stretch my season. That's why I put this one together: For all those who feel the same as I do about the sport and want a book that reflects their interest and dedication to it.

If you're like me, you're probably reading this one in front of the fire, when the day's or week's work is finished and the toddy has been poured and you're ready to let your mind slip away for a while to other days, other hunts.

Your companions in the pages ahead will be men you will like—that I promise.

ACKNOWLEDGMENTS

Coward-McCann, Inc.: "White Deer Are Bad Luck," by Arthur R. MacDougall, Jr., originally appeared in *Where Flows the Kennebec* by Arthur R. MacDougall, Jr., published in 1947.

Outdoor Life magazine originally published "Three Men and a Buck," by William A. Miles. The following stories originally appeared in *Outdoor Life* magazine and later in *Outdoor Life's Deer Hunting Book,* published by Outdoor Life and Harper and Row in 1974: "The Arizona Coues Deer," by Jack O'Connor, "Day of Stealth and Grappling," by Ken Crandall, "Mississippi Backwoods Buck," by Charles Elliott, "Northwestern Whitetail Trophy," by Jack O'Connor, "Finding Wounded Deer," by Ray Beck. "The Secret Life of the Cottontail Deer," by John Madson, originally appeared in *Outdoor Life* magazine and later in the book of Madson stories, *Out Home,* published by Winchester Press. "Palace in the Popple" also appeared in *Out Home.* "Portrait of the Whitetail Deer" and "Portrait of the Mule Deer," by Jack O'Connor, originally appeared in *The Big Game Animals of North America,* by Jack O'Connor, published by Outdoor Life. "The Whitetail Challenge," by Lew Dietz, originally appeared in *Yankee* magazine and later in *Outdoor Life* magazine.

The Stackpole Company, Harrisburg, Pennsylvania: "You've Got to Suffer," by Gordon MacQuarrie, is from the book *Stories of the Old Duck Hunters and Other Drivel,* edited by Zack Taylor and published in 1967. "Making the Drive," by Francis E. Sell, is from *The American Deer Hunter,* by Francis E. Sell, published by the Stackpole Company in 1950.

Amwell Press, Inc., Clinton, New Jersey: "Stalking Snow," by Walt Sandberg, is from the collection of Sandberg stories, *The Turn in the Trail,* published in 1980. "First Buck," by James C. Rikhoff, originally appeared in *Field and Stream* magazine and was later included in an anthology of Rikhoff stories, *Mixed Bag,* published by Amwell Press in 1979. "Truthful Sam," by Charley Dickey, was originally published in *Petersen's Hunting*

Magazine and in the book, *Backtrack,* published by Amwell Press in 1977.

Alfred A. Knopf, New York: "Woodcraft and Whitetails" and "Still-Hunting the Whitetail," by Lawrence R. Koller, are from the book, *Shots at Whitetails,* published in 1948. "The Swamp Buck," by Sigurd F. Olson is from *The Runes of the North* by Sigurd F. Olson, published by Alfred A. Knopf in 1963.

The Whitetail Press, Duxbury, Vermont: "Sign the Trophy Buck Leaves," and "On the Track," by Larry Benoit with Peter Miller, originally appeared in the book, *How to Bag the Biggest Buck of Your Life.*

Doubleday and Co., Inc., New York: "Jake's Rangers Hunt the Whitetail," by Edmund Ware Smith, appeared originally in *Field and Stream* magazine and later in the anthology, *Jake's Rangers* published by Doubleday. "The Lady in Green," by Archibald Rutledge, originally appeared in *Hunter's Choice,* published by Doubleday. "That Christmas Buck," by Archibald Rutledge, appeared originally in *Plantation Game Trails,* published by Doubleday.

Winchester Press, New York: "Great Morning," by Gene Hill, originally appeared in *Sports Afield,* then in the collection of Gene Hill stories, *Mostly Tailfeathers.* "Deer Rifles—East and West," by John Jobson, originally appeared in *Sports Afield* magazine, and "Big Bucks in the Big Woods," by Jerome B. Robinson, also appeared originally in *Sports Afield* magazine.

Henry Holt and Company, New York: "Mister Howard Was a Real Gent," by Robert C. Ruark, originally appeared in *Field and Stream* magazine and later in the collection, *The Old Man and the Boy,* published in 1953. "Old King Pin," by Harry H. Sheldon, was originally published in *Field and Stream* magazine and in the book *Field and Stream Treasury,* edited by Hugh Grey and Ross McCluskey and published by Henry Holt in 1955.

Charles Scribner's Sons, New York: "Hunting the Mule Deer," by Theodore Roosevelt, originally appeared in *Outdoor Pastimes of An American Hunter* published by Scribner's in 1905.

Holt, Rinehart and Winston, New York: "Whitetails Along the Border," by Warren Page, was originally published in *Field and*

Stream magazine and then in *One Man's Wilderness,* by Warren Page, published in 1973.

David McKay Company, Inc., New York: "The Old and the New" and "I Don't Want to Kill a Deer," by Ted Trueblood, originally appeared in *Field and Stream* magazine and later in the book *The Ted Trueblood Hunting Treasury,* published in 1978.

Random House, New York: "Race at Morning," by William Faulkner, originally appeared in *The Saturday Evening Post* magazine and then in *Big Woods* by William Faulkner.

Derrydale Press, New York: "Lost," by Burton L. Spiller appeared originally in *Firelight* by Burton L. Spiller.

A. S. Barnes and Company, New York: "The Clearing Buck," by John S. Martin, originally appeared in *Field and Stream* magazine and in the anthology *Outdoors Unlimited,* edited by J. Hammond Brown, published in 1947.

The Ridge Press, Inc. and the American Broadcasting Company, New York: "The World of the Whitetail Deer," by Angus Cameron was originally published in *The American Sportsman,* copyright, 1967.

ONE

The Challenge and the Prize

THE WORLD OF THE WHITETAIL
Angus Cameron

The man who opens The Deer Book *with this engaging portrait of America's favorite game animal is one of those multi-talented individuals who makes a success of every project he turns to.*

A superb woodsman, hunter and angler, Angus Cameron spent a good part of his professional life at the Alfred E. Knopf Publishing Company in New York as an editor specializing in the outdoor field. Working with prominent writers like Jack O'Connor, Russell Annabel, Sigurd Olson, Ray Bergman, and Harmon Helmricks, Angus produced many of the most outstanding hunting and fishing books published during the past forty years.

He retired from the position in 1979 to devote himself full time to his other passion: writing.

This piece from The American Sportsman, *that beautiful hard-cover magazine of the sixties that did not survive the tough economic realities of modern publishing, shows the Cameron form in full fig—writing crisply, informatively and with great depth of knowledge.*

Angus once became so fed up with the New York scene that he and his wife Sheila spent a several-year sojourn at a cabin deep in the Alaska wilderness. Good thing for us readers that he didn't strike gold and give up the craft that produces great pieces like this.

THE WHITETAIL DEER lives in fascinating country and he is surrounded by most engaging neighbors. For the observant, *interested* hunter, an intimate knowledge of those woods and animals is almost as rewarding as the stalk itself. He sees and feels himself to be not simply a deadly interloper, but an integral part of the life of the forest. His own role in the vital balance of nature becomes clearer to him.

Deer woods often seem untenanted, especially in the fall when their bird life is scanty and their mammals are mostly nocturnal. Yet there is always much for the careful hunter to see. If he hunts as he should, spending more time watching than traveling, he'll not only see more deer, but more of everything else. Squirrels, chipmunks, mice, and voles are most visible, but once the hunter attunes himself to watch for the little private dramas in the ro-

] 3 [

dents' lives, he'll see uncommon creatures, too. If he hunts in a true wilderness, or if he canoes the stream-lake chains to get to his hunting areas, he may occasionally see exotic animals as well as common ones.

Whether the late John Alden Knight's "Solunar" theory accounts for the phenomenon or not, there is some factor that periodically controls or, at least, strongly influences the activity of birds and mammals. Observant hunters often have encountered "dead woods"—that curious autumnal period when all seems lifeless. Nothing moves. The leafless trees stand mute. No bird calls. Even the squirrels are silent. The hunter feels utterly isolated. His very animate, sentient nature seems out of place. If ever the deer hunter should feel encouraged to move around, rather than stand or sit, this is the time, for the deer seem as scarce in these dead periods as their fellow creatures.

These spells of inactivity may come at any time of the day. Often the morning hours are the silent ones. On other days the afternoon is blank and still. Eventually the mood changes, and when it does it is exciting to observe, for the woods come to life suddenly. Perhaps one hears a jay or nuthatch; then a red squirrel may be seen scurrying along a log. The woods seem to stir, to release their hidden potential motion. Downy woodpeckers dart from tree to tree; the nervous siskin begins his seedy search. The hunter senses a change even in himself; his presence will be discovered by a keen-eyed squirrel that churrs and barks at the unwelcome intrusion.

Now is the time for the hunter-naturalist to make hay. Now the creatures of the woods fill him with expectation, for when they show signs of activity, hope is justified that whitetail may be present, too.

A deer hunter's day should begin before sunup. He should be on his way to watch a likely runway in the first light, while the hunting owls are still awing. If he's lucky he may see the blunt-headed, great horned owl fly away on mothlike wings, silent as a shadow. Sometimes he will flush one of these night hunters watching his own runway in a snowshrouded alder bottom. He may even hear the clatter of wings against dry twigs and see the

] 4 [

snow flurry from the disturbed branches as the dark figure accents itself against the white-gray monochrome of morning light. The curious hunter should mark the perch and later examine the ground beneath it for one of the pellets owls disgorge to rid themselves of the fur, feathers, and bones of their victims. These tightly packed, feltlike pellets give clues to the owl's diet and his success as a hunter; the skulls of mice, birds, and shrews; the bones and feathers of grouse, jays, and other birds; the fur and bones of the snowshoe rabbit; and sometimes the black, shiny fur of the skunk. Once in the wintry, dark green gloom of an Ontario spruce swamp I saw where an owl had killed and eaten a skunk on the snow. The skunk, whose only defense does not daunt the great

horned owl, had been seized just a few feet from where his shredded remains were found. The sweep of the owl's wing primaries could be traced in the soft snow, revealing how the silent hunter had mantled his victim, propping and bracing himself with his five-foot wingspread while he tightened his grip and drove his talons into the victim's chest cavity. The skunk had thrown his scent, but to no avail. He had waddled a few feet in a half circle of desperation, carrying his nemesis, and had soon succumbed.

The chipmunk is one of the more diverting of all the woodsy creatures. When the beechnuts are in plenty, this little fellow becomes a tireless worker, scurrying from his neat and smoothly rounded burrow entrance to the sources of supply. The observer who singles out individual animals to watch will soon discover that the chipmunk's foraging area is surprisingly small, as little as ten yards square. Once I watched the activity of an open beech hillside for an hour and a half. On occasions there were as many as two dozen foragers in view at the same time. One, which had a den near the base of a white pine quite close to my own position, collected beechnuts assiduously for forty minutes, his contours changing with each busy trip. When he returned to the smooth-edged hole his cheek pouches swelled with nuts; when he re-emerged he had lost his mumpsy look. Once he perched on a nearby stump to preen himself. Then, to my surprise, he wiggled his nose and produced a beechnut he had held out from storage and ate it daintily, extracting the meat with tiny, practiced nips of his chisel-edged incisors.

On one occasion as I watched a gleaming chipmunk forage for fallen beechnuts, I noticed that the tree under which he gathered was a beech whose top had died. While the chipmunk filled his pouches on the ground, a blue jay scurried back and forth on a branch, picking the nuts that had not exploded from their burrs and catching them with hammerlike strokes in the niche where the branch grew from the tree. That same tree showed black, three-lined scars where in some past autumn the black bear had left his claw marks as he climbed to feed on the fat and abundant nuts. The trunk's upper surface, the dead area, was pocked with the huge, oval holes made by a great pileated woodpecker that had found in the beech's deadened pith a source of delectable ants.

The most charming companion of the November woods is surely the chickadee. When he and his fellows first announce themselves, they seem to be deployed as skirmishers, making their way by infiltration, and "dee-deeing" in animated conversation. When the lively company has passed on, it leaves the woods a little lonely. Sometimes kinglets join these bands, and occasionally the nuthatch. But the chickadee is most welcome at the noon tea fire. A gleaner of crumbs, he comes close with nervous courage, sometimes venturing onto one's sleeve or shoulder if one remains motionless, with just the right feeling of approachability. One can almost will friendliness to which the little bird invariably responds.

Noon tea provides one of the hunter's finest moments. That quick, hot little fire is a prime refresher. Produced from kindling of fat pine, split and then resplit from stumpy remnants of an old burn, it cheerfully divides a hard day into two easier parts. A green poplar pole is cut and trimmed, the heavy end shoved into the dirt, and propped and weighted with two stones, so the blackened tea bucket will hang nicely just over the flames. A scoop of fresh water from lake, spring, or brook, and the hunter settles down on the windward side to escape the smoke and to nudge fresh sticks in and around the pail's bottom to keep the fire hot and hasten the boiling. A sandwich or two and a tin cup with its handle wrapped in string to reduce the heat on his fingers are set out handy to a plastic container holding the tea leaves. While the water comes to a boil, he takes a jackknife and cuts an alder branch, leaving a small snag untrimmed at the butt end. When the water bubbles this tea stick catches the tea pail's bail and lifts it off to receive the brown leaves. Then, ceremoniously, he holds the pail over the flames to toll it a second or two. Then a dash of cold water reserved in a tin cup to settle the leaves and the tea is ready. Plenty of tea should go into that pail to give it strength and color, lest the guide should say, "Hell, a man could see to spear eels in thirty feet of that!"

Unlike the chickadee, who always seems a guest at these noon repasts, the Canada jay, or whisky-jack, as he is somehow properly nicknamed, comes not as a guest but as a panhandler. One always feels conned by these well-tailored gray and black birds, but few can resist tossing out a piece of sandwich meat or a crust of surplus bread. Often the jay will perch in a dead spruce stub high overhead and cock his head this way and that for signs of provender. Nothing escapes his black beady eye, and once he has spotted a morsel he sets his wings and glides to the food in an accurate and purposeful motion, seizes his portion and flies away, as often as not to cache the offering and return for another.

The evening grosbeak and the rose-breasted grosbeak add a

touch of color to the chilly grayness of the deer hunter's woods, but the raven accents their somber quality. This great bird, whose call is more often a silvery, bell-over-water sound than the croak so often associated with it, appears to me as a kind of gloomy deacon. His great size and ragtag scruffy neck feathers give him the wonderful down-at-the-heels look of a Dickens character. His black hat and his tattered scarf make him seem dressed for the winter that will follow. "Tuloo-ak," he says, in a kind of falsetto register, a single comment with a pessimistic tone that belies its curiously musical quality. It's a lucky deer watcher who sees and hears the raven.

The deer hunter's woods can seem quite depressing at first, but it is a passing emotion, for one knows that, in spite of the coming cold, the frost-covered leaves soon to be mantled in deep snow, the winter woods house creatures who successfully make their livings despite the desolation. The dark reaches of hemlock and spruce, the unrelieved grays and blacks of the leafless hardwoods and shrubs, the wet deadness of the leaves—these things are skindeep only. Every rotting blow-down, the leafy mold, the musty earth itself shelter a myriad of creatures from the mouse to the hibernating insect. The fall woods of the deer hunter are throbbing habitats; only the surface seems lifeless.

The bewildering variety of trees, shrubs, grasses, and flowering plants that presses in upon the hunter is a world of its own, but it is also the deer's world, indeed his very livelihood. A man ought to have some respect for these things—for their own sake and because knowing about them can make a man a better hunter. It is an indignity offered to living things if one can't name them. But there is a practical reason for the hunter to know plants, for his success can depend on his ability to see what deer are feeding on. Scuffed leaves, dark and wet on the underside turned up by a pawing deer, can often show feeding areas in beech woods. The clipped twig ends of the red or striped maple, always a favorite food, can also show the observant hunter a feeding area—if he can identify his maples. The bracken fern, like everything else in the deer's habitat, relates to both deer and hunter. In woods covered with early snow a casual observer can see torn fronds greenly decorating the patches churned by the deer's searching hooves. It is good for the soul—and for the chase—to know these revealing things.

A small Bausch & Lomb engraver's glass is a fine item for the deer hunter's shirt pocket. With it he can extend his appreciation of his sport enormously. If he is a traveler, he may use the glass seldom, but if he sits as much as he walks (as he should), he can explore the miniature, as well as the larger, natural world around him. I remember once becoming restive with curiosity about a nuthatch's pertinacious exploration of a maple trunk a few feet from a deer stand I was watching. I feared to move, for my hunting partner was still hunting a ridge toward my runway and my position was a likely one. The nuthatch, in that crazy up-side-down style of his, busily probed the bark, adding to my growing tension. Finally, when my friend's head showed above the ridge-top and I thought he had moved away, I hunkered down to examine with my glass the crevices under the bark's corrugation and found the tiny pear-shaped eggs of the insect that had provided the nuthatch with his protein. The nuthatch, always a deer hunter's neighbor, also finds hibernating adult insects in his tireless search. Considering the millions of these tiny, animate bits of fat that lie dormant in the winter woods, it is no wonder the nuthatch need not migrate. The nuthatch is fascinating to watch, but sometimes he has another function for the deer hunter. Hugh Fosburgh, the novelist-naturalist, says he trusts the *rapid* "yank-yank" alarm call of this bird far more than he does the noisy shrieks of the blue jay or the nervous churr and bark of the red squirrel as an indicator of the presence of some other creature in the area. The slow, tin-horn call of the nuthatch means nothing, but the rapid nervous yanking often indicates a deer in the vicinity.

The pocket glass also will reveal the beautiful abstraction of a birch bud's cross section, or the design of the vagrant snowflake, marvelous before it melts on the sleeve of your stag shirt. And it will transform a jay's feather, enabling you to see clearly the barbs of the shaft and to note how the barbules hook on to each other to hold the interlocking strands against the rushing air in flight. The little glass is an educational companion for the deer hunter; its extension of the hunter's world is limited only by the hunter's degree of imagination and industry.

The observant deer hunter will see a surprising variety of animals during a hunting career. For the fun of it, my wife and I made up lists of frequencies. My list included, in order, squirrel, chipmunk, mouse, rabbit, porcupine, muskrat, weasel, fox, otter, mink, beaver, skunk, raccoon, bear, shrew, bobcat, fisher. My wife, not surprisingly, listed the same animals, with slightly different frequencies of appearance.

Not only the forest but the campsite itself can provide a setting for nature's small dramas. Here, too, an observant hunter will see the life cycle of the forest in full chase.

Roy Smith's one-room camp, a reasonably roomy, peeled-cedar cabin, overlooked a gracefully descending, low and smooth rock slope to the water of the west bay of a lake called Horseshoe. It was surrounded by a few spruce and hemlock, firs and birches, and squatted comfortably with a low seemliness, as if a Frank Lloyd Wright had designed and planted it on the one spot where it belonged. Its low peaked roof had an overhang at the front to shield a man who might have to get into the breadbox nailed on the front wall or take down a tool on a mean, rainy day. The roof was made of corrugated metal, canoed and portaged in awkward sheets, but worth the trouble because it would be far better than tar paper in the long run. And, besides, it was bear-proof.

One night the Coleman gas lantern had finally blinked out its last diminishing light, but had given a respite of illumination between the turning off and the actual blackout. (That time is so brief it must be planned for. It is a tiny contest to wriggle quickly into one's sleeping bag and be settled in time to watch the extinction of the light.)

Silence came with the loss of light, broken only by the slow fizz of the dying fire in the wood range. In a matter of seconds, the darkness would bring out the white-footed mice that had gratefully moved in when we did to share our grub with us. Welcome though these little, large-eared beauties were as companions, they were troublesome, too (as when they left their tracks in the carelessly uncovered butter). We reduced their numbers with back-breaker traps baited with butter and oatmeal, and were careful to set our mink traps at a distance from the cabin, so as not to catch the camp weasel who invariably showed up after a day or two to take advantage of the fine mouse supply. In the dying light of evening, I often watched his camera-shutter movements as he raced in and out of the spaces of the woodpile. Sometimes we'd hear his hunts in the cabin after dark. A wild, noisy, scrambling race and a high, abruptly stopped squeak of the little victim invariably told the tale. There would be silence again, then more tiny furry scurryings of the rummaging mice, and soon, when the weasel had cached his first mouse somewhere outside the camp, he'd return and take another. The camp weasel was better as a mouse hunter than we were as mice trappers.

Night sounds came from outside the cabin as well, and one cold, wet November we had a barred owl for a neighbor. We'd hear his muffled hoots, and though an owl's hoots have a curious quality that makes them hard to locate, we could tell from the volume that he was close. Finally one evening in the weak gray light, I flushed the round-headed bird as I hurried toward the warm cabin from the chilly discomfort of the log outhouse. All I saw was the level, flat trajectory of the gliding owl as he picked his way through the hemlock stand.

So, the influx of mice in our camp had beckoned a second mouser. Sad to say, once the owl took up residence near us, we lost the services of the camp weasel. Though the white-foot supply seemed inexhaustible, the weasel's visits ceased and I concluded that probably the slim, swift, four-footed mouser had been picked up by the winged one.

In the evenings, after we had returned from the trap line or from the day's hunt, I began to search out this owl's feeding roosts and from a lucky discovery of his pellets I located one perch, at least, in a big hemlock a hundred yards back in the bush from the cabin. I spotted him fairly regularly during that three weeks' period, usually perched on a limb halfway up and quite close to the bole of the hemlock, but often I found him tucked away on a spruce limb where he suffered me to observe him. This owl appeared a most mild-mannered bird when perched, seemingly little disturbed by my pokings about and persistent observations. When sometimes he flushed, he displayed a light buoyant flight. He slipped his way among the trunks and saplings with a delicacy that was most pleasing for such a big bird, for the barred owl is fully crow-sized.

One night as I lay on the top bunk in the silent, pitch-dark camp I heard a dull thump on the corrugated roof directly above my head and not three feet away. The creature was undoubtedly a flying squirrel that had glided to a noisy landing on the roof from some higher limb that had served him as a launching pad. I listened a moment to the scratchy bumpings and scurryings of the squirrel. Suddenly there was only silence, and as suddenly a soft brush of wings on the metal surface. Instantly there was a loud, anguished squeal from the squirrel. I held my breath and listened for further evidence of the little tragedy out there in the dark, but the owl had evidently plucked the flatbodied squirrel from the roof and made off without a formal landing. I lay there scarcely daring to breathe, for the closeness of the drama had raised my own hackles. As I dozed off, I visualized "my" barred owl perched on a limb of his feeding station beheading the hapless flying squirrel. The owl was a hunter, too.

Hunting is a way of understanding the natural world we live in by participating in that world. In the hunt one becomes a part of the life process that the hunter and the hunted daily and nightly reenact. There are psychic relationships involved here that arise out of these natural processes, and a hunter senses them by participation in the chase. It is said by some that this participation brutalizes, but of that I am very doubtful. As my then-eight-year-old daughter once said from the half-darkness of her bunk in Roy Smith's Ontario trapping shack: "You know, even though Roy kills animals and traps them, he is still the best animal-lover I ever knew." The little girl had sensed the same thing that had caused my wife and me to return there fall after fall to live the hunting and trapping life with a man whose relationship to the wilds was surpassingly simple and at the same time infinitely complicated.

When Roy spoke of otters he used a kind of folk terminology.

He always referred to "The Otter" or "The Mink" and no matter how often the stories ended in the tragedy of death by some predator or accident, the creature lived on, timeless and inextinguishable. Roy Smith took a crop off the wilderness every fall, but the species, himself included, persisted and reenacted their dramatic ways, generation after generation.

"Why is it," asked my fifteen-year-old son the year we introduced our children to Roy and his world, "that game you yourself have shot, skinned, packed in, butchered, cooked in crude utensils, and eaten on a plank table covered with scratched oilcloth tastes so much better?" One can say that the reason lies in the extra hunger one feels from hard exertion, or that this feeling shared by most hunters is a sentimental rationalization. One can say that, but it will not be true. Living the hunting life, absorbed in the world of the hunter and the hunted, is a special kind of experience. Hunting is a natural pursuit; it is deeply ingrained in men (and women), but it is hidden only skin-deep. What hunter has not seen most unlikely men who have gone on a first hunting trip, for business reasons, perhaps, suddenly respond to the profound urge to hunt, in a manner that surprises themselves most of all?

The "other rewards" of hunting, the communion with and participation in nature, to put it blandly, are not at all unconnected with the pursuit and killing and eating of game. They are not static pleasures of nature observation; rather they are integral to the hunting act itself, a not-unnatural need of the psyche of man.

The relationship between nature, game, and hunting man has nowhere been more penetratingly analyzed than by Paul Shepard, Jr., a professor of biology at Smith College. In a paper read before the twenty-fourth North American Wildlife Conference in 1959, Shepard observed: "If the real value of hunting is to get a hearing, its spokesmen must insist on greater perspective by all concerned. The essential point must clearly be understood to turn on a broader philosophy of man in nature. Opposition to hunting for sport has its accusing finger in the morality of the act of killing. The answer is not a matter of forming the admission that we are all human, bipedal, carnivorous mammals, damned to kill, but consists in showing through anthropology, history, and the arts that the superb human mind operates in subtle ways in the search for an equilibrium between the polarities of nature and God. To share in life is to participate in a traffic of energy and materials, the ultimate origin of which is a mystery, but which has its immediate source in the bodies of plants and other animals. As a society, we may be in danger of losing sight of this. It is kept most vividly before us in hunting."

The reason why my young daughter recognized the trapper, Roy Smith, as an animal-lover, and why my son found the eating of game a special delight, and why a closely observing relationship with the deer woods is important is found in the last two paragraphs of Shepard's paper. "It follows," he wrote, "that hunting is not, as even hunters sometimes claim, just an excuse to get out of doors, to which killing is incidental. Killing and eating the prey are the most important things that hunters do. The successful hunt is a solemn event, and yet it is done in a spirit of joy. It puts modern man for a moment in vital rapport with the universe from which civilization tends to separate him in an illusion of superiority and independence. The natural environment will always be mysterious, evoking an awe to be shared among all men who take the trouble to see it. . . .

"Regardless of technological advance, man remains part of and dependent on nature. The necessity of signifying and recognizing this relationship remains. The hunter is our agent of awareness. He is not only an observer, but a participant and receiver. He knows that man is a member of the natural community and that the processes of nature will never become so well understood that faith will cease to be important."

PORTRAIT OF THE MULE DEER

Jack O'Connor

He's gone now, but before he passed away suddenly in 1978, Jack O'Connor produced a body of work unparalleled in hunting and sporting firearm literature—both in volume and reader appreciation.

Jack wrote more books, and sold more copies of those works, than any outdoor writer ever. His magazine articles in Outdoor Life *played the leading role in making that publication the number one newsstand seller of sporting magazines during O'Connor's entire career there.*

My personal relationship with Jack began late in his life, but I was extremely fortunate to share several dove hunts with him in the company of Jim Rikhoff—founder of Amwell Press—and writer Gene Hill.

In his introduction to the Amwell Press limited edition, The Best of Jack O'Connor, *Jim wrote eloquently of the man with whom he had shared hunts and campfires for many years around the world and, most importantly, two final sheep hunts in the Canadian Northwest. Later, after Jack's death, he modified that introduction and added a new ending for a memorial in his monthly column, "Mixed Bag," for* The American Rifleman:

"Very few men are legends in their own lifetimes, which is probably a pretty good thing when one considers the possible consequences of too many egos abroad at one time. A lot of people think they are legends, but very few are genuine bonafide "living legends," and even fewer are nice about it. Jack O'Connor, who died a year ago this month, was one of the rare last ones.

It's taken me that year to sit down at this typewriter and write an obituary on Jack. And now that I'm at it, I guess I'll have to admit that this short, inadequate piece isn't going to be any sort of a conventional obituary. When Jack had his first and last heart attack on board a cruise ship coming back from Hawaii last winter, he was working on his last book. Yes, I mean the last book he intended to write, not just "last" because death made that decision for him. That book will be his definitive memorial because it is something different from anything he ever wrote.

I knew Jack for some twenty years. We hunted quite a number of states and a couple of Canadian Provinces. We also hunted Mexico, Scotland, Spain and Italy—sometimes even with a little success. We always planned to take an African safari together but somehow the years passed and we never did. While Jack hunted the world over—from Alaska to Zambia— his primary identification was always with his native Arizona and the Southwest, including, very significantly, Northern Mexico. He was an expert on African safaris and Indian shikars, but old timers and young whippersnappers alike still picture Jack's familiar Hibernian mug peering through wirerimmed glasses out from under an old beat-up cowboy hat. And well it should be for, regardless of all his world travel and sophisticated cultural and educational achievements, he remained the quintessential Southwestern hunter.

Few of his fans knew that Jack served in both the United States Army and Navy for some years at the tail-end of World War I, including a memorable stint as a 15-year-old, obviously under-age, private in the Arizona National Guard, activated as the 158th Infantry. He was known as "Cactus Jack, the Ass-less Wonder"—a description, I might add, that remained incredibly apt right up to the end. (One recalls an historic occasion a few years back when Winchester took the gun writers to Italy to view their new ammunition plant; on the way over we were standing in the plane's aisle discussing ballistics when a stewardess had to go by Jack, who promptly pulled in his stomach to allow this pleasant passage and found to his dismay that his pants fell down).

Perhaps Jack was most closely identified with his many years (starting in 1937) with *Outdoor Life,* primarily as Arms and Ammunition Editor from 1941 until his retirement from that position in 1972. He stayed on as Hunting Editor after his retirement until 1973, when he grew weary of changing editorial policy and took his talent and prestige to Petersen. He still contributed a full feature article every month right up and past his death, because he always stayed well ahead on his assignments, something his editors cherished.

Jack died just two days short of his seventy-sixth birthday; strangely, his old rival-friend, Warren Page, the long-time shooting editor of *Field & Stream,* had died on Jack's seventy-fifth birthday the year before. Jack and I were hunting sheep together in the Cassiar range of British Columbia and the Pellys of the Yukon when he was in his early seventies. We both took a stone sheep in the Cassiars, but Jack never fired his gun in the Yukon on what was to be our last hunt together, which I think now we both knew.

We were with a brand new outfit, Teslin Outfitters, who had just taken over a country that had not been hunted for six years. They also had not had a chance to do much more than put in an excellent base camp on Francis Lake, so when we took off from there with our pack string, we were really striking out into new country. It was just as if we were old mountain men pushing around that next bend, through that next stream, over that last ridge. Jack was exhilarated. After a day or two on the trail, as we made camp at dusk, he told me that of all the places he had hunted—from Africa to India and beyond—he guessed that he loved the high country of the Northwest the best.

We pressed on for five days and saw no game. Finally even the last rudimentary man-made trails petered out and we followed increasingly narrow and steep game paths. There were so many blowdowns and so much buck brush that we had to get down off our horses and cut our way through. It soon became obvious that Jack, partially crippled from a bad automobile accident years before and circulatory problems from plain old age, couldn't make it any further in that country.

He insisted that we make a camp by a stream in the open and that I go on with one guide while he remained with the rest. I went off and a couple of days later took a sheep. We returned and Jack was overjoyed. We had made the trip a success—for myself obviously, but also for Teslin's first hunt and

lastly for him on what he knew might be his last trip to his beloved high country. We packed up and headed back and once
almost got another sheep for Jack. He didn't care about not
getting the shot, but seemed strangely content to be once more
on horseback, with friends, in another country, with a river to
cross and maybe some trees to rest under.

I have no doubt that he has found those trees."

In this, the first of four O'Connor pieces in The Deer Book, *Jack portrays the mule deer, the West's most popular big game animal. The piece is
from the book* Big Game Animals of North America, *published by*
Outdoor Life.

WHENEVER anyone assures me that all mule deer are morons, I
think of the first really big buck I ever shot. I knew of a chain of
hills where early in the season I had always seen a good many
does, fawns, and young bucks. One year I turned down easy shots
at two or three perfectly legal males, knowing that late in the season a big fellow would probably show up to boot out the small
bucks and take over the harem.

So it came about that one afternoon when the Arizona season
had only a couple of days to go, and when every morning white
frost glinted on the grass and the brooks up in the mountains were
frozen at the edges, I hit my little chain of hills again. By taking a
game trail up the side of a wide canyon I had an easy walk to the
top. When I got there I planned to work along the ridge and hunt
the points and the heads of the draws.

I hardly started up the trail when I saw a movement in the
buckbrush and junipers about 400 yards ahead of me and toward
the top of the ridge. It was a doe. Then I saw more shadowy gray
forms, and I could tell that about a dozen deer were going over
the top. Then a larger form detached itself from the group and
sneaked off to the left. Even at a quarter of a mile or so I could see
a big gray body and heavy, many-pointed antlers. Here was the
buck I had been looking for, the old boy himself. He had collected
his harem and chased the young bucks out, but now that danger
threatened he was abandoning the ladies and looking after his
own sleek hide.

] 18 [

I felt that he'd cut over the ridge into the head of the next draw. So the moment he was out of sight, I ran over the ridge that separated the two canyons and stopped in a spot that gave me a good look at the far side. I hadn't got my wind back when I heard a stone roll, and in a moment I saw him slipping through the scrubby junipers and pinons with his head up and his great antlers laid back so they would get through the brush easier. If he kept on coming he would go by me on the opposite side of the draw, so I switched off the safety of my Springfield and waited.

It was the first time I'd ever been close to a really big trophy buck, and I'll never forget the sight he presented—the blocky, dark-gray body, the heavy brown antlers with the many points polished sharp and bright, the massive neck swelled from the rut, the maniacal look of lust and excitement in his eyes. I had the wind on him and I could smell the oily rancid odor of the rutting mule deer, a smell at once fascinating and repellent, heavy, musky, greasy. He saw the movement when I lifted the rifle to my shoulder, and stopped less than 50 yards away. Winded, and shaking with excitement though I was, I couldn't very well miss him. There was nothing wrong with that buck's brains. In the grip of the strongest of instincts, he was yet smart enough and cool-headed enough to leave his does as decoys and try to slip out to one side and around the danger.

The mule deer is no boob, but I must admit that he generally isn't as smart as his cousin the whitetail, or as hard to get. Part of this comes from the fact that he is more of an open-country animal and hence is easier to see and hunt. But part of it also comes from the fact that he does not lie as close, that he takes longer to make up his mind, and that he often is addicted to the fatal habit of stopping for one last look before he gets out of sight.

A whitetail will conceal himself in a patch of brush hardly big enough to hide a pheasant. If he thinks he can't sneak off unseen, he'll sit tight with hunters all around him. When he thinks he has to move, he's off like a rocketing grouse and he doesn't stop for a backward look. The mule deer, on the other hand, has a tendency to move off and reveal himself in the face of danger, to jitter around, unable to decide which way to run, and to stop for one

] 19 [

good look. But old trophy bucks get cautious. They select their beds with care, and get almost as good as the whitetail is at slipping away from the hunter.

A very smart and close-lying buck mule deer I'll never forget was one I shot in northern Arizona in 1934. I had made a long trip to hunt an area I knew well, and I was after a trophy head. I turned down several small bucks and a couple of good average ones with four points to a side. About two p.m. of my last day I stopped on the brink of a canyon to eat a sandwich. I was still without a deer, and was kicking myself for passing up the two four-pointers. Below me I could see the trail that led to camp about five miles away. I was going to have to start back, pack up, and leave empty-handed.

After I finished my sandwich, I drank from my canteen, smoked a cigarette, and started to lead my horse down the side of the canyon which was too steep and rocky to ride down safely. I hadn't gone more than 30 yards when a tremendous buck got up from beneath a juniper below me about 300 yards away and took off. On my second or third shot he fell head over heels and lay in the scrubby sage. When I got to him I found he needed another shot. The bullet that dumped him had passed through the knee joint of his left front leg. He must have had most of his weight on this leg when it was struck, and the fall must have stunned him. He had seven points on one side, six on the other, and a spread of

] 20 [

34½ inches. A right fair buck. All the time he'd been lying there getting more and more nervous, and when I started toward him he must have thought he'd been seen. If I'd gone the other way, I'm sure I would never have known he was there. All mule deer aren't dumb.

The fact that they have adapted themselves to great varieties of climate and terrain also shows they have their share of brains. They are found from the Dakotas to the crest of the Coast Ranges, from the hot subtropical deserts of Sonora, Mexico, to the subarctic tundras of northern British Columbia. I have seen mule deer in country rough enough for mountain sheep and have, in fact, seen bighorns and deer feeding on the same hillside. I have likewise seen them in the cactus and brush on the level deserts of northern Mexico. When I was hunting antelope some years ago around Gillette, Wyoming, there were many mule deer in the brushy coulees where little streams wandered through the antelope plains. When they were frightened they'd take right off across the sagebrush flats with the antelope.

In most areas mule deer have increased enormously in the past thirty or forty years, so much so that they have starved on their winter range. They have invaded the suburbs in many Western cities, particularly in the winter when feed is scarce. In the north they have followed the Alaska Highway up into southern Yukon, where they have never been known before. So plentiful have the mule deer become in some states that in certain areas hunters have been able to take two, and even three, deer.

The mule deer got his Latin name of *hemionus* from his large ears, *hemionus* being the Latin word for mule. In general, the muley is a different breed of cat from his whitetail cousin. Instead of having the whitetail's large, floppy tail—generally body-colored on top and snow-white beneath—the mule deer has a small, thinly haired tail of dingy white with a black tip. He does not throw it up when frightened, as the whitetail does. He always keeps it hanging down. The tail of the muley's near relative, the Columbian blacktail, is about halfway in size between the small one of the mule deer and the large one flaunted by the whitetail. It is black on top, and instead of tossing it up when frightened, as

] 21 [

the whitetail does, he carries it horizontal. In many ways the blacktail looks like a compromise between the mule deer and the whitetail. It's an odd fact that in areas where both mule deer and whitetails range, one occasionally comes across bucks that look like Pacific Coast blacktails. They are crosses between whitetails and mule deer. I have never shot one, but I have seen several that were taken in southern Arizona and northern Sonora.

The mule deer has a strongly marked face with a dark V on the forehead and a light muzzle, as compared with the whitetail's fairly uniformly dark face. All the points of the whitetail's antlers come off of one main beam, but the antlers of the mule deer are evenly branched. The brow tine of the whitetail's antlers is always conspicuous and large, but that of the mule deer is smaller and sometimes absent altogether. Pacific Coast blacktail antlers look like those of mule deer, and both differ so much from those of the whitetail that it is almost impossible to confuse them. In the West the brow tine is not counted, and only the points on one antler are referred to. A four-pointer by Western count would be a ten-pointer in the East.

An odd thing about the facial markings of mule deer that I have never seen referred to in print is that the latitude from which the deer comes can pretty well be told by the black line around the lower jaw. In the northern portion of the range in Alberta and British Columbia, the black line goes completely around. Somewhat farther south the line is divided in the middle, and at the lower end of the range—in the deserts of southern Arizona and northern Mexico—the line has degenerated into two dark spots on either side of the lower jaw.

In favored localities mule deer grow tremendous antlers, and a fine muley head is one of the most beautiful of all North American trophies. These big heads are found wherever there is plenty of lime in the food and water. Colorado has produced many great heads, and so have the limestone ranges of Alberta. Many spectacular ones have come out of Arizona's Kaibab National Forest north of the Grand Canyon. I have not hunted there for many years, but I believe I have seen a higher proportion of exceptional heads there than anywhere else. I once measured a Kaibab head with a spread of 47½ inches and about 20 points to the side. Another region of fine heads that is little known is in Sonora south of the town of Altar, and I have seen some beauties from southern Idaho. In the 1971 edition of *Records of North American Big Game,* the world record typical mule deer head came from Alberta.

On average the mule deer is the largest of American deer, but many tales told of their size are on the giddy side. For the past forty years I have been following up rumors of bucks that are supposed to have field dressed at 400 pounds and more, but I have yet to find an authentic instance of one. Apparently the very largest mule deer and the heaviest northern whitetail from Maine and Michigan are about the same size, with dressed weight running something over 300 pounds and live weight at close to 400.

For many years all deer brought into the hunting camps of Arizona's Kaibab were weighed, and in years of good forage the heaviest bucks would weigh something over 300 pounds hog dressed. The largest bucks I have authentic weights on all go about like that, with records running from 300 to 335 pounds. I have heard of many bucks that weighed more, but when I investigated I found the weight was estimated. I have shot two bucks that went 175 and 176 pounds in the quarters (the four quarters weighed without skin, head, or entrails). One was shot northwest of Flagstaff, Arizona, and the other down in the Sonora desert. The Arizona buck had been hit in the ham as he ran away from me and I had cut away 10 or 12 pounds of bloodshot meat. How much would they have weighed field dressed? I don't know. They might have gone 250 pounds or so and well over 300 on the hoof.

I have only seen one buck I thought would weigh 300 pounds field dressed, and it was shot in exactly the same area: Slate Mountain northwest of Flagstaff, where I killed my heaviest Arizona buck. He was distinctly larger than any other buck I've ever seen. But anyone who gets a buck that weighs 175 pounds field dressed has a large one, and anyone who gets one that weighs 200 has a very large one. A Western game warden I know has weighed hundreds of mule deer and says he has never seen one that weighed more than 250 pounds dressed. I have yet to see a buck mule deer as large as a spike bull elk.

] 23 [

In most areas with which I'm familiar, the mule deer begin to show signs of the rut by the end of the first week in November, and by the middle of November most of the bucks have swelled necks and are starting to get interested in the does. The height of the rut for most Rocky Mountain mule deer is probably about the last week of November and the first week of December. Then each big buck collects as large a harem as he can and defends it from other bucks.

The desert mule deer of southern Arizona and northern Sonora are not well into the rut until about the middle of January, apparently a provision of nature for the does to be in milk during the summer rains. The old bucks have a grim time. Each will have from four to twelve does, and the bunch will move endlessly, restlessly. Hanging around the outskirts will be from two to four smaller bucks. Now and then when one of these approaches too closely, the big herd buck will chase it away. Occasionally one of the hangers-on will do battle, but generally they turn tail and run. On many occasions I have seen a small buck slip in and cover a doe while the lord of the harem was chasing off another one, but I have yet to see the big, heavy-horned bucks in the act of mating. I have a notion that most of the breeding is actually done by the young bucks, and that big fellows have all the responsibility and little else.

At the height of the rut the old buck is a sight awesome yet piteous, and at that time he's easily killed. He has a wild and desperate look in his eyes—as anyone would who had twelve wives ready to two-time him—and he looks gaunt and ragged. Generally he has a point or two broken off his antlers and skinned and bleeding places on his neck. The ones I've seen have always been running around with their mouths open as if they had difficulty in breathing, and I have had them go by me within 20 feet and pay no attention to me.

A Mexican cowboy I once knew was sitting on a hillside one January day brewing a can of coffee and heating up some tortillas when he saw a desert mule deer doe trot by about 50 yards away. A minute or so later a big buck, following her trail with his nose to the ground, came into sight. The vaquero had a little Winchester

Model 92 .25/20 carbine on his saddle. He unlimbered it and shot the buck in the neck. Before he could get to it a smaller buck came along on the trail. He shot that one and a moment later yet another—this an ardent little forkhorn. I went by his place a week afterward and he had jerky strung up everywhere.

Once the rut is over, the bucks leave the does and start putting some fat on their ribs. Sometimes one sees solitary bucks, but generally a couple will travel together, often a large buck and a small one. Occasionally before the rut I have seen several together, and one time near Slate Mountain I saw a herd of about thirty fine big bucks. But that was exceptional.

The gestation period of the mule deer is seven months, and in the Rocky Mountains the young are born in late May and early June. In the deserts, of course, they are born later. Young does generally give birth to single fawns, but mature does almost always have twins. In areas where food is plentiful and predators are not numerous, around 40 per cent of the deer should be taken annually if the herd is to be kept within the limits of its food supply.

Coyotes and bobcats take fawns, and some are even killed by golden eagles. But the greatest natural predator of the mule deer is the mountain lion. Every one of these big cats, the most skillful deer hunters in the world, will kill from 100 to 150 deer a year—a lot of deer. Compared with the incredibly stealthy mountain lion, man isn't a very good hunter.

One factor in the astonishing increase of mule deer throughout the West has been the thinning out of the lion population in certain areas. In Arizona's Kaibab, which for years was open to lion hunting but closed for deer, the explosion of the deer population came about because there were too few lions. The result was that tens of thousands of them starved to death and the range was permanently damaged. In the West today there are many problem deer areas because there is not only a shortage of lions but because the coyotes have been poisoned off.

As is the case with most other game meat, mule deer venison varies enormously with the time the deer was taken, his condition, the manner in which he was killed, and what he'd been eating. No deer taken during and right after the rut is much good to eat, and no deer is good if he's been wounded and chased all over the country before being dispatched. The deer of some localities produce fine venison and of others they do not. I think the answer lies in their food.

The desert mule deer of southern Arizona and northern Mexico (like the bighorn sheep and whitetails that occupy the same country) are almost always fine eating. The answer probably lies in what they eat—mild and nourishing plants like jojoba, mesquite beans, leaves of the ironwood, and cactus fruit. Some mule deer in the Southwest spend the entire year on the winter range, and without exception these are poor eating because of the bitter plants, such as juniper and quinine brush, they devour. Deer that have fattened on mild morsels such as aspen leaves, mushrooms, and piñon nuts are as good as the best beef. I have shot several deer on the Salmon River upstream from Riggins, Idaho, and I have yet to find one that furnished first-class venison. On the other hand, all the deer I have taken off the Snake River upstream from Lewiston, Idaho, would melt in your mouth.

One of the worst bucks I ever ate was a fine, fat three-year-old I took in the piñon-juniper belt in northern Arizona, and one of the most delicious was an old-timer I shot in the Kaibab. He was hog fat with 4 inches of lard on his rump, and I think I must have taken him right after he came down from the summer range where he'd been feasting on mushrooms and aspen leaves. He was blind in one eye, and so old I think he'd lost his interest in the gals. Although I shot him on Armistice Day—a time when the necks of most of the bucks were swelled and some of them were showing interest in the does—he gave no sign at all of the rut. His meat was so tender you could cut it with a fork. But once the rut has begun the venison is strong and musty.

Some of my most pleasant memories are of hunting mule deer. I have hunted them right at timber-line in the Rockies, where they can be glassed and stalked like sheep. On those lofty ridges right at the limit of trees it has been my experience that the deer are almost always bucks—generally big ones—as the does and young bucks like to summer lower where there is more cover. And

] 26 [

I have still-hunted them down in the flat deserts of Sonora so close to salt water that I could see the blue Gulf of California by climbing a little hill. It's a great joy to sneak quietly along upwind in the fresh, chilly hours of early morning watching through the cholla and palo verde for the glimpse of gray that means a deer. It is easy tracking country, and often I have taken up the fresh track of a buck as he fed along.

But some of the most interesting hunts I have ever had have been on horseback for the great bucks of Arizona's north Kaibab. I used to like to hit it late in the season after a snow on the summer range had pushed the big bucks down onto the semi-open winter range. It is easy riding country for the most part—wide, shallow draws and long ridges clothed with a scattering of junipers. A couple of horsemen riding down a ridge will usually push deer off the points. The action can be fast and furious when a big buck comes tearing across an open flat or trotting along a hillside flashing in and out of the junipers. That used to be a great deer country, and I presume it still is. Many times I've seen from ten to twenty big bucks in a day, and well over one hundred deer, and the man who could pass up the ordinary heads had a good chance of finding a trophy to be proud of.

Once a friend and I were hunting there on horseback when we saw a tremendous buck just going over a ridge. The footing was good for horses, so we dug in the spurs and went after it. We chased it over about three ridges, never having it in sight long enough to jump off and shoot. Then the buck (no dumbbell he) cut to the left up a draw and turned left again about 300 yards away in an effort to get into heavy timber. I jumped off my horse, grabbed my .30/06 out of the scabbard, swung ahead of him, and let drive. I saw him go down at the front quarters, and then he was out of sight.

We jumped on our horses again, took after him, and found him down. He looked not long for this world, but he was still breathing. Foolishly I decided to cut his throat. At the prick of the knife he came frantically alive. I dropped the knife and threw myself on his head, with a hand on each antler. The buck dragged me in a 50-yard circle, bumping me against every bush and tree around.

When he finally collapsed I was skinned, dusty, and covered with blood. From that time on I have never tried to dispatch another animal by attempting to cut its throat.

Because mule deer are usually found in open, hilly country, and because they tend to move out ahead of danger, they are generally shot at longer ranges than are whitetails. As I look back on fifty years of hunting them, I'd guess the average range at which I've shot muleys has been well over 200 yards—maybe 250. I have shot a good many at 300 or a little over, but doubt very much if I've ever shot more than one or two at 400. Those I have taken in the brushy desert have been much closer.

I believe I've taken more mule deer with a .30/06 than with anything else, and because they usually open up quicker I like the 150-grain bullets better than the 180s. Compared with a moose or an elk, even a large mule deer is lightly constructed, offering no great amount of resistance to a bullet, and country, and because they tend to move out ahead the heavily constructed bullets don't open quickly enough to nail deer in their tracks. The .30/30 with the old soft-point bullet with plenty of lead exposed is good deer medicine up to about 150 yards, but beyond that distance it won't anchor a deer unless the shot is placed just right. With the 150-grain bullet in the .30/06 or .300 Magnum, or the 130-grain bullet in the .270, quick and spectacular kills are the rule.

Oddly enough I have killed more deer with fewer shots with the 7 x 57 Mauser than with anything else—all with 140-grain bullets. I believe I have killed twelve deer with twelve hits. In Mexico, over a score of years ago, I once had to shoot a desert mule deer twice with a 7 mm., but a few years ago I let fly at a fat doe at about 300 yards and the bullet went through her and killed a spike buck on the far side. Both came rolling down the hillside at the same time.

Once I literally killed a big buck in his tracks with the 7 mm. I was out with my wife, who had shot a buck earlier, when we saw this beautiful buck standing by a tree about 200 yards away across the canyon. I dropped into a sitting position and let one go. He collapsed like a paper deer in a puff of wind. When we went over we could see that his feet were still in his last tracks. I have a lot of respect for that little 7 mm.

Much as I like old *Odocoileus hemionus,* I have to admit that he doesn't have as much in the way of gray matter under the antlers as an elk or a white-tail, and that he won't give the hunter quite as much of a run for his money. We all can't be geniuses, though, and the mule-deer hunter who confines himself to the hunting of big bucks will get all the action he could want. And when he gets a real trophy head he has something—the finest antlers worn by any American deer.

PORTRAIT OF THE WHITETAIL DEER

Jack O'Connor

Since our introduction to Jack's first piece, which immediately precedes this selection, is by far the longest for any author in this anthology, we will spare you further comment on this second selection except to point out that Jack knew whitetails as well (or maybe better) than muleys. Most of his early big game hunting experience in pre-World War II Arizona and Mexico was for the southwest's whitetails and Coues deer. This article also first appeared in The Big Game Animals of North America, *published by* Outdoor Life.

THE WHITETAIL DEER is the most widely distributed big game animal in the United States, the most plentiful, and the smartest. So crafty is the whitetail, and so much joy to hunt, that no one whose hunting is confined to the whitetail deer should feel very sorry for himself. He's got the best.

Whitetails are found, or have been found, in every state of the Union, in all the southern provinces of Canada, and throughout Mexico, with the exception of the peninsula of Lower California. Today he is still hunted over most of his original range, even in such prairie states as Illinois, Iowa, and Nebraska. Whitetails are shot even in tiny Delaware, and the ancient commonwealth of Pennsylvania, with an annual kill of over 100,000, is one of the best whitetail states in the Union. The middle-aged states of Michigan and Wisconsin have almost as large a whitetail kill each year as does Pennsylvania.

Give the whitetail a little cover, some food and water, and protection from year round hunting, and he'll take care of himself. He can get along with a minimum of even these essentials. In the deserts of Sonora, Mexico, whitetails live and die without ever tasting water; they get all their needed moisture from dew and the sap of plants. One of the best whitetail countries I have ever seen is a chain of low hills of decomposed granite near La Cienega,

Sonora. Rain sinks into the ground the moment it strikes, and any open water in the country is found in deep wells that are fenced off and used for cattle and not available to deer. But this does not bother the whitetails at all.

And whitetails can get by with very little cover. Although they are traditionally animals of thick brush and forest, they'll often surprise you. I remember one time in Idaho when I was hunting pheasants in an enormous stubble field. There was not a tree in sight, but through the field ran a shallow draw which had been planted with grass about two feet high to check erosion. Mike, my Brittany spaniel, went on point at the edge of the grass. He had a sneaky, shifty-eyed look about him. I knew he wasn't on a pheasant because when he has one of the gaudy birds under his nose he wears the all-gone expression of a hepcat digging some sharp clarinet work. I suspected he was on a porcupine, something which surprised me because he hadn't paid any attention to porcupines since he'd got well stuck up by one when he was a pup. Anyway, I walked in on the point, and out from under my feet barreled the biggest, fattest, sleekest, most beautiful whitetail buck I have ever laid eyes on. The evidence showed he had been lying up in that grassy little draw for weeks. Adaptable? You're telling me.

Some of the whitetails in southern Arizona and northern Mexico are found in country rough enough for mountain sheep. Nowhere can they negotiate solid rock the way sheep can, but I have found these deer far up in sheep mountains wherever there was sufficient soil and broken talus to give them footing. Yet in the great plains, whitetails have been found in the brush and trees along the river bottoms. I have seen whitetails in wilderness country where man seldom comes, and in the outskirts of Westport, Connecticut, that haven of commuters. Many deer are killed annually in New Jersey within sight of the towers of Manhattan.

There are undoubtedly more whitetails in North America now than there were when Columbus discovered the New World. The reason is largely that the virgin forests have been cut down and light has been let in to bring up plants and brush suitable for deer fodder. Deer almost always multiply when forests are cut over or burned off.

] 31 [

For many years deer were hunted hard twelve months of the year, and their numbers in the older states decreased to the point where the sight of a wild deer was a rarity. Then, along about 1900, game laws began to have a few teeth in them, and with some protection and more forage the whitetails began to increase. In Pennsylvania, for example, only two hundred were killed in 1907. By 1923, 6,452 legal bucks were taken. At the turn of the century Maine was a land with great areas of wilderness and afforded the best deer hunting in the East. In 1899, 7,579 whitetails were killed there, compared with 38,413 in 1958.

Most states passed buck laws around sixty years ago, and there

] 32 [

is no doubt that protecting the does did much to speed the come-back of the whitetails. However, deer are prolific animals. The does breed young, and if they're in good condition they generally produce twins.

During the years of the buck law, the doe became a sacred ani-mal to the American hunter, and his attitude toward the doe was about as rational as the attitude of a Hindu toward the sacred cow of India. The man who would shoot a doe (even legally) was in the same class as one who would rob widows and orphans or swindle his aged mother. I grew up in Arizona under the buck law and as a youngster was thoroughly indoctrinated. In my day I have shot a few fat does for meat, but in spite of the fact that they have all been perfectly legal, I have not enjoyed it and have al-ways felt a nagging sense of guilt.

About 1920, game rangers and foresters began to see that in many areas deer were too plentiful for their own good. In places the second-growth forests that had furnished plentiful deer forage had grown up to the point where they no longer made good deer range. As the years went on the situation became acute, and in bad winters there was wholesale starvation among the deer.

Then the game managers began to tell license-buying sports-men there were too many deer for their range and that does should be shot to hold the increase in check. A generation raised under the buck law reacted in shocked alarm. Too many deer? That was like saying a man had too much money, or that a woman could be too beautiful or too virtuous. Shooting does was like desecrating the American flag, casting doubt on the morals and motives of George Washington, or sneering at mother love. A violent controversy raged in Pennsylvania between those who op-posed the shooting of does and wanted more and more deer and those who felt that to preserve the forage and the deer themselves, does had to be shot and the herd reduced to the carrying capacity of the range.

The management of game is a difficult proposition because every man who has ever shot a deer becomes an authority on deer, and every man who has shot a duck knows all about ducks. In general, sportsmen have always opposed any reduction of deer numbers, and the rhubarb that had Pennsylvanians at each other's throats over the deer situation back in the nineteen twenties has been repeated elsewhere. When he becomes too plentiful, the whitetail is his own most serious enemy. Throughout the East the situation has been complicated by the fact that all the natural predators of the whitetail have been killed off. The mountain lion and the wolf are extinct there, and bobcats and wild dogs are the only things, besides man, that prey on the deer.

However, today's sportsmen are better educated in the realities of game management than they were a generation ago, and game departments are better staffed, have more revenue, and more skilled and convincing technicians. Whitetail hunting in the United States should remain good for generations.

Not only has the adaptable whitetail increased in the East, but he has also come back in the Midwest and the South. A generation ago, deer were very rare in Missouri, but in 1950 the kill there was almost 14,000, and does are shot in some areas. In Kentucky and Tennessee the whitetail is coming back, and the annual Texas deer kill of around 100,000 is composed largely of whitetails.

The wide distribution of the whitetail, his vast numbers, and his nearness to civilization make him by far the most important game animal in the United States. Many hunters can only dream of a hunt for sheep and grizzly bears, for white goats or caribou, but they have whitetail hunting right next door. More rifles are purchased especially for whitetail hunting than for any other, and more man-hours are spent in the woods for whitetails than for any other game. The next most important animal is the mule deer, and after it would come the elk, the Pacific Coast blacktail, and the antelope.

Because whitetails are so widely distributed and range in so many different kinds of country—from chilly Maine to the semitropical everglades of Florida, and from the hills of Pennsylvania to the deserts of the Southwest—they are found in many subspecies. However, all have the same sort of a white tail, the same pattern of antlers, and the same coloring. A New Yorker hunting for the first time in northern Idaho or Mexico would instantly recognize his old friend, the whitetail deer.

The antlers of a whitetail are different from those of the mule and blacktail deer in that all the points come off the main beam, and that the eye guard, or brow tine, is long and conspicuous. The antlers of the mule deer and the blacktail, in contrast, are evenly forked, and the brow point is smaller and sometimes absent altogether. Normally, the mature and well-fed whitetail buck of the East has four points and a brow point and would be what an Easterner would call a ten-pointer. In the West, where the brow tine is not counted, and where points are counted only on one side, the same buck would be called a four-pointer.

The whitetail found in Arizona and northern Mexico is the subspecies with which I am most familiar. He is a smaller deer on the average than those of the East, and the normal, mature Arizona whitetail head has an eye guard and three points, rather than four. Farther south in Mexico some bucks have only two points besides the brow tine.

As is the case with any deer, the antlers of old whitetail bucks often freak. They grow abnormal numbers of points. Often the antlers flatten, or palmate. Once in Arizona a hunter brought me a widely palmated, freak whitetail head and assured me it was a cross between a whitetail and a caribou. I tried to tell him there wasn't a caribou within 1,500 miles, but it made no difference. He knew a deer-caribou cross when he saw one. Freak heads are a sign of glandular imbalance and lagging sexual powers. If by accident or design a buck is emasculated, he never sheds the velvet from his antlers, and the antlers stay on until they are broken off or frozen. Glandular imbalance is responsible for the antlered doe that is shot now and then, and also for the antlerless bucks that one hears about occasionally.

Whitetails do not grow the tremendous antlers one finds on the best mule deer, but a big whitetail head is a handsome and impressive trophy. The new world record, entered in the Boone and Crockett Club's 1958–59 competition, is from Minnesota and was killed in 1918. It has a main beam of 31⅜ inches and eight points on each side. Of the other heads in the first ten, two are from

Canada and one each from Minnesota, New York, South Dakota, Iowa, Texas, Montana, and Ohio. The number one and number two freak heads are from Texas. The record has twenty-three points on one side, twenty-six on the other.

I have always felt that the Black Hills of Wyoming should produce some excellent whitetail heads, because when I drove through there one time I saw excellent ones taken from local deer nailed up on the walls in every garage and filling station. Some excellent heads are also found on the northwestern whitetails of northern Idaho, Washington, and southeastern British Columbia.

In the summer, whitetails wear their "red" coats. Generally it is a soft, reddish-tan, but in the winter this is replaced by the "blue" coat, in most subspecies a salt-and-pepper, brownish-gray. In some areas the top of the whitetail's tail is body color, but in others the top of the tail is brick red. The inside of the front legs, belly, buttocks, and underside of the tail are pure white.

As anyone who has ever seen a whitetail knows, the animals throw up their tails when frightened, and to a jittery hunter the big, white "fan" sometimes looks as large as the deer. The tail is the most conspicuous thing about the animal and is, of course, responsible for the name. The mule deer, on the other hand, does not elevate his dinky, thinly haired little tail, and the Pacific Coast blacktail (which in many ways looks as if it might be an ancient cross between the mule deer and the whitetail) compromises and holds his medium-size tail horizontally.

It is commonly believed among hunters that when a whitetail is wounded he clamps his tail between his legs as he runs off. Often this happens, but on at least two occasions I have seen mortally wounded whitetail bucks run off with their flags flying gallantly in the air.

The mule deer has a black V on his forehead and a light muzzle, but the whitetail's face is dark almost to the nose. No one who knows the two species will ever mistake any whitetail scalp for that of a mule deer, and a freak set of mule deer antlers will resemble those of a whitetail.

The metatarsal glands of the whitetail are much smaller than those of the mule deer, and those of the Pacific Coast blacktail are

] 36 [

about halfway in size between the two. In areas where mule and whitetail deer range in the same country, an animal occasionally is shot that is plainly a cross between the two species. Oddly enough, these hybrids look just about like Columbian blacktails. In the northwestern Sonora desert, where the mule deer range out on the flats and the Coues whitetail is found on all the little hills, these crosses are fairly common. When I lived in Tucson, Arizona, several specimens were brought to me by puzzled hunters who wanted to know what manner of animal they had shot.

In some places whitetails have degenerated because of poor range conditions until they are much smaller than their ancestors. In parts of Pennsylvania, where the range has long been over-browsed and the deer are half starved a good part of the year, they are skinny, slab-sided, little animals that compare very poorly with the fine, sleek, and chunky bucks from the same state that come out of agricultural areas where they find plentiful food. Whitetails from the Texas hill country around Kerrville are scrawny little fellows, and from what I have seen of them it takes a big buck to weigh 85 pounds field dressed. Presumably the deer in the brush of south Texas along the Rio Grande are the same subspecies, but they are much larger deer that will weigh almost twice as much.

The Coues, or Arizona whitetail of southern Arizona, southwestern New Mexico, some mountains of west Texas, and northern Sonora and Chihuahua, is a small whitetail, but not as small as many of those who have written about him claim he is. The average buck will dress out at from 85 to 100 pounds. One weighing 110 is a large one, and the largest of several dozen that I have shot myself weighed 118½. The largest I have actually seen went 128½. I have heard of one that weighed 135, but I'm a bit skeptical of the report.

How heavy are the very largest whitetail bucks? About as heavy, from all I can find, as the largest mule deer. The average mature buck from Virginia will weigh about 150 pounds on the hoof and the average doe about 100. In the North the deer are heavier and in the South lighter, with the tiny Florida Keys deer the smallest of all.

] 37 [

I have heard of many whitetail bucks that were said to have weighed as much as a spike bull elk, well over 460 pounds field dressed. I wrote the State Conservation Commission for verification, but, like most stories of such deer, the tale blew up. No biologist saw the buck, I was informed, until it was cut up and partly eaten, and no one who would make an affidavit of the weight could be located. I was told that the largest Missouri whitetail the commission had any record of weighed 369 on the hoof. That's a walloping big whitetail, but it's a long way from 460 pounds field dressed.

As in the case with the mule deer, a whitetail buck that will weigh 200 pounds field dressed is a big buck. And also like the mule deer, an occasional, extraordinarily large whitetail will field dress over 300 pounds and weigh 400 pounds or so on the hoof. Maine and northern Michigan have produced many heavy bucks, and some very large ones have been shot in northern Idaho, Montana, Washington, and British Columbia. But even in the Northwest a buck that will dress out at 200 pounds is an exception. A buck from Michigan was recorded with a dressed weight of 354 pounds—a tremendous buck but within the realm of reason.

The owner of a locker plant in Lewiston, Idaho, reports that the heaviest deer ever brought into his place was a whitetail, not a mule deer, and that its field-dressed weight was about 325 pounds. I have never laid eyes on a buck of any sort that heavy.

As one goes south in Mexico deer are smaller, with those of Sinaloa running lighter than the Coues deer of the northern part of the state. I have shot several of these bucks, and I doubt if the largest would dress out to 60 pounds. Still farther south, around Acapulco, deer don't go much over 40, I have been told.

Whitetails are generally animals of small range, and as they increase they move into new country slowly and experimentally. The average deer lives and dies in a few square miles of territory, and often deer will starve in an overpopulated area a few miles from good forage.

Even if hard hunting pushes a whitetail out of the little area which he regards as home, he'll come back as soon as he thinks the coast is clear. A frightened mountain sheep or an elk will travel for miles if he's had a good scare, but the whitetail buck will run a little way, sneak into some thick brush, and hide. In whitetail areas with which I am familiar, I find the same deer in the same canyons day after day, week after week.

I remember one very fine buck that lived all his life in an area not over two miles square. He grew an exceedingly fine head with, if I remember correctly, ten points on one side, nine on the other. His haunts were well known, and many hunted him. He was easy to see but almost impossible to get a good shot at. No matter which way hunters came at him, he had his escape routes all figured out. If he thought he had not been seen, he'd sneak off with his tail clamped between his legs. If, however, he was sure the hunter had glimpsed him, he'd tear out rapidly, giving his pursuer only a quick look at gray-brown body, flaunting white flag, and shining, many-pointed antlers. I finally learned his habits so well that a couple of friends and I ganged up on him and nailed him. He must have been twelve to fourteen years old at the time because he had been an exceptionally fine buck for six or seven years.

I remember another big buck with a very restricted range. A Mexican cowboy had seen a large, desert bighorn ram on a low and isolated but rough little chain of hills down on the Sonora desert about twenty-five miles from the Gulf of California. It looked like an easy sheep hunt, so every day for three days I would ride about five miles from the well where I was camped to the foot of the hill, tie my horse, and hunt.

Every day a big whitetail buck would get up from under a certain tree and trot off. I never did manage to see the ram. His tracks were all over the place, but there was a good deal of brush all over those hills and, because he would lie down where he was screened by brush, I could never get him in the glasses. One day I found where he'd come off the hill in the morning, fed for a time on cholla fruit on the flat, and had then left for the Sierra Las Mochis. He had apparently been traveling from the Sierra Picu toward Las Mochis and had used the little chain of rugged hills as a rest house. There was a sheep migration route that passed right by the hills, and sheep commonly rested there.

When I learned that my ram had left, I decided to see if I could get the buck. Before that, I hadn't wanted to shoot because I was afraid I'd spook the ram. I rode over from camp and tied my horse about a half mile from where I usually saw the buck. There was a good cross wind from the sea, so I pussyfooted quietly along, approaching a little higher than I usually did so that when the buck came out I would be on the same level and not below him. The buck did not disappoint me. When he finally heard me I wasn't over 75 yards away. He looked at me as if wondering what in the world I had done with my horse. I nailed him.

The tales of the craft and cunning of the whitetail are legendary. He can sneak away more silently, lie quieter, and outwit the hunter better than any other game animal in North America. I remember one occasion when my wife and I were hunting in southern Arizona. At noon we stopped, tied our horses at the edge of a brushy canyon, and prepared to eat lunch. Deer sign was everywhere, so, while the little woman was getting out the food, I picked up some rocks and tossed them into the brush below. Nothing moved. Finally I gave up. We ate our sandwiches, drank our coffee, and stretched out for a brief snooze in the warm and pleasant midday sun.

Eventually, it was time to move on. I still couldn't get the notion out of my head that there should have been deer in that particular canyon. Again I started half-heartedly tossing rocks. Finally one slipped from my hand and fell almost directly below us. The brush popped, and out came a handsome, whitetail buck. We almost dislocated our shoulders getting to our rifles. That darned buck had been lying within 50 feet of us for an hour.

Another time I was hunting the Chiricahuas in Arizona. I had walked 10 to 12 miles, hunting as I went, but about a mile from the ranch house where I was staying, I came across an oak that had been cut down, probably so it would dry for firewood. The leaves were still on it, but dry, and it was right out in the open with no tree or brush nearby. The night before it had been cold enough to freeze water, but it had warmed up during the day, and I was hot, thirsty, and leg weary. I sat down on one of the branches of the oak, took a drink of water from my little canteen, and smoked a cigarette. Finally I decided to move on. My rifle was leaning against a limb about six feet from where I had been sitting, and as I reached for it a buck exploded out of the branches and threw dry leaves all over me. I shot the buck as he scooted for cover. Then I went back to the place where he'd been lying. To save my life, I couldn't figure out why I hadn't seen him before.

And can a whitetail be sneaky. Once in Sonora a pal and I were hunting a brushy, star-shaped hill with seven or eight ravines that came together toward the top. Both of us had horses, and we were accompanied by a Mexican vaquero. One of us would stay at the head of a ravine and the other, with the Mexican lad, would go around and come up the bottom, riding through the brush and making plenty of noise to move deer. My pal had shot a buck in the morning and now it was my turn.

On this particular occasion I saw something gray about a half a mile away moving ahead of my pal. The glass showed it to be a good whitetail buck. It would sneak quietly off, stop, and listen. Then it would move on again. Because I was above, I could see both hunter and buck. Finally the buck edged around and went into some thick brush between the vaquero and my partner. Then, when they were about 50 yards past, he sneaked off until he got to the mouth of the ravine. He then tossed up that white tail and the last time I saw him he was making knots across the flat.

And here's a story with a better ending—at least for me, if not for the deer. Two pals and I decided to hunt a brushy hill. I was to go low on the left side, one companion was to be low on the right, and the third up on the top. We thought one of us would surely move a deer to one of the others. We hadn't gone far when I glimpsed a movement about 50 feet in front of my friend on top. It was a big whitetail buck, and he was sneaking along with his tail between his legs as if he were walking on eggshells. I sat down, held the crosswires on a little opening the buck would have to cross, and when he got there I put a .270 bullet right through his lungs. To make the story even better, the shot spooked a second buck that had been sneaking off and that I hadn't seen. Frightened into losing his caution, he exposed himself and my pal nailed him. If I hadn't been fairly bright eyed and caught a glimpse of that first buck, none of us would have known there were deer so close.

Incidentally, that whitetail buck I shot had two complete antlers on one side, each with three points. I gave it to the zoology collection at the University of Arizona, and presumably it is still there.

Because of the many different types of country that whitetails inhabit, there are many different ways of hunting them. In the wooded East, I have been told that the deer are usually driven, with the standers placed on runways and the drivers working through the brush to move the deer. I hunted deer that way once in Pennsylvania. In South Carolina I hunted deer driven by dogs and beaters. In some areas the deer feed low and then move up to the hardwood ridges to lie up during the day, and the smart hunter is out as soon as he can see to catch them while they are moving. I have a lazy friend who gets his buck every year simply by waiting in a saddle back where deer come through and letting other hunters move the bucks over him.

In country where a man can move quietly and where deer lie up for the day, I like to pussyfoot along upwind, going 50 yards at a time, and then stopping to look and listen. If a hunter barrels right along as if he were competing in a walking contest, the deer will let him walk right past them. It is this business of stopping that upsets them. They begin to wonder if they haven't been seen, and often they lose their nerve and take off.

It areas of thick brush in the southern Arizona mountains, I used to like hunting with a companion. One man would take one side of a canyon and one the other. Usually the hunter would not see the deer on the same side of the canyon that he was on, but would shoot the deer his companion jumped. Generally it is more successful for two to hunt together and have a plan. Like most animals, the whitetail deer has a one-track mind, and as he sneaks away from one hunter he's often been known to walk right over another.

In thinly brushed country, the queen of all ways of hunting is to work out the canyon on horseback, riding up the cattle trails that usually go along the sides and pausing occasionally to roll stones down into the brush. It makes for some pretty fast and fancy shooting.

Whitetails are shot with everything from single-barreled shotguns taking buckshot and rifle slugs to .300 Weatherbys and .375 Magnums. They are shot at 20 yards and at 400, by dubs and by crack shots. Generally in the wooded East they are killed at ranges under 100 yards, but some crack shots shoot deer in openings across wide ravines, and in thin brush.

The .30/30 is the classic deer cartridge, and with bullets of proper construction it does very well to 150 yards or so. Other widely used cartridges for short and intermediate ranges are the .35 Remington and the .300 Savage. The .308 and the .358 are coming up in popularity. For short-range whitetail shooting the .30/06 is a lot of cartridge, but it is widely used, even in the East.

The average whitetail is a small animal, as big game animals go, with thin skin and fragile bones. Whatever the caliber used, the bullet should be one that will open quickly against light resistance. In rifles of the .30/30 class I am convinced that the best medicine is still the old-fashioned, soft point with soft lead core and thin jacket. Some bullets of the controlled-expanding class open up too slowly to do the job right.

In the Southwest, where I've done most of my whitetail hunting, I have got the quickest kills with relatively light bullets at high velocity—the old 139-grain open point in the 7 mm., the 150-grain in the .30/06, the 120- and 130-grain bullets in the .270, and even the 87-grain in the .250/3000. With these a shot in the chest cavity usually means an instantaneous kill, and even a gut shot will generally disable a deer so that it will not go far. I don't recommend gut shots with anything, but sometimes they cannot be avoided.

The whitetail is a grand animal, and the man who hunts him owes it to himself and to the deer to use good equipment, shoot carefully, and kill cleanly.

PORTRAIT OF THE
ARIZONA COUES DEER

Jack O'Connor

The third consecutive "Portrait" on deer by Jack is devoted to the diminutive Arizona Coues or Sonora deer. Since Jack's native stomping grounds for over 50 years was Arizona and Northern Mexico, it is no wonder that he was probably one of the world's experts on that distinctive member of the deer family. This piece appeared in the Outdoor Life Book of Deer Hunting, *published by Outdoor Life and Harper & Row.*

MOST INTELLIGENT GAME animal I have ever run into on this side of the world is the pint-size Coues deer, also known as the Arizona whitetail. He's a little guy, about half as large as the mule deer he often ranges with. He is, on the other hand, about five times as smart as the mule deer. The little rascal makes up his mind quickly and gambles coolly with his life. When he knows he can no longer stay concealed, he comes out like a quail, depending on his sudden and noisy appearance to befuddle the hunter.

The only North American animal I've hunted that I'd put in the same strategy class with the little Arizona whitetail is an old desert bighorn, one that has learned the facts of life by dodging the bullets tossed at him by prospectors, fishermen, and vaqueros. Yet the wild sheep get smart the hard way. The Coues deer imbibes craft and cunning with his mother's milk.

He's a great fellow to size up a situation, work out an escape plan, and stick to it. On one hunt I used binoculars to watch two distant whitetails go into a little patch of chaparral under a rimrock about thirty feet from a spring. Soon after that a cowboy rode his horse up to the spring, where he made a fire, boiled a can of coffee, ate his lunch. Then he snoozed in the sun for about fifteen minutes before he mounted and moved on. The Coues deer stayed put. I hadn't been able to see antlers even with my 8X glasses, but the color of the deer and the way they carried their heads made me think they were both bucks.

I approached the chaparral where the bucks lay upwind and

inconspicuously, but both deer sneaked out ahead of me. I just caught a glimpse of one, moving like a gray shadow with his head down and his tail clamped between his legs. Before I could shoot he was out of sight. Those deer knew the cowboy's heart was pure as driven snow but mine was full of guile. How, I'll never know, but they did. That's why so many Coues bucks live to a ripe old age.

The only animal I ever ran into anywhere that seemed smarter and harder to hunt than the Arizona whitetail is Africa's greater kudu. This elk-sized, spiral-horned antelope has many things in common with the little whitetail—super hearing, coolness, a gambler's instinct. He's considered one of the very top African trophies and the hardest of all the fairly common antelope to bag.

The little whitetail, although tough to hunt and about as smart as a kudu, is not so famous. In the United States, he's found only in a strip near the Mexican border, and his head is a very rare one, in trophy collections.

One afternoon years ago another hombre and I were hunting in southern Arizona. We had separated, and in late afternoon I saw him pussyfooting down a point about 400 yards from me. Presently I saw a deer jump ahead of my friend, and from his obvious excitement I knew it was a buck.

The deer continued off the point as if to run along under the rimrock toward the main mountain. My friend hurried out to the brink of the ridge and stood there with his rifle ready. He was watching the spot where the oaks ended, where the buck was sure to break out of cover on his way to the mountain beyond.

But instead of doing the obvious, the buck put on his brakes as soon as he was out of sight in the scrubby little evergreen oaks under the rim. Then he turned back around the point, sneaking along under the rim with head down, tail plastered between his legs. He came out in the open about 200 yards to the left of where my pal was expecting him. Then, with the last concealing bush behind him, he flirted up his big white tail and ran. My friend threw a hasty shot at him and missed. It was difficult to make him believe that this deer he shot at was the same one he'd jumped a few minutes earlier.

] 45 [

I know of no animal that's better at finding a strategic bedding ground than this smart little whitetail. This was firmly impressed on me one fall day when I was hunting a long ridge on horseback. I saw four bucks, but every single one of them was bedded so that he needed but one jump to be out of sight.

I have never seen an animal make better use of cover than the Coues deer. I recall a time years ago when I was hunting with two friends in the Canelo Hills not far from Patagonia in southern Arizona. We were climbing up a trail toward the top of a low range. When we got to the top we'd figure out how to team up and work out the heads of some canyons. Then one of my friends saw a buck flip up its white tail and jump over the ridge toward a big canyon.

Yelling for us to follow, he took after it. We knew the country and thought it highly probable that we'd get another look at the deer. The big canyon into which he'd gone was quite open— golden slopes of frost-cured grama grass with an occasional ocotillo and oaks in little groves in the side draws. There was so little cover that it would be almost impossible for a deer to move without one of us seeing it.

But nothing did we see. That deer hadn't possibly had time to run out of sight, yet he was. A couple of us searched the valley with binoculars. Not a thing could we find except a couple of crows slithering along with a lofty wind, cawing and snarling at each other against the flat blue of the sky. We decided the deer might have stopped directly below us, where the contours of the ground and a few scattered patches of mountain mahogany and cliff rose would afford cover. We rolled big stones that went crashing through that growth. Nothing moved.

Right beside us was a little patch of brush about large enough to conceal a cock pheasant. We hadn't given it a thought. Presently one of my pals decided to roll a cigarette, so he walked over and leaned his rifle against a bush. Instantly a fine whitetail exploded out of the little patch, head up, antlers back, snowy tail looking as large as he was. His first jump kicked leaves and twigs all over us. He passed so close to me that if I'd been less astonished

I might have grabbed him by an antler. (Don't ask me what I'd have done after I got such a hold.)

Meanwhile the man who'd leaned his rifle on the bush made a lunge for it and fell flat. The other hunter and I were so busy bumping into one another that the buck buzzed over the ridge without a shot being fired at him. We agreed that this buck was too hard on our nerves and set out to find a more docile one.

The career of a mossy-horned old buck that lived near Patagonia, Arizona, illustrates the amazing ability of these little deer to survive heavy hunting without much cover. The buck's home range was a canyon-cut ridge that ran about three miles from north to south. Thin brush grew along the talus slopes below the rimrocks. Oak, mountain mahogany, and cliff rose was fairly thick in a few places in the draws. The rest of this long ridge was

open—slopes of grama grass, limestone outcrops, an oak here and there. The ridge was within half a mile of a ranch house containing three hunters, within three miles of the village, and a mile from a good automobile road.

The buck lived out his long, long life almost as publicly as a goldfish in a bowl. He probably was born on the ridge and he lived about five years after his antlers had grown so large and many-pointed as to cause comment. Deer hunters came down from Tucson to try for him. High school kids matched wits with him after school and on weekends. Cowhands sniped at him.

It wasn't difficult to see the buck. Almost anyone could see him. But armed men only saw him just as he was disappearing into the brush, crossing a ridge at 400 yards, fading around a point. Yet I'm sure two-hundred shots were fired at that buck, maybe more.

] 47 [

I had a hand in this buck's undoing. Arizona rancher Frank Siebold and I knew the buck had a habit on chill fall mornings of taking the sun on a flat between a big canyon and the south slope of the mountain. If hunters came up the canyon, the deer faded over the south slope and hugged a belt of oaks as he eased away. If hunters came up that south slope, he dropped over into the canyon.

Frank and I framed him. We sent his sister Doris and my wife Eleanor up the canyon while we skirted the bottom of the south slope of the hill. When the buck came sneaking along through the belt of oaks, I took a crack at him. The bullet struck a bit low in his left shoulder. He went down, but got up as we were scrambling toward him, and climbed over the rimrock. There he ran into Doris, who nailed him.

The old buck had a beautiful head with nine points to a side, but the meat was so tough it was only edible in a stew. His teeth were about gone and he showed every sign of extreme age and decrepitude. He was probably somewhere between twelve and fourteen years old and probably would have died of old age within a year.

Arizona whitetail is a misleading name for these little deer. That's a handle they got when they were first classified from specimens taken near Fort Crittenden, Arizona, in the days when that old army post was on guard against Apaches. Coues (pronounced *cows*) is a more accurate name for these little deer, and the scientific name for them is *Odocoileus virginianus couesi*. Other common names are fantail, Sonora whitetail, Arizona whitetail. Mexicans call it the venado, which simply means deer. They keep things straight by calling the mule deer the burro.

Coues deer are found in southern Arizona in all the hills and mountains high enough to support live oaks from the little border town of Sasabe east to the New Mexico line. Their range is by no means continuous, but there are scattered herds as far north as central Arizona along the Mogollon rim. In New Mexico they are found in mountain ranges west of the Rio Grande as far north as the Datils and are quite plentiful in the Mogollons and San Franciscos. Some are found in the Davis Mountains in the Big Bend of

Texas and in the Glass and Chisos Mountains in the same area.

They are most plentiful in the Mexican states of Chihuahua and Sonora, and there are many in western Choahuila. In the United States, Coues deer are generally found at altitudes above 4,000 feet, but in Sonora they range from 10,000 feet in the Sierra Madre clear down to little hills that are in sight of the Gulf of California. Distribution maps do not show them down near the salt water, but I have seen them there by the hundreds and shot many.

Outside of the Southwest, these wonderful little deer are almost unknown. They have also undergone the ordeal of being written about by people who knew but little about them. I mentioned that distribution maps do not list them as occupying the western desert portion of their range in Mexico. Writers often promote another error by making Coues deer seem smaller than they actually are. One piece I read about them says to imagine a jackrabbit with horns. That's silly. Vernon Bailey, Fish & Wildlife Service biologist, wrote that bucks reached a maximum weight of a hundred pounds (presumably live weight) and does seventy-five.

I have weighed dozens of them. The average grown buck will weigh from eighty to ninety pounds after he's field dressed, and hundred-pound bucks are common in any area I have hunted. It's true that a buck weighing more than a hundred pounds field dressed is large, but a hundred pounds is certainly not a maximum weight. I wrote a story some years ago about a 117½-pound Coues buck. I killed it in the Tortolita Mountains near Tucson, Arizona. I thought I'd win a rifle in a heavy buck contest, but the next day my shooting pal Carroll Lemon brought in one that weighed 128½.

Generally speaking, the little whitetails are just about half the size of Southwestern mule deer or the larger varieties of Virginia whitetail. Coues bucks weighing a hundred pounds are just about as common as buck mule deer that dress out to two-hundred.

Coues deer look like Eastern whitetails done in miniature, except that their skulls are smaller and shorter in proportion. Does and young bucks are a beautiful dove gray, but old bucks are grizzled and darker. Their antlers, ears, and tails are larger in proportion to their bodies than those of their Eastern relatives. Tails range from a grizzled brown on top to a bright orange, and when they toss them up to take off the deer appears to be all brilliant white tail.

Although the little fantail is only about half the size of his Northern and Eastern cousins, his antlers are larger in proportion to his body. As is the case with all whitetail deer, all the points on the antlers of the fantail come off one main beam and the eyeguard points are long and conspicuous as compared with the short ones of the mule deer. However, whereas the mature Eastern whitetail generally has four points to the side in addition to the eyeguard, the Arizona deer has three. On the other hand, I have shot Coues bucks with as many as five points to a side and have seen one with nine on one side and eleven on the other.

The heads do not freak as much as those of mule deer, and are generally very regular and symmetrical. A head with a 16-inch beam usually will have about a 16-inch spread, and so on, and a four-point buck with a 16-inch beam is a good one. A buck with a 17-inch beam is extraordinary, and an 18-incher is getting far up in the records if the antlers are massive. The heads may not knock your eye out, but they are one of the rarest trophies in North America. Because they are an entirely different animal from the orthodox whitetail, they are given a separate classification in Records of North American Big Game.

No matter where he's found, the little Coues deer is a hill animal. On the Sonora desert, the mule deer like to range out on the flats, but the whitetails cling to the hills like ducks to a pond. The long, rather narrow tracks of the desert mule deer are found all over the flats, but usually the hunter doesn't run into the smaller heart-shape tracks of the whitetail unless he's close to a hill.

The most heavily populated whitetail area I ever ran into was in the Sonora desert—a chain of low, rolling hills southwest of the little placer-mining town of La Cienega. I was in there for a hunt during the winter of 1937-38, and the deer were so thick that they obliterated the horse tracks on a trail between dusk and dawn. Apparently they soon got too plentiful and died off. I was in there a few years later and didn't see one where I had formerly seen ten.

In spite of their wide distribution in respect to altitude, I always think of the little whitetails as creatures of what scientists call the upper Sonoran climatic zone, which means a zone with the climate and vegetation common to the higher elevations in Sonora. This is one of the most pleasant regions on earth, a zone where it seldom gets very hot or very cold, a land of eternal fall and eternal spring. In the warmest months the nights are always cool, and in the coldest months the sun is out bright and warm at noon. This is true of high and hilly Sonora, and also of the Arizona hills running along the Mexican border clear to the Big Bend of Texas.

All of this area has hills and mountains rising from grassy, rolling plains. It's a region where the ocotillo and the prickly pear of the desert meets the oaks of the mountains, a land of piñon and juniper, cliff rose and mountain mahogany. In this belt of country the animals of the Rockies meet those of the semitropics. From the far north have come the bighorn sheep, the mule deer, the elk, the black bear. Up from the south have come our little whitetails, the peculiar coati-mondi, the mountain lion, the wild turkey. Once the grizzly ranged this country in good numbers, but it has been hunted out in the American Southwest and survives only in a few parts of Chihuahua. Of all these animals, to me the most typical of the region is the little fantail. I always think of him as running along a grassy hillside, waving his snowy flag, and disappearing into the head of an oak-filled draw.

Because the little whitetails occupy many different types of country, there are many different ways of hunting them. Down on the Sonora desert I have hunted them by walking around the bottom of the little hills, where they bed down, and letting my rising scent flush them out. When they're found in brushy canyons, a good way to get venison is for two hunters to work together, one hiking up one side of a canyon and his companion taking the other. The hunter seldom sees deer that he himself moves. Instead he can nail bucks on the other side of the canyon that have been put up by his pal.

As I write this I can still see in memory one of the finest whitetails I ever shot. A friend and I were hunting together, he on one side of a draw and I on the other. I saw a buck get up about fifty feet in front of my companion and sneak off, head down, tail between his legs. He was almost as inconspicuous as a cock pheasant sneaking through the stubble ahead of a dog. My pal wasn't aware that he was in pebble-tossing distance of a fine buck, but I could see both of them on that steep hillside opposite me. I sat and carefully put a bullet right behind that buck's shoulder.

But the sportiest and in many ways most pleasant whitetail hunting is done with horses, riding cattle and game trails along the sides of the draws and canyons. Then every time a deer flashes a white tail and takes off, the hunter has to see if it's a buck or a doe and take action accordingly. I always carry my rifle in a scabbard on the left side of my saddle, with the rifle butt to the rear and pointing up at about a 45° angle. It takes only seconds to get off the horse on the left side, grab the small of the stock with the right hand, and yank the rifle out of the scabbard. Then you sit down and open up.

Fantails are small deer, and their light, tender bodies don't offer much resistance to bullets. This calls for relatively light, easily expanded bullets traveling at high velocity. More often than not the bucks are shot running, and fast bullets make it easier to figure the right lead. I have used the 87-grain bullet in the .250/3000 Savage and have found it excellent on these diminutive deer. The 7 mm. Mauser with the old Western 139-grain open-point bullet was powerful whitetail medicine, and so is the .257 with good 100-grain bullets. The new .243 Winchester and .244 Remington with bullets weighing from 90 to 100 grains should be made to order—fast, flat shooting, and quick opening. The 150-grain bullets in the .30/06 and the 130-grain bullets in the .270 are poison on fantails. Generally, 180-grain bullets for the .30/06 open up too slowly. Some of the 150-grain bullets are excellent.

I did a lot of whitetail hunting in Mexico, from one to four trips a year for many years. I have no exact record of how many whitetails I shot there and in Arizona, but I took a good many. One thing I learned for sure is that they call for a fast-opening bullet. Back when the .257 was newly hatched, the bullets for the most part had thick, heavy jackets, and when I used them I spent half my time chasing wounded whitetails that were well hit but still going.

The main enemy of the fantail is the mountain lion, and until hunters get more skillful and are allowed to shoot does as well as bucks, predation by lions is necessary for healthy whitetail herds. In areas where lions are kept killed down, the deer become too plentiful, destroy their own browse, and die off from disease. The best Mexican deer ranges have a lot of lions—and a lot of deer. Coyotes take many fawns, and I have found where they have killed grown deer. Bobcats are likewise fawn killers.

But nature has seen to it that the little whitetails can survive. The twin fawns, born in the off-beat months of July and August, mean a great rate of increase. The stealth and cunning of the deer make them difficult for predators to get. Because of their size, an area can support about twice as many whitetails as mule deer.

The hunting pressure Coues deer can stand is amazing. There's excellent whitetail hunting, for example, in the Catalina mountains overlooking the city of Tucson, the second largest city in Arizona.

If a country is brushy, the little fantails like it. If it's open, they can make a little cover go a long way. Many times when hunters are working out the brush in the draws and along the rimrocks, fantails bed right out in the grass where no one would expect to find them. I once jumped a dandy buck out of tall grass under a lone oak on a big grassy slope. I shed my surprise in time to nail him, but I had no more expected a shot at a whitetail than at a tiger.

Another time I was sitting on a ridge glassing some country below when it dawned on me that some dark points sticking out of the grass about fifty yards in front of me looked more like antler tips than dead sticks. I turned my 9X binoculars on them. They were antlers. The buck had been lying there in the grass taking the sun when I came over the ridge, and he apparently decided the smart move was not to move at all. He didn't jump until I was almost on top of him.

A Coues buck in Sonora jumped out of the grass so close in

front of my horse that he frightened my poor beast of burden almost out of his wits. By the time the resulting rodeo was over the buck was long gone.

I've seen grown fantail bucks sneak along in tall grass with their knees so bent they appeared to be crawling. Once I missed getting a shot at a fine buck I'd watched for five minutes as he crept through tall grass and thin brush. I couldn't believe it was a deer, it was so close to the ground I thought it must be a coyote.

I can think of no hunting more pleasant than a November or December shoot for fantails in Mexico. It's a hunt for a rare trophy worn by a shrewd and intelligent animal.

The deer don't rut until February and March, so the late-fall venison is always good, one of the choicest pieces of big-game meat in North America. The weather is perfect then—crisp nights and balmy days full of sun. Generally the dude will hunt from horseback and cut the deer down on the run, which takes some doing. Then there are always the nights around the campfire of fragrant mesquite, the coals cooking steaks from the little venados and a pot of frijoles. Ah, me!

THE OLD AND THE NEW

Ted Trueblood

To me, the name Ted Trueblood has always been synonymous with two things: Field & Stream *magazine and some of the best writing the outdoor field has ever seen.*

I have never had the privilege of actually being in the field with Ted, but as an editor and writer myself I have never ceased to be amazed at his integrity for accuracy, information depth, and colorful no-nonsense language that lets me share and feel everything he has known in his days afield. Very few, and I really mean very few, *outdoor writers can match Ted's facility for imparting information through* sharing *it* rather than *preaching it. It is a talent to treasure.*

This piece, from Field & Stream *and published in the superb collection of Trueblood pieces,* The Ted Trueblood Hunting Treasury (*McKay*), *evokes the mood of the hunt with considerable feeling and is one of two Trueblood efforts we're proud to include in* The Deer Book.

EACH AUTUMN when the nights grow longer than the days and the aspens turn to gold on the hillsides, I am faced by an annual dilemma: Should we explore some new area or should we hunt once more in the old, familiar spot? There are strong inducements for both alternatives, and all deer hunters must answer the same question.

There are advantages in hunting country you know, but there might be more deer somewhere else. Besides, it is exciting to explore new territory. I will never forget the thrill of topping a ridge on my first deer hunt to look down into a mountain basin I had never seen before.

After a long climb, the cool breeze in my face was as fresh as the Arctic. It breathed a hint of the winter that was soon to come. I knew it couldn't be, of course, but it was easy to imagine that my companion and I were the first white men to cross this particular ridge at this particular point and so enjoy this particular view of the granite-rimmed basin below.

There were alders along a trickle of water in the bottom. A

stringer of lodgepole pine, trunks as straight and slender as pickets in a fence, came up along one side of the basin. Beneath them the grouseberry bushes had taken on the blush of fall. Along the ridge on which Don Hill and I stood, here and there on the slope below, and on the opposite slope were scattered clumps of alpine fir. The hillsides were partly clothed by grass and low brush, and partly by barren slides and jagged outcroppings of clean, gray granite. A towering peak, still streaked with hard banks of last winter's snow, jutted into the blue sky beyond.

It was a wild and free and thrilling sight, and before we had even caught our breath Don said, "Boy! Look at that!"

At his words the biggest buck I have ever seen sprang from his bed in the shadow of some firs, not 20 yards below, and bounded into the open. I heard Don gulp. My heart leaped into my throat and by the time I could raise my rifle I was trembling like an aspen leaf. I could no more keep my dancing sights on the deer than I could fly. In desperation I fired shotgun style as they jerked across his chest. I imagine Don was equally unstrung, though naturally neither of us ever admitted to such boyish weakness.

The buck started around the hillside. We each fired several shots. By some miracle the buck went down. By an even greater miracle, there were two bullet holes in his rib cage—a fortunate thing since we were, it developed, to share both the venison and the glory. We saw no more deer that trip.

We dressed him where he fell, then strung him on a pole and tried to lift him. We couldn't do it, so we cut him in two, tied one half to the pole, and started to camp with it. When we came back for the second half we were so tired we decided to leave the head where it lay. We didn't even take the antlers. They were wide, heavy, and well shaped, with six points on one side and seven on the other, but we didn't realize what we had. Don was sixteen and I was seventeen years old.

So each fall when I must make the decision where to hunt I remember that first hunt—plus many others in new country since. Obviously, none of us in the 1970s can explore in the sense that Daniel Boone or Jim Bridger did, yet any hunter in an area he has never seen before is really exploring. Within its confines each bend of the stream and each view from a ridge top are as new to him as they were to the first pioneer who saw them.

Still-hunting in new country, watching carefully for sign to learn where the game is using, exploring each new vista, and finally succeeding offer real proof of hunting ability, provides a success of thrills climaxed by well-deserved satisfaction. To breathe the clean air of the high places and glory in each new panorama, completely removed from any sight or sound of man, is in itself reward enough. Whatever game we may bag is an extra bonus.

Yet at the very time I am tempted by such thoughts I remember the familiar spot near home where my wife and I have camped and hunted for more than thirty years. I can smell the clean campfire smoke that drifts down the river bottom in the evening, mingling with the lush odor of overripe elderberries and the fresh smell of the pines. I can see the mountain maple ablaze on the hillsides and the billion diamonds of the frost when the sun first touches the meadow beyond our camp.

We have camped there, sometimes to hunt grouse, but more often deer, since before our sons were born. When they were tiny they played for hours with their little cars, building roads around a dirt bank near the tent and zooming the cars over them. When they were older, maybe ten or twelve, they built a platform in a nearby tree and perched on it to read while we hunted. The day came when they hunted with us. Now we go back alone.

Sentiment influences me, of course. The place has a thousand memories. But there is a practical reason for hunting here, too: We know the area surrounding it better than we do the town in which we live. We know every thicket where the sleek deer hide. We know every trail they follow and every saddle they pass through on migration. We know where they feed early and late and where they bed down during the day. We know the best time of the season to be here and the best time of the day to hunt each spot—and *how* to hunt each one. For example, Ellen's favorite hunt is a short one after dinner to the basin at the head of a long draw.

Our usual routine deer hunting is to leave camp before daylight and be where we expect to find game by the time it is light enough to shoot. We then still-hunt, sometimes together but more often separately, until 10 or 11 o'clock. (We hunt longer on snowy days because the deer don't brush up so early then.)

After our morning hunt we wander back to camp, have a bite to eat, and loaf or go fishing for a few hours. We eat dinner about 4 o'clock. After dinner we go out again and stay until it is too dark to see the sights.

Ellen likes to take her rifle and climb up to this basin, a steep half mile from camp. Once there, and if the wind is right, she sits quietly a few yards below the west rim and waits for the deer to come out to feed. (If she sat on top of the rim she would be silhouetted against the sky and easy to see.)

The basin is about 250 yards across and without trees, but it has an abundance of bitterbrush, snow brush; bitter cherry, and other choice deer food. Over the rim to the east there is a 100-acre thicket of Douglas fir, a safe retreat for deer during the day, but devoid of food. So at dusk any deer that may be there are likely to wander out into the basin to feed.

We have lost track of the number Ellen has killed by waiting patiently here as night descended, but I do remember her best shot. A young buck—three points on each side—came out of the timber but stopped on the opposite ridge and started nipping the leaves off some tall snow brush. Ellen could see only his head, and

that only occasionally. It was nearly dark. She wouldn't be able to see the crosshairs in her scope much longer. She decided to try for a head shot, a small target at 250 yards.

At the crack of her rifle, however, the buck disappeared. She found him dead. She had to dress him and prop him open to cool before she could leave, and it was long after dark when she got back to camp.

This is an evening spot; we have never found deer here in the morning. Then they prefer to feed on the east-facing slope, on the other side of the timber, where the first rays of the rising sun drive away the chill—though they never linger in the open for long after the sun comes up.

There are other evening spots and others that are good in the morning. We know them all and so we no longer make the hard, all-day hunts we once did. We kill our deer close to camp—and we don't have to work hard to do it.

This is the practical side. You may be sure that any deer using an area knows it very well, and it gives a hunter a great advantage if he knows it as well as they do.

There is another reason for going back to the same deer camp year after year, preferably with the same companions. Every time you return you add to the store of memories that make each new hunt that much more rewarding. You recall the good times around the camp itself, the great meals, the funny things that happened on past hunts.

In the woods you remember the crossing where you caught the big buck dead to rights—and missed him clean. You recognize the spot where you made the best shot of your life.

So while I like to explore new country, I must admit that if I had only one more hunt to make I would surely go back to our old, familiar camp. And if I had to kill a deer, which, fortunately, I don't, I'd go there, too.

HUNTING THE MULE DEER

Theodore Roosevelt

No collection of big-game pieces could be complete without including the man who loved and lived the hunting experience with the same energy and zeal that were manifested in every area of endeavor in his life.

Theodore Roosevelt's voluminous accounts of hunting in the American west and the far reaches of the world are all mellow classics now. Still, they are so alive with the account of the stalk and the shot, the freshness of the then-untouched game fields, that they will always occupy an honored spot on my library shelves.

I am particularly fond of this one—from Outdoor Pastimes of An American Hunter.

If you haven't had a full-course Roosevelt reading experience, you're in for a treat with this.

THIS IS THE LARGEST and finest of our three smaller deer. Throughout its range it is known as the blacktail deer, and it has as good a historic claim to the title as its Pacific coast kinsman, the coast or true blacktail. In writing purely of this species, it seems like pedantry to call it by its book name of mule-deer, a name which conveys little or no meaning to the people who live in its haunts and who hunt it; but it is certainly very confusing to know two distinct types of deer by one name, and as both the Rocky Mountain blacktail and Coast blacktail are thus known, and as the former is occasionally known as mule-deer, I shall, for convenience' sake, speak of it under this name—a name given it because of its great ears, which rather detract from its otherwise very handsome appearance.

The mule-deer is a striking and beautiful animal. As is the case with our other species, it varies greatly in size, but is on the average heavier than either the whitetail or the true blacktail. The horns also average longer and heavier, and in exceptional heads are really noteworthy trophies. Ordinarily a full-grown buck has a head of ten distinct and well-developed points, eight of which consist of the bifurcations of the two main prongs into which each antler divides, while in addition there are two shorter basal or frontal points. But the latter are very irregular, being sometimes missing; while sometimes there are two or three of them on each antler. When missing it usually means that the antlers are of young animals that have not attained their full growth. A yearling will sometimes have merely a pair of spikes, and sometimes each spike will be bifurcated so as to make two points. A two-year-old may develop antlers which, though small, possess the normal four points. Occasionally, where unusually big heads are developed, there are a number of extra points. If these are due to deformity, they simply take away from the beauty of the head; but where they are symmetrical, while at the same time the antlers are massive, they add greatly to the beauty. All the handsomest and largest heads show this symmetrical development of extra points. It is rather hard to lay down a hard-and-fast rule for counting them. The largest and finest antlers are usually rough, and it is not easy to say when a particular point in roughness has developed so that it may legitimately be called a prong. The largest head I ever got to my own rifle had twenty-eight points, symmetrically arranged, the antlers being rough and very massive as well as very long. The buck was an immense fellow, but no bigger than other bucks I have shot which possessed ordinary heads.

The mule-deer is found from the rough country which begins along the eastern edges of the great plains, across the Rocky Mountains to the eastern slopes of the coast ranges, and into southern California. It extends into Canada on the north and Mexico on the south. On the west it touches, and here and there crosses, the boundaries of the Coast blacktail. The whitetail is found in places throughout its habitat from east to west and from north to south. But there are great regions in this territory which are peculiarly fitted for the mule-deer, but in which the whitetail is never found, as the habits of the two are entirely different. In the mountains of western Colorado and Wyoming, for instance, the mule-deer swarms, but the whole region is unfit for the whitetail, which is accordingly only found in a very few narrowly restricted localities.

The mule-deer does not hold its own as well as the whitetail in

the presence of man, but it is by no means as quickly extermi-
nated as the wapiti. The outside limits of its range have not
shrunk materially in the century during which it has been known
to white hunters. It was never found until the fertile, moist country of the Mississippi Valley was passed and the dry plains region
to the west of it reached, and it still exists in some numbers here
and there in this country, as, for instance, in the Bad Lands along
the Little Missouri, and in the Black Hills. But although its limits
of distribution have not very sensibly diminished, there are large
portions of the range within these limits from which it has practically vanished, and in most places its numbers have been woefully
thinned. It holds its own best among the more inaccessible mountain masses of the Rockies, and from Chihuahua to Alberta there
are tracts where it is still abundant. Yet even in these places the
numbers are diminishing, and this process can be arrested only by

better laws, and above all, by a better administration of the law. The national Government could do much by establishing its forest reserves as game reserves, and putting on a sufficient number of forest rangers who should be empowered to prevent all hunting on the reserves. The State governments can do still more. Colorado has good laws, but they are not well enforced. The easy method of accounting for this fact is to say that it is due to the politicians; but in reality the politicians merely represent the wishes, or more commonly the indifference, of the people. As long as the good citizens of a State are indifferent to game protection, or take but a tepid interest in it, the politicians, through their agents, will leave the game laws unenforced. But if the people of Colorado, Wyoming, and Montana come to feel the genuine interest in the enforcement of these laws that the people of Maine and Vermont have grown to take during the past twenty years, that the people of Montana and Wyoming who dwell alongside the Yellowstone Park are already taking—then not only will the mule-deer cease to diminish, but it will positively increase. It is a mistake to suppose that such a change would only be to the advantage of well-to-do sportsmen. Men who are interested in hunting for hunting's sake, men who come from the great cities remote from the mountains in order to get three or four weeks' healthy, manly holiday, would undoubtedly be benefited; but the greatest benefit would be to the people of the localities, of the neighborhoods round about. The presence of the game would attract outsiders who would leave in the country money, or its equivalent, which would many times surpass in value the game they actually killed; and furthermore, the preservation of the game would mean that the ranchmen and grangers who live near its haunts would have in perpetuity the chance of following the pleasantest and healthiest of all out-of-door pastimes; whereas, if through their short-sightedness they destroy, or permit to be destroyed, the game, they are themselves responsible for the fact that their children and children's children will find themselves forever debarred from a pursuit which must under such circumstances become the amusement only of the very rich. If we are really alive to our opportunities under our democratic social and political system, we

] 63 [

can keep for ourselves—and by "ourselves" I mean the enormous bulk of men whose means range from moderate to very small— ample opportunity for the enjoyment of hunting and shooting, of vigorous and blood-stirring out-of-doors sport. If we fail to take advantage of our possibilities, if we fail to pass, in the interest of all, wise game laws, and to see that these game laws are properly enforced, we shall then have to thank ourselves if in the future the game is only found in the game preserves of the wealthy; and under such circumstances only these same wealthy people will have the chance to hunt it.

The mule-deer differs widely from the whitetail in its habits, and especially in its gait, and in the kind of country which it frequents. Although in many parts of its range it is found side by side with its whitetail cousin, the two do not actually associate together, and their propinquity is due simply to the fact that, the river bottoms being a favorite haunt of the whitetail, long tongues of the distribution area of this species are thrust into the domain of its border, less stealthy and less crafty kinsman. Throughout the plains country the whitetail is the deer of the river bottoms, where the rank growth gives it secure hiding-places, as well as ample food. The mule-deer, on the contrary, never comes down into the dense growths of the river bottoms. Throughout the plains country it is the deer of the broken Bad Lands which fringe these river bottoms on either side, and of the rough ravines which wind their way through the Bad Lands to the edge of the prairie country which lies back of them. The broken hills, their gorges filled with patches of ash, buck brush, cedar, and dwarf pine, form a country in which the mule-deer revels. The whitetail will, at times, wander far out on the prairies where the grass is tall and rank; but it is not nearly so bold or fond of the open as the mule-deer. The latter is frequently found in hilly country where the covering is so scanty that the animal must be perpetually on the watch, as if it were a bighorn or prongbuck, in order to spy its foes at a distance and escape before they can come near; whereas the whitetail usually seeks to elude observation by hiding—by its crouching, stealthy habits.

It must be remembered, however, that with the mule-deer, as

] 64 [

with all other species of animals, there is a wide variability in habits under different conditions. This is often forgotten even by trained naturalists, who accept the observations made in one locality as if they applied throughout the range of the species. Thus in the generally good account of the habits of this species in Mr. Lydeker's book on the "Deer of All Lands" it is asserted that mule-deer never dwell permanently in the forest, and feed almost exclusively on grass. The first statement is entirely, the second only partly, true of the mule-deer of the plains from the Little Missouri westward to the headwaters of the Platte, the Yellowstone, and the Big Horn; but there are large parts of the Rockies in which neither statement applies at all. In the course of several hunting trips among the densely wooded mountains of western Montana, along the water-shed separating the streams that flow into Clarke's Fork of the Columbia from those that ultimately empty into Kootenay Lake, I found the mule-deer plentiful in many places where practically the whole country was covered by dense forest, and where the opportunities for grazing were small indeed, as we found to our cost in connection with our pack-train. In this region the mule-deer lived the entire time among the timber, and subsisted for the most part on browse. Occasionally they would find an open glade and graze; but the stomachs of those killed contained not grass, but blueberries and the leaves and delicate tips of bushes. I was not in this country in winter, but it was evident that even at that season the deer must spend their time in the thick timber. There was no chance for them to go above the timber line, because the mountains were densely wooded to their summits, and the white goats of the locality also lived permanently in the timber.* It was far harder to get the mule-deer than it was to get the white-goats, for the latter were infinitely more conspicuous, were slower in their movements, and bolder and less shy. Almost the only way we succeeded in killing the deer was by finding one of their well-trodden paths and lying in wait beside it very early in the morning or quite late in the afternoon. The season was August and September, and the deer were astir long be-

---

* I call particular attention to this fact concerning the white goat, as certain recent writers, including Mr. Madison Grant, have erroneously denied it.

fore sunset. They usually, but not always, lay high up on the mountain-sides, and while they sometimes wandered to and fro browsing on the mountains, they often came down to feed in the valleys, where the berries were thicker. Their paths were well beaten, although, like all game trails, after being as plainly marked as a pony track for a quarter of a mile or so, they would suddenly grow faint and vanish. The paths ran nearly straight up and down hill, and even when entirely undisturbed, the deer often came down them at a great rate, bouncing along in a way that showed that they had no fear of developing the sprung knees which we should fear for a domestic animal which habitually tried the same experiment.

In other habits also the deer vary widely in different localities. For instance, there is an absolute contrast as regards their migratory habits between the mule-deer which live in the Bad Lands along the Little Missouri, and those which live in northwestern Colorado; and this difference is characteristic generally of the deer which in the summer dwell in the high mountains, as contrasted with those which bear and rear their young in the low, broken hill-country. Along the Little Missouri there was no regular or clearly defined migration of the mule-deer in a mass. Some individuals, or groups of individuals, shifted their quarters for a few miles, so that in the spring, for instance, a particular district of a few square miles, in which they had been abundant before, might be wholly without them. But there were other districts, which happened to afford at all times sufficient food and shelter, in which they were to be found the year round; and the animals did not band and migrate as the prongbucks did in the same region. In the immediate neighborhood of my ranch there were groups of high hills containing springs of water, good grass, and an abundance of cedar, ash, and all kinds of brush in which the mule-deer were permanent residents. There were big dry creeks, with well-wooded bottoms, lying among rugged hills, in which I have found whitetail and mule-deer literally within a stone's throw of one another. I once started from two adjoining pockets in this particular creek two does, each with a fawn, one being a mule-deer and the other a whitetail. On another occasion, on an early spring afternoon, just before the fawns were born, I came upon a herd of twenty whitetails, does, and young of the preceding year, grazing greedily on the young grass; and half a mile up the creek, in an almost exactly similar locality, I came upon just such a herd of mule-deer. In each case the animals were so absorbed in the feasting, which was to make up for their winter privations, that I was able to stalk to within fifty yards, though of course I did not shoot.

In northwestern Colorado the conditions are entirely different. Throughout this region there are no whitetail and never have been, although in the winter range of the mule-deer there are a few prongbuck; and the wapiti once abounded. The mule-deer are still plentiful. They make a complete migration summer and winter, so that in neither season is a single individual to be found in the haunts they frequent during the other season. In the summer they live and bring forth their young high up in the main chain of the mountains, in a beautiful country of northern forest growth, dotted with trout-filled brooks and clear lakes. The snowfall is so deep in these wooded mountains that the deer would run great risk of perishing if they stayed therein, and indeed could only winter there at all in very small numbers. Accordingly, when the storms begin in the fall, usually about the first of October, just before the rut, the deer assemble in bands and move west and south to the lower, drier country, where the rugged hills are here and there clothed with an open growth of pinyon and cedar, instead of the tall spruces and pines of the summer range. The migrating bands follow one another along definite trails over mountains, through passes and valleys, and across streams; and their winter range swarms with them a few days after the forerunners have put in their appearance in what has been, during the summer, an absolutely deerless country.

In January and February, 1901, I spent five weeks north of the White River, in northwestern Colorado. It was in the heart of the wintering ground of the great Colorado mule-deer herd. Forty miles away to the east, extending north, lay the high mountains in which these deer had spent the summer. The winter range, in which I was at the time hunting cougars, is a region of comparatively light snowfall, though the cold is bitter. On several occasions during my stay the thermometer went down to twenty degrees below zero. The hills, or low mountains, for it was difficult to know which to call them, were steep and broken, and separated by narrow flats covered with sage-brush. The ordinary trees were the pinyon and cedar, which were scattered in rather open groves over the mountain-sides and the spurs between the ravines. There were also patches of quaking asp, scrub oak, and brush. The entire country was thinly covered with ranches, and there were huge pastures enclosed by wire fences. I have never seen the mule-deer so numerous anywhere as they were in this country at this time; although in 1883, on the Little Missouri, they were almost as plentiful. There was not a day we did not see scores, and on some days we saw hundreds. Frequently they were found in small parties of two or three, or a dozen individuals, but on occasions we saw bands of thirty or forty. Only rarely were they found singly. The fawns were of course well grown, being eight or nine months old, and long out of the spotted coat. They were still accompanying their mothers. Ordinarily a herd would consist of does, fawns, and yearlings, the latter carrying their first antlers. But it was not possible to lay down a universal rule. Again and again I saw herds in which there were one or two full-grown bucks associating with the females and younger deer. At other times we came across small bands of full-grown bucks by themselves, and occasionally a solitary buck. Considering the extent to which these deer must have been persecuted, I did not think them shy. We were hunting on horseback, and had hounds with us, so we made no especial attempt to avoid noise. Yet very frequently we would come close on the deer before they took alarm; and even when alarmed they would sometimes trot slowly off, halting and looking back. On one occasion, in some bad lands, we came upon four bucks which had been sunning themselves on the face of a clay wall. They jumped up and went off one at a time, very slowly, passing diagonally by us, certainly not over seventy yards off. All four could have been shot without effort, and as they had fine antlers I should certainly have killed one, had it been the open season.

When we came on these Colorado mule-deer suddenly, they

generally behaved exactly as their brethren used to in the old days on the Little Missouri; that is, they would run off at a good speed for a hundred yards or so, then slow up, halt, gaze inquisitively at us for some seconds, and again take to flight. While the sun was strong they liked to lie out in the low brush on slopes where they would get the full benefit of the heat. During the heavy snow-storms they usually retreated into some ravine where the trees grew thicker than usual, not stirring until the weight of the storm was over. Most of the night, especially if it was moonlight, they fed; but they were not at all regular about this. I frequently saw them standing up and grazing, or more rarely browsing, in the middle of the day, and in the late afternoon they often came down to graze on the flats within view of the different ranch houses where I happened to stop. The hours for feeding and rest-ing, however, always vary accordingly as the deer are or are not persecuted. In wild localities I have again and again found these deer grazing at all hours of the day, and coming to water at high noon; whereas, where they have been much persecuted, they only begin to feed after dusk, and come to water after dark. Of course during this winter weather they could get no water, snow supply-ing its place.

I was immensely interested with the way they got through the wire fences. A mule-deer is a great jumper; I have known them to clear with ease high timber corral fences surrounding hayricks. If the animals had chosen, they could have jumped any of the wire fences I saw; yet never in a single instance did I see one of them so jump a fence, nor did I ever find in the tell-tale snow-tracks which indicated their having done so. They paid no heed whatever to the fences, so far as I could see, and went through them at will; but they always got between the wires, or went under the lowest wire. The dexterity with which they did this was extraordinary. When alarmed they would run full speed toward a wire fence, would pass through it, often hardly altering their stride, and never making any marks in the snow which looked as though they had crawled. Twice I saw bands thus go through a wire fence, once at speed, the other time when they were not alarmed. On both occasions they were too far off to allow me to see exactly their mode of procedure, but on examining the snow where they had passed, there was not the slightest mark of their bodies, and the alteration in their gait, as shown by the footprints, was hardly perceptible. In one instance, however, where I scared a young buck which ran over a hill and through a wire fence on the other side, I found one of his antlers lying beside the fence, it having evidently been knocked off by the wire. Their antlers were getting very loose, and toward the end of our stay they had begun to shed them.

The deer were preyed on by many foes. Sportsmen and hide-hunters had been busy during the fall migrations, and the ranch-men of the neighborhood were shooting them occasionally for food, even when we were out there. The cougars at this season were preying upon them practically to the exclusion of everything else. We came upon one large fawn which had been killed by a bobcat. The gray wolves were also preying upon them. A party of these wolves can sometimes run down even an unwounded black-tail; I have myself known of their performing this feat. Twice on this very hunt we came across the carcasses of blacktail which had thus been killed by wolves, and one of the cow-punchers at a ranch where we were staying came in and reported to us that while riding among the cattle that afternoon he had seen two coy-otes run a young mule-deer to a standstill, and they would with-out doubt have killed it had they not been frightened by his ap-proach. Still the wolf is very much less successful than the cougar in killing these deer, and even the cougar continually fails in his stalks. But the deer were so plentiful that at this time all the cou-gars we killed were very fat, and evidently had no difficulty in getting as much venison as they needed. The wolves were not as well off, and now and then made forays on the young stock of the ranchmen, which at this season the cougar let alone, reserving his attention to them for the summer season when the deer had van-ished.

In the Big Horn Mountains, where I also saw a good deal of the mule-deer, their habits were intermediate between those of the species that dwell on the plains and those that dwell in the densely timbered regions of the Rockies farther to the northwest.

In the summer time they lived high up on the plateaus of the Big
Horn, sometimes feeding in the open glades and sometimes in the
pine forests. In the fall they browsed on certain of the bushes almost exclusively. In winter they came down into the low country.
South of the Yellowstone Park, where the wapiti swarmed, the
mule-deer were not numerous. I believe that by choice they prefer
rugged, open country, and they certainly care comparatively little
for bad weather, as they will often visit bleak, windswept ridges in
midwinter, as being places where they can best get food at that
season, when the snow lies deep in the sheltered places. Nevertheless, many of the species pass their whole life in thick timber.

My chief opportunities for observing the mule-deer were in the
eighties, when I spent much of my time on my ranch on the Little
Missouri. Mule-deer were then very plentiful, and I killed more of
them than of all other game put together. At that time in the cattle country no ranchman ever thought of killing beef, and if we
had fresh meat at all it was ordinarily venison. In the fall we
usually tried to kill enough deer to last out the winter. Until the
settlers came in, the Little Missouri country was an ideal range for
mule-deer, and they fairly swarmed; while elk were also plentiful,
and the restless herds of the buffalo surged at intervals through
the land. After 1882 and 1883 the buffalo and elk were killed out,
the former completely, and the latter practically, and by that
time the skin hunters, and then the ranchers, turned their attention chiefly to the mule-deer. It lived in open country where there
was cover for the stalker, and so it was much easier to kill than
either the whitetail, which was found in the dense cover of the
river bottoms, or the prongbuck, which was found far back from
the river, on the flat prairies where there was no cover at all. I
have been informed of other localities in which the antelope has
disappeared long before the mule-deer, and I believe that in the
Rockies the mule-deer has a far better chance of survival than the
antelope has on the plains; but on the Little Missouri the antelope
continued plentiful long after the mule-deer had become decidedly scarce. In 1886 I think the antelope were fully as abundant as
ever they were, while the mule-deer had woefully diminished. In
the early nineties there were still regions within thirty or forty

miles of my ranch where the antelope were very plentiful—far more so than the mule-deer were at that time. Now they are both scarce along the Little Missouri, and which will outlast the other I cannot say.

In the old days, as I have already said, it was by no means infrequent to see both the whitetail and the mule-deer close together, and when, under such circumstances, they were alarmed, one got a clear idea of the extraordinary gait which is the mule-deer's most striking characteristic. It trots well, gallops if hard pressed, and is a good climber, though much inferior to the mountain sheep. But its normal gait consists of a series of stiff-legged bounds, all four feet leaving and striking the ground at the same time. This gait differs more from the gait of bighorn, prong-buck, whitetail, and wapiti than the gaits of these latter animals differ among themselves. The wapiti, for instance, rarely gallops, but when he does, it is a gallop of the ordinary type. The prong-buck runs with a singularly even gait; whereas the whitetail makes great bounds, some much higher than others. But fundamentally in all cases the action is the same, and has no resemblance to the stiff-legged buck jumping which is the ordinary means of progression of the mule-deer. These jumps carry it not only on the level, but up and down hill at a great speed. It is said to be a tiresome gait for the animal, if hunted for any length of time on the level; but of this I cannot speak with full knowledge.

Compared to the wapiti, the mule-deer, like our other small deer, is a very silent animal. For a long time I believed it uttered no sound beyond the snort of alarm and the rare bleat of the doe to her fawn; but one afternoon I heard two bucks grunting or barking at one another in a ravine back of the ranchhouse, and crept up and shot them. I was still uncertain whether this was an indication of a regular habit; but a couple of years later, on a moonlight night just after sunset, I heard a big buck travelling down a ravine and continually barking, evidently as a love challenge. I have been informed by some hunters that the bucks at the time of the rut not infrequently thus grunt and bark; but most hunters are ignorant of this habit; and it is certainly not a common practice.

] 72 [

The species is not nearly as gregarious as the wapiti or caribou. During the winter the bucks are generally found singly, or in small parties by themselves, although occasionally one will associate with a party of does and of young deer. When in May or June—for the exact time varies with the locality—the doe brings forth her young, she retires to some lonely thicket. Sometimes one and sometimes two fawns are brought forth. They lie very close for the first few days. I have picked them up and handled them without their making the slightest effort to escape, while the mother hung about a few hundred yards off. On one occasion I by accident surprised a doe in the very act of giving birth to two fawns. One had just been born and the other was born as the doe made her first leap away. She ran off with as much speed and unconcern as if nothing whatever had happened. I passed on immediately, lest she should be so frightened as not to come back to the fawns. It has happened that where I have found the newly born fawns I have invariably found the doe to be entirely alone, but her young of the previous year must sometimes at least be in the neighborhood, for a little later I have frequently seen the doe and her fawn or fawns, and either one or two young of the previous year, together. Often, however, those young deer will be alone, or associated with an older doe which is barren. The bucks at the same time go to secluded places; sometimes singly, while sometimes an old buck will be accompanied by a younger one, or a couple of old bucks will lie together. They move about as little as possible while their horns are growing, and if a hunter comes by, they will lie far closer than at any other time of the year, squatting in the dense thickets as if they were whitetails.

When in the Bad Lands of the Western Dakotas the late September breezes grow cold, then the bucks, their horns already clean of velvet which they have thrashed off on the bushes and saplings, feel their necks begin to swell; and early in October—sometimes not until November—they seek the does. The latter, especially the younger ones, at first flee in frantic haste. As the rut goes on the bucks become ever bolder and more ardent. Not only do they chase the does by night, but also by day. I have sat on the side of a ravine in the Bad Lands at noon and seen a young doe race past me as if followed by a wolf. When she was out of sight a big buck appeared on her trail, following it by scent, also at speed. When he had passed I got up, and the motion frightened a younger buck which was following two or three hundred yards in the rear of the big one. After a while the doe yields, and the buck then accompanies her. If, however, it is early in the season, he may leave her entirely in order to run after another doe. Later in the season he will have a better chance of adding the second doe to his harem, or of robbing another buck of the doe or does which he has accumulated. I have often seen merely one doe and one buck together, and I have often seen a single doe which for several days was accompanied by several bucks, one keeping off the others. But generally the biggest bucks collect each for himself several does, yearlings also being allowed in the band. The exact amount of companionship with the does allowed these young bucks depends somewhat upon the temper of the master buck. In books by imperfectly informed writers we often see allusions to the buck as protecting the doe, or even taking care of the fawn. Charles Dudley Warner, for instance, in describing with great skill and pathos an imaginary deer hunt, after portraying the death of the doe, portrays the young fawn as following the buck when the latter comes back to it in the evening.* As a matter of fact, while the fawn is so young as to be wholly dependent upon the doe, the buck never comes near either. Moreover, during the period when the buck and the doe are together, the buck's attitude is merely that of a brutal, greedy, and selfish tyrant. He will unhesitatingly rob the doe of any choice bit of food, and though he will fight to keep her if another buck approaches, the moment that a dangerous foe appears his one thought is for his own preservation. He will not only desert the doe, but if he is an old and cunning buck, he will try his best to sacrifice her by diverting the attention of the pursuer to her and away from him.

By the end of the rut the old bucks are often exhausted, their sides are thin, their necks swollen; though they are never as gaunt

* While the situation thus described was an impossible one, the purpose of Mr. Warner's article was excellent, it being intended as a protest against hunting deer while the fawns are young, and against killing them in the water.

as wapiti bulls at this time. They then rest as much as possible, feeding all the time to put on fat before winter arrives, and rapidly attaining a very high condition.

Except in dire need no one would kill a deer after the hard weather of winter begins or before the antlers of the buck are full-grown and the fawns are out of the spotted coat. Even in the old days we, who lived in the ranch country, always tried to avoid killing deer in the spring or early summer, though we often shot buck antelope at those times. The close season for deer varies in different States, and now there is generally a limit set to the number any one hunter can kill; for the old days of wasteful plenty are gone forever.

To my mind there is a peculiar fascination in hunting the mule-deer. By the time the hunting season has arrived the buck is no longer the slinking beast of the thicket, but a bold and yet wary dweller in the uplands. Frequently he can be found clear of all cover, often at midday, and his habits at this season are, from the hunter's standpoint, rather more like those of the wapiti than of the whitetail; but each band, though continually shifting its exact position stays permanently in the same tract of country, whereas wapiti are apt to wander.

In the old days, when mule-deer were plentiful in country through which a horse could go at a fair rate of speed, it was common for the hunter to go on horseback, and not to dismount save at the moment of the shot. In the early eighties, while on my ranch on the Little Missouri, this was the way in which I usually hunted. When I first established my ranch I often went out, in the fall, after the day's work was over, and killed a deer before dark. If it was in September, I would sometimes start after supper. Later in the year I would take supper when I got back. Under such circumstances my mode of procedure was simple. Deer were plentiful. Every big tangle of hills, every set of grassy coulees winding down to a big creek bottom, was sure to contain them. The time being short, with at most only an hour or two of light, I made no effort to find the tracks of a deer or to spy one afar off. I simply rode through the likely places, across the heads of the ravines or down the winding valleys, until I jumped a deer close enough up to give me a shot. The unshod hoofs of the horse made but little noise as he shuffled along at the regular cow-pony fox trot, and I kept him close into the bank or behind cover, so as to come around each successive point without warning. If the ground was broken and rugged, I made no attempt to go fast. If, on the other hand, I struck a smooth ravine with gentle curves, I would often put the pony to a sharp canter or gallop, so as to come quickly on any deer before it could quite make up its mind what course was best to follow. Sooner or later, as I passed a thick clump of young ash or buck brush, or came abruptly around a sharp bend, there would be a snort, and then the thud, thud, thud, of four hoofs striking the ground exactly in unison, and away would go a mule-deer with the peculiar bounding motion of its kind. The pony, well accustomed to the work, stopped short, and I was off its back in an instant. If the deer had not made out exactly what I was, it would often show by its gait that it was not yet perpared to run straight out of sight. Under such circumstances I would wait until it stopped and turned round to look back. If it was going very fast, I took the shot running. Once I put up a young buck from some thick brush in the bottom of a winding washout. I leaped off the pony, standing within ten yards of the washout. The buck went up a hill on my left, and as he reached the top and paused for a second on the sky line, I fired. At the shot there was a great scrambling and crashing in the washout below me, and another and larger buck came out and tore off in frantic haste. I fired several shots at him, finally bringing him down. Meanwhile, the other buck had disappeared, but there was blood on his trail, and I found him lying down in the next coulee, and finished him. This was not much over a mile from the ranch house, and after dressing the deer, I put one behind the saddle and one on it, and led the pony home.

Such hunting, though great fun, does not imply any particular skill either in horsemanship, marksmanship, or plainscraft and knowledge of the animal's habits; and it can of course be followed only where the game is very plentiful. Ordinarily the mule-deer must be killed by long tramping among the hills, skillful stalking, and good shooting. The successful hunter should possess good eyes, good wind, and good muscles. He should know how to take cover and how to use his rifle. The work is sufficiently rough to test any man's endurance, and yet there is no such severe and intense toil as in following true mountain game, like the bighorn or white goat. As the hunter's one aim is to see the deer before it sees him, he can only use the horse to take him to the hunting ground. Then he must go through the most likely ground and from every point of vantage scan with minute care the landscape round about, while himself unseen. If the country is wild and the deer have not been much molested, he will be apt to come across a band that is feeding. Under such circumstances it is easy to see them at once. But if lying down, it is astonishing how the gray of their winter coats fits in with the color of their surroundings. Too often I have looked carefully over a valley with my glasses until, thinking I had searched every nook, I have risen and gone forward, only to see a deer rise and gallop off out of range from some spot which I certainly thought I had examined with all possible precaution. If the hunter is not himself hidden, he will have his labor for his pains. Neither the mule-deer nor the whitetail is by any means as keen-sighted as the pronghorn antelope, and men accustomed chiefly to antelope shooting are quite right in speaking of the sight of deer as poor by comparison. But this is only by comparison. A motionless object does not attract the deer's gaze as it attracts the telescopic eye of a prongbuck; but any motion is seen at once, and as soon as this has occurred, the chances of the hunter are usually at an end. On the other hand, from the nature of its haunts the mule-deer usually offers fairly good opportunities for stalking. It is not as big or as valuable as the elk, and therefore it is not as readily seen or as eagerly followed, and in consequence holds its own better. But though the sport it yields calls normally for a greater amount of hardihood and endurance in the hunter than is the case with the sport yielded by the prongbuck, and especially by the whitetail, yet when existing in like numbers it is easier to kill than either of these two animals.

Sometimes in the early fall, when hunting from the ranch, I have spent the night in some likely locality, sleeping rolled up in a blanket on the ground so as to be ready to start at the first streak of dawn. On one such occasion a couple of mule-deer came to where my horse was picketed just before I got up. I heard them snort or whistle, and very slowly unwrapped myself from the blanket, turned over, and crawled out, rifle in hand. Overhead the stars were paling in the faint gray light, but the ravine in which the deer were was still so black that, watch as I would, I could not see them. I feared to move around lest I might disturb them, but after wiggling toward a little jutting shoulder I lay still to wait for the light. They went off, however, while it was still too dusk to catch more than their dim and formless outlines, and though I followed them as rapidly and cautiously as possible, I never got a shot at them. On other occasions fortune has favored me, and before the sun rose I have spied some buck leisurely seeking his day bed, and have been able either to waylay him or make a running stalk on him from behind.

In the old days it was the regular thing with most ranchmen to take a trip in the fall for the purpose of laying in the winter's supply of venison. I frequently took such trips myself, and though occasionally we killed wapiti, bighorn, prongbuck, and whitetail, our ordinary game was the mule-deer. Around my ranch it was not necessary to go very far. A day's journey with the wagon would usually take us to where a week's hunting would enable us to return with a dozen deer or over. If there was need of more, I would repeat the hunt later on. I have several times killed three of these deer in a day, but I do not now recall ever killing a greater number. It is perhaps unnecessary to say that every scrap of flesh was used.

These hunts were always made late in the fall, usually after the close of the rut. The deer were then banded, and were commonly found in parties of from three or four to a score, although the big bucks might be lying by themselves. The weather was apt to be cold, and the deer evidently liked to sun themselves, so that at midday they could be found lying sometimes in thin brush and sometimes boldly out on the face of a cliff or hill. If they were unmolested, they would feed at intervals throughout the day, and not until the bands had been decimated by excessive hunting did they ever spend the hours of daylight in hiding.

On such a hunt our proceedings were simple. The nights were longer than the days, and therefore we were away from camp at the first streak of dawn, and might not return until long after darkness. All the time between was spent in climbing and walking through the rugged hills, keeping a sharp lookout for our game. Only too often we were seen before we ourselves saw the quarry, and even when this was not the case the stalks were sometimes failures. Still blank days were not very common. Probably every hunter remembers with pride some particular stalk. I recall now outwitting a big buck which I had seen and failed to get on two successive days. He was hanging about a knot of hills with brush on their shoulders, and was not only very watchful, but when he lay down always made his bed at the lower end of a brush patch, whence he could see into the valley below, while it was impossible to approach him from above, through the brush, without giving the alarm. On the third day I saw him early in the morning, while he was feeding. He was very watchful, and I made no attempt to get near him, simply peeping at him until he finally went into a patch of thin brush and lay down. As I knew what he was I could distinctly make him out. If I had not seen him go in, I certainly never would have imagined that he was a deer, even had my eyes been able to pick him out at all among the gray shadows and small dead tree-tops. Having waited until he was well settled down, I made a very long turn and came up behind him, only to find that the direction of the wind and the slope of the hill rendered it an absolute impossibility to approach him unperceived. After careful study of the ground I abandoned the effort, and returned to my former position, having spent several hours of considerable labor in vain. It was now about noon, and I thought I would lie still to see what he would do when he got up, and accordingly I ate my lunch stretched at full length in the long grass which sheltered me from the wind. From time to time I peered cautiously between two stones toward where the buck lay. It was nearly mid-afternoon before he moved. Sometimes mule-deer rise with a single motion, all four legs unbending like springs, so that the four hoofs touch the ground at once. This old buck, however, got up very slowly, looked about for certainly five minutes, and then came directly down the hill and toward me. When he had nearly reached the bottom of the valley between us he turned to the right and sauntered rapidly down it. I slipped back and trotted as fast as I could without losing my breath along the hither side of the spur which lay between me and the buck. While I was out of sight he had for some reason made up his mind to hurry, and when I was still fifty yards from the end of the spur he came in sight just beyond it, passing at a swinging trot. I dropped on one knee so quickly that for a moment he evidently could not tell what I was—my buckskin shirt and gray slough-hat fading into the color of the background—and halted, looking sharply around. Before he could break into flight my bullet went through his shoulders.

Twice I have killed two of these deer at a shot; once two bucks, and once a doe and a buck.

It has proved difficult to keep the mule-deer in captivity, even in large private parks or roomy zoological gardens. I think this is because hitherto the experiment has been tried east of the Mississippi in an alien habitat. The wapiti and whitetail are species that are at home over most of the United States, East and West, in rank, wet prairies, dense woodland, and dry mountain regions alike; but the mule-deer has a far more sharply localized distribution. In the Bronx Zoological Gardens, in New York, Mr. Hornaday informs me that he has comparatively little difficulty in keeping up the stock alike of wapiti and whitetail by breeding—as indeed any visitor can see for himself. The same is true in the game preserves in the wilder regions of New York and New England; but hitherto the mule-deer has offered an even more difficult problem in captivity than the pronghorn antelope. Doubtless the difficulty would be minimized if the effort at domestication were made in the neighborhood of the Rocky Mountains.

The true way to preserve the mule-deer, however, as well as our other game, is to establish on the nation's property great nurseries and wintering grounds, such as the Yellowstone Park, and then to secure fair play for the deer outside these grounds by a wisely planned and faithfully executed series of game laws. This is the really democratic method of solving the problem. Occasionally even yet someone will assert that the game "belongs to the people, and should be given over to them"—meaning, thereby, that there should be no game laws, and that every man should be at liberty indiscriminately to kill every kind of wild animal, harmless, useless, or noxious, until the day when our woods become wholly bereft of all the forms of higher animal life. Such an argument can only be made from the standpoint of those big game dealers in the cities who care nothing for the future, and desire to make money at the present day by a slaughter which in the last analysis only benefits the wealthy people who are able to pay for the game; for once the game has been destroyed, the livelihood of the professional gunner will be taken away. Most emphatically wild game not on private property *does* belong to the people, and the only way in which the people can secure their ownership is by protecting it in the interest of all against the vandal few. As we grow older I think most of us become less keen about that part of the hunt which consists in the killing. I know that as far as I am concerned I have long gone past the stage when the chief end of a hunting trip was the bag. One or two bucks, or enough grouse and trout to keep the camp supplied, will furnish all the sport necessary to give zest and point to a trip in the wilderness. When hunters proceed on such a plan they do practically no damage to the game. Those who are not willing to act along these lines of their own free will, should be made to by the State. The people of Montana, Wyoming, and Colorado, and of the States nearby, can do a real service primarily to themselves, but secondarily to others also, by framing and executing laws which will keep these noble deer as permanent denizens of their lofty mountains and beautiful valleys. There are other things much more important than game laws; but it will be a great mistake to imagine, because until recently in Europe game laws have been administered in the selfish interest of one class and against the interest of the people as a whole, that here in this country, and under our institutions, they would not be beneficial to all of our people. So far from game laws being in the interest of the few, they are emphatically in the interest of the many. The very rich man can stock a private game preserve, or journey afar off to where game is still plentiful; but it is only where the game is carefully preserved by the State that the man of small means has any chance to enjoy the keen delight of the chase.

There are many sides to the charm of big game hunting; nor should it be regarded as being without its solid advantages from the standpoint of national character. Always in our modern life, the life of a highly complex industrialism, there is a tendency to softening of fibre. This is true of our enjoyments; and it is no less true of very many of our business occupations. It is not true of such work as railroading, a purely modern development, nor yet of work like that of those who man the fishing fleets; but it is preeminently true of all occupations which cause men to lead sedentary lives in great cities. For these men it is especially necessary to provide hard and rough play. Of course, if such play is made a serious business, the result is very bad; but this does not in the least affect the fact that within proper limits the play itself is good. Vigorous athletic sports carried on in a same spirit are healthy. The hardy out-of-door sports of the wilderness are even healthier. It is a mere truism to say that the qualities developed by the hunter are the qualities needed by the soldier; and a curious feature of the changed conditions of modern warfare is that they call, to a much greater extent than during the two or three centuries immediately past, for the very qualities of individual initiative, ability to live and work in the open, and personal skill in the management of horse and weapons, which are fostered by a hunter's life. No training in the barracks or on the parade-ground is as good as the training given by a hard hunting trip in which a man really does the work for himself, learns to face emergencies, to study country, to perform feats of hardihood, to face exposure and undergo severe labor. It is an excellent thing for any man to be a good horseman and a good marksman, to be bold and hardy, and wonted to feats of strength and endurance, to be able to live in the open, and to feel a self-reliant readiness in any crisis. Big game hunting tends to produce or develop exactly these physical and moral traits. To say that it may be pursued in a manner or to an extent which is demoralizing, is but to say what can likewise be said of all other pastimes and of almost all kinds of serious business. That it can be abused either in the way in which it is done, or the extent to which it is carried, does not alter the fact that it is in itself a sane and healthy recreation.

THE SECRET LIFE OF THE COTTONTAIL DEER

John Madson

If after reading this piece you end up agreeing with me that it is an absolute gem, then I'm mighty proud to let you know that I played a small role in bringing it into being.

I was editing Outdoor Life *in the summer of 1977 and was stuck without a good deer piece for our October issue. I turned to a man I knew could give us something special, John Madson.*

John was Assistant Director of Conservation for Winchester, headquartered at Nilo Farms at East Alton, Illinois, and an old friend. I had published many of his pieces at Sports Afield *while I was editor there, and the readers loved 'em.*

I asked John if he had ever tried a story that put all of his feelings about the whitetail into words. "Nope," came the reply. He had thought about it all his life but had never moved on it. "Maybe it's time," he said.

This article is the happy result of that conversation. It ran in the October, 1977, issue of Outdoor Life *and later was included in the collection of John's stories,* Back Home, *published by Winchester Press.*

Today John has retired from his Winchester post and has become a contributing editor to Outdoor Life, *where he is on board almost every issue. With work like this, he'll keep winning new fans for a long time.*

IF THERE'S ANYTHING DULL ABOUT A WHITETAIL DEER, I don't know it. I like everything about him. His biology is fascinating. So is his management, his history, and the old legends and grandpa yarns. I like to talk about whitetails with hunters, and with such seasoned deer men as Jack Calhoun of Illinois and Bill Severinghaus of New York. I admire a deer rifle that shoots true and handles easy. I've got a hunch that good tracking snow and prime roast venison may just help a man live forever. And as the years go by, I become more and more absorbed with the essence of the whitetail—the cunning thing inside that makes him what he is.

The whitetail is the only big-game animal that has succeeded in our woodlots and field edges, and he's made it because he's sharp. His senses of smell and hearing are acute beyond belief, and his vision is probably as keen as ours even though it's in black and white.

His success, however, doesn't just depend on the sensory information that he soaks up but on the ways that he plugs it in. Those keen senses detect the slightest changes in the deer's home range. And how he knows that home range! He knows every little break in terrain, the open ground and its edges, each windfall, thicket, rootwad, spring seep, berry tangle, cutbank, and mire. No human hunter can possibly know the deer range as well.

Knowing that range, and sensing an alien presence there, the whitetail reacts in many ways. He may lie doggo, watchful and waiting, or sneak catlike around an intruder. He may explode into action, white banner astern, making spectacular leaps over obstacles and racing headlong through heavy timber—only to stop somewhere just beyond and fade into a thicket off to one side to resume lurking and spying. He has a particular genius for melting into cover that couldn't possibly conceal a deer.

A few years back, my old friend Keith Kirkpatrick was on a whitetail hunt with several friends. They were driving some farm timber known to have deer, but they hadn't seen any. One of the group, a young man who had never hunted deer, asked the farmer where the deer were. The farmer didn't know, but he figured that somebody ought to hunt a brushy draw that ran from the timber out into the fields.

The hunter worked through this cover, coming out into an open field where there was a little pond. It didn't look like much. But as he stood there wondering what to do, he heard quail chirping in the fringe of foxtail and sloughgrass. He shucked the deer slugs from his shotgun, slipped in some bird loads, and stepped into the grass. The covey roared up. And at the same instant a big buck broke cover a few yards away. He tore across the fields and vanished, leaving our hero with a gun full of bird loads and egg on his face.

It was a standard whitetail trick. We should be used to it by now, especially out in the Midwest where good deer populations thrive in woodlots, thin fringes of creek brush, and all manner of little cover scraps. Still, it's always a surprise to find deer there.

] 85 [

Even more surprising are the people who share their land with these superb animals and never know it.

There was a certain place in central Iowa where I usually could count on a pheasant or two late in the season—a little dimple in the rolling farmland that couldn't be seen by road hunters. It was in the exact center of the mile-square land section, half a mile from any road, the remnant of an old farm dump that was set about with sumac and undergrown with giant foxtail.

I hunted up to it one day in late December, working into the wind on an inch of snow. By the time I was within gun range of the little covert I could sense that empty, birdless quality that a long-time pheasant hunter learns. But I played out the hand anyway. I stood in the fence corner for a couple of minutes, looking things over, knowing that this might do as much to flush a hiding rooster as any cover-kicking. Nothing. I jacked open the Model 12 and swung up on the fence.

He came to his feet in one fluid, powerful movement and was instantly on his way with that buoyant grace that even very large whitetails have. He had been lying beside a roll of rusty fencewire, his antlers melting into the sumac around him. He couldn't have been 50 feet from me. If he'd been a pheasant's head I might have seen him. I was hunting pheasants. I hadn't expected anything like him.

I knew him for what he was. I was a professional wildlifer by

that time. In fact, I had just finished working at the Lansing check station for five days, and we had weighed and aged many deer, including a dozen bucks that would take any hunter's breath away. But nothing like this one.

His broad back looked as if it might hold water in a heavy rain, the gray neck seeming as thick as a Holstein bull's. He wore a typical rack, though I haven't the slightest idea of how many points there were. It was the sheer weight of antler that stays in my mind. Between burr and brow tine each main beam was as thick as my wrist, arching out and forward in great curves, with broad webbing where the tines arose. Ten days before we had weighed a buck that would have gone 250 pounds, and this one was bigger.

He rose weightless out of his bed and ran off down the fence line, making no sound that I can remember. It was easily the largest whitetail I had ever seen. He left me there on the fence, heart pounding, breath coming short, and legs trembling.

I casually asked two farmers living on that square mile if they'd seen any deer around, especially anything big. Yeah, they'd seen a few deer earlier but the hunters must have killed them all. I told the local game warden, a good friend. He was keenly interested, but hadn't seen such a buck nor heard of anyone who had. Same with several good local hunters.

That deer was probably never taken by a hunter. There'd have been no keeping it out of the record books. Nor was he killed on a road during the antlerless season. We'd have known that, too, for no car could have survived it. The point is this: an incredible stag was living in an intensely farmed and hunted region and had not been detected. For all I knew, I was the only person who ever saw him up close.

The secret of the whitetail's success is simply his success at keeping secret. Given an option, he'll always play it sly.

I once started a whitetail buck near the head of a timbered valley. Flag up, he ran out of sight around a bend of the creek. I tracked him in the new snow. As soon as he was out of sight, he began walking slowly uphill, stopping now and then to look down his backtrail. At the top of the hill was a three-wire fence that the deer had crawled under. The bottom wire was just 17 inches from the ground. I measured it. To appreciate this, try crawling under a low fence with a small rocking chair strapped to your head. That buck did. He could have jumped that fence from a standing start. It would have been far easier, but it just wasn't the sly way to handle a fence with me coming up behind.

In manner of escape and evasion, the whitetail deer can be remarkably like the cottontail rabbit. (It's not unusual for deer to hide in big brushpiles in heavily hunted farm country.)

The cottontail starts with a burst of speed that quickly outdistances men and dogs. Then he slows or even stops and ambles around in a circle to his starting point, even though a couple of beagles may be singing down his trail. It's much the same with the cottontail deer—the flashy start and the sly circling back to home base.

Hunters long experienced in chasing deer with hounds report that such deer may not even run. At least not flat-out. Archibald Rutledge once said that in all his years of hunting he had seen only two or three deer in full flight before dogs, and in each case the deer was wounded and about to be caught. In front of hounds, Rutledge said, deer usually loaf along, dodge, make a few showy feints and spectacular jumps, but generally play it cool. He once watched a big buck at the head of a drive suddenly "appear like an apparition and then, with extraordinary skill, efface himself from the landscape." It was later found that the deer had turned and sneaked to safety between the hounds and the hunters.

I once played tag for four hours with a buck on a Mississippi River island. It was only about eight acres, but heavily covered. I was alone, hunting steadily and carefully, and I had one quick glimpse of the deer at the beginning and another just before I quit. So I knew that he hadn't left the island during the hunt. We were perfectly synchronized; if we hadn't been I might have killed him. But when I stopped, the deer stopped; when I sneaked, he sneaked. We must have cut each others' tracks a dozen times. By the end of the day I was kicking willows and saying things not for the young to hear. I came back the next day with Joe Martelle, my old river friend. You guessed it. The buck had left.

The whitetail's ability to adjust to man's doings is uncanny. A deer can even adjust to gunfire—if it's not being directed at him.

My son Chris and I were bowhunting one late October morning in the Glades, a wild tangle of Illinois River backwaters and bottomland not far from the Mississippi. We were on tree stands in big silver maples looking out over a cornfield that had been sharecropped.

There were local mallards and woodies back in the swamp, and duck blinds only a couple of hundred yards behind us. We hadn't counted on that. In the frosty dawn the big shotguns were thunderous. And yet, stealing down a cornrow toward us came a fat whitetail buck. At each salvo of the 12-bores back in the Glades, the buck lowered his head a notch and kept walking directly toward the guns. He was alert but not particularly nervous. He must have had a good reason. Probably trailing a doe. Anyway, it was clear that he knew the shooting wasn't at him, and when we last saw him he was still heading back into the swamp in the direction of the gunfire.

The whitetail is one of a kind, a big-game species that thrives in small-game habitats. No other large mammal could have done it; none has that unique set of qualities and responds so well to management. In most states today, this deer is the biggest and most prized of wildlife. It has special meaning to the ordinary hunter, not just as big game, but as available big game. It is the common man's chance for high personal adventure—and often his only chance.

There's all that, and something more.

Whitetails aren't often hunted in real wilderness. They are often hunted in the tamest of farmlands. But even in a horseweed patch at the edge of a cornfield, a deer lends special wildness to the land so that whenever the deer is found it is a truly wild place. Deer carry wilderness entangled in their antlers; their hoofprints put the stamp of wildness on tame country.

When I was growing up in the mid-1930s, our part of central Iowa held a lot for an outdoor boy. But deer weren't part of it. About the only deer we had was a little fenced herd in the Ledges State Park on the Des Moines River. They were interesting, but they didn't offer much to small boys who loved to prowl the woods. They were park deer, kept deer. They were not real deer, if you see my meaning.

I was about 14 the time dad and I were fishing the Des Moines River, and I took a shortcut across the inside of a big sandbar. There was a dead buck lying there at the edge of the willows. There was no sign of injury. The buck was just dead, maybe four or five days dead, fly-blown and swollen. It was the first wild deer I had ever seen, dead or alive, and it instantly changed my world.

He was imposing. His rack, still with some tatters of dried velvet on them, seemed huge. I had never been so close to a deer. There was no fence around this one. He had been ranging free, leaving his great heart-shaped prints at muddy creek edges, and finally leaving his corporeal being here for a boy to find. Buzzards and possums would soon remove that, but something of the deer's presence would stay to renew the spirit that faded from the valley 60 years before.

An almost tangible change had come over the sandbar—the thing that comes when a boy is touched by genuine wildness for the first time. It's something like falling in love. Windows had opened in my horizons, revealing wonders out back of beyond. Up until then I had played at imagining this valley to be a wild place, though I knew it wasn't. But to find a wild deer there!

That has been 40 years ago, and I still vividly remember the quality of light on the sand and the striped willow-shade that lay across the dead deer's flanks. There suddenly seemed to be a dusty quality to the light, and a hush and suspension of all moving things. It was the old spell of wildness that other boys have felt in all other times, and it must always be the same.

I dropped my fishing rod and tore off to fetch dad. He was as impressed as I. We must have hung around there for an hour or more, marveling and speculating and not knowing what to do about it. Dad told me all he knew about deer, which wasn't much, but it was impressive at the time. So was the sudden revelation that inside my stern, graying father there was a boy my own age. I suspected then, and know now, that men and boys are about the same when confronted with genuine wildness. It makes boys older somehow, and men younger, and they may come together at a common point on common-ground.

I prize the whitetail as huntable game. There is none better. I prize his fine meat and soft leather, and I waste neither. But even more, I cherish the whitetail deer for breathing wildness into our bland, tame countrysides—reminding us of old times and old doings and the meaning of being young and free.

TWO

Skills and Crafts

THE RIGHT DEER RIFLE—
EAST AND WEST

John Jobson

Although he had been camping editor for Sports Afield *for many years before I became editor in 1970, the late John Jobson had one more passionate interest—big game hunting and rifle shooting. Like his close friend, Jack O'Connor, he loved all the arguments that popped up in the hot-stove league about the merits and flaws of various calibers and could back up his own opinions with worldwide field experiences few could equal. Also like O'Connor, he tended to reserve his highest forms of praise for one caliber, the .270.*

One of the first things I did at the magazine was to urge John to begin wearing two hats, taking on both the camping department and hunting editor assignments.

This piece is one of many John produced during the seven years of my editorship. Moving into the territory that had been dominated by O'Connor, Warren Page, Pete Brown, and Pete Kuhlhoff, John quickly established his credentials as a very strong new boy on the block. His gun and hunting pieces were superb, showing freshness and wit seldom seen in that sometimes-tired area of outdoor writing.

John's death from illness in 1979 saddened many who admired the man and his work, including Jim Rikhoff, founder and owner of Amwell Press. Now Jim has contracted to publish a deluxe anthology composed of John's best pieces. It will appear sometime in 1981 and should bring considerable support and rejoicing from those who love the kind of fresh interesting writing we're presenting here.

For a full course of John's camping stuff, check out his The Complete Book of Camping *(Winchester Press).*

THE WIDESPREAD ASSUMPTION regarding the preferred stratagem for the tyro to adopt in selecting the ideal deer rifle goes: If seeking wily whitetails east of the Mississippi, it's not only stylish but positively *de rigueur* to turn out with a fast-repeating short-range affair which "comes up nat'rally" enabling one to "snap shoot." It should propel buxom round-nosed bullets which cleverly negotiate brush, saplings, stumps and other dratted impedimenta like a bowling ball hurtling through a set of pins. Traditionally, it seems mandatory for the proper eastern deer rifle to have a trajectory like a basketball arching for the hoop.

Should some untutored churl cloddishly show up in certain Maine or Michigan deer-hunting camps with a high-velocity, minute-of-angle precision-scoped *bolt action* capable of dependably putting the quietus on a 12-pointer at any range exceeding a sporting 89 yards, the local in-crowd would recoil with expressions akin to the purple-mottled visage of a Scot Laird when the inevitable Yank arrives on his ancestral estates packing an automatic shotgun with which to pot driven grouse.

On the other hand, westward of Father Of Waters, the exact opposite holds true . . . supposedly. No mule deer with normal intellect are thought to offer a decent shot at less than 367 yards. Often as not, Old Mossy-horn will be on the next mountain with nothing intervening except undefiled ozone of such clarity that you can, through the 3/9X scope of your .257 Weatherby Magnum, plainly see him bat his eyelashes. To make the scene here with a buckhorn-sighted brush-bustin' pumpkin roller would definitely not be Playing the Game. It might even be crass.

One October long ago, down in Georgia when I was 19, my Grandfather Phillips was in his favorite rocking chair meditatively giving me a few highlights from his 80 years of accumulated wisdom. I was an eager listener. This time he ruminated at length over idosyncrasies he'd observed in the human race, particularly how the most sensible men are subject to inexplicable flights of frailty, particularly in the selection of guns, dogs, women and whiskey. "For instance," Grandfather confided as I hunched my chair closer, "take the average man's approach to buying a new deer rifle. He doesn't consider the problem as if he was selecting a tractor or a goober plow. He may ask advice, but won't take it. With rifles, he wants to learn, but doesn't wish to be taught."

Not one prospective hunting-rifle buyer in 20 will organize facts and from them arrive at an impartial, unbiased opinion. Rather, he first forms a concrete opinion, then selects all the data he can to support that opinion. It seems that with guns some men lean toward the *objet d'art* rather than the functional aspect. "And we know," Grandfather snorted, "that 'true art' is in the eye of the beholder. Thank God," Grandfather went on with a benevolent air of open-minded fair play, "we don't have that problem with bird guns. Any fool knows the *only* gun for bobwhite partridges is a double barrel made by Purdey, Holland or Parker." So from that time I've attempted (with some noble restraint) to select deer rifles from a practical and aesthetic approach.

I dote on beautiful rifles, but, by gum, they must perform as well. When a neighbor blossoms forth with a spankin' new smoke pole for deer which does not exactly make me swoon in an ecstasy of avarice, I button my gob. Should he ask my opinion, the favored ploy here is to mutter something ambiguous like "By George, that *is* a lot of gun, ain't it?"

This armchair consensus about all eastern white-tailed deer hunting being short-range snap shooting through brush and all western mule-deer hunting being ultra-long-range precision shooting in open terrain is by no means a true picture. In Pennsylvania, riflemen take their deer; many of them often away off on another mountainside. The ranges are plotted to a blonde ha'r, and their rifles are accurate bolt actions.

When I lived in New York City and Philadelphia, I successfully hunted white-tailed deer in upper New York State (out of Stoney Wold, Lower, near Copake Falls, mostly); Watsontown, Pennsylvania; Caribou, Maine; and Woodstock, New Brunswick. The hunting was excellent. I have, of course, at other times hunted whitetails in most of the classic regions of the East. Also in Florida, Georgia, the Carolinas, Ontario, Quebec, Michigan and northern Minnesota. All that time (excepting a few areas where rifles were illegal), being as I was primarily a fan of versatile low-trajectory long-range calibers; I used, with monumental success, my first .270, a bolt-action Model 54 Winchester with a Zeiss Zielklein scope.

I adored this obsolete rifle (the forerunner of the great Model 70). It had some faults, chiefly among them an abysmally lousy trigger pull. It seemed some factory efficiency-expert decided to use the trigger mechanism for the bolt stop. I had heard that a gunsmith at the Hart Gun Shop out in Cleveland, I believe, could accomplish a miracle and civilize it. It was like sending a child parcel post, but when it came back, it had a separate bolt stop and a no-creep trigger with 3½-pound pull. False modesty aside, familiarity on countless 'chucks made the pair of us exceedingly deadly afield. So it followed naturally that I sought out eastern deer-hunting situations affording open, long shots.

During my summer woodchuck shooting then, I cased the countryside for apple orchards, particularly abandoned ones. I'd heard on good authority that at dawn deer could be seen during early season chomping on windfallen apples. I remember one long-deserted farm in the Catskills we found while in quest of woodchucks located at the end of a dirt lane which luckily our Bantam roadster made without high-centering. A Bantam, by the way, was an excellent, miniature automobile about half the size of a VW. Green as Ireland was this halcyon setting, and lush as a rain forest. Frosting on the cake was, too, that it had to be near "Tom Slade's" old locale, Temple Camp, written of in the wonderful old boys' books by Percy Keese Fitzhugh. All one summer the farm was "ours," excepting for a handful of trout fishermen who waded the icy hard-bottom brook which bubbled cheerily

through the property, and with whom we exchanged amiable greetings.

There was an ancient pasture of many acres, laboriously hand-cleared of boulders with which former owners had constructed stone fences. The effect was a woodchuck Shangri-La. The snows of many winters had collapsed the roof of the old barn. Sheds were in a heap. But the house stood four-square in a garden long gone wild. From the shade of the back porch we'd shoot across green fields at multitudes of 'chucks. Clear across the main pasture, 350 yards away abutting a mixed forest of hardwood with a sprinkling of conifers, was a hoary-with-age neglected apple orchard.

As August waned, my bride and I strolled over there several times, once packing a discarded 4x8-foot panel of "beaver" board, and set it up in the orchard. From the porch I sighted-in the .270 with 130-grain Winchester Pointed Expanding bullets (the bullets that made the .270's reputation) to cluster a satisfactory group in the center of the board. We had the ingredients for the kind of deer hunting I like best: A shelter for a "stand" hunt; a spot known to be frequented by deer. All we needed now was a magnificent apple-craving dream buck, and dream of him we did, with fingers crossed.

The night before the season opened was ominously black with tendrils of Baskerville-moors' fog. We were snugly huddled together in nervous readiness on that old back porch. Warm and cozy with an enormous comforter over our shoulders, we nipped at a half-pint flask of Martell cognac, ate a staggering quantity of goodies which we'd snatched on the fly from an Eighth Avenue delicatessen, and nuzzled hot coffee from a vacuum bottle.

At the first gray-blue light we indeed saw deer cavorting in the orchard. A ragged old piece of folded carpet on the glassless window sill made a thick, resilient rifle rest. A decrepit cream can provided a stool. One outsize buck was bossing things. I watched him through the Zeiss scope, as unblinking as a cat at a mousehole. Ann held her breath. It was the magic moment. He stepped clear of two does, and I touched off.

How we got this drawn but unskinned 12-point buck to Man-

] 99 [

hattan coupled with the attitude of our friendly neighborhood butcher when we conned him into letting us invade his walk-in with, to him, our "uncouth wild meat" (we finally had to convince him we were pulling an illegal caper—the only reason he did it) is an agreeble recollection, of poignant tenderness.

While I had a lot of fun with it, my own modest long-range success in typical short-range deer country only proves that pet rifles are adaptable and versatile. Eastern deer hunting has some long-range opportunities, the same as western mule-deer hunting has some short-range hunting. If I was recommending a rifle for my best friend to be used for most eastern whitetail hunting it would be one of the following: A Browning Auto Rifle in .30-06, a Ruger 44 Autoloading Carbine, a Remington Woodmaster in 30-06 or .308, a Winchester 100 in .308, a Harrington & Richardson 360 Auto in .308, a Remington Gamemaster slide action (pump) in .30-06 or .308, a Savage Model 170 Slide Action in .30-30, a Ruger No. 3 Carbine in 45/70, a Savage 99 Lever Action in .308 or .300 Savage, a Winchester 88, 94, 64—.30-30 and in the 88, .308. Also, the Browning Lever Action BLR in .308 and the Marlin 336C LA with perhaps the best eastern deer caliber of all time, the 35 Remington cartridge. The Marlin 444 should be an excellent whitetail rifle, but I have no personal knowledge that it is. I profusely mention .30-06 and .308 because in most of these high-powered modern rifles that is the best *available* for the purpose.

A few years ago *Sports Afield* commissioned me to meticulously cover and report the Trans Canada Highway from its western to eastern termini. It was quite an undertaking, and my wife and I explored every reasonable side road, all the hunting and fishing guides and outfitters we could unearth, as well as bush pilots and fish and game officials. We shot 1100 pictures and filled several hundred large pages in our journals.

What interests us here are the deer guides I interviewed in the Maritime Provinces, Quebec and in our New England states. I asked them questions like the weights of current whitetails, ratio of hunter success, and for my own amusement, what they thought was the best deer rifle of all time. By overwhelming majority, and enthusiastic nostalgic acclaim, the most favored deer rifles were the Remington Gamemaster Model 141 in .35 Remington, the Remington Woodmaster Model 81 in .35 Remington, the Winchester 07 in .351, the Winchester Model 71 in .348, the Winchester in .32 Special, the Winchester 64 in .32 Special, and the Winchesters 86 and 95 in .33 and .35 Winchester.

The amusing angle is that most of these old pros conservatively chose obsolete rifles. The "Gamemaster" Model 141 WAS the great favorite. This is a nicely balanced old slide action, not thought to be particularly strong, but it is fast, reliable and it does come up "like lightning," and it *is* a "natural pointer." I handled many of them on the trip. Odd thing about the obsolete Model 141: Years ago I had some correspondence with a maker of custom scope mounts. You had to send your firearm in for this custom fitting and mounting, and part of his service was to carefully sight them in. He kept records and targets. He said I probably wouldn't believe it, as scarcely anyone else did, but some of the most accurate rifles passing through his shop were these pump-action 141s. Obsolete or not, if a fellow could buy one in .35 caliber, reasonably, he could do worse. I would like to see Remington chamber their modern Gamemaster and Woodmaster in .35 Remington.

If I was getting a rifle for short-range eastern whitetail hunting. I'd look around for an old .35, preferably the 141. Other goodies would be an 86 Winchester in 45/70, and my first-quality British double rifle in .405 Winchester, though that one doesn't grow on every bush. Once again, it won't hurt to remind Easterners that there's lots of short range shooting in the West, too, at mule deer, and at blacktail and whitetail. Instances are areas of high thick sage; the impenetrable manzanita and chaparral of California; the devil-club, fern and rotting-vegetation mossy undergrowth of the Pacific coastal northwest, ubiquitous lodgepole and cottonwood-willow stream bottoms. All the above rifles would serve.

The features that go into making the best rifle type and calibers for mule deer are neither involved nor open to a lot of debate. Most stretched-string-trajectory enthusiasts would rather be smote with a cestus than admit their own gleaming, scoped, bolt-action 300- to 400-yard treasure is anything less than the epitome of mulie harvesters. Yet, possibly more mule deer have been collected in the past 75 years with a little seven-shot, lever-action .30-30 Model 94 Winchester than any other. Some say this is because ranchers and their employees preferred these or something similar as particularly in the carbine style they are superb saddle rifles. The 6¼ pounds does not cause the saddle to shift, and the flat, thin receiver with no projections fits under the leg with comfort. Some, I'm sure, are sold so the proud owner can emulate movie and TV cowboy heros, but the hardcore reason is simply that the 94 Carbine is light, handy, fast and among the most effective short-range deer guns of all time.

The best mule-deer hunting in the West, that is, the most satisfactory for most sportsmen, and especially *riflemen,* is in open and semi-open country, of seemingly interminable vistas where long shots predominate. You should have an accurate rifle that will, if need be, put them down out to 350 yards or so, yet do them in at 75 yards. The answer for most is of course a bolt action with scope sight. They are overwhelmingly so excellent it is impossible here to mention all makes of worthwhile bolt actions. For instance, there are quite likely so many custom jobs on Springfield 03-A3, military Mauser 98s, Enfields and several other breech actions— to comprehend it would titillate the intellect to such frenzy our poor nerves would never recover.

The better factory rifles include the Weatherby Mark V and Vanguard, Winchester Model 70, Remington Model 700, Browning High Power, Ruger 77, Savage 110, Smith & Wesson Model A, Harrington & Richardson 301, Colt, Ithaca LSA-55, Sako Finnbear and Forester, Steyr-Mannlicher, FN Mauser, PSA Monarch, Mauser 3000. In passing, more and more Westerners are taking to the Browning Auto Rifle as a long-range deal. And, bolt actions notwithstanding, there are no flies whatsoever on the Ruger No. 1 Single Shot as a mule-deer rifle. When you hear a barrage laid down, it generally means all the intrepid nimrod has smoked up is the mountainside. When you hear one shot, it usually means venison.

Any of these precision rifles should be equipped with a top-quality 3X, 4X, 6X or variable scope, and a carrying-shooting sling. It would be tough to beat the reticle consisting of four bars ending toward the center in cross wires. Leupold calls theirs the Duplex. I have shot some mule deer at extreme long range when the situation called for it, but the truth of the matter is that most of my mulies have been 200 yards or under; a great many, taken at 60, 70 and 80 yards! Yet I still want a long-range rifle, as those long shots do present themselves with satisfying regularity.

In bolt actions, I'd bet the .30-06 has taken more than any other. With modern, up-to-date bullets, choose the 150 grain. The .270 is the great, classic, romantic mule-deer rifle. 'Tis said it was conceived for mule deer and for sheep (though it has proved, like the .375 H&H, to greatly exceed its designer's most fond expectations). Use the 130-grain bullet, always, for mule deer. You will see some ill-advised advice to load (or buy already loaded) the 150 grain. This is another one of the slap-stick paper-computation things which look peachy but seldom prove out. Take my advice and load a strong 130 grain to about 3200 fps. Every real .270 expert I've ever known or corresponded with goes through these stages. First, he uses the 130 grain with which the great .270 got its fantastic reputation. Then he reads about the 150 grain, tries it, brags about its virtues in public, and like the guy who has given up booze and cigarettes, tries to brainwash his pals. If he *shoots* a lot of .270, several thousand rounds annually, rather than merely *thinking* about shooting .270, or reading about it, inevitably he will see the light and go back to the 130 grain. The 300 Holland & Holland magnum substantially beats the .30-06, yet doesn't get into the heavy-kicking super-powerful 30 calibers. You can load a 150-grain bullet to 3300+, a 180 grain to 3000. It slightly "over-kills" but it's a wonderful deer rifle, and loyal owners, real *riflemen,* will use nothing else. The Weatherby .257 WM with 100 grain @ 3600 fps, .270 WM with 130 grain @ 3450 and 150 grain @ 3200+ (*here* the 150 grain is useful as a deer load), 7mm WM with 154 grain @ 3200 fps. The 7mm Remington Magnum with 139 grain @3300+ and 154 grain @ 3100 fps. The last five are needlessly powerful from a kill standpoint, but are superbly "flat"-shooting calibers, easy to hit with.

I've read where an emerging deer-expert advises that he cannot tell the difference in killing power, on mulies, between a .270 and a .25-06, and I lay this magnificently salient observation to the fact that he's yet to shoot his first deer with a .270. This silliness can be carried to extreme. We could say, in considerable honesty (at this stage) that the rifleman cannot tell the difference in killing power between a 25-06 and a .257 Roberts. Then some grizzled ole rancher will lean around the hot stove and declare he can't tell the difference between a .257 and a .25/35. Another pipes up and virtuously vouchsafes that his .25-20 will do anything the .25/35 will. With this, gran'pappy leans forward, pounds the floor with his cane, and shouts, by cracky, his faithful ole Winchester Low Wall in .25 rimfire will do anything that goldurned ol' .25-20 will. With this reasoning, we could assume the .25 rimfire is about equal to the .25-06 as a deer rifle. It isn't, and the .25-06 is not a .270, either. The .25-06 *is* an excellent mule-deer rifle. Use 100 grains if you go for the chest shots, 120 grains if you like to take 'em at all angles. I was not kidding when I mentioned the .257 Roberts as a choice candidate. If you want an incredibly, effective *light-weight* pair of calibers to choose from, it is tough, if not impossible, to beat the .257 Roberts and the 7/57 Mauser cartridges. I've seen gigantic mule deer taken out of the old Kirk Ranch near Wyoming's Green Mountains which weighed on a beam scale well in excess of 300 pounds, taken with a light .257 Roberts (the two ranch rifles, used for everything from pronghorn to bull elk). A malignant killer of mulies is the lightweight 7/57 with 139-grain bullet. The advantage of the 7/57 is that on top of being a superb deerslayer, it's good for elk and bear.

Believe it or not, a .30/40 Krag cartridge is preferred by a coterie of highly successful long-time expert mule-deer hunters. They still-hunt (which means gumshoeing along quietly upwind or crosswind) quaking aspen coulees and have learned that due to some inexplicable combination of circumstances, nothing beats the 220-grain bullet at 30/40 velocities. Though they own other rifles, they keep beat-up ol' Krags and Model 95s in the rack for that sole and unique purpose. If you're hunting *small* mulies, like the subspecies of South Dakota between the Missouri and the Black Hills, you could well use a 6mm Remington or .243. These elfin treasures are sleek, fat, gray as a wolf and weigh about the same as a pronghorn. They're my favorite mulies, these lovelies, just as the miniature Sonoran/Coues is the favorite whitetail of a few whitetail connoisseurs. But the smallest effective caliber I recommend on normal, average mule-deer bucks is the .257 Roberts. It's light, with inconsequential recoil (nonexistent, for most), and it is one real deer killer. Other calibers which some prefer, but which I have never used and probably won't on deer, are: 250-3000, 6.5 Mannlicher-Schoenauer (I know this to be a good one), 6.5 X 55, 6.5 Remington Magnum, .264 Winchester, .284 Winchester, .280 Remington, 7 X 61 S&H, .300 Savage, .308, 7.65 Belgian-Argentine, .303 British, .303 Savage, 7.7mm Japanese, 8mm Mauser (8 X 57), .358 Winchester, and .350 Remington Magnum.

What is the best all-round mule-deer rifle? Let's see—we have a wildcat in the .35 Whelen with 180- or 200-grain bullet. There's the .270, of course, and the .30-06. Then there's the .300 H&H to which many are devoted (for life), and the 7/57 and .257 Roberts. I will play that hand, amigos.

Oh! You say, what is the one best deer rifle for *ME?!* If I could only have ONE? It's the .270.

] 105 [

WOODCRAFT AND WHITETAILS

Larry R. Koller

Larry Koller's death in 1967 stunned the world of outdoor publishing with a tremendous sense of loss. Koller was not only one of the most respected writers and editors in the field, he was also one of the most loved and appreciated—for his friendly easy style, his wit and sense of humor, and his companionship. A superb outdoorsman, dedicated to every phase of sport, he was also a gourmet cook, gunsmith, and tackle maker.

When Larry's book Shots at Whitetails *was first published by Knopf in 1948, it was immediately regarded as a classic. Superbly illustrated by Bob Kuhn, the book today is still worthy of the praise bestowed upon it. This excerpt, and the chapter to follow, will give you an idea of what Jack O'Connor had in mind when he wrote the introduction to Knopf's republication of the book in 1970:*

"I read and enjoyed *Shots at Whitetails* some years before I ever met the late Larry Koller. I liked the book because it was practical, well organized, and clearly and interestingly written from a wealth of practical experience and a great deal of enthusiasm, intelligence, and common sense. All too many books about guns, shooting, and hunting are hasty jobs by people who are shy on experience and have little common sense. But this book was solid. As I read it I realized that this was the best book on deer hunting since Van Dyke's *The Still-Hunter.*"

During his career, Larry Koller was Outdoor Editor of Argosy, *Editor-in-Chief of* American Gun, *and at the time of his death, editor and columnist for* Guns and Hunting. *He is also known for his* Fireside Book of Guns, Treasury of Hunting, Treasury of Angling, *and the now-classic* Taking Larger Trout.

OF THE MANY TALES that have been written around the drama of hunting the whitetail, each and every one tends to stress the importance of woodcraft to the success and enjoyment of the hunt. Aside from the deer taken each season by pure luck—and believe it, that number is substantial—a knowledge of woodcraft plays a most important part with every sportsman to a greater or lesser degree. The still-hunter draws heavily on his knowledge of the woods during his every moment on the hunt, for on this knowledge hinges the entire result of his trip. Even the deer hunters who gang up on deer drives following the accepted practice of most club hunting, need to possess the fundamentals of deer tactics and behavior to qualify on the score sheet.

Perhaps the original interpretation of our word "woodcraft" goes back to pioneer days when its literal translation—craft of the woods—stemmed directly from its place in the economic picture of that day. During those times familiarity with the woods and its wild people had a direct bearing on the survival of early civilization. Food in abundance, clothing and shelter were provided for the woodsman with enough knowledge and skill to avail himself and his family of these benevolent gifts of Mother Nature, all there for the taking. Our present-day thoughts of woodcraft still swing back unconsciously to the early days; even though today's woodsman applies his knowledge only to increase his recreational pleasure and further appreciation of Nature's gifts, still here abundantly.

Much of the thrill and charm of deer hunting is influenced by our conscious knowledge of the whitetail's role in the romantic days of the Indian and buckskin-clad woodsman. Any glimpse of these splendid creatures along our wooded highways and parks will stop even the most blasé individual, sportsman or not, with a quickening of the pulse and a tiny thrill of secret pleasure, as though he had been favored by an intimate glance into the pages of Nature's book.

Much of this same effect is captured by the deer hunter. Of all our outdoor pursuits none is so wreathed by the aura of romance, none so connotative of our hidden pride in our American ancestry during its uphill climb for world recognition. The whitetail possesses every quality of a top notch game animal—a position it undoubtedly commands—sufficiently to place it on the top shelf in every hunter's library of game birds and animals. No other game is so well able to adapt itself to changing conditions and the increasing spread of mankind's so-called civic improvements. The automobile and good highways, accused of ravaging the country of its small game and fish, seem to have simply awakened the competitive spirit in the whitetail—he flourishes now in many regions where he was unknown before the days of the machine age.

Our point is that the whitetail is so skilled in self-concealment and self-reliance that it requires the best of woods skill to beat him at his own game. In addition, most hunters of long experience agree that the deer of today is infinitely wiser than his ancestors of fifty or even twenty-five years ago. Just as the hunter has increased his knowledge of the hunt, successive generations have planted new, or newly sharpened, instincts in our present deer herd. Thus, we must indeed know our deer if we would eat venison.

The study of woodcraft in its general sense offers an enormously widespread field, of such scope that a lifetime of effort would scarcely scrape off the top surface of possibilities. Still, the richer we are in this knowledge, the richer we become. Each action and habit of wild creatures dovetails inescapably into the lives of its brethren, so that each new bit of information gleaned in trips afield adds immeasurably to what we have seen before. Unfortunately most of us are so situated that we can devote but little time to days in the woods and fields, spent simply in studying wildlife, however desirable this may be.

Our actual hunting trips, then, must be the sole means of enriching our knowledge of woodcraft; and fittingly enough it is this absorption of woodlore on our hunting trips that forms the major

part of our deer-hunting pleasure. Action in deer hunting, unlike other sports, occurs quickly, exists for only a few seconds—thrill-packed though they may be—then it's all over, ending in a successful bag or a heartbreaking miss. These few seconds of action may have been days or weeks in preparation, for bucks aren't seen every day in the woods by even the best hunters. These days, though, should have been made profitable by observation of deer signs, tracks, runways, antler rubs and bed-downs, giving the hunter further information for subsequent days in the woods.

In this chapter we will confine our discussion to that branch of woodcraft which deals directly with deer and deer hunting. We shall attempt to interpret the signs and existing knowledge of whitetails to the hunter's advantage. We must qualify these observations by stating that the whitetail is often a most paradoxical animal. The one statement of fact that can be definitely and unequivocally made is that no one knows exacty what any one deer will do under any given set of conditions, not even the deer itself. The best that we can hope to do is anticipate probable reactions with knowledge gleaned from previous experiences.

In strange deer country both novice and expert hunter are faced with the problem of finding the deer. The novice usually elects to find a high spot overlooking as broad an expanse of territory as possible, in the hope that a deer will walk out within his line of vision if he waits long enough. If by lucky accident he happens on a spot near feeding grounds or a well-defined crossing he may get his shot—if he waits long enough. But as a rule this hit-or-miss method of deer hunting produces little other than cold feet and discouraged impatience.

The deer hunter of experience wastes no time in watching barren ground. His first move in new territory is to locate feeding grounds, bed-downs, runways and crossings to the best of his ability. He understands that movements and behavior of the whitetail under normal conditions are influenced by just three factors: food and water; suitable cover for daytime hideouts and the process of moving from bedding grounds to food and returning once again to these bedding grounds. The logical course to follow is to locate these runways and feeding grounds and wait from some vantage point at those times when deer are most likely to be feeding. All this of course is under normal conditions but there are two factors which exist during hunting seasons that may induce some wide changes in whitetail behavior. These are the presence of heavy concentrations of hunters, and the rutting season.

With hunters tramping through almost all available cover and feeding grounds throughout the day, deer will be constantly on the move from one hideout to another, breaking their normal routine sufficiently that no rules of conduct apply. Then, during the height of the rut, all deer, bucks in particular, are constantly on the move, spending little time in feeding or resting. Any hunter who has killed a buck just after the rutting season can readily appreciate the tremendous amount of energy a buck must expend during this period, taking but little food in the process. Almost without exception, bucks taken after this period are exceedingly thin, almost to the point of emaciation, young bucks being affected to a greater degree than the older individuals.

The whitetail hunter must bear these two facts in mind, for they control hunting conditions to a great extent. However, there are many times when neither of these influences are present, and the hunter must employ straight woodcraft methods to find his deer.

First, the matter of feed. It's a recognized fact that deer feed very little, if at all, in heavily timbered areas, for the heavy top foliage discourages the promotion of undergrowth. Deer are browsers almost exclusively, feeding on the tender tips of second-growth timber and underbush, although they're not adverse to grazing off a farmer's young wheat or rye. Whitetails don't favor any one type of food to the exclusion of any other, rather they select a varied diet from among the existing hardwoods and evergreens; among these are white cedar, hard or rock maple, black ash and black birch, white birch, scrub oak, ground hemlock, beech, poplar or aspen, yellow birch, dogwood and many others. The small, pyramid-shaped nuts of the beech and acorns of all species of oaks are especially favored by deer during the early fall, perhaps to the partial exclusion of other available diet at this time. The important point to bear in mind is that deer can only obtain good browsing on low second-growth stuff, regardless of its species. It's quite useless to look for feeding grounds in heavy timber, unless large numbers of acorns or beechnuts are dropping to the ground in these areas.

In looking for feeding grounds the deer hunter goes through all the heavy second growth bordering heavy timber or in locations that are close to good deer cover. He examines the tips of low-growing branches at about his waist level, which is the preferred browsing height, looking for freshly nipped-off ends, evidence of recent feeding. He goes through heavy timber areas looking for beech trees bearing nuts or oaks laden with acorns. If there is evidence to indicate that both nuts and acorns are dropping yet none can be found on the ground, this is also indicative of deer feeding but it's not conclusive. If these areas are well populated with squirrels it may be the squirrels and not the deer that are reaping the harvest. As a rule, though, the hunter can detect squirrel workings quickly by the breaking of the acorn shells and the pulverized results of nibbling. The feeding deer makes a thorough cleanup of acorns, shells and all.

These observations, plus fresh deer tracks on feeding grounds, are certain proof of recent deer activity; but the novice may have some trouble in determining just how fresh are the tracks. If autumn leaves are falling it's simple, for some of the older tracks will be covered with leaves; if the ground is mossy, none but very fresh tracks will show; in firm, moist ground the fresh track will show a glazed appearance at the bottom, old tracks will be dull. Almost the same holds true for deer droppings. These little, dark, elongated pills are dropped in bunches, and their freshness can be determined by their shiny surface coating. Old droppings are invariably dull on the surface and are firm and hard. It's good practice to pick up these little pills and squeeze them. If they're soft you can bet they haven't laid long on the ground.

Locating bed-downs is a somewhat tougher problem, for in most cases the terrain influences the deer's choice of a resting place as well as the weather. Normally the whitetail inhabiting an area of good feed and cover leads a well-ordered life. He feeds in much the same areas every day; low ground between ridges, valley slopes and along the edges of heavy timber. As a matter of fact the best all year round deer feed is found in low places, with the exception of scrub oak and acorns. Most whitetails prefer high ground for bed-downs—ridges, hillsides and knolls, where they can be sure of detecting the approach of danger well in advance of its arrival. Now this procedure of traveling down to feeding grounds, and back up to higher ground for bedding, is the most common of whitetail characteristics. It usually results in some well-defined runways connecting in some measure the two areas, for deer are creatures of habit. However, they seldom use the same spot twice running for a bed; but they frequently use the same general area, perhaps the same slope or ridge. These spots can only be found by the most thorough search of likely ground, and even then only the freshest beds will remain as evidence.

Fresh beds are well defined. Leaves will be pressed flat in an oval-shaped area about three feet long and two feet wide; fresh droppings are almost always found near the beds as well as fresh tracks. But after a day or two the leaves once again fluff up to their original shape, aided by wind and moisture, destroying all the evidence. Of course the easiest way to locate a bed is to jump a deer, but this requires some skill in still-hunting and approach, else the deer will sneak off without being seen.

With bedding grounds and feeding areas located it's a simple matter to find well-defined runways somewhere between the two. (Right here might be a good time to offer a little explanation of the difference in deer "runways" and "crossings." Deer hunters constantly use these terms interchangeably, yet they are not quite the same. A runway is a well-defined path followed by deer, whereas a crossing is a limited area where deer are likely to pass through.)

Whitetails, with customary caution, dislike traveling in the same beaten path day after day unless it is most convenient for them to do so. We find runways, then, through very thick cover—scrub oak, laurel, rhododendron, and other tough going where travel is almost impossible except on beaten paths. Runways often follow brooks hemmed in by deep gullies, or go under rocky ledges and through swamps where deer have little choice except to follow a single path. On the other hand, when more open timber or cover is reached, they will wander off a few yards on either side of the line of travel, still keeping within the limits of a crossing, but not following any definite line. These crossings are often found in ridge "saddles," below knolls, through narrow strips of timber between open fields or meadows, or between heavy swamps or dense thickets. At no time will a whitetail reveal himself completely in open fields willingly, unless it be after dark or near sundown or sunrise. When he approaches these clearings he skirts the edges, taking as much protection as the cover will afford.

Runways are easily found simply because they are more or less beaten paths. In heavy scrub oak or laurel they show up at once, in less dense cover they can best be located by watching for fresh tracks following definite lines. In soft ground along brooks or through swamps they are at once apparent, but on mossy ground or hard-packed soil it requires closer scrutiny to pick them out. As a rule though, deer keep their runways clear of twigs and branches by browsing as they travel, and this browse line is at once a dead giveaway.

Crossings aren't quite so easy. Perhaps the best plan for their location is to look over the territory for the spots previously mentioned—"saddles" over or between ridges, and such. Then minute examination of the ground in these areas should reveal clues: fresh tracks and old tracks in profusion, droppings, indications of feeding and, during the rutting season, antler rubs on saplings. These antler rubs are perhaps the most obvious hint of deer travel in any location, and usually they are numerous during the open season.

The general opinion on antler rubs is that the bucks use this method to remove the velvet after the antler has hardened and to polish and stain the antlers in the process. I cannot subscribe to this theory, for it is my belief that the rubbing occurs only when the rutting season is about to begin or has already started. The buck's antlers start to harden early in the fall, and by the end of September or early October are usually free of any signs of velvet. Yet the rutting may not begin until late October or November, and if the observant hunter takes a trip through the woods before the period begins he will find few, if any, rubs on the saplings and brush.

Later on, however, during the hunting season and after the rutting season, rubs will be noted in profusion through the same areas. I believe that this rubbing is performed by the bucks while leading up to the mating process, merely to show off their various good points to the courted doe. In much the same manner, the deer hunter will often see shallow holes about two feet round dug through the leaves down into the soil for an inch or two, with the leaves and soil thrown to one side and scattered for several yards. This the buck performs with his front feet, pawing at the ground like an angry bull, again to give himself a good build-up with the susceptible female.

Observations made at various game farms throughout the country indicate that the velvet is removed by the buck's digging it off with his hind feet. This velvet is attached to a thin skin and once this is broken through with a sharp hind foot it peels off quite readily. In my years in the deer woods I have examined thousands of these rubbed saplings and I have yet to find any trace of velvet or skin on the ground below, although plenty of the rubbed-off bark is present. As an additional point, every experienced hunter has noted flat spots rubbed on the antlers just forward of the burrs, indicating still further that all, or nearly all, of the rubbing is done with the bases of the antlers at or near the burrs. If removal of the velvet were the primary object, the antler would show no concentration of rubbing at one point.

Now if many of these rubs are noted throughout deer country it is almost conclusive evidence that the rut is on or has already passed. This can only be determined by close observation of the peeled area itself and the condition of the peeled-off bark on the ground at the base of the tree. I usually peel some bark off the first rubbed sapling I see at the beginning of the season's hunt and leave it lying on the ground with the bark that has already been rubbed off. I come back to it in a day or two and compare its condition with the rub, and from this I can form a fairly accurate idea as to how old the rub may be.

All this may seem like unimportant detail in a small matter, but the success of a deer hunt often is made or broken by the rutting season. While the rut is on, deer are constantly on the move; bucks are chasing does over a wide area, and those does which have been already bred are running and hiding from the bucks. Likewise, the whitetail buck loses a great deal of his natural caution during this period and will blunder along runways and through crossings in pursuit of the doe with much less than his usual caution. A high percentage of the odd deer stories that come out of the woods each season can be directly attributed to the effect of the rutting fever when it is at its height.

With light snow on the ground all the problem of locating feeding grounds, runways and so on is at once simplified. It resolves itself into the single operation of finding tracks and following them, watching surrounding cover for evidence of feeding; and of course runways and crossings are at once evident. However, when snow covers the ground deer are much more on the alert; they realize that they can be seen more easily, so they take special pains to stay close to good cover in all their daylight movements.

In all our heavily hunted areas—which include most of our best deer-hunting territory—the larger bucks stay off by themselves. They find a safe hiding place for their daylight bed, usually on a ridge top covered with scrub oak or laurel, moving off this bed only after dark or at dusk. They travel down to low ground for their nocturnal feeding, then return again to the ridge for rest. These big fellows are lazy and unsociable throughout the year, with the single exception of the rutting season. At that time they single out one or two older does and stay with them for the greater part of the season, protecting them from the attentions of the younger bucks until their job is done. Then they retire to their old stamping grounds until the next season. Most of their travels are made after dark, regardless of moonlight or pitch-blackness, and as the restless urge of early fall seeps in they become more and more furtive until the mating season actually begins.

Throughout the year they permit no intrusions by young bucks into their chosen bailiwick and they demand no company of the opposite sex. All of these old bucks seem to realize that the often-careless female brings bad luck, and they fight any of the association except for the few weeks of the actual mating season. Needless to point out, these bucks carry the heaviest heads and often the fattest venison and are highly prized by the hunter. But it requires the best of skill and utmost patience to take these trophies by fair means. A "lone wolf" buck knows all the answers to a hunter's bag of tricks, but with a little luck on his side a good hunter can bring him to earth.

If a big buck is located in a given area much missionary work must be done before the season in the attempt to locate his habitat and feeding grounds. All runways and crossings must be carefully examined for the imprint of heavy feet. If the buck is a large one, he will have a much longer stride than the average deer as well as leaving a deeper impression of hoofs. This can only be determined by comparison with other tracks, but it's a good rule. When a definite runway is located somewhere near his bedding ground, a black silk thread can be tied across it at waist level. If it can be conveniently done, the thread should be examined every night and morning to determine whether he leaves his bed by that route or approaches by it, for often separate runways are used for coming and going. Of course, if the ground is soft enough a preponderance of tracks in one direction will give this information.

From then on, killing one of these big bucks is a matter of watchful waiting, taking a stand at daylight or moving in late in the afternoon, in the hope that he will leave his bed before dark or delay his return until after dawn. It may require much patient waiting, but these big fellows aren't taken every season and the time is well spent.

Discussing woodcraft and deer hunting at once brings up the subject of the whitetails' powers of sight, scent and hearing. There is little doubt that their hearing and sight are better than our own, and their powers of scent very keen. The most careful observers agree though that the scent power of the whitetail is highly overrated. Deer always seem to have trouble in establishing the identity of visible foreign objects unless these objects make some slight movement. In the case of a hunter on a stand, if a deer is within only a few yards even the winking of an eye is enough to start him off in a hurry. On the other hand, I have had deer approach within twenty-five yards and pass me by with hardly more than a glance, even though I was in full view, when I was virtually motionless.

The whitetail places little faith in any one of his several senses unless alarmed; that is, if he hears a strange noise he usually waits to see just what has caused it. If the wind brings him man-scent he bides his time until sight or sound confirms his suspicion. This natural curiosity has contributed directly to the untimely demise of more than one nice buck. Perhaps in strictly wilderness areas or regions rather remote from human activities the whitetail is much more conscious of man's intrusion and is alarmed more easily. But in those areas where deer are taken in cover near farm lands or in any populated section, the scent of man is so often in a deer's nostrils that he pays little attention unless the scent is accompanied by more tangible evidences of danger. In most cases, this is a matter either of territorial location or of one individual deer's previous experiences.

Any whitetail that has had a few close brushes with unfriendly Nimrods possesses a much higher I.Q. rating than his less sophisticated relatives. Such deer learn very rapidly with little teaching, with the result that their senses either become more acute or they develop a keener recognition of facts established by the life processes of seeing, hearing and smelling.

Five or six years ago I had located a nice buck by means of a little pre-seasonal work. I found that he bedded-down on the top of a densely thatched scrub-oak ridge. In that refuge he was completely safe from any still-hunter, for the most careful stalking couldn't bring an approach within a hundred years without alarming the deer. By a bit of good luck I found a well-defined runway approaching the bedding grounds, following up a tiny ravine, and it was here that I elected to head him off if possible.

I picked for myself a nice stand at the base of an uprooted red oak, giving me a view down the little ravine of about fifty yards and far enough off from its edge for any deer using the run to pass

] 117 [

by with little possibility of spotting me. With a definite project in mind I quite eagerly awaited opening day, almost sure of a good shot; but my luck didn't hold out. Just the day before the season opened our deer-hunting territory was blanketed in a nice snow-fall of several inches followed by a cold rain which quickly formed a most unsatisfactory crust over all. This made still-hunting in any form out of the picture entirely, and tramping through the woods rather a hardship.

Nevertheless, at daybreak of that first day I crunched up the hillside for a noisy half-mile to my chosen site. The dead air hung heavily over the hillside, sharply cold and pleasantly tingling on my cheeks. Hoarfrost formed lacy fringes on tree trunks and branches soon to sparkle with the first rays of the sun. Away off across the valley a blue jay sounded an early alarm as he policed his beat, his coarse, excited shrieking cutting crisply through the heavy silence and echoing among the white-bearded hemlocks along the slope. A beautiful morning to park quietly on a stand to listen and watch, I reflected, but that would be all.

On my stand, or seat—for I had snuggled down against the huge oak roots, well concealed—I amused myself by watching big clouds of vapor streaming out from my nostrils and lips. Trees were cracking and popping gently in the cold and a red squirrel chattered peevishly across my ravine. Soon the sun rose, spreading a deep pink over the white-blanketed forest floor, magically electrifying the frost-covered tree trunks and branches.

About half an hour after sunup I heard faint crunchings down in my ravine. As I listened they increased in volume and came nearer. Just a steady mixed crunch, crunch—sounding like a whole herd of deer in the quiet air. Then quickly they material-ized into deer; first a sleek doe, head bobbing, ears waving an out-of-step beat as she daintly lifted a slim hoof for each quick stride. At her tail was another doe, somewhat smaller, just as sleek, just as dainty but with erect head and ears laid back. Stead-ily the procession grew until five tawny-coated does drifted by, closely followed by a tiny spike buck. Directly in front of my tree the leading lady stopped, halting the line momentarily. She swept me with a quick glance, then lifted a slim hind leg and scratched her right ear. The red disc of the morning sun behind them made a striking tableau, for each one had suddenly stopped all movement.

As I held my breath momentarily they all swung their heads over their shoulders and looked back down the ravine. Ah! I thought, here follows the object of my main interest. Then without another glance in my direction they moved by on up to the ridge. I waited with pounding pulse for my buck to make some sound to indicate his approach but after ten minutes had gone by, I gave up hope. Then I again heard the confident crunching step as my buck came up the ravine, but when he was almost within sight his footstep faltered, then stopped. I knew he couldn't wind me in that dead air, and I was sure he couldn't see me. I tucked my chin still farther into the collar of my coat to keep the telltale breath vapors from fanning out before me. Hesitantly now his crunching feet came on until I could just see a faint movement through the saplings, then he stopped. There he stood, stamping his feet, suspicious now but not quite sure just what to do.

My view offered no possibilities for a shot until he emerged from those saplings, so I resigned myself to rigid immovability, but it was of no use. He snorted twice, stamped his feet again, then turned and jumped down the runway.

I never saw that deer again, alive. But as a matter of record one of my hunting pals killed him two days later from this same stand. That morning had brought a gentle, warm rain and at about the same time this buck came up the little ravine without hesitation to meet his doom; he was a nice specimen carrying ten big points. To this day I am convinced that he could see my breath through those saplings and so took alarm, but he was an old-timer, wise in the ways of hunters and cautious in the extreme. This incident is unusual and proves nothing beyond the fact that the big bucks don't get that way by being careless.

It is quite possible that this buck was well aware of the noisy progress of his travels through that deep, well-crusted snow. Perhaps this alone made him doubly cautious; so cautious that his senses were more than usually alert to possible danger. He may have picked up a tiny wisp of man-scent drifting from my stand;

may have seen some slight movement through the saplings caused by breath vapors. At any rate he was sufficiently alarmed, giving me no opportunity to place a shot. But two days later, when a warm rain had softened the crust, melted the snow and beaten down any possibility of drifting man-scent, he walked unconcernedly past this same stand, giving my partner a perfect, deadly, broadside shot through the neck.

The matter of the whitetails' keenness of vision is more closely associated with hunting methods than with woodcraft, yet it is sufficiently important for discussion here. It is hardly possible that their sight powers are more acute than the normal human animal's. It is more logical to attribute their ability to pick out a hunter quickly to their intense familiarity with their daily haunts. Any foreign object in their home woods and covers must be as apparent to them as would be a frog on our living room floor. Yet if the hunter remains quite still their attention will wander and they forget about the strange object.

Many authorities on the subject of deer maintain that deer are not color-conscious and that it does no harm to wear red clothing in the woods. This theory I personally reject. It is incredible to me that the creative force which so lavishly spreads such vivid coloring throughout the land could at the same time create any creature without inherent ability to absorb it visually. I do subscribe to the opinion that the wearing of red in any form has little effect in alarming deer, but not for the same reason. During our fall season the home covers of the whitetail deer are blotched in many ways with brilliant reds—the red oak and the sumac, to name two. What is more natural than to assume that a deer glancing casually at a hunter on his stand should mistake his red cap and coat for a scrubby red oak or a low sumac?

Deer are much more sensitive to alarming sounds than to the sight of unmoving strange objects. Many times I have had does stand, quietly watching me from distances of only a few yards. But a single snap of my fingers would be enough to produce a quick, frightened reaction that would send them bounding and snorting to safety.

A decade or more ago, when old Abe Wykoff conducted the

] 120 [

Buck Mountain Hunting Club in Sullivan County's Oakland Valley region, I was almost run to earth by two does. One morning Abe and I were hunting together, still-hunting the slopes on a long narrow hogback. Following our usual custom I was covering the river side of the slope, Abe the back side which sloped over to the Hartwood Club. I had just discovered a well-defined runway coming down the slope in a long angle and was investigating the runway at a point where it passed between two husky oak trees only about a yard apart.

At this precise moment Abe's rifle cracked once, then again, and in a matter of seconds two deer came over the hill in full flight, pounding down the runway toward my somewhat untenable position between the big oaks. My first glance labeled both deer as does, both badly frightened and in bounding high gear. When the leading doe was three jumps away I waved an arm enthusiastically, thinking this would shy her off. Quickly then I jumped behind one of my oak trees, barely clearing the run for the two deer as they bounced by.

I suppose that a good loud yell would have frightened them enough to swerve them off, but I didn't want to alarm any buck that might be following. Both these deer were blindly alarmed and might easily have knocked me down if I had stood in the run. Minutes later I found that Abe had neatly dispatched the six-point buck that had been escorting these does, so my pains to keep quiet were unnecessry. Normally of course both these deer would have spotted me at once, but I am convinced that only a loud shout or a shot from my rifle would have swerved them from this runway. In like manner many frightened deer, both bucks and does, have been known to run headlong into danger even though such danger was visually apparent.

Inversely, though deer are highly sensitive to strange sounds, the usual woods noises bother them not at all. This too is fortunate for the still-hunter, else he would rarely get close enough to see a deer. Any deer must be hard put indeed to distinguish the step of the hunter's foot from the myriad rustlings of squirrels, the dropping of nuts and acorns and the clamorings of blue jays and crows. Such sounds of the hunter's progress as he must necessarily make to move at all in the woods are not in themselves alarming unless the deer can at once confirm them by seeing the hunter himself. Snapping of heavy twigs under foot, breaking branches and rolling rocks are, of course, all taboo. Such noises form no part of the usual woods complement, and deer instantly detect them as foreign.

It is regrettable that of the hundreds of thousands of deer hunters spread throughout our whitetail deer country only a few spend sufficient time in the woods for absorbing some knowledge of deer habits. Most of the hunters of my acquaintance seem to be quite content with their knowledge after they feel that they can definitely establish the identity of the bucks' tracks from that of the does. And strangely enough, each hunter of some experience has decidedly definite ideas on this subject. For my part, although I have spent almost two decades in hunting the whitetail deer in some of the best covers of the East, I am never positive of the buck's track unless I have seen the deer making it.

Perhaps I have heard as much discussion of the subject from the hunter's viewpoint as any other individual in the East. Over the gun counter, in hunting clubs, at sportsmen's meetings, in the deer woods and in mountain taverns my ears have been bent with numerous positive rules for such identification. But still I remain unconvinced, for no two sets of rules seem to be the same.

It is this writer's experience and steadfast opinion that no man can by examining the single track of a deer thereby determine the sex of the deer making it. The best that we can hope to do is to make a reasonable deduction, considering all the factors involved, and then form an opinion. The shape of the foot alone is not enough. Neither is a large foot evidence of a buck. We have many does wandering our deer covers with feet as large as the biggest buck in the Catskills.

I have been told in perfect sincerity by certain of my deer-hunting friends that the buck always has a long slender foot. I have been told by fully an equal number of my friends that the buck has a short broad foot. Likewise I have been informed on numerous occasions that the toes of a buck always spread. Perhaps they do, but I have tracked numerous does which displayed this not too unique characteristic. There exists also a group of hunters who believe that the buck always leaves the imprint of dew claws directly behind the hoof. Perhaps no other item of deer lore carries more misinformation than this question of buck and doe tracks.

The best that any of us can hope to do to settle this problem of sex differential in the footprint is to observe all the visible evidence, then make logical deductions. Snow or soft earth is the ideal and perhaps only medium in which this can be done. It is absolutely necessary for the observer to find enough tracks in continual line to be able to establish a trend toward the identity of the animal making them.

First of all, the size of the track is no criterion. The larger females will most certainly have hoofs of greater length and width than the small bucks. Another factor is the type of terrain which the animal uses. Deer living in soft, swampy ground or an area of heavy coniferous timber will develop a larger hoof. Deer which climb rocky ridges and rock-studded slopes will have smaller, sharper hoofs. I have killed several large bucks on the Shawangunk mountain range in Lower Sullivan and Ulster Counties all of which had comparatively small hoofs. This mountain range is of heavy limestone with many jagged outcroppings and generally rock-covered. Deer living and feeding on this range keep their hoofs in a well-trimmed condition. In the swampy Wolf Pond area of Sullivan County, only a few miles north of the Shawangunk Range, the deer have somewhat larger feet.

During the latter part of December '46 one of my hunting friends and I skinned out our two bucks at the same time. One of these deer was unusually large, carrying a dressed weight of 212 pounds; the other was a normal eight-pointer which dressed out at 131 pounds. In the normal process of skinning and butchering we had disjointed the legs and thrown them into a single pile. Later, when we came to sorting out the respective feet, we would have been forced to pick at random were it not for the slightly longer and heavier leg of the larger deer. Certainly there was no apparent difference in the hoof sizes. In addition I have had ample opportunity during the past two decades to examine the carcasses of thousands of whitetail bucks. I am still unconvinced that the larger bucks carry the largest feet.

Depth of footprint is the more obvious indication of a buck's weight, plus the length of stride, both of which must be compared with other tracks made in the same vicinity by other deer. This gives an initial foundation for the hunter's deductions. Next, if the deer has been walking quietly, and a line of prints can be found, we must try to determine how closely each print will come to a center line, drawn lengthwise and between the tracks. The doe and young buck walk with feet placed close to this common center line, and are usually precise in placing the hind foot directly within the print of the front foot. Mature bucks are careless in this respect; often the hind foot is placed closer to the center line than the front footprint or fails to come quite as far forward as the location of the front print.

The fat and heavy buck shows a marked tendency to walk with front feet wider apart than the doe or small buck. Also these bucks usually show an inclination to toe-out with the front feet.

In following a group of tracks (in snow) there are some distinguishing characteristics which will help the hunter to pick out the buck's track—if there be one in the herd. The does have a tendency to wander aimlessly when the herd is moving; the buck is more purposeful and direct in his movements. The doe track will wander off the runway, then weave back. Often she'll playfully jump over a small bush or log, seemingly just for the fun of it. Her whole attitude as evidenced by the dainty hoofprints is much less concerned with a direct objective than is the buck. The buck seldom engages in the female frivolities. His walking stride is calm and purposeful; he seldom turns abruptly in his directional line to feed on a shrub off the run. Rather he walks directly to the feeding spot. He engages in no playful antics such as the doe tracks indicate; there is little bush- or log-jumping to be found in the evidence of a buck's footprints.

Often the entire group of does in the herd will fan out through crossings, covering an area fifteen or twenty yards wide, as they precede the buck. The buck's track will usually be found, firm and purposeful, following up through the center of this welter of trails. Then again, the more wary old-timers will follow the doe herd but at a distinct distance apart. If the hunter discovers one of these lone trails showing a marked tendency to stray off a bit to right or left from the rest of the herd, he can bet his stack that there is a buck ahead.

In snow less than four inches deep the buck consistently will give away his sex by dragging his front feet. The doe lifts each foot daintily, then places it quite carefully down. A buck carrying heavy neck and shoulders will not trouble to lift his feet clear of the snow. His dragging forefeet leave a distinctive line behind each print. Of course in heavy snow any deer will drag its feet, so the hunter must use judgment in making a decision of this kind.

Much has been said about the spreading of a buck's toes as a distinguishing characteristic. To me a spread-toe print means only a heavy deer, whether it be buck or doe. Any running or loping deer will leave a spread-toe print, particularly in firm soil. Neither does the shape of the hoof itself have a definite bearing on the sex of the deer. Short, broad hoofs will be found at random on both bucks and does. The nature of the terrain underfoot has much to do with slight differences in shape of hoofs. Hard rocky ground and generally rocky deer-areas contribute to wearing-off the front of the toes. The swamp areas and coniferous timberland allow the hoof to grow a much more pointed toe.

The woodsman who has opportunity to observe all the points we have mentioned will add up all of them before drawing any hasty conclusion. As a matter of fact the whole thing is not too important, because we must find the buck himself. Many times, though, we are forced to decide whether or not to follow a set of fresh tracks and we may be able to save a day's wasted hunt if we can make a logical and accurate interpretation. At any rate, the study of deer prints never loses its charm for a deer hunter. Rather it adds to the fun of a day in the woods.

There exists still another item of sex differential in deer which has caused many a clubhouse argument: the "snort" of the whitetail. Almost every hunter who spends much time in deer country has heard a deer snort. The sound is simply a whistling blast from a deer's nostrils and may be caused by the deer's alarm or anger. Of greater importance, it is often caused by the deer's effort to rid the nostrils of the nose-bot. The deer bot is one of the factors resulting in high deer mortality in certain areas. Commonly, it is the deer's ability to rid themselves of these bots by blasting them out through the nostrils that will mean whether or not the deer will be able to survive the vitality ebb of a hard winter.

However, it is a prevalent belief among hunters that only the buck snorts. As a matter of fact, this idea is so widespread that any snorting deer faces immediate danger during the hunting season.

During one of my still-hunting trips in the lower Catskills I was working a big beech ridge. I had been in the woods about an hour and not yet heard or seen any other hunters, so I was unprepared for a sudden burst of rifle shots which crashed out directly ahead of me, farther along the ridge. Seconds later two does crashed by just below me, unaware of my presence. Just beyond me they stopped, looked over their backs in the direction they had left, then, shaking their respective tails, they quietly trotted off down the ridge slope to the valley below.

A light powdering of snow covered the ground, so soon I could see two red-capped hunters following along the trail just left by the two does. They were so occupied that neither of them saw me and would have passed me by if I hadn't whistled. I dropped down the hill then to talk with them.

"How long have you been standing there?" they both asked. "Didn't you see those two bucks go by?"

"Well," I said, "I certainly saw two deer go by, but if there had been any bucks you'd have heard some shootin'. Just what made you fellows think they were bucks?"

Both shifted their feet a bit and looked at each other before the older man spoke up. "Well, we had just come up on this ridge and these deer were bedded-down in some brush. When they heard us they both snorted and jumped on up the ridge. We could see their flags for quite a ways, so we started to pump it at 'em. We're glad that we didn't connect, but that's the first time either of us heard of a doe snorting." And so it goes. I have heard numerous incidents parallel to this one, and from widely separated whitetail regions, so the idea is by no means peculiar to a few deer hunters.

In this same connection, 'way back in the early '30's I had joined an Oakland Valley deer-hunting outfit called "The Beaverdam Club." On my first day's hunt, just after daybreak I had found a tiny scooped-out gravel bank up on the mountainside, near the camp. The boys had been taking gravel out to repair the winding wood road over the mountain to Beaverdam Pond. The bank was just so deep that I could barely look over the rim from a spot within the scooped hole.

I had a good view from this spot. With only my head exposed above ground level, I could cover the little ravine running down the steep slope to my left. The whole white-birch slope to my right and the valley below was in easy view for just a shift of the eye. This I decided would be a good spot to spend an hour while the deer still would be on the early-morning feed.

Hardly had I settled down to wait when two deer came into view, gently picking their way down the ravine edge toward the valley below. They were not alarmed, and would wander a bit from the ravine to the low second growth to nip off a tender bud now and then as they progressed, ever coming closer to my stand in the gravel pit. Finally they were only a few yards from my head, when the leading doe discovered me. At once her head was thrown erect, sensitive ears cocked in my direction. Then she lowered her head slowly and, at the close range, I could fairly see her nostrils quivering as they sucked in air, filtering it for a taint of danger.

But the wind was right and she could find nothing for fear. Still, she was mighty curious; so she raised a slim foreleg and stamped it to the ground with an audible thump. Finding that I could not yet be frightened into moving, she again stamped. Meanwhile her companion doe had inched forward cautiously until they were nose to flank. Then, incredible though it may seem, they each stamped and thudded their dainty forefeet into the hard ground, no doubt still expecting to frighten a move out of me.

] 127 [

At last, satisfied that no buck was tagging along behind, I broke the tableau quickly by yanking off my cap and waving it. The response was electric. Both does jumped into the air with loud snorts, reversing their field as they headed back up the slope, bounding as though they were on springs—tails flying erect—and snorting at every jump. At the top of the ridge they stopped, shook their heads, snorted a final blast and walked off into the white birches, snapping their flags in evident disgust.

Deer of either sex seldom make any vocal noises other than this common snort, yet there have been many instances of bleating deer recorded. Bert Sauer, old-time deer hunter and once charter member of the Iroquois Hunting Club in mid-Sullivan County, has reported to me that many times he has heard of female deer bleating, particularly when wounded. I have no firsthand knowledge of this, but I have heard the doe make tiny bleating noises to the fawns, as they nestled against her flank. I doubt if the noise could be heard, in this instance, at a distance of over twenty-five yards.

I remember a tender scene up the Beaver River section of the Adirondacks. I had taken a stand at daybreak near the foot of a low spruce ridge. The morning was crackly cold; all was dead-still but for the chatter of chickadees and a red squirrel. After a while I became aware of slight rustlings that materialized first into a small fawn, just out of the spotted coat, then another fawn and the mother doe. The three stood at the edge of the birches, tiny wisps of steam fanning out from their shining black noses. The old doe then took the lead until she stood directly before my big spruce-tree stand, but the fawns hesitated. She turned her head and gave a little grunting bleat—almost a purring sound. I could see her flanks heave slightly and the vapor come from her mouth as she made this sound, so I could be certain that it was not a low snort. Then the fawns hopped over to her and one touched noses with the mother while the other nibbled playfully at her ear.

Again the mother gave this little purring bleat and the fawns moved off into the spruces, followed closely by their fond parent. Even after the little group had passed from my view I could hear the doe bleat gently now and then until at last all was still again.

* * *

In bringing out some of these more intimate details of deer behavior the writer has a definite purpose. There is a growing tendency among the great bulk of the deer-hunting clan to pursue the whitetail deer in a hit-or-miss manner. For any man to gain the fullest success and enjoyment from his hunting each year the whitetail must be made a hobby—a hobby of study which is as gratifying as the killing of the deer itself.

True, many men are fortunate enough to kill a deer the first time they set foot in deer country. This is not exceptional. Purely by the law of averages alone some small percentage of greenhorns will kill their buck, because with thousands of hunters in the woods each season some are bound to run across a deer. But the man who can kill his buck year after year is he who possesses a keen knowledge of woodcraft and deer behavior. No detail of deer lore is too insignificant to be overlooked. With the passage of years and the successive seasons no one more than the deer hunter himself will appreciate this fact.

There is much more to killing a buck than finding good deer country and spending a few days hunting therein. Any woodsman worthy of the name covers his deer-hunting grounds with hawk eyes. He studies his topographical maps (in strange territory) and from these alone—virtually without seeing the land itself—he can often locate the sections where deer will cross from valley feeding grounds to hiding places in swamps and bedding grounds on ridges. These maps are invaluable to the deer hunter in familiarizing him with areas to be hunted. Such maps may be had from the United States Geological Survey, covering in quadrangle sections almost any area in the country. The maps show elevations as contour lines, and all roads, trails and streams in any given areas.

It is a far cry from covering alder thickets with a good English setter or crouching in a duck blind on the Sound to the successful hunting of whitetail deer. The writer does not wish to disparage small-game hunting, for no one else enjoys that sport to a greater degree. However, I have always felt that such hunting calls more for good shooting ability and good dogs than for an abundance of woodlore. Successful deer hunting is the true test not only of a sportsman's shooting skill but of his specific knowledge of woodcraft and of his intelligent application of this knowledge.

A knowledge of woodcraft in deer hunting includes much more than a thorough understanding of deer habits and movements. The hunter himself must be at home in the woods, be able to detect good cover and feeding grounds at a glance, know his territory well enough to account for the movements of his pals, and above all be sure of his own position through every minute of the day. In small covers near farming lands and settled communities this is no problem. In the "back-country" and semiwilderness areas, it is not so easy. Individuals vary much in this quality of directional sense, but every hunter can acquire enough of it to give him perfect freedom of movement in any territory he might like to explore.

STILL-HUNTING THE WHITETAIL

Lawrence R. Koller

Continuing the work of a master is this second excerpt taken from Shots at Whitetails. *Personally, I have always found the expression "still-hunting" to be a strange one. As a kid who spent a lot of time in Georgia, I think I was almost ready for college before becoming convinced that a largemouth bass was not a trout—as we called them—and that still-hunting did not mean sitting on a stump and waiting for a deer or squirrel.*

SUNUP was but moments away as I stood on the roadbank near the little old schoolhouse. Earl and Eddy had just dropped me off and had gone up the winding dirt road to the next farmhouse. They would park the car there and hunt up on the big hardwood ridge that parallels the course of the majestic Delaware River. I was to hunt on up this ridge, and meet them a mile or so beyond.

How quiet and lifeless were the slopes and valley below me! The quiet gray beeches stood like guardians among the little white birch and sumac by the roadside, gleaming damply in the early daylight. Now and then a heavy water drop would fall with a *thunk* on the dead-leaf carpet below. It had rained the night before—a soft, warm fall rain, bringing off the last reluctant leaves and opening the door to the hunter.

It was opening day some ten-odd years ago. We had decided to hunt here, in the Cahoonzie area of southwest Sullivan County, purely on my say-so . . . that it was good deer country. Of course all of us knew there were deer in this general area, but we had not yet hunted here for deer. I had, however, been over the section we were to hunt a few weeks before, with the setter. I had combined grouse-hunting with a little exploration, and had decided that the country offered good possibilities.

At that time I had been more or less driven out of my old stamping grounds near Wolf Pond by the heavy infiltration of new and reckless deer hunters. I had decided that this year I would seek new hunting fields, where still-hunting would once again be practical and enjoyable.

Perhaps no one can say just why he picks a definite spot for a new hunting ground. On my grouse-hunting trip I had found many tracks, some well-defined runs, and evidence of deer feeding on acorns and beechnuts up on the big ridge, now above me. But I knew many other places where signs were just as abundant. Perhaps on the day I had been here before, the beauty of the country impressed me and now had lured me there again.

It had been a glorious, golden fall day. Riotous color had filled the woods—the warm reds of the young oaks, the pastel yellows of the beeches. Waxy-orange bittersweet berries clung to the tumble-down stone fences and clambered over dark green cat-briers like living drapes. Here I had found grouse and the delicate heart-shaped prints of deer.

Topping the ridges were long lines of towering hemlocks, standing guard over their progeny in the struggle for sunlight among the heavy white birch. Groundpine and creeping hemlock carpeted the white birch grounds, almost concealing great beds of wintergreen and partridge berries. And over all was the heavy rich glow of October sunlight. In the valley below, the Shinglekill gurgled and chattered on its journey to the Delaware. Both brook trout and the heavier browns were even now lying in the gravel-bottomed rifles, ready to spawn. To me trout and whitetail deer have always been closely associated. Perhaps it is because many of my deer have been killed near trout waters, or perhaps because in both there breathes the never-ending beauty of the wilds.

The first pink rays of sunrise bathing the top of the ridge above stirred me from my reverie. It was time now to get up on that ridge and look for my buck. Behind the little school ran a low ridge, gently sloping upward to meet the big ridge that I felt should be the resting place of at least a few deer. Slowly, reluctantly, fearful of making any sound that might break the spell of silence, I began the climb.

My shoe-pacs fell softly on the sodden leaves—I brushed through little hemlocks whose evergreen feathers dropped tiny showers at my intrusion. Every half-minute or so I stopped to look down each slope of the ridge, watching for deer sign as I progressed. Soon I headed into the base of my big ridge. Now the

timber changed abruptly from small white birch and poplar to the heavy-trunked red oaks and big beeches. The beech is ever a lovely tree. Its smooth gray bark gives an impression of quiet, firm dignity, a strong contrast to the rough, black trunks of oak and hard maple.

The woods were indeed quiet that morning. The air had but a touch of chill; no breeze moved the last remaining leaves of the aspens—nothing but a *put!* as an overburdened raindrop dripped from a high twig.

Now I struck a fresh track, and I stopped to study it. The prints were deep in wet leaves, wide-spaced and toed-out; they were heading for the ridge. It was apparent that this deer had spent the rainy night before down in the valley hemlocks, either feeding or in shelter from the rain, and was making for the ridge to bed-down.

I took the trail to the top; it was easy to follow in the sodden leaves. But at the top of the ridge, the trail became fainter as it led through long stretches of moss and over rocky ledges. Finally, I gave it up altogether to concentrate on covering the long hogback before me.

For an hour I carefully walked the ridge-top, swinging first right, then left, that I might watch both sides of the slope. Much of the time I stood to listen and watch, but I heard nothing more than the scurry of a gray squirrel as he dashed for a den tree, or the distant *Pow! Pow!* of a rifle. Then I turned to step around a big stump, and a movement in a white birch stand off to my left brought me to a halt. I could see moving bodies in the brush and now and then a slim foreleg, but no heads.

In a moment, though, two deer came out of the white birch and headed up the ridge. Both were does, or at any rate no antlers showed. I decided to wait right there for a bit and watch their back trail for any following buck. But for a quarter of an hour no other deer showed, so I took off again following the ridge and, in a sense, following the two does.

My route crossed many deer signs; fresh tracks coming up from the valley below and crossing over the ridge; many droppings sprinkled in the runs through laurel and rhododendron. Almost every visible track must necessarily be fresh, for the rain would have successfully obliterated all those before its coming. Here on a small poplar near a rocky ledge a buck had rubbed the bark—long shreds lay on the ground at the butt. No tracks were visible here; it must have been rubbed some days before. All these signs were heartening—perhaps this ridge would develop into a deer hunters' Utopia.

At last I reached the crest of the hogback. Beyond, the ridge sloped gently down to the valley of the little farm near where my pals were to be hunting. Quietly and slowly I worked down the slope, aware now of a gentle breeze fanning my left cheek and murmuring in the topmost hemlock boughs. The sun was much higher now—the early rose glow had changed to a pale yellow, penetrating to the forest floor in the beech and white birch stands, but failing to dispel the moist and morose shadows of hemlock and buck-laurel. Deer should be bedding now, I thought—not much chance to find any yet on the move.

In my musing way, I had passed a big windfall of white oaks, lying off the shoulder of the ridge, heavily leaved tops pointing down the slope. The uprooted trunks lay crisscrossed upon each other with the thick, brown dead leaves clinging to the branches in a high mound. I had stopped then for a moment, to wonder at the perversity of a flighty wind in singling out for destruction this particular clump of white oaks. And as I stood here my eye dropped to fresh deer tracks, tracks that headed toward this windfall.

Obeying the normal urge, my feet turned toward the fallen trees. No more than two steps did I make, when, with a bursting crash, a fine buck bounded out from behind the screen of leaves, high-tailing it for the crest of the hogback. As he jumped, his antlers had flashed in the sunlight, and even as my rifle came up, both antlers and long white flag were bobbing over the low brush.

My first fright over, I settled down to stopping him short of the ridge-top. Swinging with him, my front sight touched his knees as I tightened off the trigger. With the crash of the .250 his forelegs crumpled on that last bound; his nose slid to the leaves and his chunky body swept over in a high arching somersault. He made one game effort to regain his feet, but the second bullet threw a tuft of hair from the far side of his neck and he thumped to the ground again, stretched out in death.

As he lay on the damp forest floor, I marveled, as I do over every deer I have killed, at the dead-whiteness of his white hair and the tawny gray of his body coat, so like in color to the leaves in which he lay. His antlers shone dully, hinting of many rubbings on the soft-barked saplings on his ridge. The main beams swept forward and upward, topped with ten-inch-long tines. His was not a magnificent head of wide spreading beams and many points, but simply the grand, sturdy crown of an adult eight-point buck.

And now, I reflected, as I dropped down on a log to steady my quaking knees, my hunting was over and the hard work—yet a labor of love—must begin. I had to get him out.

An experience such as this is the deer hunter's dream. On the day that I have related, still-hunting conditions were ideal. Each circumstance had been in my favor—quiet, damp woods, a gentle breeze favoring my direction of hunting and the common, natural tendency of the whitetail buck to remain hidden even at the close approach of the hunter. It was mere chance that I discovered the fresh tracks, turning me towards the deer's hiding place; and at once he knew the jig was up—therefore his mad dash for safety.

It is in such a fortuitous hunt, when Lady Luck smiles, that the deer hunter reaches the greatest heights of hunting thrills and pleasure. True still-hunting will ever be a solitary effort, one in which the successful hunter can take the greatest pride of accomplishment. He has outwitted our most cautious and instinctively clever species of wildlife at its own game. The satisfaction of taking a whitetail buck by still-hunting methods alone can never be approached by killing a buck that has been driven to the stander to be killed.

Of course, still-hunting poses a myriad of problems. Much of our good deer-hunting territory is not well suited for still-hunting. For example, the heavy scrub-oak territory of many Pennsylvania counties makes a close approach to deer almost an impossibility.

A large portion of New York's Sullivan County is heavily thatched with scrub oak, laurel and rhododendron, so the hunter can never approach deer without driving them ahead, far out of seeing or shooting range. Many sections of representative deer country abound in similar obstacles to the still-hunter.

The ideal type of cover for still-hunting is the rolling, many-ridged hardwood lands, where timber is heavy enough to discourage dense undergrowth. This is not to say that virgin-forest growth is good deer country, for generally it is not. Rather the best still-hunting country is a combination of big hardwood ridges and small valleys covered with good, low undergrowth for deer feeding grounds. An example of such country can be found in the Northville area of New York State. Here, in the southern foothills of the Adirondacks, at the northern extremities of Sacandaga reservoir lies just this type of rolling hardwood country. The tiny valleys lying within these hills are well thatched with small white birch, cedar, poplar and alder, as well as many other types of good deer feed.

The Catskill area offers many good still-hunting sections: Slide Mountain near Phoenicia; the Red Hill section farther south near Claryville; the whole Upper Neversink River Valley—just to name a few.

Heavy spruce areas such as we find in the western Adirondacks are difficult to hunt. Vision is limited to the extreme in such areas by the constant walls of evergreens. Under these conditions deer can gain a safe hiding place in a few bounds, in almost any direction, giving little opportunity for a shot.

But good still-hunting areas can be found in any state where the whitetail is numerous—Vermont, New Hampshire, Michigan or Maine, or whatever state happens to be the hunter's choice. In my own experience most of my deer country is discovered on my fishing trips, for actually a deer hunter never stops hunting, even on his summer jaunts. Many of my best hunting experiences have been enjoyed in areas that I scouted during the summer months. After arming myself with topographical maps of my chosen area I would be ready to hunt when opening day came around.

Another and perhaps more important problem for the still

] 137 [

hunter is the abundance of other hunters in his area. Still-hunting is hardly practical when many hunters are tramping the woods in groups of two, three or even more. The deer become highly alarmed in any section where hunters are on the move all day; so much so that the slightest noise will tend to send them off at top speed. Deer under these conditions of heavy hunting have had their routine of natural habits broken. They feed little, if at all, during daylight hours and they bed-down in the heaviest thickets they can find.

There is a personal element too, under such a setup. It is hardly advisable for any hunter to go pussyfooting through deer country if there are many hunters strewn throughout the area. There is ever the thousand-to-one chance that a slowly moving hunter may be mistaken for a deer by one of his brethren. It is highly important, then, to pick your still-hunting grounds with a view to hunting pressure as well as abundance of deer and favorable terrain.

However, we do have many sections of good deer country where straight still-hunting methods are the only practical means to kill your buck. We speak now of the great wilderness areas of the Upper Michigan Peninsula, the North Woods of Maine, a great portion of the Adirondacks, or any true wilderness area accessible to the hunter only by trails or waterways. Here the deer live continually in a wild state, unfamiliar with the sight or scent of man. Perhaps many deer are born, live a normal span of existence and die without ever having seen a man. Hunting these deer successfully requires the best of woods craftsmanship.

It is just this type of hunting that the writer prefers, but unfortunately few of us have the time to devote to such a trip. Wilderness hunting involves considerable preparation, complete camping gear and a knowledge of woods lore in sufficient quantity to make an extended stay out of doors a pleasure rather than a hardship. Its great compensation rests in the hunter's opportunity to disassociate himself from the humdrum existence and the platitudes of normal living. Here the hunter must be virtually self-sufficient. He must walk many miles over dim trails, carrying his camping and hunting gear on his back. He must depend on his wits and ability to provide a good bed, good food and reasonable living comfort in camp. But most of all he must lean heavily on his still-hunting knowledge and ability to bag his buck. Any whitetail buck killed under these conditions will ever be the most highly prized trophy in a sportsman's collection.

And in these wilderness areas there is no other way to kill deer. No methods of deer hunting other than still-hunting are practical. The terrain is of great scope. There may be many deer but they are scattered over thousands of acres of timbered woodland. The still-hunter must seek until he locates his deer.

Many times I have thought that our deer hunters are becoming soft. Most of us can find deer within a few hours' drive of our homes. We drive into the deer country, park our cars and in five minutes are hunting in productive country. I must admit that this is good. In many cases it means that a man is able to hunt deer where otherwise he would never be able to enjoy this sport.

But in another sense, much of the true hunting spirit is lost if we hunt deer only under these conditions. The man who has the initiative to seek deer in the wilderness areas is the hunter who gains the most from his deer hunting. Still-hunting is becoming a lost art in many sections, primarily because of unfavorable local conditions but often because of general inertia on the part of the hunter. To those who say that there are too many hunters coming into their favorite haunts, or that the deer are being killed off, we can advise turning to wilderness areas. There still are many thousands of acres of wonderfully scenic forests, abundant with deer, that have scarcely felt the tread of a deer hunter's foot. Let these men get maps of the areas they would like to hunt, study them well, prepare the necessary camping gear, and when the season is at hand "go back in" for a week or two where there are still many wild deer for the taking if the hunter possesses the necesary skill and intestinal fortitude to make the grade.

"Still-hunting" is, as a term, slightly ambiguous. It is not to be confused with the common practice of sitting on a deer run all day—day after day—hoping that a buck will come along, sooner or later. This method can be a highly successful one but it should never masquerade as still-hunting. Rather it might be more aptly named "ambushing."

This difference in terminology was driven home to me quite a number of years ago—during my early days of deer hunting. I had driven up to Wolf Pond, right in the heart of Sullivan County's best deer hunting, one morning in the early part of the open season. When I reached the old hand-laid stone dam, there was a large party of hunters gathered atop the dam, waiting for good daylight before taking to the woods.

Sitting apart from this group was another hunter—advanced in years and no doubt, I thought, well learned in the art of deer hunting. I struck up a conversation by asking him if he was hunting with the gang.

"No," he said. "This bunch are going up in the scrub oaks and drive the hell out of 'em. They've been doin' it all week. Guess they killed one buck so far. But I'm going to take it easy and do a little still-huntin'."

I looked him over pretty carefully after that remark. He was bundled up in a heavy sheepskin coat, covering layers of wool shirts and sweaters. His feet were well covered with a pair of huge felt boots into the tops of which were stuffed at least two pairs of trousers. He carried a huge lunch basket in one hand with a giant-size "Thermos" bottle resting upright in one corner; in the other hand hung a double hammer-gun of ancient vintage. Quite an outfit, I decided, for a still-hunter. Then I made off up the trail to do a bit of hunting myself.

Later that day I happened on this same character, sitting a few yards off the trail but not more than a hundred yards from the Wolf Pond Dam. I stopped to ask him if he'd seen anything yet and he told me, "Only a couple of does."

"Thought you were going to do some still-hunting to-day," I remarked casually.

"Well, by God," he replied, "don't you think for a minute that I ain't been. I been here all day—haven't moved a bit since sunup. This here's a mighty good run and I know I'll get a shot if I sit here long enough." So much for that brand of still-hunting.

This writer does not intend to ridicule those who prefer to hunt deer by careful watching and waiting near runways and feeding grounds. Many times it is the only way to kill a wary old buck that has been outwitting still-hunters and deer drives for season after season. The true still-hunter, as a matter of fact, does a great deal of watchful waiting as he moves over deer territory. Looking, stopping, and watching with patience and care has many times filled a deer license, oftener indeed than has barging through deer country without regard or respect for a deer's keenness of vision, hearing and olfactory senses.

The principal drawback in this ambush style of modified still-hunting is that the hunter sees but little deer country. More valuable in deer hunting than patient waiting is a true, firsthand knowledge of the movements of deer in the area. This can only be gained by moving quietly through the woods and swamps, studying tracks, runs, bedding grounds and all the many signs that the experienced woodsman can interpret in terms of deer lore. This is still-hunting's greatest boon.

Add to this that in cold weather only the most Spartan courage can keep a hunter on a stand hour after hour throughout even the shortest fall or winter day. Such hunting limits the scope of a sportsman's knowledge. I know a goodly number of men who hunt deer year after year and of this group none have yet seen for themselves the telltale rub of a buck on a green sapling. These hunters lose most of the charm of still-hunting. Deer hunting for them becomes a battle with the elements—often highly antagonistic during the open season in any of the northern zones of deer hunting.

Frankly, this writer lacks both the infinite patience and courage to face a bitterly cold day on a runway stand. Feet become painfully inanimate lumps of frozen flesh, fingers almost crackle with frost and the entire human frame soon vibrates like a strummed harp. The entire picture is out of tune with the normal theme of deer hunting thrills and pleasure.

The hunter who follows the still-hunting game alone adheres to a typical ritual. He works the lower feeding grounds during the early morning and late afternoon hours. When the sun climbs above the treetops he begins to look for bedded deer on ridge-tops or along the edges of heavy swamp or thickets of evergreens. In any case he covers ground slowly, traveling the route which will permit motion through the woods with a minimum of noise. Feet are placed carefully on moss or rock at every opportunity, keeping away from the noisy rustlings of dead leaves. He travels wood roads wherever possible to keep clothing from brushing noisily through the small branches.

Many times a hunter will give up still-hunting entirely when the woods are dry and noisy. This can be a serious mistake. Deer are not instantly alarmed at the noise of a hunter's footfalls in dry leaves. Logically such a noise could be made by other deer, squirrels, partridge, wood mice or a myriad of other wood creatures. It is to be expected that deer will usually take off if they see the hunter after their attention is aroused by such noises. On the credit side of the ledger, we can say that a smart still-hunter will often spot his deer before their alarm sends them crashing away. Again, whitetail deer have a habit of standing quite still at the hunter's approach, if they feel that they are well concealed, or that the hunter will pass them by.

I recall an incident that illustrates this tendency to hide by remaining quiet in the hope that they would be undetected. I was not hunting deer at the time, for the season was still a few days away. Following one of my customs, I was hunting partridge in a favorite deer cover up on the Shawangunk Mountain range. It was a windy day with a decided fall bite in the air. The birds were wild, and my setter was ranging out a bit more than he would have been normally. Now and then he would pass completely out of sight and I would whistle him in. The air was filled with falling leaves, setting the whole mountain slope in motion. There were many deer signs, but so far I had not jumped a deer. Nor did I expect to, for I had taken no pains to conceal either my movements or the dog's.

At last there was a time when I failed to see Pep for several minutes. I found myself near a high ledge which dropped away below me for fifteen or twenty feet. I was not yet near enough to the rim of the cliff to see beyond, so whistling and calling as I went I came to the edge for a look below it. I searched the long slope stretching down through the big timber below for several minutes, still whistling and calling for the dog. Suddenly he appeared by my side and at once he stiffened and looked down over the cliff.

Following his lead, I too looked down, directly below the ledge. Right at the base of the rock lay two deer, a fat fork-horn buck and a doe, both flattened out on the leaf-strewn ground as though they would like to sink still further into concealment. For a space of several seconds they lay still, then in a single motion they leaped from their beds and disappeared along the ledge. The appearance of the dog was the factor that routed them out. I had stood for quite a bit just above them, shouting and whistling like a maniac, and there is no doubt in my mind that they would have remained right there in frozen immovability had not the dog suddenly appeared on the scene. I am certain that I would not have been aware of their presence if they had remained quietly huddled there at the base of the ledge and had not the setter come at that moment. At no time was I more than thirty feet from these deer while I was on the ledge-top calling and looking for the dog, but they managed to fight off any wave of nervous timidity with the knowledge that they were well hidden.

Deer continually follow this practice, of allowing the hunter to pass, and then making off quietly in the opposite direction. It is fully as important for a lone still-hunter to watch his back trail occasionally as it is for him to be alert for deer ahead. Every time the hunter passes a heavy thicket or clump of evergreens or rhododendron he should stop and watch behind for a glimpse of brown, sliding and shifting away through cover. And it's amazing to observe the ability of a sneaking deer to move with little noise, whether it be through scrub oak, tangled cat-briers or over crusted snow.

Weather has a direct bearing on a still-hunter's success. Ideal conditions are damp weather or the period immediately following rain or light snow. Dampness softens all woods noises and at the same time makes fresh deer sign more apparent. Connected also is the tendency of deer to hide away during periods of storm and to move about for feed directly after the storm has cleared. A quietly damp day with little wind and with all dead leaves fallen clear of trees and brush makes an ideal day for still hunting. I personally dislike still-hunting in windy weather. The thrashing of wind-whipped branches, the heavy sighing of evergreens and the constant motion and rustling of dead leaves fills the ears to the exclusion of all other noises.

Yet I have several highly successful still-hunting friends who much prefer still-hunting during periods of windy weather. They maintain that the noise of windswept forest effectively covers smaller noises made by their movements. Add to this the fact that with trees and brush constantly in motion the hunter's movements are more or less concealed or at least made less apparent. I can see the logic, but so far it has not worked out for me. I find that deer behavior on a windy day is skittish in the extreme and that often they dash off at any slight alarm.

In my mind the hunter who is most benefited by windy weather is one with defective hearing. Under normally quiet weather conditions such a man is at a disadvantage—the deer can hear him long before he can detect their movements by sound alone. But on a windy day every hunter must depend virtually on his eyes alone and this factor places the sportsman with poor auditory senses on an equal footing with those of us who are more fortunately equipped.

Old George Drake, well known to fishermen and hunters alike in the Lower Catskill region, had poor hearing during his last few years in the woods. But he continued to kill his buck with astonishing regularity. George was a woodsman of outstanding skill, carried over from his market-hunting days with the old muzzle-loader. Several times he confided to me that the wind had helped him get close enough to a buck to be able to get his shot. Until the time of his death a few years ago, his vision in the woods was of the best, even though he could barely read the local newspaper at a close range. Nature may have helped to balance the scales by enabling his old eyes to see well enough to overcome his other loss.

All other things being equal, the quiet day offers the best possible opportunities for the still-hunter. It is then that he may match wits with the whitetail on a more equal footing. I say "more"

] 144 [

equal advisedly, for none of us can hope to be as familiar with any deer country as are the deer.

An intimate knowledge of the terrain to be hunted is mandatory if the still-hunter would kill his buck by not merely trusting to luck. In wilderness areas of wide scope no hunter will have the time to spend in making preseasonal trips to learn the layout. It is here that the topographical maps come into their own.

If the sportsman has a definite idea as to where he intends to hunt it is advisable to send to the *United States Geological Survey, Department of the Interior, Washington, D.C.* for an index map of his state or the state in which he intends to hunt. Then from this whole master layout he will be able to select the proper quadrangles to cover the area he plans to hunt.

I remember one of the incidents that proved to me the infinite value of these little maps. Quite a few years ago a friend took me on a deer-hunting trip up into Warren County in the Adirondacks. We planned a week's stay back in the woods, so we prepared our camping gear and started off. After getting in to the end of the road we packed in and made camp. We had a grand hunt; each of us had his buck at the end of the fourth day. We packed them out after breaking camp and started for home after a week of glorious weather and ideal hunting in some of the best still-hunting territory I have ever visited.

The years passed, and my partner of this trip had moved out to the Middle West. Once again I wanted to make the trip back to this hunting spot, but I had no accurate idea how to reach it. The topographical map came to my rescue. I picked out two quadrangles covering the general area and together with a state highway map I was able to locate accurately not only the exact route by car, but even the very trail which we had taken to the camping spot. Many times since I have had occasion to seek new hunting and fishing grounds with these maps. Indeed I am never without a complete set, covering most of my hunting and fishing grounds.

I believe that over half of the United States has been covered in this Geological Survey, begun some time back in the early 1880's. Most of the territory of interest to Eastern sportsmen has been mapped, and maps are available. Of course, many of the maps are not up to date as to highways, but the country is still just the same as it was the day it was mapped. By intelligent study of the individual quadrangles an accurate mental picture of the terrain can be visualized. Streams, lakes and swamps are accurately detailed; contour lines show every elevation. Valleys and ridges, steep hillsides and cliffs are graphically detailed. In a word, no area can be strange to the hunter who studies well one of these topographical maps.

Any still-hunter of experience can virtually pick out on these maps the areas to hunt. Crossings through ridge saddles can be determined, and swamp hiding places brought to light. Watering places and streams are of course at once evident, and if the still-hunter plans a camping trip he is able to pick out the exact trail to carry him to good water. The maps are roughly 16½ by 20 inches, and if they are to be carried on a trip, as they should be, they can be pasted on cheesecloth or muslin, rolled up and carried in a mailing tube. Reposing on my den wall is a large map of the Catskill area, made up by joining quadrangles together, the whole mounted on muslin. I have it covered with various colors of map tacks pointing out deer areas, trout and bass waters, and any other facts of interest to my sportsmen visitors. I consider it one of the most interesting additions to my equipment.

It has often been advised by authoritative writers that the still-hunter should always hunt upwind. The purpose, of course, is to prevent man-scent from reaching the game in advance of the hunter. No doubt a deer can pick up scent for two hundred yards if it's carried by a stiff breeze. Generally speaking it is good advice to keep downwind of any game, particularly deer. I fear, however, that in some areas the hunter will be hunting up hill and down dale all day long if he sticks to the letter of the rule. If the ridge we propose to hunt runs north and south and the wind blows east to west, we have little choice but to follow the ridge. Certainly we will never hunt straight up the side of the slope and down over the other side merely to keep head into the wind.

In every hunting problem rules must be tempered with good

judgment, and in this matter of hunting against the wind there can be no hard-and-fast rule. A hunter's entire strategy is dictated for the most part by the lay of the land. And in rolling, hardwood whitetail country, the contours of the land are broken up in many ways by cliffs, ravines, pinnacles and knobs. Wind direction over such terrain is fitful and flightly. One moment we will feel a touch on the right cheek and as we move past a rock ledge the breeze will come directly toward us. In the mountainous areas the bright sunlight, beaming down on a southern slope, will create a heavy updraft, nullifying wind direction on this slope. Many times in a single hunt I have found the breeze shifting in every conceivable direction.

If the wind velocity is fairly stiff these modifying factors will be overcome, but in any case the hunter will abide by the influence of the terrain. He must keep a general upwind direction if possible, but it is not vitally important that he face forever into the wind. A good crosswind, either to right or to left, is every bit as effective in keeping away man-scent from the game, at least until the still-hunter is abreast of the quarry.

In hunting a ridge I prefer a cross-breeze, keeping on the downwind shoulder of the ridge as I move slowly along. Deer often keep constant watch along the very top of the ridge in both directions. They seem vaguely to expect a higher incidence of danger along the crest of a ridge. It is wise then to keep just far enough away from the top of the ridge to yet be able to see any movement upon it. In no instance, however, will a still-hunter move in a deliberate down-wind direction—this simply advertises his presence to every whitetail in the area ahead.

The term "still-hunting" is in itself connotative of the hunter's actions while in the woods. Every effort must be made to move slowly, and with a minimum of noise underfoot. The cracking of dead branches, the rattling of loose rocks and other carelessly made noises are definitely foreign to the progress through the woods of any wild animal, except possibly a black bear or a frightened deer. Primarily, the still-hunter is most concerned with seeing or hearing his deer before the deer sees him. His every movement must be directed to this end.

] 147 [

The thought that much territory should be covered in a day's hunt must be abandoned. This single factor has contributed many an unsuccessful day to a deer hunter's season. No one, even the best woodsman, can cover five or six miles of territory silently and with caution and see the movements of game within his travels. The watchword must ever be: Move slowly, watch carefully and listen closely. Each time the hunter comes to a strategic spot where deer may cross, let him stop, first picking a suitable background where his silhouette will not stand out in bold outline. Deer are highly conscious of any new object in their home covers. If the hunter is foolish enough to permit his body to be seen against an open skyline or atop a rock-ledge or big boulder he cannot, in all honesty, complain if he fails to get a fair shot at his buck. The best policy is to stand against a neutral background—a scrub-oak patch, a big tree trunk or a boulder, first being certain that the background is large enough to cover his outline. Suitably placed, a passing deer may see him, but if he remains quiet and the wind favors him, there is every possibility that the deer will not be alarmed.

There is still another and important factor in watchful waiting. Often the most careful approach and intelligent observation will fail to give the hunter a look at his deer before it makes off. If the cover is good, and the buck has been making the area his regular hangout, the chance is great that he will return shortly. Any prime wise buck is ever reluctant to leave his home bailiwick unless he is badly frightened. The mere passage of an occasional hunter seldom routs a buck for long from his home coverts. The wise still-hunter who discovers fresh tracks leading away from an obviously good hideout will do well to spend a quiet hour waiting for the buck to come sneaking back home.

In any heavily hunted deer territory the older bucks have a habit of selecting a good high ridge, a heavy scrub-oak thicket or some other spot where a hunter cannot approach without the deer's being aware of the danger. When one of these bucks does locate such a safe spot for his hideout, it requires plenty of hunting to keep him away from it. He may be scared off by a still-hunter or driven out by a drive, but ten to one he will make every effort to get back again, provided always that the source of danger has apparently left the area. In my own experience, I have had the opportunity to kill several bucks in just this way, after locating their hideaways.

One of these deer bedded-down on a narrow scrub-oak ridge. Through the middle of the scrub oaks and lying along the crest of the ridge ran an old abandoned wood road. Many years of disuse had filled the road with tangled blow-downs and small brush, making quiet progress impossible. By the process of elimination, I discovered that this buck would take to this scrub-oak patch just as soon as the first rifles began to crack after the opening day sunrise.

Twice in as many days I jumped him out of the scrub but never caught a glimpse of him. Then I decided it might be good strategy to drive him out to a stand, giving someone a shot. I gathered together six of my hunting pals and mapped out a still-drive, thinking that he would run the top of the ridge, follow it to the end and give a shot to the standers I had posted at the top of the ridge where it sloped down to the creek bed. But he was too wise for us. Twice we jumped him but he failed to run the ridge. He went down the slopes to the nearest swamp, and of course there was never a stander near his route. He successfully eluded all our efforts that year, but I had decided to try for him again next season if he still used that scrub-oak ridge.

Before the season came around next year, I looked over the ground carefully for his tracks; they were sprinkled all over the ridge. I found two rather fresh beds in the scrub oak and near a well-defined run this buck had rubbed and gouged a small maple tree in pre-mating exuberance. There were many signs that he had been active on the ridge, but no tracks of other deer were evident. Apparently the ridge was not used by any other deer, or else this buck had driven off outsiders.

I decided to wait for him on one of his runways right after daylight on opening day. I waited and waited for two days but he made no appearance. I believed then that he was leaving the ridge after dark each night, feeding in the lower valley areas and then returning before daylight each morning. His fresh tracks were very much in evidence each morning so I could make no other deduction. Accordingly, at dark of the second day's hunt I tied my black thread across the runways in two different places. Next morning both threads were hanging limply.

By this time I was a bit desperate, so I decided that I'd jump him out of his bed anyway, just to make him "git." I swung up over the ridge, fighting my way down the wood road. I went through to the end of the cover—about a quarter of a mile; then I swung back through the scrub oak itself. At no time did I hear the buck leave but I found fresh tracks leading down toward the runway, and it seemed from their appearance, he was in a hurry.

Satisfied that I had at least disturbed his siesta, I came out to the edge of the scrub and dropped down on a mossy patch near his runway for a little rest. Plowing scrub oak and brush for an hour had taken a little pep from my legs and shortened by breath to little pants. I soaked in a bit of November sunshine, listened to the red squirrels chattering and the little mountain brook gurgling below me. Suddenly a gang of blue jays set up a raucous chorus over on the next little ridge, and then just as suddenly flew off in silence. Disturbed by a hunter, I thought idly, wondering meanwhile if he had heard the buck come down off the ridge.

I passed many minutes in this fashion, planning new stratagems to outwit this deer, for by this time he had become a major obsession. In fact, I dreamed one night that I had killed him, but unfortunately I did not dream in sufficient detail, so it wasn't of much help. I had not yet set eyes on this buck, but I could easily visualize a great spread of antlers crowning a massive head and neck, an idea no doubt implanted by the deep gouges I had observed in the trunk of the little maple he had rubbed.

Somewhat lost in this haze of thought I gradually become aware of tiny noises, foreign to the normal sound pattern, filling my ears. I glanced across to the other ridge but could see nothing strange. Again I heard a mumbling footfall and rustling of twigs but could not make out any movement in the low second growth that separated me from the other hardwood ridge across the valley of the little brook. But quite without warning I saw the flash of sunlight on antlers as a buck moved slowly through the underbrush toward the brook, moving ever in the direction of the runway. He paused now and raised his head in my direction, lifting it until I could see the full wide spread of his long-tined antlers and the tips of his ears.

I waited, then, until he began to move again; I shifted my position slightly until I could bring the short-barreled Krag into line with his path. He was in no hurry. He stopped many times, probably to test the wind and listen for noises up on his scrub-oak ridge. Now he was quartering toward me, only fifty yards off, and still I could see no part of his body through the underbrush. Approaching the brook, he stopped dead-still in a little alder clump on the far bank.

For many minutes he stood there, his antler-tips shifting to right and left as he looked over the area ahead cautiously. Then in a single leap he cleared the brook and walked into a big white-birch clump; and at the edge of the white birch lay his runway. My front sight rested on the runway where he should emerge, held at knee level; my breath again was short but for a different reason; my heart click-clicked in my throat. I thought he never would show himself—the suspense was frightful.

Slowly he poked a black nose out of the birches, head low now, as he sniffed at the runway. His front feet came into the opening and my front sight lifted to his neck as he quartered toward me. I squeezed off the shot. The muzzle blast blotted him out of my vision for just a fraction of an instant and then he lay across the runway, all four feet in the air, kicking out his last moments. He never regained his feet nor moved from the spot where he first came to earth. The open-point bullet had blasted a two-inch section from his neck vertebrae.

It was evident that this buck never moved far from his hiding place in daylight hours. When alarmed he simply moved off the ridge, crossed the brook and went up on another ridge, very likely staying there until things quieted down, when he would again carefully pick his way back to safety. He was a fine animal with long wide beams and carrying 8 long points; his dressed weight was just over 180 pounds. A splendid buck added to my list of trophies—simply by watching and waiting in the luckily chosen proper spot.

Often a buck will be aroused by a prowling hunter and his natural caution will dictate moving from the spot. But until he has precisely located the hunter he may remain hidden until he is certain in which direction the danger lies. On two occasions I have jumped whitetail bucks while still-hunting, bucks that jumped only at the noise of my approach and who then stood quietly waiting to spot the danger. One of these moved into a heavy spruce thicket and stood there for many minutes. When I alarmed this deer I had been fighting my way through some of this same spruce and any progress that I had made was far from silent. However, when I heard the deer jump just ahead I stood very still and watched carefully all about me on the ridge-top. I was aware that after the deer had jumped I had heard only a few bounds, then complete silence. I suspected that he might still be hiding in the heavy evergreens, so I waited for him to move out. The air was motionless, the day damp, giving any man-scent that may have carried from me, a limited range.

As I stood there in the quiet of the spruces I thought I could hear a faint sniffing noise. At first it puzzled me but it at last dawned on me that my buck was just a short way ahead, screened effectively and most likely wondering where I had gone. Perhaps a quarter hour passed before he decided it was safe to move on, and he chose to move out at right angles to his original flight. I could hear him moving through the heavy spruce off to my right and then I caught a quick glimpse as he crossed a small opening in the green curtain. He moved slowly, stopping often to listen and watch, but at last he came out of the spruce thicket, giving me a standing shot at its edge. This was another buck I did not have to trail after the shot.

Normally, of course, a buck fully aroused will move quietly away and will never be seen by the hunter, but every so often we'll run across one who pulls just such a trick as this. It pays then to play these little hunches when we're still-hunting.

* * *

] 152 [

In rainy weather many hunters are content to stay indoors and leave the deer hunting to the more hardy souls. But I remember vividly several occasions when I have been able to walk up on deer during a steady downpour.

The day that comes most clearly to my mind was in the Oakland Valley section of the Lower Catskills back in the early 1920's. At that time I was a member of a little group of good, old-time deer hunters who had a comfortable camp up on the mountainside above the Neversink River Valley. In those days, perhaps even more than now, my deer hunting was strictly secondary to making my living. I could hunt the opening day, perhaps, and a couple of week ends. That made up my deer-hunting season. My fellow club members were more fortunate. Deer hunting to them was a two weeks' vacation—the entire season—and how I envied them! For myself, I must hunt when I could find time, and had no choice about the weather.

Before daylight of this morning I had driven up into the Valley in a warm, steady fall rain. I was prepared to hunt, though, for I had brought oilskin trousers, laced rubber knee boots and a light rubber raincoat. When I hit the camp not a light showed. The gang were all still enbunked. I tried to rouse out a few, but I was turned down with much profane emphasis. The entire gang were in accord on late sleeping that morning. I gathered that they planned a leisurely breakfast, then a session with cards and a five-gallon demijohn of red Italian wine to keep up their morale; they graciously consented to give me the freedom of the entire mountain for my hunting.

I'll admit I was a bit downcast as I hit the long winding wood road leading to the top of the big hardwood ridge above camp. The gaunt black limbs of rock oak and hard maple dripped water steadily. The rain beat a steady tattoo on the flat dead-leaf woods floor. Tiny wisps of fog gathered in the tops of the big pines and beeches. Little rivulets slithered over the dead leaves, making their way down the mountainside. It was a dreary, dismal day, hardly one to fill a hunter's heart with the joy of the outdoors.

I managed to make the top of the ridge and here I encountered heavy patches of fog. I was carrying a 'scope-sighted .250 Savage, but I had the leather lens-caps in place to keep out the rain. However, I had mounted the 'scope high enough so that I could use the iron sights if need be. I had had this in mind when I picked this rifle for the day's hunt, rather than one of my other pets. I felt that I might have need of the 'scope's definitive qualities on such a gloomy day, but if the rain held on I could still use the iron sights below the 'scope.

As I reached the ridge-top I swung toward the west, heading for the big rhododendron clumps that I knew were sprinkled along the ridge-crest. I suspected that there might be a deer or two hiding in the shelter of the big flat, rubbery leaves, hoping to keep off some of the rain. I was not in the least concerned with walking quietly for the pelting raindrops covered any small noises I might have made.

I had covered only a few hundred yards when my eye picked out a slight movement at the edge of a laurel clump. The fog had again come down and it was difficult to make out anything over thirty yards away. But I stood quietly under a big, sheltering hemlock and waited for the concealing vapors to clear off. Again I saw that flick of motion—which evolved suddenly into a deer's tail, twitching now and then. The deer was headed away from me into the heavy laurels and it stood with its head down, much as cows will do out in an open pasture lot during a summer storm.

Carefully I removed the lens-caps from my 'scope and caught the deer in its field. Now I could see it distinctly but could not see anything but the hindquarters and that drooping tail, which still twitched every few seconds. At last when I saw that the deer had no immediate intention of moving, I put the 'scope post on its back and whistled sharply. At the sound the buck—for buck it was—threw up a startled head, giving me a perfect opportunity for *coup de grâce* through the neck.

Several times since then I have been able to approach to within close shooting range of deer during a fairly heavy rain. The drumming of raindrops effectively covers all movements of a hunter's approach and at the same time has the effect of dampening scents to a negligible factor. Deer hunting in the rain certainly is far from comfortable, but if the hunter equips himself with light waterproof clothing it isn't unbearable. We must concede that at many times it is highly effective. In such wet weather the whitetail moves around but little and if he does move he will skirt the heaviest covers, favoring the more open glades and bigger timber. Presumably the whitetail has no greater liking for traveling through the rain-sodden brush than does the hunter seeking him.

Thus far we have been still-hunting alone, but some of the finest days a man can spend in the woods will be with a well-chosen hunting partner—a man as well-versed in whitetail lore as is he himself. Two men hunting the ridges and slopes together in the right co-ordination can develop into a deadly deer-killing combination. Old Abe Wykoff, of the Buck Mountain Club, and I had some fine hunting days up along the rugged slopes of the Neversink River Valley. Abe knew the haunts of most of the deer in that area and soon I learned to match my pace to his, studying his movements and absorbing some of his skill. Together we jumped many a deer from the long slope above Kitchen Eddy and not all of them got away to safety in the scrub oaks of the high ridges.

Before Old Abe and I would start our hunt he invariably instructed me to take the high side or even the crest of a ridge. He himself would work the lower ground, knowing that a jumped deer most often runs uphill. He would insist that I keep about a hundred yards ahead of him as we moved along, and to help me keep his location he carried a crow call. Every few hundred yards he would give out with a few short caws and I never would be in much doubt as to his whereabouts. Each of us would follow the same hunting system—walk fifty yards or so, then stop to watch for several minutes. In this way I would have a crack at any deer moving out ahead of Abe as well as a jump shot in my own territory ahead. Often it worked out beautifully.

One time we started a still-hunt just above Barber's Eddy. Abe went down the trail to the river's edge and he left me to follow the old wood road crossing the face of the valley slope. I waited in the road until I heard Abe's call down by the river, then I moved in, watching carefully. This slope of cover between the river and the

] 155 [

wood road which lay parallel to it along the mountain is thatched heavily with laurel and small hemlock. It's a great hideout for deer in the morning hours, before they have worked up from the river to the mountaintops.

Not long after we had started I heard Abe give a couple of short blasts on the call, quickly followed by two sharp reports from his little .32-30 Winchester. Then, with a great crashing of laurel and thumping of hoofs a whole herd of deer—seven in all—came bouncing up and across in front of me. A big doe was leading, followed closely by a small buck, with the rest of the herd right behind. I riveted my attention on the fork-horn and managed to throw three shots just ahead of him, piling him up a rod short of the wood road. The rest of the herd scattered off into the heavy laurel without my having been able to locate another buck in the bunch.

It developed that Abe had connected with this buck as the deer first moved off. His bullet had ranged up after entering the back ribs and no doubt would have dropped him shortly even if I had not luckily broken his neck with my third shot. Abe stoutly maintained that there had been another and larger buck in the herd and that he had taken a crack at this one too, not knowing that he had hit the fork-horn. But we went back to the spot and looked it over thoroughly without finding any evidence of a hit. There is no doubt in my mind that I would have seen the second buck if I hadn't been so intent on stopping the first one. But such is deer hunting.

We both were well pleased to have bagged this buck so easily, and within a matter of a few days I had killed mine, again with Old Abe's help. This time we were on the flats upriver, about a mile from Barber's Eddy. Here the river makes a wide sweep, leaving a flat several hundred yards wide between the foot of the steep slope and the roaring, boulder-strewn stream. The cover is good, mostly white birch and poplar. Again, Abe elected to work along the riverbank and I kept to the far side of the flat right at the foot of the slope.

We had almost completely covered this flat strip—about half a mile long—when I decided to stop under a big hemlock to watch for a bit. Glancing down through the white birch toward the river I saw the movement of two deer. They were sneaking through, stopping now and then to look back in Abe's direction. The cover was heavy and dark enough so that I failed to see antlers till the two deer were within forty yards. Then I could pick out the points on the second deer. As I raised my rifle, both deer spotted me but it was too late for the buck. My bullet struck him low in the chest. He made two bounds and collapsed; he was quite dead when I reached him. Abe had started these deer but had not caught a glimpse of them. They had started for the safety of the mountain-side and it was my good luck to be in just the spot to intercept them.

In a like manner I have had some wonderful still-hunting trips with a partner in Pennsylvania's Pike County, on the ridges along the Delaware River. This lad had a full quarter-share of Iroquois Indian blood in his veins and his skill in the woods left little to be desired. His knowledge of deer behavior was uncanny. Many times he could call the spot where he would jump a buck and, even more remarkable, he would be able to tip me off to where the deer would run. If I followed his advice I soon would get a shot.

Strictly speaking such two-man hunting is not simon-pure still-hunting, but it produces good results. It is made to order for a couple of good friends who like to camp out in the wilderness, rough it for a week or two, and help each other to kill their bucks. And when it comes to bringing out that heavy old buck from over behind a small mountain, four hands are many times more efficient than two.

An additional point for the still-hunter: often in hunting over lowland country, where feeding deer may be wandering and browsing, it is good policy to hunt over small ridges and knolls. By this I mean to hunt up to the top of these high spots, then look over the little valleys in between for feeding deer, then move across and up to the top of the next little ridge. Feeding deer spend much of their time in such little valleys in low ground, and often it is easy to come up on them from over a slight rise. Under these circumstances a hunter has every advantage. He can approach unseen and virtually unheard until his head clears the top of the rise. Then, with only his cap visible, he can scan the whole terrain beyond with little chance of being seen by the feeding deer. Such "crossing" of the lay of the land produces excellent still-hunting results in the lower deer areas.

In wilderness sections, the still-hunter covers not only the slopes and ridges, looking for resting and bedded deer. The edges of slashings in heavy forest are always favored by feeding deer just after sunup and before sundown. In the heaviest of timber many deer find all their available browse in these slashings—the big timber discourages the growth of small brush and offers little for hungry deer except acorns or beechnuts. Cedar swamps are regular feeding grounds too, and in deer country where high ridges are lacking any swamp ground may be the hideaway of a resting buck. It pays off to spend plenty of time in looking over these spots during the normal daylight feeding hours.

Thus far, we have been hunting our whitetail buck on bare ground. But in almost all of our great expanse of whitetail deer covers, the magic of snow-covered ground can reasonably be expected during some part of the open season. Snow in deer hunting changes many things; many a fervent prayer has been offered by the deer-hunting fraternity that the all-revealing blanket of white may cover the ground next morning.

How strange it is that a deer hunter can become so snow-conscious that the first few flakes on his camp roof will strike a hidden chord in his being! He will stir uneasily in his bunk or sleeping bag, get up and throw another stick in the fireplace; then, prompted by some inner urge, he will throw open the door and find the first crystal flakes sifting to the ground. I can offer no explanation but many times I have seen it happen. Its coming is unheralded; it drops softly and silently, yet seldom is a deer hunter surprised at dawn by the nocturnal visit.

The snow transforms the hunter's familiar slopes and ridges into a new world. Gone are the brown carpet of dead leaves, the gaunt nakedness of leaf-stripped hillsides, the crisp cracklings and rustlings of the fall woods. Instead, with the coming of the fresh, all-concealing blanket, a new brightness and a tender hush sweep the deer country. The deep shadows and gloom of dense poplar and birch thickets are lightened by the new white base; the evergreen stands are limed to overloading with the contrasting spread of puffy snow on the outermost branches. The sweeping panoramic change wrought overnight is miraculous.

Now is the time for the still-hunter to venture forth into this revealing medium to read the pages of winter's new book. Every movement of land animals and of many birds is at once apparent to the woodsman who can read the signs. Here a squirrel has dropped from his den-tree, making a lacy four-point pattern in the snow as he searches for the acorns hidden early last fall. A ruffed grouse has alighted from his hemlock tree roost, ready to try his new snowshoes along the hidden wintergreen beds. Now something has startled him—perhaps our approach. He bursts from the ground, leaving only a sweep of wing tips at either side of his trail's end to mark his flight.

The deer have been moving after the storm. Tracks fan out from the fringes of swamp and spruce thicket as the hunger urge prompts them to leave these shelters. The dainty heart-shaped prints move aimlessly here and there as the deer feed on tender buds of poplar and black birch. We can see the freshly nipped ends. Here three deer have been feeding; two sets of prints are much smaller than the third. It may be a doe and two first-year fawns; perhaps it is a trio of two does and a buck. At any rate we follow the prints for a while to detect indications of buck behavior in the larger prints. Thus we begin another interesting day in the deer woods, following and watching, anticipating the deer's movements, hoping to get a quick look at the game before it takes off in alarm.

The whitetail on the snow becomes almost a different animal. His senses, if anything, become keener. He is alert at all times for any danger approaching on his back trail. He stops frequently to scan the cover behind and in snow-filled woods his vision is as much improved as is the hunter's. Fortunately, the snow covering the earth deadens the noise of the hunter's footsteps and with proper caution he has a good chance of coming within shooting

] 159 [

distance of the deer before being heard. The game resolves itself into a chess battle between the hunter and the hunted, anticipating each other's moves.

The problem, as always in still-hunting, is to see the buck in time for a shot. If the trailing hunter can keep always upwind of his deer he will in time get his chance. But as soon as a buck is aware of a following hunter he picks a good location to circle around, both to pick up a trace of man-scent and to throw the hunter off the track. A wise old buck is full of tricks to fool the tracker. He will often head for a small brook, follow it downstream for several hundred yards, then come out again to the same bank and circle back to some higher ground where he can watch the hunter following the brook. He may even lay a straight trail for several rods, then reverse his field, stepping carefully in each footprint of his back trail. Then with a tremendous leap he will leave the trail at right angles, often landing on a higher bit of ground. Many times the novice hunter will be fooled by the apparently abrupt end of such a trail.

Some years ago I followed a buck in a six-inch fall of snow for several miles. He tried several times to throw me off the track by heading into a herd of does, traveling with them for a while, then jumping off to the side, hoping that I would keep on after the does. He tried backtracking, going through the heaviest swamps and scrub oak, but always I was able to pick up his track and keep up the chase. Finally he headed for a heavy clump of rhododendron. This patch was almost round, covering at least an acre of ground. His track led directly into it, past a big yellow pine standing at the edge of the cover. Of course, I kept on his track even through this thick stuff. I knew that if I didn't overtake him soon, darkness would come to his rescue—there was but a short period of good light left for the day.

I had reached the middle of this heavy rhododendron thicket when I heard him moving ahead, perhaps forty yards off. He would move when I moved, stop when I stopped, but always kept a safe distance ahead. When I reached the edge of the cover his track swung around, circling the outer fringes, back to the big lone pine. He then had gone right in again over my tracks. This had me stumped. I knew he could keep this up forever and I'd never get a look at him.

I stood near the pine while I thought out a plan. Finally, I dug in the snow for some loose rocks small enough for throwing. I hung my rifle on a dead stub and began to heave rocks into the clump. I threw perhaps a dozen, then grabbed my rifle. With my back to the big pine I waited, watching his back track—and my own. Within two minutes I could see him picking his way around the fringe of the rhododendron, watching over into its center and looking behind him every few steps. Twice he stopped to listen, ears cocked in the direction of the noise he last had heard. Thus it was that he never felt or suspected the shot that dropped him with a broken neck.

The major problem in tracking deer through snow is to anticipate when they are preparing to find a resting place after feeding. When deer tracks have been meandering through heavy second growth in little valleys and ravines or in cedar swamps and open slashings it's a clear indication that they are feeding. Then when the tracks head for higher ground it's equally clear that they are looking for bedding grounds on a sloping sidehill or ridge-top. If the hunter has a reasonably accurate idea that his game will choose a certain ridge for a bed, then it is wise to leave the track and circle ahead and beyond the probable bedding spot. Quite often deer can be more easily approached by circling ahead rather than by following the trail directly. Again, if the hunter knows his country well, he may be able to determine just where his deer is heading and, by circling around behind a covering ridge or swamp, get into a good position to head off his buck. If no deer appears after a reasonable wait, then the hunter will again take the track, planning new strategy. It requires much hunting to head off a whitetail buck on the snow—for every buck killed there will be a dozen failures. This type of hunting demands the utmost in perseverance and patience.

Of all the advantages that snow-covered ground has for the hunter, undoubtedly its greatest boon lies in the reading of deer movements. The still-hunter who is willing to expend a little energy can, within a period of two days' exploring, uncover all the major feeding grounds, resting places and the connecting crossings and runways. Since these areas remain more or less unchanged from year to year in deer country such information gained in one season will form the basis of the hunter's strategy for years to come in such an area.

In the late '30's word came to me of a big buck that had been seen for several seasons in the Roosa Gap section of Sullivan County's Shawangunk Range. For two years I failed to gain an inkling as to just where this buck fed and rested, even though I spent several days each season in the region hoping to jump him or at least find a bedding ground that he used. He had been seen several times during the summers down in the valley, but so far as I knew no one had ever had a shot at him during the hunting season. Legend had given him a huge body and heavy, wide-spreading antlers, but for all I could tell he was due to die of old age.

One day in the early fall two young lads came into my shop and asked for a box of .38-40 cartridges. I had the shells but reluctantly I had to tell them they were both too young to buy ammunition. It was evident that neither of the two had seen more than twelve summers. I wondered out loud why two young lads would need a box of center-fire rifle cartridges of this caliber. So they told me that a big buck had been coming down through their Dad's meadow night after night just at dusk. They were going to be prepared for him when the season opened. After probing a bit more I learned that these boys lived quite close to the Roosa Gap road and their glowing description of the buck seemed to fit all the stories I had heard before.

Then I told them I would be glad to drive up to their farm with the ammunition and deliver it to their Dad, provided they would show me where this buck came down off the mountain. It was a deal. The following Sunday I went up into the valley to the farm, and after I had delivered the shells the boys guided me to the little ravine where a tiny mountain brook tumbled down the mountainside to the valley below. In the soft earth at the roadside were deep tracks, widely spaced in stride, indicating a really big buck. I thanked the boys and drove home, planning to make another visit a few days before the opening day of the season.

In that year our New York State opening Catskill date had been advanced to December first. On Thanksgiving Day we had a ten-inch snowfall, so on the intervening week end I went up to the mountain to do a little investigating. At once I found the big tracks coming down the mountainside along the little brook. They crossed the dirt road and went off down into the open valley fields. But here I could find no returning tracks, so rather than cover the whole valley by following his feeding trail, I walked the road hoping to cut his track on the return trip up on the ridge.

Only a hundred yards beyond, a rocky gulch butted into the road. And again here were his tracks, an identical set, heading up the slope through heavy alders and white birch. I took the track and followed it to the mountaintop about a mile off. At this spot the Shawangunk Range has a flat plateau for a crest; a plateau half a mile wide and every foot of this half-mile covered with the thickest sort of scrub oak, jack pine and laurel. Through all of this went the buck's track, heading for a swamp which lay in the middle of this flat plateau. The swamp was a forbidding place, filled with tangled cat-briers, piles of windfalls, thick, heavy swamp huckleberry and crowded stands of pin oak.

Just within the edges of the swamp I found beds—one for each day the snow had been on the ground. One bed fairly steamed—I had jumped the buck in my snooping! I took the fresh track and followed him throughout the length of the swamp; leaving the swamp he had circled and gone off into the scrub-oak morass surrounding the whole place. But I was satisfied—I had located this buck's hangout. On the way down the mountainside I picked up his coming-down runway. It closely followed the brook outlet of the swamp and continued all the way down the mountainside running parallel to the stream.

On the way up the mountain I had followed the buck's trail through the corner of a little clearing. Many years before there had been a house far up here on the mountainside but all that now remained was a crumbling foundation and the stumps of a few apple trees long since rotted away. Here, I thought, would be an ideal stand to kill this buck; I could crouch down against the old foundation and pick off the deer the moment he came near the clearing on his way up the mountain. But I had neglected to include Lady Luck in my plans.

Long before all this I had invited Jim Deren, of the Angler's Roost, to hunt with me that fall. The night before the season opened Jim hit the shop about eight o'clock, loaded down with baggage and prepared for a week's stay. I outlined what I had learned about this big buck, so together we planned to hunt for this deer alone, to the exclusion of any other deer that might be in the area.

The next morning dawned bitter cold—six above zero, with a gale whipping through the treetops. Jim decided not to climb the mountain so he waited on a good stand at the foot of the ridge while I swung up over in a wide circle, following a wood road.

I took my stand just at good daylight; I huddled down in the snow trying to gather as much protection from the wind as the old foundation would give. For an hour I sat and watched—the roaring wind precluded any change of hearing a deer approach, so I had to keep both eyes riveted on the runway.

After an hour of this my feet were tingling bitterly. I knew I must move or once again suffer frozen feet. I headed for the mountaintop only a few hundred yards away; by the time I had plowed my way up to the top I was thoroughly warm, I turned around then and dropped back to my stand at the old foundation. Once again settled, I began to look around.

About thirty feet away I suddenly noticed a track that had not been there before. I rose and walked over, to discover that my buck had come up in my absence of a few minutes. He had stopped only thirty feet from my stand. From the nature of the tracks I could visualize him standing there, shifting his feet and testing the wind until he had located man-scent from my stand. Then with great leaps he had bounded down the slope and, making a wide circle, had gone up on the mountain to the safety of the swamp. I had missed my chance by a matter of minutes. I knew there was no further use hunting for him that day, so I went down the mountain to where Jim was shivering on his stand.

Daylight the following morning found me on the same stand, but as soon as it was light enough to pick out tracks I found that my buck had already made safe passage up the hill. Again I brushed out the tracks and resigned myself to coming up the next morning.

Overnight the thermometer rose slowly. The first rays of the morning sun softened the top layer of snow. I had again taken my stand after learning that the deer had not yet come up the mountain, at least not on this runway. There were no fresh tracks leading up the mountain this morning, so this time I waited with high hopes. The day was Sunday and an army of hunters roamed the mountaintop and the valley below. From my stand I could hear talking and shouting above me and shots from widely scattered areas up and down the mountain slopes.

The sun rose high and still there had been no sign of my buck coming up the hill. I decided to walk across the ravine and look over his other runway, which up until now he had only used for coming down from his swamp hideout. But there were no tracks here going up the mountain. I decided then to swing down to the valley below and try to cut his track. There was now no doubt in my mind that the noise of many hunters on the mountaintop had kept him down in the lower ground where cover was good.

Halfway down the mountain I cut into his fresh track, heading up the ravine. I stopped then and watched above me but could see no movement. Slowly I moved up, following the trail until I came up over a little ledge. From here the timber above me was more open and as I glanced up the slope I saw a movement as the buck sneaked up through the big oaks and beeches about two hundred yards away. I knew then that I would never get a shot at him, for he had undoubtedly spotted me and would soon be within the safety of the screening scrub oaks.

Disappointedly, I stood there for a while looking at the depth and span of those big footprints, wondering if ever I would get a crack at the buck making them. Even as the thought crossed my mind, there was a staccato flurry of shots from just above me on the mountaintop. With the sound of the shots I was off like a sprinter at the starting gun. I raced across the ravine, jumped the brook and planted my feet in the runway coming down the mountain.

Hardly had I stopped for breath when, with a great clatter of rocks, my buck came crashing down the hillside directly toward me. Now I could see the huge rack of antlers flashing over the tops of the underbrush. His feet hit the opening through the brush at the foot of the slope, thirty yards away, and my bullet met his chest as it emerged from the curtain of undergrowth.

Never did he falter in his stride. He made a mighty leap to my left, bounding over the brush. Fifty feet away stood a high stone wall; beyond, the ground sloped down to the valley. Frantically I threw the Krag bolt and as he left the ground in the last leap to clear the wall and to safety, my front sight swung with him. As the report cracked out there was a heavy thump; then all was still. I ran to the wall and looked over. There in a mass of bloody snow lay my buck, on his back, all four feet kicking. His wide-spreading antler points were buried in the snow—preventing him from turning his head in the least. The white throat-patch gleamed in the morning sunlight, offering my favorite target, so I ended his struggles quickly with a shot through the neck.

This was the largest buck—not quite the heaviest—that it has been my good fortune to kill. His antlers are wide, covering a 2-foot spread. The main beams are over twenty-six inches in length. His body was huge, but he was in extremely poor flesh, with hardly a bit of fat visible on the skinned carcass; yet he weighed in, dressed, at 202 pounds. I doubt very much if I would have killed this buck had there been no lucky snowfall to give away his habits.

For several years Jim Deren had the mounted head of this deer hanging in the entry to the Angler's Roost. Of the many sportsmen who saw it and admired it none would suspect that such an innocent happening of Nature as a snowfall contributed to its capture. But without snow there never would have been an opportunity to learn that this deer followed such a precise routine to get from feeding grounds to his hideout in the safety of the mountaintop swamp.

From the viewpoint of the conservationist and true sportsman snow in hunting has a much more important value. Few badly wounded deer need ever escape to die a lingering death with snow covering the ground in hunting season. Any hunter with even a slight degree of woods skill can follow and find his wounded deer on the snow. It would be a highly conserving factor if all our open seasons in the Northern States would coincide with the first snowfall, but it would be a hopeless goal for legislators. I believe, too, that far fewer hunting accidents would occur under such conditions. The visibility of game is much more distinct in snow-filled woods.

The choice of clothing has a direct bearing on the still-hunter's comfort and success in the woods. It is impossible to recommend the exact outfit for a still-hunter, because of the wide variation in weather conditions throughout deer areas. Likewise there is always considerable variance in seasonal temperatures in any one section. I have hunted deer in the early part of the Adirondack season when the temperature at midday rose to eighty degrees. However, early morning hunting in the Adirondacks is always chilly, sometimes downright cold.

Sensibly, all garments worn in still-hunting should be of wool. There should not be any heavy, bulky overgarment to hamper freedom of movement or to load down a hunter who climbs the steep ridges of mountainous terrain. Two suits of wool underwear or a good Duofold garment are efficient, much more so than a shirt-and-shorts outfit covered over with sweaters and a blanket-type coat. As much wool as can be comfortably worn should be next to the skin. In warm midday, perspiration will be effectively absorbed and the wearer will still be comfortable after the late afternoon chill sets in.

If a still-hunter were constantly on the move throughout the day, proper clothing would be no problem. But a good still-hunter moves but little during the early morning hours when the air is cold. Then throughout the day he pauses many times to watch, wait and listen. During these periods of inactivity he must have sufficient wool clothing near the skin to retain body heat. So over the woolen underwear should go a pair of dark woolen trousers, or roomy hunting breeches. Trousers, however, are much to be preferred, for they give greater freedom of leg-action. A still-hunter does a good bit of climbing—up steep slopes, over windfalls and rocky ledges. Any confinement of leg muscles brings on quick fatigue. The trouser is much more comfortable in this respect, although if a pair of breeches are selected with wide, roomy knees and worsted cuffs they will be entirely satisfactory. Dark-red plaid makes a good color for hunting pants, but this writer prefers the Oxford gray. Woolrich makes a "felted" line of trousers and of hunting breeches in this Oxford gray; both are durable, warm and comfortable. By all means use a wide pair of suspenders to support trousers. If a belt is required, to carry a belt-ax, hunting knife or cartridge holder, then wear both. A full day's walk in the woods with only a belt holding up sagging trousers has left many a still-hunter with painfully sore hips.

A good solid wool plaid shirt is standard equipment. It should be a hard weave and all wool as heavy as can be found. Flannel shirts are much too light for woods wear, unless a hunter prefers to wear a heavy jacket over them. If the weather can reasonably be expected to be cold throughout the day, then a heavy sleeveless sweater should be worn over the underwear and under the wool shirt. Sheepskin vests under the shirt, too, are entirely practical. For normal temperatures—which, in most deer-hunting sections, means somewhere between freezing and forty above—the above outfit is sufficient for still-hunting comfort. In weather colder than this, add a light, short Mackinaw. It is of prime importance to have no more clothing than is required to keep comfortably warm. Too much causes excessive perspiration, so that as soon as a hunter stops for a while to watch a crossing he begins to freeze.

Another garment that this writer favors for still-hunting is the light, water-resistant parka. For windy weather or rainy, damp days the parka over proper underwear and wool shirt is extremely practical. Of course it will not keep the wearer dry in a steady rain, but for foggy, drizzly weather or during a light snowstorm it's a most effective garment. The close, water-repellent weave turns a good deal of moisture and gives comfort against a chilling fall wind. Another advantage: for those cold, early-morning stands the parka can be slipped on to take advantage of its heat-retaining close weave. Then when the hunter takes to the ridges and hills, he rolls up the parka and slips it under his suspenders behind his back. If he makes another lengthy stand he unrolls the parka, slips it on and is prepared to wait and watch, with some degree of comfort.

The most important item of wearing apparel in the still-hunter's duffel is footwear. Foot comfort is of the utmost necessity in still-hunting. Much walking over all types of terrain must be done—through swamps and slashings, over rocky ledges and steep slopes, crashing through scrub oak and laurel—and through it all the hunter must have both good foot protection and comfort. The soles must be sensitive, so that he can feel a dead branch under-foot soon enough to prevent cracking it. The uppers must be tough, to withstand the ripping, tearing action of briers and scrub. The entire shoe must be reasonably water-repellent, so that the normal amount of moisture encountered in a day's hunt will still not reach the feet.

Many hunters prefer the rubber-bottom, leather-top shoe-pac, the so-called "Maine Hunting Shoe." In most respects these are good. They are light, quite waterproof and fairly comfortable, but they have two objectionable defects. One, they do not offer good foot support to the man who is accustomed to wearing street shoes for fifty weeks of the year; they lack support to the arch, and are so soft in the foot that the foot lacks confining control. For the hunter who does much walking rough country they are not as de-sirable as an all-leather shoe. Two, the full rubber foot in this style of shoe-pac causes excessive perspiration. To many hunters this contributes to extreme foot discomfort—among these is the writer.

The writer searched for a number of years before finding the ideal type of dry weather hunting shoe for still-hunting. My re-quirements were rigid. I needed an all-leather shoe to overcome any excessive sweating caused by rubber; I wanted a shoe-pac type for comfortable and quiet walking, with a sensitive sole yet one which gave good protection agains sharp rocks. I wanted reasonably light weight so that I could cover plenty of ground without undue leg-fatigue. It was desirable, too, to use a boot sufficiently water-repellent for wading a small brook or hunting through swampy areas without soaking the feet. The entire boot should be tough, to withstand enough hard usage for the investment not to be lost in two or three seasons of hunting.

The first shoe that I found to meet these requirements was Russell's "Ike Walton." These have been so highly satisfactory during my last ten years of hunting that I have never had occasion to look further. There are other shoe-pacs which may meet my requirements, but so long as I am able to get Ike Waltons I will be content.

For hunting in rain or melting snow there is only one type of footwear that will keep feet dry—*all rubber.* Of the many types available the twelve-inch snug-leg or ankle-fit with the short lacing at the top is by far the most desirable. They should be purchased large enough, at least a full shoe-size larger than your size, in order to hold a light woolen sock and a heavy woolen sock easily. These boots are light and comfortable, but are not well adapted to long hikes over rough country. Neither do they give good foot support or adequate foot protection over rough, rocky ground. But they are the only medium for keeping feet dry under wet weather conditions. In wet weather the still-hunter does not cover much territory as a rule, so these boots will be practical for this type of hunting. I always throw a pair in the duffel bag when I plan a hunting trip for several days.

Further to assure foot protection the still-hunter must obtain boots—whatever the type—sufficiently large to accommodate a light wool ankle-sock and a heavyweight pair of full-length socks. Warmth is a reason for providing plenty of socks, but equally important is the cushioning effect that heavy socks give to the foot.

In cold weather, gloves are a problem. The all-leather, lined glove is too bulky to permit easy handling of the rifle. The unlined leather glove is hardly warmer than no glove at all. I have solved the problem—to my satisfaction at least—by using a light wool glove with full leather palm and finger facing. All-wool gloves are warm but are so slippery that handling the rifle and operating the action can be uncertain. Leather-faced wool gloves are both warm and sufficiently high in friction coefficient for shooting with them not to be much different from shooting with bare hands.

The still-hunter's headgear can be left to personal choice. By all means let it be red in color; likewise, the still-hunter should avoid any white in his clothing, even a white handkerchief. It's surprising how many hunters are ready and willing to blast a shot at a white flash in the deer woods. Better stick to somber grays and plaids for a general color scheme, and top it off with a red cap.

Add to the above outfit a small-bladed, sharp knife and a pair of rawhide shoelaces (for getting out your buck), and we are ready for a still-hunting trip. In wilderness areas we will need to add a small pocket ax, waterproof matchbox, and a floating dial compass (this we will deal with in a later chapter).

It is with some reluctance that the writer closes this chapter on still-hunting. No doubt a full book could be written about this one aspect of the deer hunting sport, but space limits such expansion. I have endeavored to show some of the thrill and satisfaction which lives forever in the mind and heart of the successful still-hunter. Deer driving and club hunting, while highly productive, never reap the reward of glowing inner satisfaction gathered by still-hunting.

There will always be, in the still-hunter's memory, the song of a little mountain brook, discovered in his wandering; the heart-stopping clutch as a magnificent buck bounds from a windfall hideaway; the triumphant moment when, by wits and woodsmanship alone, he has tracked down his whitetail buck and sent forth the well-placed shot that has brought his trophy to bag.

MAKING THE DRIVE

Francis Sell

Most readers will probably remember Francis Sell for his excellent and pas-
sionate magazine articles touting the twenty-gauge as the all-around scatter-
gun. But Sell's early book, The American Deer Hunter, *published by*
Stackpole in 1950, is still regarded as one of the finest. This excerpt will
show you why.

A HAPHAZARD BEATING of the brush does not constitute a deer
drive, and it is a fruitless effort. The driving of game by hunters is
successful only to the extent that it is well planned. Neglect of but
one small detail of the plan can cancel an otherwise expert drive.

Before we investigate the precise method of driving deer, it may
be well to explain more fully this type of hunting. In driving a
piece of cover—a procedure commonly called a "deer run," the
hunters move in line, each a calculated and safe interval from the
other. They progress through the cover toward other hunters who
are posted on deer stands—places where the driven game is most
likely to emerge from the cover. In most instances the drive is
commenced at a time well past the game's feeding period, after it
has retired to heavy cover and is bedded for the day. This cover
presents much the same problems to the line of drivers as it does
to a lone still hunter.

We'll examine a typical deer run to see what it actually is. The
one I have in mind has produced much worthwhile game. It is on
an abandoned farm, now well grown up to small trees and brush.
But the lichen-crested apple orchard still produces a crop of
wormy apples, and the deer feed on them in season. The run is to
one side of the once-cultivated fields, where a strip of woods
covers a long slope. This woods extends almost due north and
south and is fully a half-mile in length. It is broken by an overgrown field at the top of a rolling hill. South of this hilltop the
ground falls away in a gentle slope toward the drainage of a large
brook. One stand is in the hilltop field, another is almost directly

west of the field, about two hundred yards away. The third stand is still farther west.

Four men are needed to drive the cover properly, and these, with the three on the stands, make an easily-handled hunting party. If the party is larger the added members are posted near the old orchard, but these stands seldom produce any game. The three stands along the top of the hill are the important ones. For it is here that the game usually crosses when put up in the strip of woods. These stands were not established by arbitrary selection on our part; they were established by the game itself. In the main, we decide on the location of stands by watching the normal movements of the deer as they move out of the cover.

Always there is a definite reason for the direction taken by game in making its escape from the hunter. In that direction lies heavy cover, and new security. There is little of the haphazard in the action of game; there is a logical explanation for everything done by animals. Their need during a drive is for security.

The long slope to the north of the hilltop on the abandoned farm has a primary covering of heavy alder. Under the alder are islands of denser cover—huckleberry and hazel, and a rank growth of briars and brush. The deer bed in these thickets and usually must be flushed directly to make them move. When they are finally put up they have the choice of five stands in making an escape. The two stands beside the orchard can be ignored for all practical purposes; the three along the top of the ridge are the important ones. Jumped game can move directly up the slope, crossing the stand in the grown-over field at the top of the ridge, to escape into thickets on the south slope of the hill. They may cross the second stand and skirt the field, moving into the thickets of the south slope without exposing themselves on the more open stand in the field. On this stand most of the old moss-horns are killed. They have survived several hunting seasons and take little for granted. They cannot be stampeded into an opening, and they habitually take the least exposed route in moving out of the cover. Nice bucks have been killed in the abandoned field, but the stand is usually crossed by many immature animals and does.

Deer cross the third stand of this run with a rather sly purpose.

After crossing the stand they swing toward the west, turning north and east to regain the security of the cover after the drivers have passed. This requires clever timing on the part of the game. Many deer escaped before a watcher was placed on the stand. Such a tactic characterizes an old, woods-wise buck. He accurately gauges the drivers' movements, especially if they are making considerable noise, and then proceeds to outflank the line.

Drivers commonly try to make enough unearthly noises to stampede the game out of the cover. I believe it is best to drive the game with less noise, and even with an amount of caution. This practice serves to influence the animals' movements to a desirable degree. An undue din is almost certain to put the deer out of the immediate run, as well as putting them out of adjoining cover before it can be properly posted and driven.

In discussing the technique of still hunting, I stressed the need for personal movements and sounds that would not alarm the game, also the necessity for keeping on the trail and moving with the flow of traffic. Now, in driving game, we seek an opposite result and use appropriate methods to achieve it. The driver keeps off the trail, moves against the normal flow of traffic, and he also moves at a gait faster than that used by unalarmed game. Then, as would be expected, the game moves out at once and crosses the logically located stands.

Correct timing is very necessary in driving a piece of cover. No drive is more ineffective than the one which involves an uneven and poorly spaced line of hunters. To avoid such poor organization it is necessary for each driver to heed the sounds made by his nearest companions, as a means for adjusting his own pace and position. This is not hard to do and results in uniform and effective advance of the line.

A hunting party should not try to drive too much territory at one time. There is a limit to the distance that deer can be moved before they turn out of the runways to seek safety in other nearby thickets. It is also impossible for a line of drivers to maintain spacing and timing in an area large enough to contain numerous ridges and draws. It is best to study the cover to be driven and find the natural divisions which will allow the shorter, more efficiently handled drives. A piece of cover a half-mile long is much easier to drive successfully than one three-quarters of a mile in length. A drive of two hundred yards is better still. Most of the longer runs are, in reality, composed of several shorter drives. Once the longer pieces of cover are properly divided and driven on that basis they become much more productive of game.

Although the main effort of the individual driver is to put game across the stands, he should not ignore his personal chances to take legal game. If a shot is offered, and it can be taken with safety, he should take it. These opportunities usually come when the game attempts to turn back into the cover. These shots can be taken with complete safety when the drivers are keeping an orderly, well-informed line.

Driving is, incidentally, not quite the proper description for the phase of hunting now under discussion. Deer are not "driven," in the accepted sense of the word. About all the "driver" can do, aside from jumping the game, is to prevent it from turning back into the cover. His aim is to keep it moving toward a stand and if the stand is on a logical escape route, well and good. There is no use in manning points other than known escape routes. I know of one so-called stand on which a hopeful watcher has been posted during ten different drives, and in all that time he has seen no deer, not even a fawn. The natural aspects of this location have been ignored by hunters, year after year. The stand is selected simply because it offers a fine chance for a shot if a deer did cross it. But no deer will cross it if it can avoid doing so. There is no shelter beyond the stand, just a series of open fields. A deer would be very stupid to move out and expose itself in the fields, and the game is never stupid.

The three stands on the run at the abandoned farm have one thing in common; each stand is on a deer's path to a new place of security. If this were not so the stands would be as worthless as the one I have just described. However, not always does a natural deer crossing become a desirable stand. There are other factors to consider. The most important among these is the matter of safety in shooting. A stand which would afford shots only in the direction of the drivers must be avoided. No responsible hunter takes the chance of killing a hunting companion just for the sake of a shot at game.

The hunter going on a stand should examine it to determine if the background will safely stop his bullets. His field of fire should then be held within the evident safety limits of the stand. Any shot should be avoided which would have the slightest chance of wounding another hunter. Another and very practical benefit attends determination of this field of fire. The hunter will do much better shooting if he knows, before the game appears, just how much space he has in which to make the kill. He will then spend his limited firing time in getting this space under his rifle. He knows what his first move will be when the deer crosses the stand, and this has a steadying effect. He is not so likely to suffer from buck ague, that common ailment of the inexperienced hunter.

Wind can also cancel the effectiveness of an otherwise logical stand. Adverse winddrift may be so casual as to escape the hunter's notice. If it persists for several hours while the drive is getting under way it will warn the game before it is in sight of the hunter. I recall a very troublesome instance of this. Deer would follow the run perfectly until they gained the ridge north of the swamp where the stand was located. Then, instead of coming over the rise to the hunter, a substantial number of them would leave the runway and turn east. The hunter had no opportunity to intercept a deer as it left the runway because the cover between him and the animal was a dense mat of huckleberry brush.

The problem remained unsolved for quite a while. What made the situation more baffling was the fact that we occasionally did take a good buck on this stand. Why wasn't it a consistent producer? Then one evening, long after the deer season, I studied some field notes I had made of this run. I had a sketch of the runway, the stand, and the area lying to the north of the stand. The stand was located in a draw at the foot of a ridge, a reasonable place for a shot. Of the deer killed here my notes stated: "Cold day, sky overcast. No wind." Of the deer jumped in the swamp, but which did not follow the runway, the notes said: "Warm Indian Summer day; not a trace of wind."

I mulled over these facts; knowing also that the north winds of fall storms made the stand untenable. In some way certain deer were getting the stander's scent, even when there was "no wind" on the warm days and cold days of record. However, with the complete data at hand, the problem yielded a solution which was simple in the extreme. This involved common knowledge of conditions that set air in motion. On warm days there were always some air currents rising from the swamp toward the higher ground. The hunter would hardly notice such a faint movement, and in this case the currents had ample time to carry to the top of the rise in front of the stand before the deer was put out of the swamp. On the cold, overcast days these currents did not exist, for then the high ground was colder than the more sheltered swales and valleys. Any winddrift at that time is likely to be downhill. My review of these facts made it easy to understand the varying behavior of the driven deer.

It is well to mention at this place that the flow of air currents at a given location may change completely with periods of the day. During the early hours of morning the winddrift is likely to be uphill, and downhill in the late evening. These thermals would in no wise affect the still hunter, for even though he moves at a very slow rate he keeps abreast of any imperceptible air current. But with the hunter on a stand the case is entirely different.

I tested the solution of our problem during the next hunting season. We established a new stand a hundred yards north of the previous one. Here was a ridge which was open enough to allow the stander a good view of the game trail and at the same time keep the deer from getting a warning scent before it was under the rifle. This stand worked excellently on warm days. On cold days we posted the hunter on the original stand.

I believe that almost any stand which proves to be only partially effective is a good subject for similar study. The mysterious aspects of the situation will dissolve when the factors of terrain, weather and winddrift are placed in logical combination. Each failure and each success must be studied carefully, and no detail however small should be overlooked. This attention to detail must not be confined to the natural manifestations; it must include one's own behavior while on the stand, and even when approaching it.

When the hunter is assigned to a stand he is under obligation to make the most of his opportunity. This obligation is in full force as soon as he leaves camp and is on his way to the post. He is already moving as cautiously as possible, and is using a game trail if the situation warrants. This trail would, of course, not be one over which the game is soon expected to move, for there is too much chance of leaving the tell-tale human scent along the runway. In any case, the hunter approaches the stand with precisely the caution he'd observe if he expected to find a deer already there. And that can happen, too! Once, on the run at the abandoned farm, I walked up to the stand west of the high field and found a four-point buck lying directly on the stand. At the same stand, on another occasion, a hunter put a great buck out and didn't get a shot, simply because he felt no need for caution in moving onto the stand.

While on a stand some hunters avail themselves of the comfort of a fire. It is their fatuous belief that a small fire does not alarm game. When the fire-makers do make a kill they have only to thank the law of averages, not their hunting skill. Any fire is foreign to the cover, and game associates its presence with hunters—and danger. Just the odor of smoke or the crackle of flames are fair warnings to any deer.

The successful drive is characterized by teamwork and good conduct. Each hunter should avoid doing anything that might hold up the drive. If he is to go on a stand he should be on it promptly and remain quiet. And if he is to be a driver he shouldn't be late taking his place in the line. There is always some unavoidable delay in organizing a drive, but this delay can be cut to the minimum when each hunter is properly alert to his responsibility.

Although armed drivers may shoot game when they have a fair opportunity to do so, their main concern and function is directed toward providing shots for the standers. There is a tendency of some drivers to press ahead of the other drivers in the hope of getting a shot at the game put out by them. Of course, to do this is unsportsmanlike, and it is also probable that a driver resorting to such an action would not be overly concerned about the safety of the other hunters while shooting.

The driving of game is, withal, a very effective method of hunting. In certain kinds of cover it is the only procedure that will give the hunter a reasonable chance for a shot. And always necessary in such hunting is a good foreknowledge of the area to be driven. This information points to the proper location of stands and regulates the boundaries of the drive. These are major factors in making a successful drive. But let no one minimize the necessity for each driver and stander to do the right thing at the right time.

FINDING WOUNDED DEER

Ray Beck

Ray Holland, superb editor of Field & Stream *during the halcyon days of American hunting, was fond of quoting this silent prayer, which he attributed to gun editor Bob Nichols:*

"Lord, please let me kill clean. And if I can't kill clean, let me miss clean."

Well, the truth is that we don't always kill clean. And we must be prepared to face the painstaking, sometimes agonizing task of following up and dispatching a wounded animal.

Because that area of our sport is so important, I'm very glad to have a veteran hunter and writer like Pennsylvania's Ray Beck on hand for a discussion.

I've always admired Beck's pieces from Outdoor Life, *and this one is no exception. After its original publication in September of 1956, it was later anthologized in the book* Outdoor Life's Deer Hunting Book, *published by Outdoor Life and Harper & Row.*

THE FELLOW on the big pudding stone raised his rifle and shot. Once. Twice. Three times. Because of the young hemlocks, I couldn't see the deer he was shooting at, but I figured it would be coming my way. I eased the hammer back and waited. In a couple of seconds a frightened doe rushed by the rock I was standing on, never even noticing me. I waited, thinking a buck might be following, but none appeared.

I was as sure that doe didn't have antlers as though I had just given her a shampoo, but I knew there was no use chewing the guy out about shooting at her. He'd insist that he saw horns, and I couldn't prove otherwise.

Later, after the hunter left I back-tracked the doe to see if I could find any hair or blood spots showing she'd been hit. About 200 yards from the stone from which the stranger fired I found a six-point buck with a hole in its ribs. More back-tracking showed it had come nearly 100 yards after being shot through the heart.

Locating an unknown hunter in the Allegheny National Forest of Pennsylvania in deer season was out of the question, so a soldier in our party who had to start back to camp the following day put his tag on the buck and took it home. It wasn't the way he wanted to get his deer, but ninety pounds of venison wasn't to be turned down in those meat-shy days of 1944.

If the fellow who shot that buck is still hunting, I hope he's learned by now that it pays to investigate.

It would be hard to estimate how many fatally wounded deer are lost each season. In this and similar cases, the hunter never realizes he connected. In others, he believes the wound superficial and doesn't try to trail the deer. Most common of all is the hunter who defeats himself by driving the wounded animal too hard.

When the deer you shoot at keeps going, the first thing you want to know is whether you hit it at all. That's easy. Deer hair is brittle, and a bullet anywhere but the lower legs will knock off a lot of hair. Don't let the absence of blood fool you. The wound may not bleed for five or ten seconds, or the animal may bleed internally.

Like most condensed pieces of wisdom, the saying that a wounded deer always pulls its flag down, isn't always true. A wounded deer usually runs with its tail down, but the tail doesn't work automatically like lights on a pinball machine. A frightened deer may not feel the bullet for a few seconds. This is especially true when there's no shock of bones being struck, and when the bullet fails to expand properly. A deer hit in the legs will often run with its tail up, and occasionally a badly terrified one will run with its tail down when it hasn't been hit at all.

The deer's response to your shot gives you a pretty good clue as to where the bullet went. If the animal jumps straight into the air, you probably shot too low. A few hairs suggest that you just creased its belly. No hair means that you missed entirely but came very close—or else you shot so low the bullet threw dirt up and stung the deer. If there's considerable hair and some blood along the trail, you've paunched the animal low down.

In 1954 my nephew shot at a standing buck which reared up,

turned around, and went back the way it had come. Later in the day the deer was killed, and we found that his bullet had cut a crease through the chest hair without breaking the skin.

A deer that drops at the crack of the gun, then regains its feet and bounds away apparently unhurt was probably creased across the back. There will be plenty of hair but little or no blood, and the deer is practically uninjured. A deer which goes down and then regains its feet with difficulty is most likely paunched.

If your deer drops at the crack of the gun as though struck by lightning, you probably made a perfect shot. But don't waste any time getting to it. Every season "dead" deer come to life and get away. A bullet striking an antler, creasing the skull, or nicking a

vertebra will knock a deer cold, but when the deer comes to it's unhampered by the minor wound. Hunters used to capture wild horses by knocking them out with a bullet high in the neck.

If the deer you shoot at gives no indication of being hit, yet quantities of loose hair say otherwise, you have a problem on your hands. Not all deer flinch when hit. So did you hit it solidly or only crease it?

A lot of old-timers advocate waiting an hour to give such a deer time to calm down if it's just frightened, or to lie down and stiffen if it's wounded. A better plan is to follow the trail a quarter of a mile or so. The deer ordinarily won't stop within that distance unless it's too weak to go farther. If it keeps going, you should have a pretty fair idea of the extent of its injuries by its tracks and blood spots, if any. Then you can lay your plans accordingly, and decide what course of action to follow.

A keen student of animal behavior can predict very accurately what deer wounded in different ways will do. After deer season in 1939, Bill Best and I were hunting foxes in the Allegheny National Forest east of Marienville, Pennsylvania. It's a country of big rocks, bracken, and quaking aspens, but halfway up this particular mountainside is a five-acre patch of scrub hemlocks.

Pointing toward these evergreens, Bill said, "I'll bet a dollar there's a dead deer in there, and I'll bet another dollar I can tell you where it was hit."

I figured I was a pretty good woodsman, but I couldn't see anything to indicate a dead deer in a patch of brush half a mile away. Even so, how could anybody tell where it had been shot? We hadn't hunted that section, so I knew Bill hadn't found the deer previously. I also knew I was going to lose two dollars.

"Okay!" I said, "We'll settle the stakes when we sell the furs. Now where was it hit?"

"Gut-shot," Bill said.

The deer wasn't hard to find. The foxes had the snow tramped down all around it, but they were too suspicious to come closer than ten or twelve feet. As Bill had predicted, there was a hole back of the ribs. Near the other end of the brush patch was another doe with a bullet hole in practically the same place.

Bill said, "I guess I'll have to explain it to you so you can get your mind back on fox hunting. A gut-shot deer wants to hide. It will leave the rest of the herd, get into the thickest cover it can find, and lie down. Soon it's too weak and stiff to get up, and it dies there. But if it's kept on its feet, it can go for miles. That's why you should give a gut-shot deer time to lie down before you follow it. Those hemlocks are the only good cover within two or three miles, so any gut-shot deer in this area would be there."

"I can see that," I admitted, "but deer get shot in the legs too. How did you know we wouldn't find one in there with broken legs?"

"That's easy," he told me. "A deer with a broken hind leg can travel down hill easier, and it ends up down along the creek without the strength to climb. Deer with a broken hind leg usually die, but deer with a broken front leg get along pretty well so long as they don't have to go downhill. Any deer around here with a broken front leg will be sticking to level ridgetops or flat bottoms, not hanging along the sides of a mountain where it's likely to upset if it tries to run. Any more questions?"

"Yes," I said. "How did you know there were any deer here at all?"

"Oh, that was easiest of all," he grinned. "We're about three miles from the road, and in doe season there are a lot of hunters, and there's the creek. A deer can cross the creek, but a man would have to make a five-mile detour. So when a wounded deer gets on this side of the stream nobody chases it any more."

A paunched deer which slows to a walk within a quarter of a mile has probably been hit in the liver or kidneys and won't go much farther. The old-timers used to say that if a wounded deer wasn't chased it would walk twice as far as it had run and then lie down. The rule is fairly accurate for paunched animals, providing there's a place to hide within that distance.

A deer hit in the liver or kidneys with anything in the .30/30 class or heavier will be dead or unable to regain its feet in an hour. Shot through the stomach or entrails, it will take three times as long to stiffen up.

If you paunch a deer in late afternoon, let it go till morning. Even if there's no snow, you'll probably find it without much trouble by searching the thickets and windfalls in the direction the animal headed. It won't travel far if it isn't chased.

Where the woods are full of hunters, however, it's sometimes a matter of following the deer right away or having some other hunter cut in ahead of you. The best method under these conditions is to follow the deer till it enters a thicket, then circle around to the other side to see if it came out. If it's still in the thicket, begin at the side opposite where the deer entered, and work back, taking plenty of time, and being as quiet as possible. The deer will be watching its back trail, and it won't be as alert as an uninjured one, so you have a fair chance of seeing it first. If some other

] 184 [

hunter follows the tracks into the brush, he's quite likely to drive the deer to you.

When a party of hunters are working together, one should take the trail while the others spread out on each side, staying just close enough to keep track of the man doing the trailing. Since the deer will most likely double back to where it can watch its trail, the flankers have a better chance than the man on the track. As you approach promising thickets, at least one man should circle ahead to be in a position to get a shot if the deer runs.

If it heads for a river or creek you can't cross, stop and wait. Unless it's driven, a wounded animal is reluctant to enter the water.

I'll never forget the time a kid in our party put a shotgun slug behind the ribs of a buck along the Clarion River, a few miles below the power dam. The buck was hit hard, and if left alone he'd probably have crawled into the nearest thicket and died. But it was the kid's first deer, and he chased that buck like a greyhound after a rabbit. This foolish zeal drove the deer into the river. It fell dead on the opposite shore.

To reach that buck, we first drove to a bridge—six miles over a bumpy dirt road where the axle dragged most of the way. Having crossed the river, we hiked to the deer and then dragged it two miles uphill through laurel brush so thick a man could hardly walk.

It was after dark by the time we got the buck to the car. Then we got hung up trying to drive back another way, which turned out to be worse. We had to back-track and didn't get home till nearly midnight.

If that deer had just been left alone for an hour it would have died on our side of the river.

Deer with broken legs are less common than paunched animals, but you actually see a lot more of them. The reason is that a deer with a broken leg continues to travel about, while paunched animals crawl into a thicket and die where their remains are very seldom found.

Tracks will indicate if a leg is broken, and which one. A deer with a broken hind leg has lost a lot of its driving power, and while you can't run it down, it tires rapidly. Before long it will turn downhill. It gets along pretty well going down, but it can't climb efficiently and ordinarily won't try.

To get a deer wounded in this way, station a couple of your party where they can watch the bottom of the valley, then drive the deer toward them. Most likely it will move down the valley, keeping the levelest course possible. If it does try to climb, it will move so slowly and awkwardly that somebody should get a shot. If a deer with a broken hind leg escapes because of a blizzard or darkness, it can usually be located the next day by searching the bottoms of near-by valleys and ravines. Always do your utmost to recover a deer with a broken hind leg, as very few survive.

A broken front leg, however, is not so serious. The first deer I ever shot had a completely healed break in one front leg. It was easily keeping up with the rest of the herd at the time I shot it.

A deer with a bullet-broken front leg can run uphill or on the level nearly as well as any, but it has trouble running downhill. The best way to get a deer with a broken front leg is for one of the party to follow it while the others wait at stands chosen to take advantage of the animal's reluctance to run downhill. If this strategy fails, chances are you'll never catch up with the deer. Unless there's a tracking snow, an extended hunt for a deer with a broken front leg is usually hopeless.

Sometimes a deer is wounded in the brisket, or the fleshy parts of the legs without breaking any bones. Such wounds aren't serious, but they may bleed enough to mark the track plainly. One of the party should follow it while the others wait at likely locations. If the deer escapes, it will most likely recover.

A deer wounded in the fleshy part of a leg will use the leg, but not lift it as high as the other. If one leg is being dragged through the snow after each step, you can figure there's a hampering flesh wound on that leg.

We can't possibly recover every wounded animal, but spending a little time and effort could cut the losses considerably. There's no excuse for such shameful sights as I saw in the spring of 1952 while trout fishing—seven dead deer within a mile, in the brush along Little Salmon Creek.

An outdoor column in a local paper had recently told of large numbers of deer starving in the Allegheny National Forest, so I examined these seven with that in mind. Two of them—one an old gummer doe whose teeth were too worn to chew browse—apparently starved. But three had been paunch-shot, and two had broken hind legs.

By using the systems we've just discussed, hunters could have recovered these five wounded deer, converting them into venison instead of leaving them as carrion in the woods.

SIGN THE TROPHY BUCK LEAVES

Larry Benoit with Peter Miller

Peter Miller had been producing excellent articles and photography for Sports Afield *for some time when he came to New York for a visit in the summer of 1970, and told me about an unusual deer hunter named Larry Benoit.*

Benoit, it seemed, was obsessed by the art of hunting big bucks. In the past five years in Vermont he had killed four bucks over 200 pounds, including two over 230! A superb woodsman, Benoit more or less specialized in the art of hunting until he found the track of a buck he wanted, then staying on it, mile after mile, through swamps and hills, until he made a kill.

Though I knew that Peter's relationship with Larry would lead to some excellent articles, I was not prepared for the impact they made on our readers. The four Benoit pieces that Peter produced for Sports Afield *were the most-commented-upon, most-remembered in my entire seven-year editorship of the magazine. Peter's words and photographs and the magazine's pages made Benoit into a cause celebre in the hunting world. Later Peter teamed up with Larry to produce the book,* How to Bag the Biggest Buck of Your Life, *published by* The Whitetail Press, Duxbury, Vermont.

The next two chapters of The Deer Book *are excerpted from that excellent book.*

Peter is a former Life *magazine staffer who now freelances in the outdoor and skiing fields. He lives in Stowe, Vermont, where there is skiing when it snows, woodcock when the flights come in, and small trout all the time.*

THE TROPHY BUCK leaves his calling card in a number of ways, and it is up to you to recognize his calling card, for it will tell you as easily as if that old buck whispered in your ear—"Hey, I'm one helluva big buck—try to catch me!"

Naturally, the first thing you have to read and understand is the track. Is it buck or doe?" If it's a buck, is it worth tracking for the next day, or perhaps the rest of the season, until you drop him? There have been times when I have passed up five buck tracks in a morning before I found one I thought was a big enough hoosier to go after.

You know, to tell a buck track at a glance is a gift that's very difficult to explain. Some people have it and some people will never learn. Once Lanny was called in by a friend to help sort out a "big buck track" that his friend claimed just disappeared. Lanny grabbed his rifle and went out to take a look, and just burst out laughing. His friend had been following squirrel tracks that disappeared when the squirrel scooted up a tree.

I started tracking deer when I was seven and just a whisker of a fellow living in northern Vermont. Tracking fascinated me. I even tracked dogs. I first started trailing bucks with my dad. He was a blacksmith, heavy of shoulder, a powerful man who loved to hunt and loved wild life. He wouldn't kill anything needless. If we had any meat in the house, he wouldn't go out looking for it. That was the Indian in him, I guess. Dad was a marvelous tracker and people often wondered how my father could tell the difference between a buck track and a doe track when snow was on top of it. Yet he wouldn't tell me any of his secrets. I just learned, and when I told him what I thought I saw in a track, and I was right, his eyes would light up. I would search his face for the answer. Sometimes he would say to me, "there's a nice looking track, Ling," and I'd take it for granted that it was a buck track and then I'd study it for all it was worth and try to figure out why it should be a buck. Dad's heaviest buck weighed in at 350 pounds. When I was eight, and hunting with him, he shot a 16 pointer.

It takes years of careful observation and lots of common sense to become a good tracker. I learned how a buck walked and a doe walked, on bare ground and in snow. I taught it to my sons. I have kept most of these secrets to myself and to my family, because I have found that a lot of hunters called me a liar when I told them. I guess that's human nature.

There are signs the trophy buck leaves for you to read. Probably eight out of ten hunters think that dew claws tell the difference between bucks and does. Well, does have dew claws too. So do pigs, for that matter. When does run, their dew claws will spread out just like a buck's. What you can tell by dew claws is the weight of the deer—not when it is running but when it is walking. If the deer is heavy, the dew claws will be well etched in the ground. Dew claws can be circumstantial evidence pointing towards a buck, but if you follow a track with large dew claws, you might surprise yourself to find your gunsights locked onto a great big bald-headed doe.

Lots of people say that a buck will drag his feet more than a doe. Bucks and does both drag their feet, particularly big does. You need a couple of inches of snow to tell for sure, for a big buck will drag its feet just a hair more than a doe. Drag marks aren't the best way to tell a buck.

There are many ways you can confirm a buck track, but when you are after a trophy buck, look for two important points—the weight of the deer, as seen in the hoof print, and the pattern of the track.

To tell the weight of the deer, see how deep the dew claws and the hoof print sink into the earth. If there is snow, brush it off and feel with your bare fingers the outline of the track. If the hoof

AB

sinks deep into the ground (often the ground is soft under a layer of snow) and is splayed, you can bet your life it's a big deer, and chances are it's a trophy buck. You take a deer over 200 pounds and you'll find there's no difficulty in tracking a deer like that. His foot really leaves an impression—on the earth and in your brain.

If the ground is bare, see how deep the hoof cuts into the leaves. A trophy buck's hoof will cut right through the top leaves. Compare that track to your own and take into consideration your weight. Compare the track to other deer tracks in the vicinity, or to your past experience of tracks you have followed that have led to a buck you have seen or shot. This will let you know quite a bit about the size of the deer.

Take another gander at that track. Really squint at it. A buck that lives in a swamp has long toes that are pointed, as there are no rocks or ledges. Mountain bucks often have stubby toes that are rounded or jagged, because they have been worn while that deer humped over rocks and ledges. It's plain old common sense that tells you that a track that is jagged and well rounded is no young little lightweight buck. It takes a few years for a buck to develop his track, and there's as much difference between a trophy buck's and a young buck's track as there is between a man and child's hand. And there's also as much a difference between a buck and doe's track as between your gnarled old hands and those of a woman.

A trophy buck's toes are more rounded. A trophy buck's track will spread out more than others, and really squish into the muck. But some deer are just like people. They have awful big feet, and don't weigh anything. Small deer with big feet have toes that don't splay out. Common sense tells me that a big deer track 8 times out of 10 means a big buck.

From these signs you should be able to tell the big deer track from a small deer track, but you still aren't certain whether it is a trophy buck or just some monstrous doe that's trying to fool you. Now to really tell the difference, look at the pattern of the track. Look at tracks—not a single track—but a number of tracks and figure how that deer sets his feet down—how that deer actually walks.

A very small deer, doe or buck, will often leave an even pattern of tracks, one track following the other almost in a straight line. A doe leaves a track in a fairly straight line; it's the way they are built. But one of those big trophy bucks, one of those long legged monsters who has heft and is broad of beam—built wide on the haunches—his tracks are staggered right and left. That's one of the strongest signs you can find for recognizing the big trophy buck. It's a sign you should never miss, and if you do, well mister, maybe you should be spending most of your time on the skeet range.

Deer amble, meander, walk, range and run. Take a close look at the gait. A small deer takes small steps. That fact stands to reason but many deer hunters don't seem to remember these reasonable, common sense facts. Does take dainty steps, as my son Lanny says, just like a teen age girl at her first dance. Now a big trophy buck—he strides. That buck lopes along, and if that track has a big gait, you know there goes one big deer. If there is snow on the ground, small deer will sort of play hoppity, skippity, jumpity through the snow. Your trophy buck does none of that—he slogs through the mush with an even gait—he has the height and the strength.

What if that deer is running? Look at the track he's left. Big, 20 foot bounds between tracks means a big deer. When a big deer is moving down a mountain like a freight train, the distance between bounds can be even greater. If the ground is chewed up something awful where that running deer set down his four hooves and took off, you can bet your last cartridge that, considering the sign you've already read, you're on to one very big buck that's worth following.

When I see all these signs, and the track tells me a buck is up ahead, strutting like a gander, God, I can feel it in my bones. I know it in my brain. It's just there, and if it's a big one, my gut gets churning and I just want to set right after him and track him right down. Oh, a good buck track just sets me to quivering!

Now if for some reason you still aren't sure that you have a trophy buck marking up the world in front of you, track the deer for a few hundred yards. Again keep a close eye on how that deer walks through the woods. A doe will meander all over the place, just like a woman on a shopping spree in a department store. The doe will flit here and there, feed a bit, circle a tree, go under a fir and dilly dally around, just like a filly at the local Saturday dance. The buck won't. A buck will follow a much straighter line, and if that is a trophy buck sporting a mighty big rack, he won't be caught ducking into thickets or under fir trees. He's mighty proud of that rack and he'll circle all the obstacles that could tangle with his rack.

When you see rubbings—where the buck has scraped his horns on a tree, you know for sure that he is a buck. A buck scrapes and hooks trees for several reasons. The head around the horns itch, just like your back does sometimes, and he rubs it. A buck can be in rut, and he will hook trees and brush, just to show his virility.

And a buck, when he's angry, particularly if you are hot on his trail, will take out his frustration by hooking trees and brush. Another buck can make him do that too. Where he hooks and scrapes trees can also tell you how big he is. Stands to that old standard of common sense that a trophy buck will scrape or hook a lot higher than some runty buck. It is also a fact I have seen a number of times that a big buck will have a favorite tree he likes to bang the hell out of, year after year. They will rip that tree into shreds, show off, and prance around. You can read the sign in the snow and on the bare ground. Take a careful look where that buck attacked the tree. If the scars on the tree are a day or so old, you know it's the same deer. Trophy bucks develop routine habits. And if that rubbing or hooking is off the ground three to four feet, mister, you're on to one big trophy buck that just ought to make your heart pound and your belly squirm, you should be so anxious to get him. If the rubbing is higher than that, you just might be onto a moose or elk.

Bucks paw the ground too, they also hook the ground. When they are in rut they often have only one thing in mind, and they're randy and belligerent. They'll paw the ground when they scent another buck, then they get stiff legged and tippy toed, as they move up to the other buck, ready to have a grand go at it. A buck in rut will most often paw the ground where it is level. A feeding deer, buck or doe, often paws on a slope, looking for fiddlehead ferns or mushrooms that are buried under leaves or snow. Remember this—a feeding deer paws a lot deeper than a buck in rut paws.

There's another thing bucks will do when they're expressing their manhood by scraping up mother earth. They'll paw the leaves something wicked, sometimes scrape up a few square feet, turning over the top leaves, so the dark, wet sides are showing, then urinate in the leaves. Mister, don't be proud. Put your nose right down there and take a whiff. If it is strong, he was there in the morning. If it is faint, it is a day or so old. Be like another buck. He's leaving his calling card for does and bucks alike. And for hunters too. Think like a deer.

All these signs can be read in snow and on dry ground. When

there is snow, the job is easier to read the sign. When the ground is bare, it is more difficult. If the leaves are damp, say from early morning frost or from rain, it is a lot easier than when the woods are dry. Then you have your job cut out for you.

A buck will often piddle while it's walking, leaving yellow drops marking the snow. A buck, excited by a doe in heat, will leave piddle marks 4 to 6 feet long. A doe leaves a big round hole where it has urinated. A buck invariably urinates when it passes another deer track—buck or doe. I have seen this sometimes 15 times a day, and a buck, if it gets a whiff of a doe in heat, will follow the doe's track. Curiously enough, a smaller buck will often follow a larger buck's track. Maybe the reason is somewhat similar to a young gun slinger going after the old pro.

A buck will often stick its nose into another deer track, to get a good scent, and if there is snow on the ground, you will see the dimple where the nose was imprinted. If there is a good six inches of snow on the ground, you might even see the imprint of his tines and read how many points this particular buck has.

If you find where the deer has bedded down, give it a very careful eyeballing. A trophy buck doesn't curl up into a ball, like a doe or small buck—he lays right out and stretches himself over the ground—he's just too big to do any small curl up when he wishes to take a snooze. If there's snow on the ground, take another close look. I mean really close. Look sharp, because you ought to be able to see the imprint of his horns in the snow and maybe the spread of the antlers. Two years ago in Maine I knew I was onto what I thought was a 14 pointer by seeing seven tine marks in the snow. He ended up a 13 pointer.

There are so many ways to tell a big buck track that it seems impossible for me not to know what I'm after. But it does take a lot of experience to tell the big buck track—the deer that goes over 200 pounds. However, if you keep snooping in the woods, remember what you saw, for you'll gain the experience to tell the 200 pound plus buck sign. It may take seasons of roaming the woods and keeping your eyes peeled and your brain sharp, but that's what trophy deer hunting is all about. Rely on your eyes, your brain, your memory and your common sense, and you'll bag that big buck, sure as shooting.

] 194 [

ON THE TRACK

Larry Benoit with Peter Miller

Continuing the adventures of the master tracker. I really love this account of Benoit's duel with the monster buck. I wish I could track. I wish I could hunt in an area wild enough for me to leave the stand and go on the track without getting shot!

NOW THAT YOU HAVE SPOTTED the big buck's track, and you know it's not only a big buck but a rangy, crafty critter sporting an awesome rack, and he's out there in front of you, you also know it's time to track him down. The most enjoyable part of the hunt begins—trailing the trophy buck.

You must have only one thing in mind, and that's bagging that trophy buck. Don't be thinking about your wife and the milkman. Don't worry if your car is going to start when you come out of the woods after tramping 20 miles. Don't worry about getting lost. Don't fret about if the cartridge is going to go off, or whether the firing pin is broken, or whether the rifle sights were bent the last time you fell down. Don't get anxious about pulling a muscle. And never get sick of chasing this buck, for when you begin to have those thoughts, that buck will just walk circles around you and you'll never see him. When I set on a track, I wonder if he's as big as I think he is. I say to myself, "That fellow must have some antlers by the imprinting in the snow . . . I want him! You got 14 days left, Mr. Buck, and if I haven't downed you by then, you're one smart buck." When you are worrying, you are no longer hunting.

Turn on your senses when you are on the track. Tune into the woods and the mountains. The hunting scent in the air and every move and everything you hear coincides with stalking your deer. If you don't turn yourself into a hunting animal, you won't get that buck.

The first thing you have to be sure of is which direction your buck is moving. This may sound foolish but in deep snow, if you don't study the track closely, you may end up tracking that buck in the wrong direction. Feel with your hand, if the track is snow covered, the outline of the toes, then you know for sure. Three seasons ago I was coming down a mountain in northern Vermont into a large basin, and I spotted the track of a large deer moving up the mountain. It had been made during the night. There was about eight inches of snow on the ground.

As I walked further down the side of the mountain, I cut onto this hunter's track, which was following the deer track down the mountain. So I followed both tracks and down a ways I came onto this hunter. I hollered at him and asked him if he was following the deer track.

"Yeah," he said, "What's it to you?"

"Nothing," I answered. "It's no skin off my nose."

So I followed along behind him and then said to him, "You're really following this deer?"

"Course I'm following it! Don't it look like it?"

"Yeah," I told him, "It looks like it, but are you trying to find out where he was born or where he is right now? You're trailing him backwards, you know."

"Mister," he said, "I'll have you know I've been trailing deer and tracking deer all my life and I don't need no smart upstart young punk telling me how to track a deer."

"Sorry I mentioned it, and have good luck, my friend. You might get him tomorrow, or the next day, if you back track him," and I left him. As far as I know, he's still tracking him. If a hunter, who has been tracking all his life can't tell the difference between a forwards track and a backwards track, then he might as well quit doing it. Deer can only walk in one direction at once, and it was pretty obvious that this particular deer was going uphill, heading into the mountains. If I'd have come on that track sooner, I'd have tracked him down.

Now you know for sure where that deer is headed, but you still have to answer a few questions. What is that buck's range? As I stated in Chapter 5, all bucks range in circles; they are just like big rabbits. You have to break down that circle the deer follows. You have to know how far he is in front of you, for that buck might have an 8 hour jump on you, and maybe more. You might

trail him all day and never see him, and you might pick up his trail the next day, kick him out of his bed within the next hour or maybe not catch up to him until late in the afternoon, when it's time to leave the woods. If you find the buck makes a complete circle in three or four days' time, and you know where, that buck is your buck. Many times we have shot our bucks before they completely made their swing. It depends upon how hard we're pushing, how fast the buck is moving, whether he is in rut and has located a bunch of does or is marching off somewhere else, looking for strays, or whether he is just ranging and feeding, or whether he is just a sly, fast moving devil that likes to play tricks on you.

Now you have to learn just how old that track is. If the track is on dry ground, take a look at the leaves that the deer has turned up. Are the back sides all dried out compared to leaves that have not been disturbed? Have dirt and leaf fragments crumbled into the track? If the track is clean and the leaves look freshly turned up, you know that buck is not far ahead. If the ground is wet, how much muck has collected in the track? How does it compare to your own track? If there is fresh snow on the ground, dust it off from the track and eyeball the outline of the track. If the track is hard and rigid it's at least one day old. Frostlines in the track can also mean it's a day old. But if the snow in the track is granular and you can move it around in your hands, the track may be a few hours old.

When there is snow on the ground and it is warm, don't get fooled. A melted out buck track may look like a whopper but could be a small 110 pound deer track. It only takes about an hour for the sun to beat down and spread out that track. Look for the outline of the original track. You may find the actual track is one half inch smaller than the outline. If you know how long the sun has been beating on the snow, you can guess the age of the track.

There is a lot to reading the age of a deer track that should be spewed out by that computer in your head. Much of it is past experience but you should keep current weather conditions in mind. Deer move at night and bed down in the morning. What was the weather like the day before? If it was warm and mushy, then cold overnight, and snowed a few inches, you should be able to tell to the hour when that track was made.

Is that buck traveling with a doe? If there is one doe with him, chances are you are going to get a shot at him. But if that buck is traveling with a group of does, nine times out of ten all you will see are the does, and your buck will be off loping to one side. It's best to split a buck away from his harem, which will happen anyway if you are on his track. Does are fickle and they will pack up and run quickly if they find their stud has the misfortune to have a good tracker dogging right after him.

Now you're ready to track that buck and find out a lot more about him. Your mind is set right. You have nothing to worry about, except that buck. Now forget about your scent. The wind blows in four directions, and sometimes in all four at once. If you worry about your scent, you'll never move fast enough to get that buck. A plus here is that deer are curious. Sure he'll smell you. But if you stay on his track, he'll get curious, angry or both. He's going to stop or back track, to get a look at just what is following him.

There's another thing you do here. You might not get that buck on the first day, and will have to pick up the track the next morning. Try to recognize that buck track. I have tracked bucks that have had a broken hoof, a limp or in one case, a rear left hoof where the right toe was ingrown more than it should be. Plant his signature in your brain so you can sort him out anytime—if it's the next day or after he's walked through and circled a herd of other deer that could include other bucks. (Sometimes, you might find a bigger buck track than the one you are following. Then I switch, naturally, to the bigger buck).

There is a time to run or dog a deer, a time to trot, a time to walk, and a time to pussyfoot.

If the track is old and you know that deer is hours ahead of you, sling your rifle and trot right after him. Noise and smell make no difference, just get on his trail. Pretty soon you'll know what that deer is doing. He might be in rut and looking for does and moving all over the place. At times like this he won't be feeding much. Sometimes bucks range—just trotting right along. Then is the time for you to jog right after him. Keep your eyes open for other signs too. As I said before, if your buck has pawed the ground and urinated on it, you can smell that urine easily. But if the odor is faint, it could be a day old. Has that buck shredded a tree? Check the scar he's made. Is it fresh looking? How about the shreds of bark on the ground? Are they fresh? Is the underside of the bark fresh or has it darkened? Are the shreds curled? If they're not, that deer could be closer than you think.

When that buck you're trailing moves from a trot to a walk, you move from a trot to a walk. When he stops to browse, nipping buds here and there, mister, you better be on your guard, then it's time to start pussyfooting, for chances are that buck will browse just a bit, then bed down. It only takes a buck about an hour to browse and bed down.

During the deer season I have found that bucks usually don't have more than a few pounds of browse in their stomachs. They don't eat much. Sex is on their minds, and their bodies are in excellent condition from stuffing themselves all summer.

When a buck is browsing and standing about, nipping buds, pawing for food, or eating mushrooms from the side of a tree, he may move just a few feet in a half hour. If it takes you one half hour to move ten feet, then take one half hour. If you make one mistake here, that buck will know it, and be off faster than you can blink, and you'll never see him.

When I start pussyfooting, I hunch down, glance at the track and where I can walk without making noise, and I keep glancing around. You can see at a 40 degree angle off to the sides and your eyes should be constantly swinging. Just because that buck is moving in a straight line doesn't mean he can't be off to the side. Many times, when a buck is ready to bed down, he'll make a small circle uphill from his bed, just checking out the security. He may be eyeballing the back of your head from above when you're looking at his track and up in front of you.

When you see by the sign that your buck is no longer browsing, then you know he is not more than 50 to 100 yards from you and you have to do more than just sneaking and peeking. You sort of flatten right out, hunch close to the ground. Many, many times I have been that close to a rangy old buck, and he's won the game. He's there giving me the eye before I spot him, then he snorts and my hair curls and my heart stops, then spurts madly and I just catch a glimpse of him tearing through the brush like a locomotive.

Well, the game is on again. I scold myself for being a dummy, sling my rifle, and start right after him full bore. I run, literally run, after that bounding deer. If I have to run up hill, I run uphill. Sometimes, when I hit the crest of a peak, around 4,000 feet, I'll be coated with rime frost and look like some grizzled snowman. But I keep after him. When he slows to a trot, I slow to a trot. When he stops to feed or to listen, I do the same, and we play hide and seek and sneaking and peeking. Now I hope to get him again.

Sometimes, I have to leave the track at the end of the day, and I'll pick it up the next morning. Hopefully, during the first day's hunt I'll have figured out part of his circle and the next day I'll hit the ridge and zig-zag up and down until I find his trail and sometimes his bed. These old bucks, as I said, have habits, and they usually bed down in pretty near the same location, night after night, even when they have had a hunter on their tail. A long winded buck might take off with you after him for 18–20 miles, then that night return to his stomping ground, going as much as 40 miles a day. Remember, he has four legs, you've got only two.

Get to know the habits of that trophy buck you're tracking. If that buck is in rut, he'll be chasing down does and anxious to fight other bucks, and, just like us, he gets a little careless when he's excited. You can read all this in the ground. You can see where your big buck has chased a doe and butted her around and mounted her. Remember, the buck gets excited because the doe is in heat. He literally goes out of his mind. His neck swells, his pride gets high, he's randy and practically insatiable. If that buck of yours is after a fight and smells another buck, he'll walk stiff legged and take little sharp pointed steps in the snow. He'll bristle right up, walk on the tips of his toes, his head will go down, antlers out, and he'll bellow right from the bottoms of his lungs. It's an odd sound, and if you hear it, your hair will curl. You'll never forget the sound. Most times though, you only hear it, because you become anxious and make a mistake. I almost came onto a fight two years ago. I heard the sound high on the mountain—an awful racket. The buck I was following tore hell out of a smaller buck. The ground was literally ripped up. Spots of blood reddened the snow and deer hair was matted on the trees. The smaller deer limped off, but I noticed he limped off at a run.

Some deer, after they know you are on their track, become awful curious as to just what it is that is bugging them. They will stop and look, sometimes a half dozen times. If you have a buck like that in front of you, you have a buck that isn't going to live very long. Other bucks will circle around you and this is another reason to keep your eyes open to the side.

Sly old trophy bucks don't want you on their track at all. Some of them will just try to run away. Others will try to lose you by milling around in a yard of deer, including bucks and does. When this happens I generally follow the buck in and figure he'll come out of the yard in the opposite direction. Other times, though, you have to circle the mess of tracks and sort out which one was yours, or which one is bigger. This is where it comes in handy to know your buck's track.

I've had bucks double back on their track and jump off, trying to lose me. Other bucks have followed streams and half a dozen years ago one did this to me in northern Vermont, following a stream right down the mountain. After a mile I thought I had lost him but on a rock I saw splashes of water and knew he was ahead of me. I tracked that deer right through a town.

Some other bucks I have tracked have followed other buck tracks, hoping to lose me. And many times, I have seen a smaller buck track a bigger buck. I have walked onto these smaller bucks, pointed my finger at them, said "Bang! Now go away and grow up, little feller" and watched them, startled out of their skins, bound through the brush. Some of them were good bucks, but never as good as the one I was on.

I have followed trophy bucks that are ornery and mean. They are mad and frustrated at this being that is following them and they will hook brush and the ground and trees and stamp their feet. Often those angry bucks spend too much time doing that and they suddenly find their rib cage is pinned to my sights.

Eight falls ago I was on a large buck track for five days. That old buck didn't like me on his track at all. He was some upset about it, I could tell, because he pawed the ground and hooked branches. He was belligerent and looking for a fight. I had put him up out of his bed on the fifth day and he roared down the mountain with me right after him. He forgot about me and rammed into three does, charging right after them. They took off to the left of a ravine, and the buck to the right. Then he ran into two does and a 7 point buck. That buck I was following just leaped down the mountain and in one mighty 30 foot leap rammed into the smaller buck.

I came on the scene five minutes later. The seven point buck was just getting to his feet. I figured he had a broken shoulder and fractured ribs, the way he was breathing so hard. One eye was punched out and when he stood, his head was down, which is a sign of an injured buck. There wasn't much blood so I also knew the injury was internal. I knew he'd live, that poor old fellow, and I kept right after the big one. I finally nailed him—a 230 pound eight pointer.

I have never had a buck charge me although Lanny has, on a deer he had tracked for several days in northern Vermont. That buck started charging from 30 feet away. Lanny, however, just loves to get gatling with his .270 and that buck didn't get too far. "Gosh, Pop," Lanny said to me when we were dragging him out.

"He sure surprised me. I figured he had more brains than that."
The deer was an old, 215 pound hoosier with eleven points.

There are other characteristics about bucks I have tracked. Some are real skitterish of humans, and these are the ones found in the lowlands. Ridge bucks often have not had too much contact with people, and are easier to track. Maine bucks, I have noticed, are not half as shy as Vermont bucks, and I think it is because they have not felt the hunting pressure. The bucks I am talking about, of course, are those high on mountains, where few hunters have dared to stray. I imagine that bucks in other states, such as Michigan and Pennsylvania and even Texas all have different levels of wariness. And each buck that you track is different, just like humans. Some cover a lot of territory in their range while others prefer a shorter circle. Some are curious, some are ornery, and a lot of those big hoosiers are sly. You can spot them sometimes when they get out of their bed, their head low to the ground, streaking away like a comet. You often see pictures of deer bounding through the woods with their heads high. Bucks don't do that. They keep their head down low, so their antlers don't get caught up.

Bucks are supposed to crawl on their bellies to hide from you. That sure is some buck tale. I've never seen a buck crawl on his belly when he could be making 25 foot leaps, putting a lot of distance between you and him. This is the same sort of tale as one I recently read—that a buck will rub his hind legs together to get the musk working from his scent glands. If you ever see one do that, lasso him and take him to a carnival, for he'll have to be some contortionist to rub his hind knees together.

There's lots you will learn on the track, much you can figure out about all bucks and about the one you are following. You will also be smart to mind the weather. If there's fresh snow on the ground, and the snow is falling, and there's little wind, and you find a buck track, you should have him before sunset. If the snow is frozen and crackly, the chances are against you. When the leaves crunch like cornflakes when you put your foot down, you might as well be home, for it takes mighty good luck to get a shot at a buck when it is noisy. The wind doesn't help either. Deer and all other wild game become very wary when the wind is up. You rarely spot a buck in this sort of weather.

But a good snow, even a blizzard, can't be beat. I and my sons have slogged after bucks in snow three feet deep (soft, fluffy snow, not 3 feet of wet snow) and there's no finer time to hunt than when the woods are freshened by a blanket of snow, the noise is deadened, the wind is still, and you know the bucks are moving. That's the best condition for hunting you'll ever find.

The buck that I tracked the longest was a wily old Vermont ridge runner who ran the mountain tops in northern Vermont. He led me on the track for 13 days before I downed him. He was a smart creature and a noble one. I wrote about that hunt in *Sports Afield* and I am running it here again. Read it carefully, because that buck pulled most of the tricks I know. You'll learn a lot on how a buck thinks.

THE THIRTEEN DAY DEER HUNT

I knew he was up there somewhere, browsing about, up on that mountain I know so well. Last year I saw his sign a bit and had a peek at him. He wasn't a barrel-chested deer—the type that look more like a buffalo with spindly legs, and he wasn't a lean or a long deer—he was just a well-built deer. He had a good pair of legs, he sure did. He was a good runner, a big, mountain top deer, living about 3,300 feet. I don't believe he came down during the summer or winter, except when the snow laid in deep. I think he lost his horns up there too. You could lay a 30-06 cartridge in his tracks sideways and it wouldn't fill it and I figured he would go over 250 pounds. His rack was heavy, wide spaced and very, very thick. He had ten points and five years of mountain running. I planned to get him.

First Day

It was two hours before dawn when Lanny, my son, Uncle Windy and I drove north to the mountain and ridges that run parallel to the road that leads into Canada. I dropped Lanny off 18 miles from where I went in. He would work over the range and

] 204 [

hunt six to eight miles from me, down in the swamp basin. We never hunt together until we have some cleanup work. Uncle Windy hunted down low and I was heading to the peak of the highest mountain. On that first day we were just scouting, looking for sign and I was looking for the big one. It was pretty black out that first morning, a slow wind whistled through the trees. It was damp and quiet walking—spongy. There was no snow on the ground but I knew there would be shortly, I could smell it, coming in with a soft wind from Canada. I walked straight up the mountain, about three miles in, up to the browse area where I thought I'd find my buck. There was good browse on this mountain, beechnuts, mountain laurel, maple, the tender shoots off birch. Birch is very sweet you know.

I was up near the top, about 10:00, when small flakes sifted down, then changed to good heavy flakes—typical high mountain early season flakes—and the snow began sticking to the ground. We never lost the snow for the rest of the hunt. I had circled the area, looking for sign but with the snow coming down heavy I hunched under one of those scrawny spruce trees, stunted by the altitude. They never have any body to them. I sat there, dry, warm, just waiting. I was about 3,400 feet and the mountain peaked out at about 3,700. I knew the deer would be moving in the storm in the afternoon, and I had lunch, brownies, a peanut butter sandwich. I met a friendly chickadee. He'd land on my finger and pick at my ring. I'd snap my fingers and he'd flutter up, scold me, then come right down and land in my hand and do it again. He liked brownie crumbs.

After lunch a couple of does trotted in sight. Nervous they were, fooling around. I didn't know why but probably there was another hunter below them—probably my son. They wouldn't stop to feed and kept looking back down the mountain. It was snowing pretty hard then and you could see about 75–80 feet. The blizzard was really setting in, and would drop about eight inches of snow that day. The storm was going full swing about one o'clock and I knew the deer would be moving and I started to move parallel to the ridge, zigzagging up to the summit, then back down, trying to find where the old boy would get up and start moving around.

I was walking slow, just more or less wasting time and sure enough I came across his track. He was with a doe and I could see right off he was a big deer and I was pretty sure he was my deer. Those big deer, they have a home and they hang right into it. You know, there's a way to tell a buck track just by glancing at it. More people get fooled by dew claws or a splayed track, but all deer got dew claws. So do pigs and goats, and all deer with weight splay their hooves. To recognize a buck track right off, well, it took me years.

These two were just browsing several hundred feet off the summit; they had come out of the spruces on the top and were working down. They didn't know I was about so I started sneaking and peeking, because I knew he was right in front of me. I could tell by his tracks in the snow, and they were feeding slow, on buds on short, sparse trees that up there are only two or three feet off the ground. You could see their nipper marks.

I was on to them for about a half hour when I felt eyes on me and I turned my head to the left. There they were, staring right down on me. The buck and his doe had probably been watching me for three minutes, just frozen up there, hidden by some spruces, peering at me through the snow flakes. They were about 50 feet up hill. They had zigzagged while browsing moving up hill. Oh, he was a big buck, he was my buck all right, and I felt like killing myself because I missed him.

My rifle was ready but I never had a chance to fire. I saw horns, a body, then he was gone. He went straight up and over the top. I called myself a dummy and all kinds of things for a few seconds, slung my rifle and took right after him.

I had been with him for about an hour and had dogged him right over the top of the mountain and down the other side to about the 2,600 foot level where I was below the snowstorm line and I could see good. He had slowed down, and wasn't taking those 30 foot jumps and I slowed down too and kept looking forward. I spotted him down about 90 yards.

I use a .30-06 carbine with an 18 inch barrel. I carved a big running deer on the stock, and it shoots where I want it to. I pulled my rifle up just as he broke into a run and I followed him, waiting for him to hit an opening and for that moment when he is still, his legs all bunched up, ready for the next leap. He got into an opening, all bunched up, and I squeezed the trigger and at the same time a tree jumped right smack out in front of the sight. It was a 10 inch birch and I hit it dead center. I don't know how they do it, those trees, but most deer hunters have chuckled at that because it has happened to them many times.

The buck headed northwest, parallel to the ridge. He would run trot, walk, browse with me right behind him. It started to snow again and sometimes I could see no further than 50 yards, but usually less because he and I were moving through thick brush. He was not following a trail but in typical buck fashion he was going where his feet happened to lead him. Oh, he knew where he was going all right, he knew the route but he was not following a trail.

And he knew I was there with him. He would cut up the mountain, then down, then back up again. He circled, twisted, and back tracked. He back tracked several times on his own trail to see if I was coming. I guess he was worried about me. He saw me several times, I could tell from his tracks. Sometimes he back tracked 50 yards. Back tracking is a mistake, because I catch them in the act and they find me in front of them, looking down the barrel.

You see, a deer doesn't always trust his nose, they just have to back track and see what is following them. They don't understand—"What is that persistent thing behind me?" And if they're in rut, why, they make more mistakes, fooling with the does and battling other bucks. This one, though, wasn't in rut. His doe left him way back on the high mountain. In typical fashion does usually start packing their bags a few minutes after they get jumped.

The buck finally headed for a swamp, a big basin, and I left his track a little before dark and walked out on a log road to the main road and waited for Lanny or my Uncle Windy to pick me up. I figured I had dogged that buck 18 miles and I knew he was smarter than I first reckoned.

Second Day

I knew that buck would be back where I picked him up the first day so I went to the same area, up about 3,400 feet and zagged around and about 8:30 I found his trail. I knew it was him by the size of the hoof print in the snow. It was murky out, the clouds were low and dark and there was a light snow falling when I started after my buck. An hour later I watched him rise out of his bed and walk away from me, right into the falling snow. He never ran. He was laying down in thick spruces, about 60 yards from me. I guess I let him go, I could have had him.

Well, then again I like to get one good shot into a deer, and I like to take my opportunity. I don't like half shots—never did—don't like shoulder shots nor neck shots. I like rib shots, right into the boiler works. When you shoot them in the boiler works they go for probably 30 yards and are practically dead on their feet and they don't even realize it. I really didn't have that type of shot at him.

So I tracked him, and he began to play some tricks on me. He got into a bunch of deer where there were four or five does, and tried to shake me onto another track. I saw sign where he ran into a small buck and didn't challenge him so I knew he wouldn't waste time with the does, or fighting other bucks. He must have walked into 15 different deer that day to see if he could lose me. He didn't and he worked northwest, the same direction as the first day. I followed him for about four hours. I was moving along at a good trot.

I let him go in the late afternoon, and walked down the mountain onto the road. I was working through the spruces half way down when I ran across a fisher cat, chasing a red squirrel. Fisher cats make the most vicious sound you ever heard when they are after anything, and that cat was trying to scare the squirrel to death. The squirrel was leaping blindly from limb to limb but the trees were small and the big cat couldn't get leverage and stayed about five or six feet behind the squirrel, screaming till he saw me and took a powder. I've come across hedgehogs a fisher has killed. They run under a limb, where the hedgehog is and open him right up across the belly and that hedgehog is dead and doesn't know it. The fisher eats the hedgehog inside out and when he's done that hide lays right out like a rug. I found them in the woods—the only thing left is the upper part of the skull, the teeth, and the hide laid out just clean, no back bone or nothing. You see a fisher cat you want to be damn thankful you saw him, because they are rare and very evasive, just like the whitetail I was after.

Third Day

At 8:oo I was onto his track again. Just like clock work that devil would be right back in the same area. He was meandering and browsing slow like and I was soft behind him, slow and peeking. But he got me again. He whistled so hard at me, it practically knocked my hat off, and took the wind out of me so fast I think I whistled back. Then he was off and so was I, trotting right after him. He would run, taking those 20 and 30 foot jumps, then he would slow right down. While he was running I would cover some ground too and I'd catch up with him right along. But I never saw him that day. I followed him for about five hours and all I saw was a smaller buck who was trailing my buck. It happens often. (Although I ran across seven bucks who were trailing my big one). Some might be trailing out of curiosity but in typical buck fashion, they probably wanted to fight. I'd catch up to them, about 60 yards, sometimes a lot closer and I'd point my finger at them and say "Bang! I got myself another buck!" and let them go. Most generally they got a good look at me and they'd take right off in a heck of a fright.

Fourth Day

I saw him this day, about 80 yards in front of me, hidden in some brush, moving away at a trot. I didn't have a good shot, so I didn't fire. He was back in his stomping ground and although he got away, I felt a little more enthusiastic about killing him and I followed him again for 18 miles. He'd zigzag the mountain and ridge always heading northwest, going up to the summit, then heading back down, trying to shake me, but never going below 2,600 feet. He had his routine and I knew if he stuck to it, I'd catch him eventually. I also knew he was upset about me being on his tail. He wasn't in rut, yet in several places I saw sign where he tore hell out of the trees and the snow, pawing, scratching, banging away. He was getting to be just a bit frustrated with me, for I was always with him.

It was damp cold that day but I wasn't uncomfortable. I dress light because I do a lot of dogging and sometimes my hair and jacket get all rimed with frost when I'm on the trail. Sometimes I moved in close to him and I could smell him, the stink would linger because he would be running and sweating. I didn't see him again that day but he was sure learning my scent.

You know, with big deer, you got to be patient, because they are smart. You can say, mister, that this buck was smart, he proved it to me. I think he was one of the smartest I ever trailed. Just to get away from me he was smart, normally I nail them right in their bed and usually, two days is about the limit I'll track a deer. Any more than two days and you know you are onto an exceptionally smart buck.

Fifth Day

I picked up his track no less than 50 feet from where I found him the day before. He had come back again, a round trip of 36 miles. It had snowed again, during the night, and it was up to my knees. I was just easing along, it was early in the morning and I was bending down to check his tracks in that deep snow. While I was piling away the snow to look at the track, I heard a crash in back of me. He cleared the trail I was on—jumped right over it— and if I moved back in my tracks six feet, he would have jumped over me. He was bedded down on my left and got a whiff of me. I was between him and the top of the mountain. No sir, he wouldn't go down the mountain, or around me; he wanted to go straight up and follow that same escape route. They have habits just like we do. Even though he was that close, I just caught a glimpse of him.

I didn't have much to say to myself and I took off after him and ran myself right into the ground. He did some wicked swinging that day. He went over the mountain, then he swung down, and slapped around and ran three or four miles straight to the top, headed northwest for awhile, then swung back down the mountain. He did that four times, following the ridge, angling his swings always to the northwest, towards the high basin. I was learning to anticipte the swings and I just cut parallel to the ridge, trying to catch him when he came down. But he always was out in front of me about 200 yards and on the last swing he stayed high, and he ran hard and he ran, and ran and ran. That was the runningest deer, and it looked like a question of who in the hell was going to run out first, and it wasn't going to be me! We did about 12 miles that day, and I left him at 4:30.

Sixth Day

I went back up to the same area, just below the summit, and for the first time in the hunt I didn't find him so I knew he was still down where I left him the day before. Rather than waste my energy going down where I knew it would cost me three or four hours of tough dogging, I by-passed him and made a big swing around a swamp and looked for sign of other bucks for future hunting. I didn't find any sign of big bucks, although I saw one medium sized buck, a four pointer.

Seventh Day

He was back that morning, right on the very top of the mountain hidden in the shortest spruces you could find. I got right on his trail at 7:30 but again I missed him coming out of his bed and he struck right off northwest. At around 2:00 I knew by the sign on the ground he was beginning to browse and I knew then that I might catch him so I was really pushing it when up from the valley, about 4 miles away, echoed five quick shots. It distracted me and I was looking down the side of the mountain, in open timber, where you could see for up to three hundred yards. I knew my son Lanny was doing the shooting, for when he shoots a deer, he likes to pepper him. Just like a machine gun he is. Also, no one else was hunting this area. I never have seen another hunter or human track, we just hunt too deep in the woods for civilized hunters to venture. Goodness, they might get lost!

So like a fool I was looking down, towards the shooting, trying to imagine the scene down there. I was standing on a runway, right on the top where the big deer cross. The runway goes northwest, along the ridge and down into the big basin, although I never caught my buck on it. But there he was, boring right to me on a collision course. I was startled at about the same time he was and when I unslung my rifle, my buck was gone and I was standing there like a fool, holding my gun.

I just wasn't thinking, and you always must keep attention in the woods. He had back tracked because the shooting startled him. He was nervous and when he saw me he reared right up, did a quick about face, roared right back where he came from. I followed him hard until about 3:30, because I thought I'd get him but it didn't work out that way. Lanny got his though. Not a big one. About 175 pounds.

Eighth Day

It was a nice day for a change, not snowing and we had some sun. I picked him up at the same time in the same place and started tracking him as he moved in the same direction at the same altitude. I tracked him for 10 miles, then swung to my car. It was this day that I heard the squeal of a rabbit. I left the trail to see what was going on. A red fox had this poor old bunny rabbit and he was giving him one hell of a drubbing. He hadn't finished him when he saw me and dropped the rabbit. The rabbit is a sensitive little animal and he died right in my hands, died of fright.

Ninth Day

I found him, tracked him and didn't get a peek at him, and I was growing a little bit disgusted. I'd come home and talk about the big deer that I was following that for some reason or another kept getting away from me. I told that to Lanny and he told me, "Fine, Frank, if you can't get him, I'll have to go up and get him for you" but I didn't want him to do that. I was bothered though.

Tenth Day

All of a sudden, there he stood, in front of me, out 60 yards, and I wasn't ready for him. I had been on his track for three hours but

I must have been daydreaming. The brush was thick and that buck back tracked like he often does. I was too nonchalant in the woods that day. Yeah, I was beginning to be careless. That day I saw where he hooked the trees, and I found where he sunk down in front of me, right before me, just looking at me. He was sneaky all right. It started to snow again and I didn't feel so sure about ever catching up with this buck.

Eleventh Day

The snow was really deep, and it was snowing a blizzard. Although I was early on his track, the snow was coming down faster than I could make out the track. So rather than spook him into an unknown country, I gave it up. I dropped down into a small plateau under the mountain and I was going through the spruces. It was quiet like in that deep snow and I came on six deer in a clearing just before a beechnut grove. I was watching them and then this buck came right up out of the snow, he just materialized, I never knew he was there, and he started browsing. These were different types of deer—mid-range deer, between the ridge runners, and the lowland deer. I was watching them and said to myself why should I shoot, I got mine to get up on the ridge, and I walked right into the midst of them. There were three bucks in the group, a spike horn, a four and six pointer. I just pointed my finger at them and went "Bang! Bang!" They sure did take off.

Twelfth Day

It was do or die this day and I humped him for every inch of his life, boy, and I mean I petered him right out—through the spruces, hardwood, and brush. He went down to the swamp again. It had stopped snowing but it was fluffy and easy to see his tracks under the spruces, where the snow wasn't so deep. I tracked him northwest until he swung back up to where I started him. I was on his tail for about 25 miles and he followed the same routine, staying high, and I proved that he came back along the same route. That night I told my son that we'd get him the next day because I knew every move he had made was exactly the same and we laid out our plans.

] 213 [

Thirteenth Day

I went up the mountain working east as I always did until I hit his track. Lanny went in east too, then swung southeast, then cut north, working slow. I jumped the buck and he rambled northwest, as I knew he would. I was still on him at about 1:00 when our mousetrap play started to work. When I was dogging him, the buck had never had human scent in front of him but now Lanny's scent drifted up from the valley. Lanny was about 200 yards below me and the deer, working towards us.

The buck didn't know what to do so he slowed down, hesitating. I was onto his sign, right behind him and I pussy footed. It was a clear day, cold, but I was working a sweat. I had that feeling. The buck just couldn't figure what that was down below him. He probably never ran against two men before; this was one trick he had never had played on him, the other tricks he was wise to. I finally saw him, about 25 feet from me hidden behind a big mountain spruce, covered with snow. He was looking down the mountain in the direction of Lanny all tense, still, suspicious looking, ears forward. I could see all his rib cage, then his shoulders and right up to his antlers. He looked bigger than ever. He was just standing there and I saw him just for a split second because my rifle was up quick. I fired, just once, and he toppled over and looked as big as a horse laying there on the ground in the deep snow. I had broken his back, I had made a poor snap shot because he was so close and also I thought he'd disappear on me. He wasn't dead when I came up to him and that is when I always have my moments of regret. He and I watched each other for a few minutes and we said a few words and I said to him, "Well, we finally caught up with you didn't we?" I had to shoot him again in the neck. I always hate to finish them off like that; I wish he was dead before I got there. Well, another big king went down; they're not many of the big deer left in the woods and you have to hunt a long time before you can find them. That buck had a 24 inch antler spread and dressed out at 230 pounds. I believe he would have weighed 260 pounds on that first day I spotted him.

BIG BUCKS IN THE BIG WOODS: THE CHALLENGE OF WILDERNESS WHITETAILS

Jerome B. Robinson

Although he labors officially in the Sports Afield *vineyards as Gun Dog Editor—and a mighty good one he is, too—Jerry Robinson is one of those hyper-active outdoorsmen who likes to do it all.*

His favorite passion—one that has produced his most memorable articles and photography—is for hunting and fishing adventures that take place in remote, big-wilderness country.

Yes, friend, the big woods are different. You can get lost out there; or frozen, drowned, starved, injured, and scared. The trick is to know what you're doing.

This story from Sports Afield *contains the only account I've ever heard personally of a deer actually charging a hunter. Because it happened to Jerry, I know it's true.*

Jerry lives up in New Hampshire on a remote spread. When he's not off to the far wild places, he walks down to the mailbox every day to see how the readers like his articles and his excellent book Hunt Close!, *published by Winchester Press.*

I remember hearing about a dog that would hunt close once. Mind you, I never actually saw the dog, but I did hear about him from a friend of a friend. Perhaps he actually exists.

TO HUNT DEER where no stranger's boot track mars the loneliness of a wild and silent forest is nothing short of splendor.

I've had it with the red-coated horde, thrashing about the woods with all the serenity of an earthquake. Frankly, I don't want to shoot a deer that's been spooked to me by some other hunter's noisy passage. Nor do I enjoy that crawling feeling I get in the dim hours of dawn and dusk when I know the woods are full of hunters. Instead of watching for deer, my tendency at such times is to worry about my general safety.

] 215 [

When I hunt deer, I want to be so far from other hunters that I can't hear a distant rifle shot. I want no drone of road traffic to interfere with my ability to hear the quiet, telltale sounds of the forest. And, most of all, I want to be able to study a big buck's pattern of movement and hunt according to where I think he wants to be.

To hunt that way means exerting extra effort and going back in farther than the other hunters. But once attained, that untouched country is where the deer will be moving according to their natural patterns, and that's what deer hunting is all about.

Hunting in country that is devoid of other hunters allows you to hunt methodically; by observing the signs you find where a good buck is moving. You scout out his trail system, noting where and how often the buck stops to rub and where the thickets are in which he polishes his antlers. Gradually, you assimilate knowledge about where that buck is most likely to be, and your hunt becomes a matter of trying to be there to meet him.

If you are back in far enough, you can be sure that no one else will mess up your hunt by spooking the buck and causing him to change his pattern. When they are really in the rut, the big forest bucks of the untouched backcountry are on the move day and night. You can find places where the buck has been a hundred times, and you can go there yourself a hundred times and never see him. But all it takes is that one time when you and the buck will be there simultaneously.

The untouched country doesn't have to be as far away as you may think. Studies have shown that the average modern deer hunter rarely goes more than a few hundred yards from a road. A small percentage hunt back as far as two miles from a road. But if you find a spot on a map that shows no roads within five miles in any direction, you can be assured that you will have that area to yourself.

Particularly in the northern forest states, these remote sections may not have been hunted since the early days when Indians or wandering trappers cruised the country. It is certain that the hunting horde never makes it back into these game-rich pockets, and that the deer have not learned to fear a constant danger as they have in the crowded hunting areas.

In 1973, I spent a week with two friends hunting deer in a remote and wild part of Maine. We came out with two good bucks and should have had a third, but the success of that hunt cannot be measured in antlers and venison alone. Our biggest success was in finding an area that had virtually never been hunted before. Certainly, no one had made a practice of hunting this area in many, many years.

To reach our spot, Gene Bourne of Brattleboro, Vermont, Paul Pray of Millinocket, Maine, and I drove 25 miles back over a gravel tote road, then unloaded two canoes where the road crossed a river (that shall be nameless) and paddled downstream eight miles. There we set up a tent camp and settled in for a week.

During the season, other hunters would travel that tote road and might even hunt along the edge of the river up around the bridge. But eight miles of thick black-spruce growth separated us from the road, and we knew we would not see or hear another hunter.

From the moment our two canoes dropped down around the first bend in the river, and we entered that long black watery corridor between walls of somber spruces, we knew this would be the best deer-hunting trip we would ever experience.

The silence was magnificent. The liquid murmur of the ripples played back off the silent forest. Once or twice, a paddle clunked against a canoe gunwale, but there were no other sounds. It was raining softly. Later it would snow.

We were well equipped, for a week in the bush can be uncomfortable when the temperatures hover near freezing, and wet snow and cold rain fall intermittently.

We carried a 12x14 canvas dining tent as well as individual sleeping tents in which each man stored his clothes, sleeping bag, mattress pad and miscellaneous small gear. In the big tent, we had a folding aluminum table and three folding deck chairs. Those chairs, by the way, are terrific on such trips. Nothing seems nicer than to be able to sit down comfortably, close to the stove, when you come in wet and cold after dark.

In one corner stood a sheet-iron wood stove that we could quickly fire up with dry cedar splits. This stove was capable of heating the tent to such a degree that steam would roll from our wet clothes. In another corner, we rigged a table of poles for the Coleman stove, and there were two wanigans filled with good food. Along one wall, we built a drying rack for wet hunting clothes. Two Coleman lamps hung from the ridgepole.

We had also brought with us a small chain saw which, although occasionally shattering the silence of the peaceful wilderness, was worth the interruption. In an hour's time every few days, we could lay up enough chunks of dry cedar, birch and green spruce to turn our wood stove cherry red whenever someone needed thawing or drying out.

With great anticipation and with the enthusiasm that begins all good hunts, we built a rugged game pole outside the tent—rugged enough to hang three big bucks and a bear. Two hours after arriving, our camp was rigged, and we were out scouting the area.

In remote country where there are no other hunters and probably never have been during the lifetime of the game in that section of forest, you have several distinct advantages.

Most outstanding is the fact that the game is not particularly afraid of you. These deer haven't been shot at before. If they have had any previous contact with man, it has been with fishermen or loggers. Thus, if you jump a buck, the odds are he will run only about a hundred yards and then stop and look back.

The deer are not numerous in remote forest regions as they are, for instance, in woodlands surrounding farmlands that provide extra feed. In the big woods, the deer are strictly browsers. They feed on twig sprouts, berries, nuts, certain leaves, brush tips and cedar. Very rarely do they graze on grass. To find preferred browse, the deer work the riverbanks and odd tote paths where new growth has appeared. They browse the edges of swamps, old burns, and, if it's a good beechnut or acorn year, the deer will work the open mature hardwood ridges.

The first thing to do when you are hunting new country is to search out and discover these open feeding areas. For, even though the deer may not be as educated or as frightened of man in remote forests, the big spruce woods are so thick that it is hard to get a good shot at a deer, even if he does only run a hundred yards and then stop.

Having gone to the trouble to avoid other hunters, it naturally follows that the three of us would want to hunt as quietly as possible once in camp. That meant hunting alone. Hence, we divided the area into six wedge-shaped sectors: upstream from the tent, downstream from the tent and straight out from the tent on both sides of the river.

No matter where you travel in big-game country, there will be a game trail along both banks of every river. Canoeists know this and use these trails for portages where no distinct portage trail has been previously made.

Game trails follow the paths of least resistance. If you have ever been stuck in a thick spruce bog, floundering around in ankle-deep water and fighting branches that claw your hat away and rake your face with every step, you know what I mean. Suddenly the thicket relents in some imperceptible way. The lay of the land changes slightly in your favor. The branches all seem to point away from you now rather than straight into your face. Your feet naturally follow this more comfortable line. Look down, and you'll find that wild-life has passed that same way.

If you let your feet guide you in a general direction without thinking exactly how you plan to pass through a big stretch of forest, you'll almost always find yourself on a faint game trail. The

] 219 [

signs will be unmistakable and it will surprise you at the time. The facts are simple enough, however. Without planning a route, you have chosen the path of least resistance. Game does the same thing.

Because deer are scarcer in the big woods, bucks must cover a wide territory leaving their marks and scent to lure willing does to remain until the buck can find them. When the rut is really upon them, the bucks move almost constantly. Their tracks tell the story.

Straight up the middle of every open pathway, the big tracks continue, rarely showing where the buck paused to snatch a fresh hardwood twig. Whatever he eats is snatched along the way. You will not find a single place where he has stopped and browsed for any period of time.

At regular intervals, he leaves his mark, almost always where an evergreen bough hangs over the trail five or six feet off the ground. Beneath this overhanging branch, the buck paws out a scrape mark, clearing the earth beneath the moss and leaves. And in the center of that torn patch of earth will be the buck's signature—the perfectly impressed print of his rear hoof. Where the path goes through a patch of hardwood saplings or an alder thicket, the buck will have stopped to polish his antlers, and the rubbed trunks and broken branches will serve as signposts to lead you through the thicket.

Rarely will you find a place where the buck has bedded or stopped to feed. He is constantly on the prowl, staking out his territory, returning over his route and freshening his scrapes and scent marks every few days. Because the bucks are so diligently on the move, you find more buck than doe sign along the game trails. However, where a doe or group of does are feeding, you will find there is a buck checking on them apparently waiting for one to come in heat.

Three days of scouting the riverbanks, low hardwood ridges and cedar swamps within a couple of miles of our tent camp told me a lot about where one old buck was working. I had followed his tracks across the river and far up through cedar swamps into the hardwoods. I had spent another entire day following his tracks as they led straight up the middle of mile after mile of old mossy tote roads that had not been used by loggers since the area was cut 40 years before. This old buck was really on the move. He seemed to have been everywhere, and his pawings were great rips three or four feet long. The track he left in the center of each scrape mark was of impressive size. Though we had not yet had a lasting snow, it rained every day, and the tracks were clear in the mud. These tracks indicated that he did not pass over the same route every day.

On the third day, I hit a mother lode of sign. I had been moving slowly along a series of old paths on the low ridge across the river from camp and broke out on the river a mile or so downstream from our tents. I had not previously scouted the riverbank in that sector, but now I decided to follow the river to check for sign.

Within a quarter mile, I came upon an alder thicket that had been absolutely ravaged by a buck. Every few feet, he had battled with the black twisted alder trunks. Shreds of bark hung from the branches. There were places where the buck had carefully polished his antlers, but mostly the alders were violently ripped and gashed. Much of the sign was very fresh. The buck had been there only hours ahead of me and had obviously spent some time in that thicket.

I slipped quietly down the riverbank, moving slowly in the gathering gloom of a light rain and approaching dusk. His sign was everywhere—tracks, scratch marks, antler rubs, droppings—some old, but much of it very fresh. Somewhere down along that riverbank, he and I would meet.

Next morning, I paddled the canoe across the river at daylight and stood waiting beside an opening in the alder thicket for more than an hour. Nothing moved.

Slowly I started downriver. The wet leaves made no sound beneath my feet, and it was gloomy and dark in the forest. Any moment, I expected to see the buck. His tracks formed a highway through park-like glades close beside the river. Great pines reached high overhead. I passed through an ancient opening where great twisted oaks scattered acorns on the ground and let daylight into the dark evergreen growth.

Every sense was alert. I moved slowly, stopping for minutes at a time, studying what was ahead, listening, smelling the heavy fragrance of wet decaying leaves and evergreen needles.

Two miles from camp, I came to a turn in the river and quietly made my way to a point where I could look around the bend and down the open water. Standing there watching the mist rising from the river, I heard the unmistakable crack of a breaking branch. A moment later the sound was followed by another crack and then the slashing of leaves and twigs being scraped from the ground.

The noise was close by, only 30 yards or so away. I dropped to one knee and peered into the thick gloom beneath the spruces just across a narrow drainage.

There, among a tangle of alders, I caught movement. A deer's forefoot came clearly into view, but I could see nothing of the rest of the deer. Suddenly, the hoof pawed the earth and threw back a scattering of twigs and leaves. As I watched, the buck's heavily antlered head came briefly into view as he lowered his muzzle to sniff where he had pawed.

I was slightly above him and across the drainage. I raised my gun but could not find a target. In the gray gloom, the deer's body was completely hidden. All I could see was the pawing hoof and his face and antlers when he sniffed the ground.

I waited. One forward step, maybe two, were all it would take to bring the buck out into the open where I would have a clear shot.

Suddenly, his head snapped up above the alders, and he looked straight at me. My scent must have drifted down to him. One bound would put him back into the gloomy spruces. It was now or never.

I slid my Winchester Model 70 to my shoulder and slipped the safety off. The bead lay just above the buck's black muzzle, halfway below the level of his eyes. I remember thinking that the bullet should go out through the back of his neck, breaking the spinal cord. I fired, and instinctively chambered another shell.

The buck went down hard but out of sight. Then, what should have been a dead deer, was up and coming fast. He disappeared briefly into the deep cut of the drainage and then came galloping up over the bank. As he cleared the top of the bank ten yards away, the buck saw me in the open woods and let out a bellow of rage, unlike any sound I have ever heard before. He wheeled my way, lowered his head and charged.

My recollection of the next split seconds are blurred. I remember the feeling of my eyes popping wide, and something hit my chest which I think must have been my jaw. I know my gun came up without any conscious direction from me. I remember thinking "neck" and firing. I remember the great buck crashing to the ground. I know it was but four steps from where I stood to where he lay dead.

The buck was big—193 pounds dressed, with an eight-point rack 24 inches across the thick beams. My first shot had not gone out the back of his neck as planned but had deflected along the muzzle doing terrible damage to the deer's jaw but not touching any mortal spot.

The reason why the deer had charged became apparent a few moments after I began dressing him out. Suddenly the sound of breaking branches came from the thicket once more. Then a deer blew the shrieking, high-pitched blast that deer emit when signaling danger. A moment later he blew again, and once again I heard the cracking of branches.

Now the story became clear. My buck had been battling with another when I chanced upon him. When I had seen him pawing and sniffing, he was working up sufficient rage to reenter the battle with this second unseen buck. When I shot the buck in the face, he saw me as yet another adversary.

I had learned another characteristic of deer found in rarely hunted areas. Once a buck has grown to maturity there is no animal in the woods that he need fear, even man.

Gashes and a deep puncture wound in my deer's neck caused speculation about the size of the buck my deer had been fighting.

If my 193-pounder had placed second, what had that other deer looked like?

With my tag filled, I was relegated to bear hunting for the rest of the week, but Paul took up the hunt for my buck's challenger. Gene had seen plenty of sign upriver and wanted to stick with that area.

That night, snow came, and in the morning only fresh tracks could be seen. Gene, moving upriver, came upon a track heading for the water and followed it to the bank. There, standing on the opposite bank looking back, stood a six-point buck. One shot through the neck was all it took, and that deer was ready for a ride in the canoe.

Paul's chance came the last day. He had found big tracks in the area where I had shot my deer and felt sure he was on the trail of my deer's rival.

Paul slipped along the side of the low ridge above the river for more than an hour trying to get above the slowly traveling pair. He finally jumped them out of a heavy spruce thicket and a got a glimpse of the buck's gigantic rack. The cover was too thick for a shot, but true to the nature of deer in unhunted areas, these two ran for about a hundred yards and stopped, looking back.

Paul said he drew a careful aim just behind the buck's shoulder and squeezed one off. "It was a perfect shot," he groaned later back in camp. "If there hadn't been a tree in the way I'd have had that buck on the meatpole for sure."

A wilderness deer hunt is not for those who like to see lots of "flags." The three of us saw three good bucks and one doe in a week of hunting separately and hard. The deer are not concentrated in the big woods in November. You've got to hunt hard to find where a deer is moving, then stay with him until you can pinpoint his general location.

You may not see a deer at all on a hunt like this. Lady Luck is a fickle gal and often winks but looks the other way. Only one thing is certain when you hunt in lonely country: You can hunt the way you want to hunt, and if your efforts fail, at least you can be assured it was not because some other hunter spooked your deer away or killed him accidentally as you plotted your approach.

I DON'T WANT TO KILL A DEER

Ted Trueblood

We introduced Ted—as if he needed it!—back in Part One. This piece, from his Field & Stream *column and book* The Ted Trueblood Hunting Treasury *(McKay), has always been one of my favorites. Don't let the title fool you.!*

I DON'T WANT TO KILL A DEER. I haven't really wanted to kill a deer for years. Yet I go deer hunting every fall and have, I suppose, shot about as many of them as most other men my age. If these statements constitute a paradox, bear with me.

Consider October, the hunter's moon. The heat of summer is over. The September rains have washed the haze of August from the air, and frosty nights have brought the first dusting of gold to the white-barked aspens. In all the arid West, from the Coast Range to the eastern slope of the Rockies, the shimmering, lovely days of Indian summer have laid their spell upon the land.

The early harvest is finished, but the orchards are still flecked with the rich red of late apples. The voice of the cornfield has changed from the whisper of summer to the dry rustle of autumn. The stubble, from which the grain had long since been taken, has the look of fall about it, and the young cock pheasants that it harbors are rapidly acquiring the full glory of their adult plumage.

Everywhere, especially in the cool of evening, the rich, ripe fruity odors of the season lie heavily upon the air. Late-curing hay; grapes hanging purple from the vine; the rich earth, disturbed to yield its treasures; melons, frost-sweetened and dead ripe—all these and many others add their savor. And always, somewhere in the distance, an eager householder, unable to wait for the deluge of leaves that will come later, is burning the first sprinkling. The smoke, thin and clean, drifts low across the countryside. It adds spice to all the other mingled odors, seasoning them with the sure proof that this is, indeed, October.

At this time we go hunting. It is a tradition. Our preparations are made pleasant by memories of past trips and anticipation of the one ahead. We are going to hunt deer, not merely to kill them. The reward is in the hunt, but since there could be no hunting were there no deer, and since the logical culmination of any hunt must lie in securing its object, we will no doubt kill one.

Thus rifles and food and bedrolls and tent are loaded, and we drive away from the rich, green valley into the brown foothills and through them, winding always upward, into the home of the mule deer in October. Yellow pines stand majestically alone on the south slopes, their trunks brick red in the late sun. Aspens line the draws along the clear brooks that trickle down and make bright splashes of yellow among the dark firs on the north hillsides.

Camp is made, water carried from the little stream nearby, a fire kindled. Soon the heartening odors of good outdoor food and coffee mingle with the tang of the smoke that rises in a thin, straight column toward the earliest stars. We eat and loaf beside the embers and plan the morrow. This first evening, loaded with anticipation, is a real part of deer hunting, and we enjoy it to the fullest.

We will hunt a country we know well. It is always a challenge to explore a new area, but it is also rewarding to hunt where you know each ridge and valley, where every little bench and pocket holds its share of memories. Here beside this patch of timber I missed a big buck way back in 1936. With a forkhorn, two does, and two or three fawns he walked out of the thick cover just at sunset. He was very close, and I thought, "I'll shoot him in the neck," but, somehow, I missed. I saw the bullet kick up the dirt behind him, a little to one side, and before I could work the bolt he leaped back among the trees and disappeared.

And down the draw from this saddle is where another fine buck eluded us by running low along the bottom, screened by alders and aspens, until he was out of range. On this bench, several deer have fallen to our rifles during the years. And down the canyon below it, where alternate thickets vie with more open browse among the boulders on the hillsides, many fine bucks have rewarded us.

There are real, as well as sentimental, values in hunting a familiar country. You know where to look for deer that are trailing through on their annual migration from the high summer range to their lower wintering area. You know the pockets where they hide during the day. You know where to look for the resident deer that spent the summer here rather than higher in the mountains. And you have learned through experience the best way to approach all these places without alarming any game that might be in them.

The alarm rang at 4 o'clock. I crawled reluctantly out of the warm sleeping bag, touched a match to the fat-pine slivers in the little sheet-iron stove, lit the gasoline lantern, and dressed. Then I stepped outside. The snapping stars were so close I could almost touch them; not even the palest hint of gray showed in the east. There were slivers of ice in the water bucket. I slopped a little into the wash pan, and by the time I had applied it to face and hands no trace of sleepiness remained.

It is during these magic hours that a hunter has the best chance to see deer undisturbed in the open. In the early morning, usually not later than 8 o'clock, they gradually feed or wander into some tight and hard-to-approach thicket where they will spend the day. About sunset they emerge to feed again.

The grass was crisp underfoot as I walked along the bench east of camp. The mountain on my left loomed black against the northern sky, and since I couldn't possibly see a deer anyway, I hurried. I had about a mile to walk and I was chilly. I wore no coat because I knew it would be warm later, but now the air was sharp.

The eastern sky grew paler, and finally there was a hint of pink and saffron to give sure promise of approaching day. Individual trees became visible on the mountainside. I knew I'd soon be able to see a deer. I slowed down and attempted to walk quietly. The spot where I wanted to be at shooting time was just ahead.

Here a little stream came gurgling down out of the hills. Its drainage was a basin, perhaps a mile long and half that wide, divided into several draws and pockets, with steep ridges between. There were bare slopes and brushy ones, dense thickets and sparsely covered benches. It had everything—food, water, thick

] 227 [

cover, and shade. During migration the deer—which followed a course generally parallel to the river in the bottom of the valley and did most of their traveling at night along the open slopes facing it—turned into this basin to spend the day. Here, finding things to their liking, they sometimes loitered for a week or more if the weather remained pleasant.

I paused at the mouth of the basin to test the wind. It was perfect, a steady, downstream breeze. I crossed the brook and started slowly up the game trail a few yards above it on the other side. It was now light enough to shoot. I took a few careful steps, paused to examine everything in sight, took a few more steps, and paused again. I tried not to make a sound.

Time was when I hunted mule deer from the ridges. I could watch a big area and cover more ground. Later—and wiser—I came to favor walking up a valley. I can't see so much country, but what I can see, I see better. I have to hunt more carefully, but any deer I see is usually in range.

I moved slowly along, alternately watching and walking. The predawn chill, which my brisk walk across the flat had overcome, caught up with me again. Shivering, I hung my rifle over my shoulder and put my hands into my pockets to warm my fingers. The light grew stronger, and at last the sun touched the highest tip of the high ridge on the west.

I was looking at it, anticipating its warmth—though the best of the hunting would be over by the time the sunlight reached the bottom of the valley—when I saw a movement halfway up the slope. It was in sparse brush along the point of a ridge that came straight down toward me from the peak. On the right, on the north slope of this ridge was a dense stand of fir. On the left, extending toward the mouth of the little valley for several hundred yards, was a sparse stand of mixed snow brush, ninebark, and chokecherry, with clumps of bunch grass in the open spots.

The movement could have been made by a bird or a squirrel— or by the flick of an ear. I watched carefully but saw nothing more for several seconds. Then suddenly a deer stepped from behind a cherry bush. It was a long way up the slope. I raised my rifle slowly and looked at the animal through the scope. A doe. Does were not protected, but I had no desire to kill one, at least not this early in the hunt. Our best venison has always come from big bucks killed before the beginning of the rut.

I lowered my rifle and continued watching. Soon a second deer materialized, farther out in the brush. It was no bigger than the first, and I assumed that it was another doe or a small buck. Then, almost at the edge of the timber, a third deer stepped leisurely from behind a clump of ninebark, moving slowly toward the trees. Even before I could raise my rifle to look at him I knew he was the one I wanted. I could tell by his size and by the way he walked that he was a big buck. I got the scope up barely in time to get a glimpse of him before he disappeared. His rack was big; certainly each antler bore the four points of a mature mule-deer buck, and maybe more.

The chill was forgotten. I sat down in the game trail and watched the edge of the timber until the sunlight reached the bottom of the valley, hoping he would come out. He didn't. The two other deer, one a small buck, went in.

Thanks to having hunted here before, I didn't have to walk on up the valley and inspect that patch of timber to learn how big it was. I knew all about it. It covered 100 acres or so, from the top of the high ridge on the west to the creek in the bottom, and it ran from the crest of the hogback down into a ravine on the north. It was big enough to hide a hundred deer, and it would be impossible for a lone hunter to push any of them out—or get a shot if he did.

] 229 [

There were several things I might do. I could go on hunting and forget about the buck. I could continue up the creek and climb the hillside to inspect a bench north of the timber in the hope that the deer might have gone on through. I could, of course, work my way into the jungle and hope for the best.

None of these possibilities seemed very attractive. I felt sure that the little band of deer had gone into the timber to spend the day. When evening came they would emerge, and with luck I might be in the right spot waiting.

Back in camp by 9 o'clock, I cut some wood, started a stew that would be ready when my partner came, and looked around for any other odd jobs that needed doing. Twenty yards from the tent, the bench on which we were camped broke away sharply to the river bottom. I walked over and looked down at the river, sparkling among the cottonwoods. Its voice, muted by distance, rose and fell softly with the vagaries of the breeze.

The jobs didn't seem very important and the blanket of pine needles on the ground was soft. I decided to sit down in the mellow sunlight and look at things. I thought about the spots where the big buck was most likely to come out of the timber and wondered whether I should go fishing—the trout season was still open. And then I decided to sort of lie back on the needles for a minute or two and put my cap over my eyes.

My partner woke me when he came in. He had seen only tracks. We ate and discussed the possibility of getting a shot at the big buck in the evening. Two of us would have a better chance than one, since there were several spots where the three deer might emerge, either to feed or to continue their leisurely migration toward the winter range.

Northwest of the patch of timber was a low saddle over which deer often crossed into the drainage of the next creek. A hunter stationed here would also be able to watch the bench that bordered the timber on the north, a likely spot for them to feed in case they decided to loiter a few days in the little valley. If they intended to continue toward the winter range, however, they would be more likely to come out of the south side of the timber probably near the spot where I had seen them in the morning, and swing around the points of the ridges that dropped sharply down toward the river.

The high point above the timber, where I had been looking at the sunlight when I first saw them, was the apex of several ridges. The good browse bordering the timber extended around to the river slope in the pockets between the heads of the ridges. It would be worthwhile to watch those pockets.

We left camp in late afternoon, not retracing my path of the morning but walking up the next creek to the west. This way we could reach our chosen stations without forewarning the deer, because the breeze regularly drifted up each valley in the evening. When we were a little beyond the saddle, we climbed the hillside nearly to it. Here we separated. My companion would find a position from which he could watch the hillside, the bench on the other side, and the northern and western edges of the timber.

Gradually climbing higher, I angled back toward the southern point of the ridge, staying on the west side, opposite the timber. Eventually I reached a spot from which I could watch a couple of brushy pockets, above and just around the corner from the southern edge of the cover. I couldn't see the cover—I was afraid to go around because the upcanyon breeze might drift my scent into it—but any deer that came out should eventually wander into my view.

I had barely settled myself down to begin my vigil when I heard a shot. Just one. It was back where I had come from. It could be nobody but my companion, since there were no other hunters in the area, and one shot usually means a dead deer.

Instantly I was torn by indecision. Had he killed the big buck? Should I go back to help dress it or should I stay here? Was there any chance of the buck's coming out now, assuming he was still alive? Well, if I returned I certainly would not get a shot, whereas if I stayed I might. So I leaned back against the hillside with my rifle across my lap and devoted my attention to the pockets below me. They were partly floored with grass and partly grown up to several varieties of browse. I searched them minutely and, satisfied they were vacant, allowed my attention to drift off across the valley.

This was the magic hour, when the night creatures begin to stir and game feeds in the long twilight. Instead of the keen anticipation that I should have felt, however, the ordeal of holding still bore heavily upon me. I was assailed by doubt. I sat there quietly while the sunset blushed and faded.

Imperceptibly the shadows grew thicker; it would soon be too dark to shoot. For the thousandth time I began a careful examination of the two pockets below me. And there, suddenly in full view and close, stood the buck of the morning! How he had arrived unseen was a mystery, but of his presence there could be no doubt. Nor did I have any question as to his identity. He was magnificent.

He was standing broadside, but his head was turned slightly away and he appeared to be looking at something farther down the little basin, perhaps at another deer that I couldn't see in the deep shadows. Slowly, quietly I raised my rifle and eased off the safety, holding it with thumb and finger so that there would be no click.

Twenty-four hours earlier I had harbored no particular desire to kill deer. I would hunt, yes, but I was not anxious to kill a deer. Twelve hours earlier I had seen this buck, and immediately, as though ordered by some remote ancestor whose very life depended upon the hunt, I had devoted every faculty to bringing about this very moment. Now, partly because my planning had been sound, but to a much greater degree because the buck had been unlucky enough to come into the open at this particular place and time, I was about to kill him. Without thought, without an instant's hesitation, I centered the crosshairs on his gray neck and squeezed the trigger.

THREE

Camps, Campfires, and Great Hunts

PALACE IN THE POPPLE

John Madson

John Madson is back (see his piece in Part One) to kick off our section on hunting camps with this little piece of nostalgia.

As you'll see in the pages ahead, deer-hunting camps are special places for special people. I hope I'll always be the kind of guy who'll be welcome in yours.

It's a smoky, raunchy boars' nest
   With an unswept, draft floor
And pillowticking curtains
   And knife scars on the door.
The smell of a pine-knot fire
   From a stovepipe that's come loose
Mingles sweetly with the bootgrease
   And the Copenhagen house.

There are work-worn .30-30s
   With battered, steel-shod stocks
And drying lines of longjohns
   And of steaming, pungent socks.
There's a table for the Bloody Four
   And their game of two-card draw,
And there's deep and dreamless sleeping
   On bunk ticks stuffed with straw.

Jerry and Jake stand by the stove,
   Their gun-talk loud and hot,
And Bogie has drawn a pair of kings
   And is raking in the pot.
Frank's been drafted again as cook
   And is peeling some spuds for stew
While Bruce wanders by in baggy drawers
   Reciting "Dan McGrew."

] 235 [

No where on earth is fire so warm
    Nor coffee so infernal
Nor whiskers so stiff, jokes so rich,
    Nor hope blooming so eternal.
A man can live for a solid week
In the same old underbritches
And walk like a man and spit where he wants
    And scratch himself where he itches.

I tell you, boys, there's no place else
    Where I'd rather be, come fall,
Where I eat like a bear and sing like a wolf
    And feel like I'm bull-pine tall.
In that raunchy cabin out in the bush
    In the land of the raven and loon,
With a tracking snow lying new to the ground
    And the end of the rutting moon.

THE WHITETAIL CHALLENGE
Lew Dietz

*Lew Dietz is a New England writer of great skill and wide outdoor experi-
ence. But I've never seen his words shine brighter than in this moving portrait of his deer camp and the interesting friends who accompany him there.*

After the piece appeared in Yankee Magazine *originally, I liked it so
much that I urged* Outdoor Life's *publishers to allow me to break the magazine's long-standing policy of publishing only original pieces and present
the piece to our readers as a reprint.*

*From the reaction that occurred when the piece ran, it became apparent
that my decision was one of the best I ever made.*

AS I HAVE FOR OVER 40 YEARS, I went into Maine's north woods
for a deer hunt last fall. I left my car at Fort Kent on the Maine-
Canada border and made the final stage of the trip with my
friend Bart in his all-terrain vehicle.

The trek entailed making a loop into Canada and crossing back
into Maine, fording a swollen river in the process. The only other
access was even more difficult. It required a punishing 35-mile
push north from the Allagash over all but impassable abandoned
logging roads.

The reward was more than commensurate with the effort. For a
week I saw no tracks save those of game and those of my two-
legged friends. The hunters, friends, and friends of friends, ranged
in age from 20 to 70. There were fathers and sons, brothers and
cousins, and as different as people can be. What they had in common was the love of the hunt and a deep appreciation of the wilds
and the privilege of hunting in them.

Arnold Toynbee in his monumental work "A Study of History"
dismissed Maine and its people as relics of 17th-century New England. After associating with Maine hunters for half a century,
I've become reconciled to that judgment.

If we are persuaded by the increasingly common notion today
that hunters are dehumanized cretins without redeeming social
assets, my Maine gunning friends and trail companions must
qualify as anachronisms—characters misplaced in time.

I expect there are hunters here in Maine and elsewhere whom I would not choose as friends. But taken as a breed, I have found hunters to be both gentlemen and gentle men. The Maine men with whom I have shared the chase hunt as their fathers and grandfathers hunted, unabashedly for the love of it. Nor do they feel any need to defend their pleasure or to apologize for bearing arms in the pursuit of this ancestral blood sport.

I much doubt that I have been brutalized by my addiction to hunting or corrupted by my long association with hunting men. I find my interludes in the Big Woods restorative and cleansing. It is a form of escape, perhaps. We live in a neurotic time, beset by exploiters, wasters, and plunderers. A few brief days with men at ease with the wilderness and at peace with themselves is a healing respite.

Perhaps only in northern New England and in certain regions of the South has the lore and love of the hunt been passed on, father to son, for centuries. An understanding of the ethos of the hunt and a respect for it's unwritten code is a matter of tradition. The sad truth is that though a man can learn to use a gun in a few easy lessons, the skills and attitudes that make hunting a rewarding human experience are not so much acquired as instilled.

And as I hunted that week in November, it was borne in upon me that should the American tradition of hunting lapse, the last remnants of our wilderness would be doomed for lack of caring.

Jake, who with Bart owns the camp, had come in the day before with his son Sam and brother Will to open the place. It was Sunday, and the three were out cruising the territory for game sign when we arrived. They wandered in as we were stowing grub and gear.

Jake, a sly leprechaun of a fellow, said the deer were there but that they weren't moving much. However, he had seen a number of buck scrapings that indicated the rut had begun. Then as an afterthought he added, "Charlie's still here. Saw his track on the ridge road."

For men who have hunted a territory over the years, there is always a Charlie, a big and wise buck deer, a patriarch that has proved too smart for mere men. Needless to say, he left moose-size tracks. That, of course, was an exaggeration. Nor was there any way to be certain that the outsize spoor could be assigned to a single antlered behemoth. More friend than quarry, a Charlie is the all-but-obligatory myth savored and perpetuated by hunting men.

Bart smiled. "Hollis tells me he has Charlie figured out," he said. "He'll arrive Wednesday, and we shall see."

Hollis was Bart's brother-in-law, and of all the group perhaps the purest of hunters. Hollis was a figurer, a theoretician, with the patience and dedication to see his strategies through. For Hollis, though venison was a welcome by-product, hunting was an end in itself.

There would be nine or 10 hunters in the camp in the course of the week. I saw little of any of them in the interim between hunts. But men who share isolation even briefly tend to form lasting

] 239 [

friendships. Sharing a hunting camp is much like cruising in a small sailing vessel. The crew is bound by common interest, and each member of the crew contributes to the small community according to his talent. The difference is that a hunting camp is more loosely structured.

There was no need to assign tasks when the hunt began. The division of work long since had been established by custom. Jake, a compulsive neatener, saw to it that the floor was broom-clean, the dishrags hung to dry, the long table rid of crumbs. Bart, a relaxed and visceral fellow whose portly construction betrayed his love of food, was the cook. Each morning he would post his menu. Some of his creations were a bit exotic for common palates, but the crew could always count on steak on Friday and beanhole beans on Saturday. And, of course, deer liver and heart, served with onions and bacon, was an expected treat.

Early in my tenure I assumed the post of Bart's assistant, a job corresponding roughly to that of a cookee in a logging camp, the difference being that I was given to offering advice, solicited and otherwise, something a cookee would venture to do at the risk of his neck.

And there was the lugger of wood and the stoker of the fires. In our camp this job fell to George, a great, lumbering hulk of a man addicted to chewing on cold cigars. There is always the mother hen of the crowd, the benign spirit who remains up until the others are bedded down to see to it that the fires are banked, the kettle purring, and the lights extinguished. For us this was John. He had spent most of his life in the Maine woods as a walking boss for jumper operators, and his knowledge of the wilderness was rich and vast. John served also as our weather prognosticator. Once the lights were out, he would step out into the night in his longjohns to sniff the air and consult the sky, returning to announce to the quiet camp his forecast.

The dishwashing assignment was left open, and for good reason. Invariably there would be an eager young guest, usually a friend of a son of one of the coterie, who innocently would volunteer for this chore. The custom was to await the initiate's unwary offer. He was never denied the honor, and the job was his for the duration, or until such time as a compassionate regular would decide to spell or assist him.

I awoke the first morning of the hunt to the rich aroma of coffee and bacon in the making. At 4:30 Bart bellowed the logging camp exhortation.

"Roll out, you tigers! It's daylight in the swamp!"

For most men, putting on pants seems the logical way to start a morning. Bart would first put on his hunting hat, a green porkpie. He was making pancakes in his longjohns and slippers. Also, he was singing a snatch from a Puccini opera. Bart had once met Ezio Pinza.

"Today is the day I will meet Charlie," he announced. "I feel it in my Irish bones. Did I tell you Hollis has Charlie figured out?"

"Yes," I said, "you told me."

At the breakfast board plans were made for the day ahead. To a man, these were stillhunters who prided themselves not so much in their shooting as in the mastery of the arts that bring a hunter face to face with the quarry. Like the woodland Indians, from whom the early settlers learned the skills of the stalk, they preferred to succeed as hunters rather than shooters.

In the predawn, each man let it be known where he proposed to hunt that day. This knowledge could be critical in the event a hunter did not come in by several hours after dark. Jake said he'd try the Green Road, Will opted for the Swing Around Road, designations that would have no meaning beyond the group. Nor would Dodge City, the remains of an old logging camp, or Jackstraws, a bad piece of blowdown, mean anything to a stranger. And then there was Hank's Bend where some years before Hank LeBlanc had shot the biggest black bear ever seen in that country.

I chose Deer Boulevard, a whimsy of my own concoction. This was a quaggy, overgrown old logging haul road at the foot of the ridge, a territory that had been productive for me the year before. Like Hollis, I am a figurer. I need to be. I judge myself to be a good observer, adequate woodsman, fair hunter, but no more than a passable shot beyond a 100-yard range. Further, I tend to wool-gather, to permit my mind to wander from the business at hand, a habit that has been the salvation of many a deer.

Typically, a hunting week will break down into three parts. The initial days are devoted to investigation, to ranging over a wide area in an attempt to locate deer concentrations and ascertain patterns of deer movements. Usually by the third day each hunter has narrowed his target area, basing his decision on his observations. Ideally the climax should come on the final days of the hunt, the denouement satisfying the expectancy developed in the early stages of the drama.

All the proper elements were present on my first day as I cruised three miles of that old haul road. Near a cedar swamp, three miles from the camp, I came upon fresh droppings in assorted sizes that suggested a deer-bedding place was nearby. On the trek back I came upon the pawings of an extremely large buck. Charlie, or a reasonable facsimile, had scraped the soft earth in five or six places. Then, to make my day replete, I had a snatch-vision of a bear as it took off up the ridge.

The rewards of the hunt are many and various for those who relish the simple creature pleasures. There is the joy of coming in out of the cold to a warm fire, the easing out of boots with the prospect of being revivified with good whiskey and branch water. And, as the others wander in, there are experiences to exchange.

On this and other nights, the talk continued on into the early evening. Stories of other hunts were told and retold. The best relished were those of misadventures. Big George inexplicably had missed a deer at 30 paces. John had dozed off on a stump and awakened to find the tracks of a deer that had walked by him in the interim. By eight, the talk tapered off to desultory exchanges. One by one the hunters wandered off to hit the sack. It was nine when I crawled gratefully into my eiderdown womb. The last thing I heard that night was John coming in.

"We'll have rain by morning," he said.

And rain it did that next day, a gentle soaking rain that filled the brooks and made morasses of the trails.

The first kill was scored by Jake that day. He wandered into camp an hour after dark with liver and heart on a green stick.

After supper a few of us went out to help him bring in the kill.

"It sure ain't Charlie," Will said, as we hoisted it into the game tree.

Hunting maturity is not a matter of years. It comes with the developing of appreciation and understanding of the multitude of things that constitute the totality of nature. Lacking the naturalist's eye, a hunter is no more than an armed interloper in the wild domain. Jake's boy Sam had spent a good hour of that hunting day watching two otters at play. Bart's day was made when he sighted a wolf crossing over the ridge.

Hollis had arrived by the time we got in from the woods that next evening. He'd no more than stowed his gear than he was called upon to resolve an accumulation of troubles. Bart's rig had clutch problems. A lifelong farmer, Hollis was by necessity a good haywire mechanic. He listened to the symptoms and offered his diagnosis.

Then George told him of missing a deer at 30 paces. Hollis asked to see George's ammo clip. He discovered that the clip held rounds of the same bullet weight, but of different manufacture. "You should use the same brand cartridges that you used to sight in your rifle, George," he said. "I've found variance in brands of as much as eight inches at 100 yards."

Later I asked him about the rumor that he had Charlie figured out. Hollis smiled. "Let's say I have one thing figured out," he said. "Charlie rides the thermals."

Hollis proceeded to explain his thesis. "As you know," he said, "the thermal currents in the early morning flow downhill from the ridges to the lake. Along about eight, or almost the instant the sun touches the top of the ridge, he waits for the thermal to reverse so he can travel into it. If he's down in the back-growth, he'll be sure to get up the ridge before the thermal switches. But he doesn't travel directly into the wind, he quarters it. This gives him a larger green sector, or that part of the circle in which he's protected by his nose. This gives the hunter a smaller green sector, or that part of the circle in which he has a wind advantage. Of course, all deer are inclined to feed into the wind. But some deer are a bit careless at times. Charlie is never careless."

George rolled a cold cigar in his teeth.

"With you on his trail, Hollis," he said, "Charlie is going to need some advanced education. Let's all chip in and send Charlie to Yale. It's the sporting thing to do."

Hollis didn't see Charlie that next day, or any other deer, but John and Jake's son Sam scored with big bucks, both 10-pointers in the 250 to 270-pound range. Bart, who had decided on the second day out that the deer were feeding and bedding in the mixed growth, had his hunch confirmed on Thursday at high noon. He jumped three deer out of a fir thicket halfway up the ridge and downed the largest, an eight-pointer.

Time was running out for me, and for Will as well. We were going out Saturday morning with Sam. As the first days of a hunt are exploratory and the middle days concerned with site selection and the establishment of a modus operandi, the hunter in the final period tends to exercise his hunches or fall back on his more esoteric strategies.

Thursday night, Will felt his five days' worth of whiskers. "It's all very simple," he said. "Tomorrow I'll take a walk in the woods. I always see deer when I'm just taking a walk in the woods. The trouble with you, Hollis, is that you think deer when you hunt. If a dog can scent emotions and pick up thought waves, why can't a deer? I'm going to take a quiet walk in the woods and think about strawberry shortcake."

Matter of fact, Will did get his deer that next morning, though he couldn't for the life of him recall what had been on his mind at the moment of truth. I missed my big chance, and I do remember what was on my mind: I was undone by a partridge. I was sitting on a log in the still of the morning when the bird dropped into a spruce thicket behind me. I turned to watch him as he fussed about. When I turned back to the trail I was covering, there staring at me was the biggest buck deer I'd ever seen. Before I could swing my body around into position, he took one great arching leap and it was good-bye Charlie.

I went out with Sam and Will the next morning. The snow we all had been waiting for had begun to fall. We made it across the swollen river, but just barely, and only by employing the expedient of disengaging the Jeep's fan belt so it wouldn't throw water over the spark plugs.

A week later, I had a note from Bart. Hollis had shot his buck in the Jackstraws. It was a deer they estimated would go close to 300 pounds woods-dressed. "Hollis wants to assure you that it wasn't Charlie," he wrote.

Though I appreciated Hollis's reassurance, it wasn't necessary. For all of us Charlie would be there so long as that piece of wilderness we shared with him remained inviolate. To preserve the myth of his immortality was an article of faith, a putting off of the day when the last of wilderness would be civilized off the face of the earth.

TRUTHFUL SAM

Charley Dickey

Charley Dickey's byline has been one of the most frequently published in out-door magazines during the past thirty years for one simple reason: readers appreciate what he has to say.

Charley's range as a writer is great. He can tell you how to rig and fish and dropper fly in a way that will be clear and interesting; he can tell you about a dog that died in a way that will bring tears into your eyes.

This piece is taken from the full banquet of Dickey pieces; the book Backtrack *published by Amwell Press. If you don't already have the book, the reading of "Truthful Sam" will probably spur you into adding it to your library.*

DEAR SAM,

It is that time of year again! My husband is planning to spend a week at deer camp, the same as every fall. I have heard many wild stories about what goes on at these camps. Some are disturbing, so much so that I am not keen about my husband going. Could you please tell me the truth about life at a deer camp? Signed, Anxious.

Dear Ann,

I realize that certain wild rumors are circulated about hunting camps. It is really a mystery to me how they get started and exaggerated.

I hear from many deer widows each fall. For 40 years, I have hunted at camps all over America. The following is a truthful description of a typical deer lodge.

Various chores are divided among the hunters. For instance, one hunter, usually with a scientific background, is named nutritionist. His main duty is to insure a balanced diet so that general health is maintained. He makes sure there are leafy foods to provide bulk and an even balance of green and yellow vegetables along with a high-protein serving. Vitamin supplements, in moderate dosage, are available at each meal.

Although pack-in conditions may preclude fresh fruit juices and whole milk, adequate substitutes of concentrated juices and powdered milk are provided. Beverages containing high caffeine content, such as coffee and tea, are discouraged. Small amounts of alcohol are permitted, but only for medicinal purposes. For instance, a hunter may arrive back at camp with aching calf muscles. The alcohol is massaged into the legs much like a linament to increase circulation and relieve tense muscles.

A few camps may allow moderate amounts of wine but this is strictly for cooking. For instance, two or three tablespoons of red wine may be added to venison a couple of minutes before serving. As you know, cooking removes the alcohol content. In essence, wine is used only as a flavoring.

Of course, there is no need for cocktails such as martinis or Manhattans. The daily exercise in the stimulating fresh air, the rejuvenation of the spirit by communing with nature, and the relief from normal urban tensions all dispel the desire for relaxants. The thought of a cocktail simply never occurs to a deer hunter.

Although the routines at different camps may vary, here is a typical schedule. At 4:00 a.m., the nutritionist quietly arises and begins preparing a wholesome breakfast. At 4:30 a.m., the physical culture instructor gently awakens everyone. He then leads the group through 30 minutes of stretching and bending exercises to condition the muscles and joints for the morning hiking.

Following the yoga-like exercises, the chaplain of the day reads a spiritual paragraph or two which is appropriate for all religions. This is followed by 10 minutes of silent meditation; each hunter is free to let his spirit roam and dwell on metaphysical thoughts.

Breakfast is leisurely partaken. There is no need to rush. The early awakening each morning insures a calm atmosphere. It is still an hour before sunrise and each hunter has time to shave and thoroughly brush his teeth.

Naturally, the terrain, cover, and general hunting conditions determine whether the hunters stay out all day or return to camp about noon. There is often a joyful contest to see who will get back first, the winner having the privilege of tidying up the camp.

Following grace, a light luncheon is served. Perhaps 15 to 30 minutes are spent in a group discussion of what wildflowers or unusual songbirds were seen during the morning hunt. The hunters then take a quiet siesta, refreshing their minds and bodies for the afternoon hunt.

As the men return to camp near dusk, they compete in a spirit of good humor to see who will have the honor of doing the most difficult chores, such as cutting firewood. When all work is completed in preparation for the next day, there is a devotional period. The hunters sit in a circle and each relates his most gratifying spiritual experience of the day.

After a strenuous day in the great outdoors, the men are ravenous. If there is one small criticism of deer camps, it is that sometimes grace is overly long. Dinner is a relaxed time of good-natured banter, the men relating humorous incidents of the day or those of other years.

Cleanliness is next to godliness at deer camps. It is an inflexible tradition. After the dishes are sanitized, the men retire to a nearby creek where they plunge in, no matter how cold the water, to bathe. In extremely inclement weather, it may be necessary to heat water in a tub for a sponge bath, but the hunters always cheerfully make do with what they have.

To me, the most pleasant part of the day seems to spring up spontaneously. Someone will begin to hum an old spiritual and in a moment he will be joined by another. A clear tenor picks up with the words and is quickly joined by a baritone. A deep bass comes in with the bum, bums and suddenly the camp bursts into song as everyone joins in.

What joyous times these are as the merry men sing "Tenting Tonight" and "It's a Long Way to Tipperary!" They gloriously go through their repertoires of Gay Nineties songs and the popular favorites of the Big Band days. You wish that it would go on all night but everyone realizes there is a long morrow ahead. The tenor leads into "God Bless America" and the rafters fairly come out of their sockets.

The farewell chorus of the evening is alway s "Swing Low, Sweet Chariot." The chaplain reads a bit of inspirational poetry and the hunters bid each other sweet dreams and climb quietly into their bunks. In a few moments, all is quiet except for gently snoring as the men sleep to restore their weary bodies.

Ann, you need have no worries about your husband at a deer camp. This is a typical day at any camp. Signed, Truthful Sam.

MISTER HOWARD WAS A REAL GENT

Robert C. Ruark

Readers who purchased my previous Amwell volume, The Bobwhite Quail Book, *will hopefully stifle their yawns when I repeat some insight into Robert Ruark's career that I covered in introducing his piece, "The Brave Quail."*

The quail piece, and others to follow, marked the beginning of Ruark's relationship with Field & Stream *in the early fifties. The magazine began running his "The Old Man and the Boy" column in 1952. The event had significance beyond the reward it brought to* Field & Stream *readers, for the column enabled Ruark to free himself from his newspaper writing chores and concentrate on his first successful novel,* Something of Value. *After that, he was off and winging with three other novels and scores of magazine pieces before his untimely death at age 50.*

The pieces from the "Old Man and the Boy" series have been collected into two books published by Henry Holt and Company, New York. They are The Old Man and the Boy *and* The Old Man's Boy Grows Older.

This excerpt is from the first volume and originally was a two-parter when it ran as a column in Field & Stream.

This superb portrait of a deer hunt is one of my all-time favorite pieces of outdoor writing. I find that it has depths and layers of feeling that are constantly worth rediscovering when I take the book down from the shelf every year or so.

THE WEEK BEFORE THANKSGIVING that year, one of the Old Man's best buddies came down from Maryland to spend a piece with the family, and I liked him a whole lot right from the start. Probably it was because he looked like the Old Man—ragged mustache, smoked a pipe, built sort of solid, and he treated me like I was grown up too. He was interested in 'most everything I was doing, and he admired my shotgun, and he told me a whole lot about the dogs and horses he had up on his big farm outside of Baltimore.

He and the Old Man had been friends for a whole lot of years, they had been all over the world, and they were always sitting out on the front porch, smoking and laughing quiet together over some devilment they'd been up to before I was born. I noticed they always shut up pretty quick when Miss Lottie, who was my grandma, showed up on the scene. Sometimes, when they'd come back from walking down by the river, I could smell a little ripe aroma around them that smelled an awful lot like the stuff that the Old Man kept in his room to keep the chills off him. The Old Man's friend was named Mister Howard.

They were planning to pack up the dogs and guns and a tent and go off on a camping trip for a whole week, 'way into the woods behind Allen's Creek, about fifteen miles from town. They talked about it for days, fussing around with cooking gear, and going to the store to pick up this and that, and laying out clothes. They never said a word to me; they acted as if I wasn't there at all. I was very good all the time. I never spoke at the table unless I was spoken to, and I never asked for more than I ate, and I kept pretty clean and neat, for me. My tongue was hanging out, like a thirsty hound dog's. One day I couldn't stand it any longer.

"I want to go too," I said. "You promised last summer you'd take me camping if I behaved myself and quit stealing your cigars and didn't get drowned and—"

"What do you think, Ned?" Mister Howard asked the Old Man. "Think we could use him around the camp, to do the chores and go for water and such as that?"

"I dunno," the Old Man said. "He'd probably be an awful nuisance. Probably get lost and we'd have to go look for him, or shoot one of us thinking we were a deer, or get sick or bust a leg or something. He's always breaking something. Man can't read his paper around here for the sound of snapping bones."

"Oh, hell, Ned," Mister Howard said, "let's take him. Maybe we can teach him a couple of things. We can always get Tom or Pete to run him back in the flivver, if he don't behave."

"Well," the Old Man said, grinning, "I'd sort of planned to fetch him along all along, but I was waiting to see how long it'd take him to ask."

We crowded a lot of stuff into that old tin Liz. Mister Howard and the Old Man and me and two bird dogs and two hound dogs

and a sort of fice dog who was death on squirrels and a big springer spaniel who was death on ducks. Then there were Tom and Pete, two kind of half-Indian backwoods boys who divided their year into four parts. They fished in the summer and hunted in the fall. They made corn liquor in the winter and drank it up in the spring. They were big, dark, lean men, very quiet and strong. Both of them always wore hip boots, in the town and in the woods, on the water or in their own back yards. Both of them worked for the Old Man when the fishing season was on and the pogies were running in big, red, fatbacked schools. They knew just about everything about dogs and woods and water and game that I wanted to know.

The back seat was full of dogs and people and cooking stuff and guns. There were a couple of tents strapped on top of the Liz, a big one and a small one. That old tin can sounded like a boiler factory when we ran over the bumps in the corduroy clay road. I didn't say anything as we rode along. I was much too excited; and anyhow, I figured they might decide to send me back home.

It took us a couple of hours of bumping through the long, yellow savannah-land hills before we came up to a big pond, about five hundred yards from a swamp, or branch, with a clear creek running through it. We drove the flivver up under a group of three big water oaks and parked her. The Old Man had camped there lots before, he said. There was a cleared-out space of clean ground about fifty yards square between the trees and the branch. And there was a small fireplace, or what had been a small fireplace, of big stones. They were scattered around now, all over the place. A flock of tin cans and some old bottles and such had been tossed off in the bush.

"Damned tourists," the Old Man muttered, unloading some tin pots and pans from the back of the car. "Come in here to a man's best place and leave it looking like a hogwallow. You, son, go pick up those cans and bury them some place out of my sight. Then come back here and help with the tents."

By the time I finished collecting the mess and burying it, the men had the tents laid out flat on the ground, the flaps fronting south, because there was a pretty stiff northerly wind working, and facing in the direction of the pond. Tom crawled under the canvas with one pole and a rope, and Pete lifted the front end with another pole and the other end of the rope. Mister Howard was behind with the end of Tom's rope and a peg and a maul. The Old Man was at the front with the end of Pete's rope and another stake and maul. The boys in the tent gave a heave, set the posts, and the two old men hauled taut on the ropes and took a couple of turns around the pegs.

The tent hung there like a blanket on a clothesline until Tom and Pete scuttled out and pegged her out stiff and taut from the sides. They pounded the pegs deep into the dirt, so that the lines around the notches were clean into the earth. It was a simple tent, just a canvas V with flaps fore and aft, but enough to keep the wet out. The other one went up the same way.

We didn't have any bedrolls in those days, or cots either. The Old Man gave me a hatchet and sent me off to chop the branches of the longleaf pine saplings that grew all around—big green needles a foot and a half long. While I was gone he cut eight pine stakes off an old stump, getting a two-foot stake every time he slivered off the stump, and then he cut four long oak saplings. He hammered the stakes into the ground inside the tent until he had a wide rectangle about six by eight feet. Then he split the tops of the stakes. He wedged two saplings into the stakes lengthwise, jamming them with the flat of the ax, and then he jammed two shorter saplings into the others, crosswise. He took four short lengths of heavy fishing cord and tied the saplings to the stakes, at each of the four corners, until he had a framework, six inches off the ground.

"Gimme those pine boughs," he said to me, "and go fetch more until I tell you to stop."

The Old Man took the fresh-cut pine branches, the resin still oozing stickily off the bright yellow slashes, and started shingling them, butt to the ground. He overlapped the needles like shingles on a house, always with the leaf end up and the branch end down to the ground. It took him about fifteen minutes, but when he finished he had a six-by-eight mattress of the spicy-smelling pine boughs. Then he took a length of canvas tarpaulin and arranged it neatly over the top. There were little grommet holes in each of the four corners, and he pegged the canvas tight over the tops of the saplings that confined the pine boughs. When he was through, you could hit it with your hand and it was springy but firm.

"That's a better mattress than your grandma's got," the Old Man said, grinning over his shoulder as he hit the last lick with the ax. "All it needs is one blanket under you and one over you. You're off the ground, and dry as a bone, with pine needles to smell while you dream. It's just big enough for two men and a boy. The boy gets to sleep in the middle, and he better not thrash around and snore."

By the time he was through and I had spread the blankets, Tom and Pete had made themselves a bed in the other tent, just the same way. The whole operation didn't take half an hour from stopping the car until both tents and beds were ready.

While we were building the beds Mister Howard had strung a line between a couple of trees and had tied a loop in the long leash of each dog, running the loop around the rope between the trees and jamming it with a square knot. The dogs had plenty of room to move in, but not enough to tangle up with each other, and not enough to start to fight when they got fed. They had just room enough between each dog to be sociable and growl at each other without starting a big rumpus. Pretty soon they quit growling and lay down quietly.

We had two big canvas water bags tied to the front of the flivver, and the Old Man gestured at them. "Boys have to handle the water detail in a man's camp," he said. "Go on down to the branch and fill 'em up at that little spillway. Don't roil up the water. Just stretch the necks and let the water run into the bags."

I walked down through the short yellow grass and the sparkleberry bushes to the branch, where you could hear the stream making little chuckling noises as it burbled over the rocks in its sandy bed. It was clear, brown water, and smelled a little like the crushed ferns and the wet brown leaves around it and in it. When I got back, I could hear the sound of axes off in a scrub-oak thicket, where Tom and Pete had gone to gather wood. Mister Howard was sorting out the guns, and the Old Man was puttering around with the stones where the fire marks were. He didn't look up.

"Take the hatchet and go chop me some kindling off that lightered-knot stump," he said. "Cut 'em small, and try not to hit a knot and chop off a foot. Won't need much, 'bout an armful."

When I got back with kindling, Tom and Pete were coming out of the scrub-oak thicket with huge, heaping armfuls of old dead branches and little logs as big as your leg. They stacked them neatly at a respectable distance from where the Old Man had just about finished his oven. It wasn't much of an oven—just three sides of stones, with one end open and a few stones at intervals in the middle. I dumped the kindling down by him, and he scruffed up an old newspaper and rigged the fat pine on top, in a little sharp-pointed tepee over the crumpled paper.

He put some small sticks of scrubby oak crisscross over the fat pine, and then laid four small logs, their ends pointing in to each other until they made a cross, over the stones and over the little wigwam of kindling he had erected. Then he touched a match to the paper, and it went up in a poof. The blaze licked into the resiny lightwood, which roared and crackled into flame, soaring in yellow spurts up to the other, stouter kindling and running eager tongues around the lips of the logs. In five minutes it was roaring, reflecting bright red against the stones.

The Old Man got up and kicked his feet out to get the cramp out of his knees. It was just on late dusk. The sun had gone down, red over the hill, and the night chill was coming. You could see the fog rising in snaking wreaths out of the branch. The frogs were beginning to talk, and the night birds were stirring down at the edge of the swamp. A whippoorwill tuned up.

" 'Bout time we had a little snort, Howard," the Old Man said. "It's going to be chilly. Pete! Fetch the jug!"

Pete ducked into his tent and came out with a half-gallon jug of brown corn liquor. Tom produced four tin cups from the nest of cooking utensils at the foot of the tree on which they had hung the water bags, and each man poured a half-measure of the whiskey into his cup. I reckoned there must have been at least half a pint in each cup. Tom got one of the water bags and tipped it into the whiskey until each man said, "Whoa." They drank and sighed. The Old Man cocked an eye at me and said, "This is for when you're bigger."

They had another drink before the fire had burned down to coal, with either Tom or Pete getting up to push the burning ends of the logs closer together. When they had a solid bed of coal glowing in the center of the stones, the Old Man heaved himself up and busied himself with a frying pan and some paper packages. He stuck a coffee pot off to one side, laid out five tin plates, dribbled coffee into the pot, hollered for me to fetch some water to pour into the pot, started carving up a loaf of bread, and slapped some big thick slices of ham into the frying pan.

When the ham was done, he put the slices, one by one, into the tin plates, which had warmed through from the fire, and laid slices of bread into the bubbling ham grease. Then he broke egg after egg onto the bread, stirred the whole mess into a thick bread-egg-and-ham-grease omelet, chopped the omelet into sections, and plumped each section onto a slice of ham. He poured the steaming coffee into cups, jerked his thumb at a can of condensed milk and a paper bag of sugar, and announced that dinner was served.

He had to cook the same mess three more times and refill the coffee pot before we quit eating. It was black dark, with no moon, when we lay back in front of the fire. The owls were talking over the whippoorwills, and the frogs were making an awful fuss.

The Old Man gestured at me. "Take the dirty dishes and the pans down to the branch and wash 'em," he said. "Do it now, before the grease sets. You won't need soap. Use sand. Better take a flashlight, and look out for snakes."

I was scared to go down there by myself, through that long stretch of grass and trees leading to the swamp, but I would have died before admitting it. The trees made all sorts of funny ghostly figures, and the noises were louder. When I got back, Mister Howard was feeding the dogs and the Old Man had pushed more logs on the fire.

"You better go to bed, son," the Old Man said. "Turn in in the middle. We'll be up early in the morning, and maybe get us a turkey."

I pulled off my shoes and crawled under the blanket. I heard the owl hoot again and the low mutter from the men, giant black shapes sitting before the fire. The pine-needle mattress smelled wonderful under me, and the blankets were warm. The fire pushed its heat into the tent, and I was as full of food as a tick. Just before I died I figured that tomorrow had to be heaven.

It was awful cold when the Old Man hit me a lick in the ribs with his elbow and said, "Get up, boy, and fix that fire." The stars were still up, frosty in the sky, and a wind was whistling round the corners of the tent. You could see the fire flicker just a mite against the black background of the swamp. Mister Howard was still snoring on his side of the pine-needle-canvas bed, and I remember that his mustache was riffling, like marsh grass in the wind. Over in Tom and Pete's tent you could hear two breeds of snores. One was squeaky, and the other sounded like a bull caught in a bob-wire fence. I crawled out from under the covers, shivering, and jumped into my hunting boots, which were stiff and very cold. Everything else I owned I'd slept in.

The fire was pretty feeble. It had simmered down into gray ash, which was swirling loosely in the morning breeze. There was just a little red eye blinking underneath the fine talcumy ashes. After kicking some of the ashes aside with my boot, I put a couple of lightwood knots on top of the little chunk of glowing coal, and then I dragged some live-oak logs over the top of the lightwood and waited for her to catch. She caught, and the tiny teeth of flame opened wide to eat the oak. In five minutes I had a blaze going, and I was practically in it. It was mean cold that morning.

When the Old Man saw the fire dancing, he woke up Mister Howard and reached for his pipe first and his boots next. Then he reached for the bottle and poured himself a dram in a tin cup. He shuddered some when the dram went down.

"I heartily disapprove of drinking in the morning," he said. "Except some mornings. It takes a man past sixty to know whether he can handle his liquor good enough to take a nip in the morning. Howard?"

"I'm past sixty too," Mister Howard said. "Pass the jug."

Tom and Pete were coming out of the other tent, digging their knuckles into sleepy eyes. Pete went down to the branch and fetched a bucket of water, and everybody washed their faces out of the bucket. Then Pete went to the fire and slapped some ham into the pan and some eggs into the skillet, set some bread to toasting, and put the coffee pot on. Breakfast didn't take long. We had things to do that day .

After the second cup of coffee—I can still taste that coffee, with the condensed milk sweet and curdled on the top and the coffee itself tasting of branch water and wood smoke—we got up and started sorting out the guns.

"This is a buckshot day," the Old Man said, squinting down the barrel of his pump gun. "I think we better get us a deer today. Need meat in the camp, and maybe we can blood the boy. Tom, Pete, you all drive the branch. Howard, we'll put the boy on a stand where a buck is apt to amble by, and then you and I will kind of drift around according to where the noise seems headed. One, t'other of us ought to get a buck. This crick is populous with deer."

The Old Man paused to light his pipe, and then he turned around and pointed the stem at me.

"You boy," he said. "By this time you know a lot about guns, but you don't know a lot about guns and deer together. Many a man loses his wits when he sees a big ol' buck bust out of the bushes with a rockin' chair on his head. Trained hunters shoot each other. They get overexcited and just bang away into the bushes. *Mind* what I say. A deer ain't a deer unless it's got horns on its head and you can see all of it at once. We don't shoot does and we don't shoot spike bucks and we don't shoot each other. There ain't no sense to shootin' a doe or a young'un. One buck can service hundreds of does, and one doe will breed you a mess of deer. If you shoot a young'un, you haven't got much meat, and no horns at all, and you've kept him from breedin' to make more deer for you to shoot. If you shoot a man, they'll likely hang you, and if the man is me I will be awful gol-damned annoyed and come back to ha'nt you. You mind that gun, and don't pull a trigger until you can see what it is and *where* it is. *Mind*, I say."

Tom and Pete picked up their pump guns and loaded them. They pushed the load lever down so there'd be no shell in the chamber, but only in the magazine. The Old Man looked at my little gun and said, "Don't bother to load it until you get on the stand. You ain't likely to see anything to shoot for an hour or so."

Tom and Pete went over to where we had the dogs tethered on a line strung between two trees, and he unleashed the two hounds, Bell and Blue. Bell was black-and-tan and all hound. Blue was a kind of a sort of dog. He had some plain hound, some Walker hound, and some bulldog and a little beagle and a smidgen of pointer in him. He was ticked blue and brown and black and yellow and white. He looked as if somebody spilled the eggs on the checkered tablecloth. But he was a mighty dandy deer dog, or so they said. Old Sam Watts, across the street, used to say there wasn't no use trying to tell Blue anything, because Blue had done forgot more than you knew and just got annoyed when you tried to tell him his business.

Tom snapped a short lead on Blue, and Pete snapped another

one on Bell. They shouldered their guns and headed up the branch, against the wind. We let 'em walk, while the Old Man and Mister Howard puttered around, like old people and most women will. Drives a boy crazy. What I wanted to do was go and shoot myself a deer. *Now.*

After about ten minutes the Old Man picked up his gun and said, "Let's go." We walked about half a mile down the swamp's edge. The light had come now, lemon-colored, and the fox squirrels were beginning to chase each other through the gum trees. We spied one old possum in a persimmon tree, hunched into a ball and making out like nobody knew he was there. We heard a turkey gobble away over yonder somewheres, and we could hear the doves beginning to moan—*oooh*—*oohoo*—*oooooh*.

All the little birds started to squeak and chirp and twitter at each other. The dew was staunchly stiff on the grass and on the sparkleberry and gallberry bushes. It was still cold, but getting warmer, and breakfast had settled down real sturdy in my stomach. Rabbits jumped out from under our feet. We stepped smack onto a covey of quail just working its way out of the swamp, and they like to have scared me to death when they busted up under our feet. There was a lot going on in that swamp that morning.

We turned into the branch finally, and came up to a track that the Old Man said was a deer run. He looked around and spied a stump off to one side, hidden by a tangle of dead brush. From the stump you could see clear for about fifty yards in a sort of accidental arena.

"Go sit on that stump, boy," the Old Man said. "You'll hear the dogs after a while, and if a deer comes down this branch he'll probably bust out there, where that trail comes into the open, because there ain't any other way he can cross it without leaving the swamp. Don't let the dogs fool you into not paying attention. When you hear 'em a mile away, the chances are that deer will be right in your lap. Sometimes they travel as much as two miles ahead of the dogs, just slipping along, not running; just slipping and sneaking on their little old quiet toes. And stay still. A deer'll run right over you if you stay still and the smell is away from him.

But if you wink an eye, he can see it two hundred yards off, and will go the other way."

I sat down on the stump. The Old Man and Mister Howard went off, and I could hear them chatting quietly as they disappeared. I looked all around me. Nothing much was going on now, except a couple of he-squirrels were having a whale of a fight over my head, racing across branches and snarling squirrel cuss words at each other. A chickadee was standing on its head in a bush and making chickadee noises. A redheaded woodpecker was trying to cut a live-oak trunk in half with his bill. A rain crow—a kind of cuckoo, it is—was making dismal noises off behind me in the swamp, and a big old yellowhammer was swooping and dipping from tree to tree.

There were some robins hopping around on a patch of burnt ground, making conversation with each other. Crows were cawing, and two doves looped in to sit in a tree and chuckle at each other. A towhee was scratching and making more noise than a herd of turkeys, and some catbirds were meowing in the low bush while a big, sassy old mocker was imitating them kind of sarcastically. Anybody who says woods are quiet is crazy. You learn how to listen. The Tower of Babel was a study period alongside of woods in the early morning.

It is wonderful to smell the morning. Anybody who's been around the woods knows that morning smells one way, high noon another, dusk still another, and night most different of all, if only because the skunks smell louder at night. Morning smells fresh and flowery and little-breezy, and dewy and spanking new. Noon smells hot and a little dusty and sort of sleepy, when the breeze has died and the heads begin to droop and anything with any sense goes off into the shade to take a nap. Dusk smells scary. It is getting colder and everybody is going home tired for the day, and you can smell the turpentine scars on the trees and the burnt-off ground and the bruised ferns and the rising wind. You can hear the folding-up, I'm-finished-for-the-day sounds all around, including the colored boys whistling to prove they ain't scared when they drive the cows home. And in the night you can smell the fire and the warm blankets and the coffee a-boil, and you can even smell the stars. I know that sounds silly, but on a cool, clear, frosty night the stars have a smell, or so it seems when you are young and acutely conscious of everything bigger than a chigger.

This was as nice a smelling morning as I can remember. It smelled like it was going to work into a real fine-smelling day. The sun was up pretty high now and was beginning to warm the world. The dew was starting to dry, because the grass wasn't clear wet any more but just had little drops on top, like a kid with a runny nose. I sat on the stump for about a half-hour, and then I heard the dogs start, a mile or more down the swamp. Bell picked up the trail first, and she sounded as if church had opened for business. Then Blue came in behind her, loud as an organ, their two voices blending—fading sometimes, getting stronger, changing direction always.

Maybe you never heard a hound in the woods on a frosty fall morning, with the breeze light, the sun heating up in the sky, and the "aweful" expectancy that something big was going to happen to you. There aren't many things like it. When the baying gets closer and closer and still closer to you, you feel as if maybe you're going to explode if something doesn't happen quick. And when the direction changes and the dogs begin to fade, you feel so sick you want to throw up.

But Bell and Blue held the scent firmly now, and the belling was clear and steady. The deer was moving steady and straight, not trying to circle and fool the dogs, but honestly running. And the noise was coming straight down the branch, with me on the other end of it.

The dogs had come so close that you could hear them panting between their bays, and once or twice one of them quit sounding and broke into a yip-yap of barks. I thought I could hear a little tippety-tappety noise ahead of them, in between the belling and the barking, like mice running through paper or a rabbit hopping through dry leaves. I kept my eyes pinned onto where the deer path opened into the clearing. The dogs were so close that I could hear them crash.

All of a sudden there was a flash of brown and two does, flop-eared, with two half-grown fawns skipped out of the brush, stopped dead in front of me, looked me smack in the face, and then gave a tremendous leap that carried them halfway across the clearing. They bounced again, white tails carried high, and disappeared into the branch behind me. As I turned to watch them go there was another crash ahead and the buck tore through the clearing like a race horse. He wasn't jumping. This boy was running like the wind, with his horns laid back against his spine and his ears pinned by the breeze he was making. The dogs were right behind him. He had held back to tease the dogs into letting his family get a start, and now that they were out of the way he was pouring on the coal and heading for home.

I had a gun with me and the gun was loaded. I suppose it would have fired if the thought had occurred to me to pull the trigger. The thought never occurred. I just watched that big buck deer run, with my mouth open and my eyes popped out of my head.

The dogs tore out of the bush behind the buck, baying out their brains and covering the ground in leaps. Old Blue looked at me as he flashed past and curled his lip. He looked as if he were saying, "This is man's work, and what is a boy doing here, spoiling my labor?" Then he dived into the bush behind the buck.

I sat there on the stump and began to shake and tremble. About five minutes later there was one shot, a quarter-mile down the swamp. I sat on the stump. In about half an hour Tom and Pete came up to my clearing.

"What happened to the buck?" Pete said. "Didn't he come past here? I thought I was going to run him right over you."

"He came past, all right," I said, feeling sick-mean, "but I never shot. I never even thought about it until he was gone. I reckon you all ain't ever going to take me along any more." My lip was shaking and now I *was* about to cry.

Tom walked over and hit me on top of the head with the flat of his hand. "Happens to everybody," he said. "Grown men and boys, both, they all get buck fever. Got to do it once before you get over it. Forget it. I seen Pete here shoot five times at a buck big as a horse last year, and missed him with all five."

There were some footsteps in the branch where the deer had

disappeared, and in a minute Mister Howard and the Old Man came out, with the dogs leashed and panting.

"Missed him clean," the Old Man said cheerfully. "Had one whack at him no farther'n thirty yards and missed him slick as a whistle. That's the way it is, but there's always tomorrow. Let's us go shoot some squirrels for the pot, and we'll rest the dogs and try again this evenin'. You *see* him, boy?"

"I *saw* him," I said. "And I ain't ever going to *forget* him."

We went back to camp and tied up the hounds. We unleashed the fice dog, Jackie, the little sort of yellow fox terrier kind of nothing dog with prick ears and a sharp fox's face and a thick tail that curved up over his back. I was going with Pete to shoot some squirrels while the old gentlemen polished up the camp, rested, took a couple of drinks, and started to prepare lunch. It was pretty late in the morning for squirrel hunting, but this swamp wasn't hunted much. While I had been on the deer stand that morning the swamp was alive with them—mostly big fox squirrels, huge old fellers with a lot of black on their gray-and-white hides.

"See you don't get squirrel fever," the Old Man hollered over his shoulder as Pete and I went down to the swamp. "Else we'll all starve to death. I'm about fresh out of ham and eggs."

"Don't pay no 'tention to him, son," Pete told me. "He's a great kidder."

"Hell with him," I said. "He missed the deer, didn't he? At least *I* didn't miss him."

"That's right," Pete agreed genially. "You got to shoot at 'em to miss 'em."

I looked quick and sharp at Pete. He didn't seem to be teasing me. A cigarette was hanging off the corner of his lip, and his lean, brown, Injun-looking face was completely straight. Then we heard Jackie, yip-yapping in a querulous bark, as if somebody had just insulted him by calling him a dog.

"Jackie done treed hisself a squirrel," Pete said. "Advantage of a dog like Jackie is that when the squirrels all come down to the ground to feed, ol' Jackie rousts 'em up and makes 'em head for

the trees. Then he makes so much noise he keeps the squirrel interested while we go up and wallop away at him. Takes two men
to hunt squirrels this way. Jackie barks. I go around to the other
side of the tree. Squirrel sees me and moves. That's when you
shoot him, when he slides around on your side. Gimme your gun."

"Why?" I asked. "What'll I use to shoot the—"

"*Mine,*" Pete answered. "You ain't going to stand there and tell
me you're gonna use a shotgun on a squirrel? Anybody can hit a
pore little squirrel with a shotgun. Besides, shotgun shells cost a
nickel apiece."

I noticed Pete's gun for the first time. He had left his pump gun
in camp and had a little bolt-action .22. He took my shotgun from
me and handed me the .22 and a handful of cartridges.

" 'Nother thing you ought to know," Pete said as we walked up
to the tree, a big blue gum under which Jackie seemed to be going
mad, "is that when you're hunting for the pot you don't belong to
make much more noise with guns than is necessary. You go
booming off a shotgun, blim-blam, and you spook ever'thing in
the neighborhood. A .22 don't make no more noise than a stick
crackin', and agin the wind you can't hear it more'n a hundred
yards or thereabouts. Best meat gun in the world, a straight-
shootin' .22, because it don't make no noise and don't spoil the
meat. Look up yonder, on the fourth fork. There's your dinner. A
big ol' fox squirrel, near-about black all over."

The squirrel was pasted to the side of the tree. Pete walked
around, and the squirrel moved with him. When Pete was on the
other side, making quite a lot of noise, the squirrel shifted back
around to my side. He was peeping at Pete, but his shoulders and
back and hind legs were on my side. I raised the little .22 and
plugged him between the shoulders. He came down like a sack of
rocks. Jackie made a dash for him, grabbed him by the back,
shook him once and broke his spine, and sort of spit him out on
the ground. The squirrel was dang near as big as Jackie.

Pete and I hunted squirrels for an hour or so, and altogether we
shot ten. Pete said that was enough for five people for a couple of
meals, and there wasn't no sense to shootin' if the meat had to
spoil. "We'll have us some venison by tomorrow, anyways," he

said. "One of us is bound to git one. You shot real nice with that little bitty gun," he said. "She'll go where you hold her, won't she?"

I felt pretty good when we went into camp and the Old Man, Mister Howard, and Tom looked up inquiringly. Pete and I started dragging fox squirrels out of our hunting coats, and the ten of them made quite a sizable pile.

"Who shot the squirrels?" the Old Man asked genially. "The dog?"

"Sure," Pete grinned. "Dog's so good we've taught him to shoot, too. We jest set down on a log, give Jackie the gun, and sent him off into the branch on his lonesome. We're planning to teach him to skin 'em and cook 'em, right after lunch. This is the best dog I ever see. Got more sense than people."

"Got more sense than *some* people," the Old Man grunted. "Come and git it, boy, and after lunch you and Jackie can skin the squirrels."

The lunch was a lunch I loved then and still love, which is why I'm never going to be called one of those epicures. This was a country hunting lunch, Carolina style. We had Vienna sausages and sardines, rat cheese, gingersnaps and dill pickles and oys-terettes and canned salmon, all cold except the coffee that went with it, and that was hot enough to scald clean down to your shoes. It sounds horrible, but I don't know anything that tastes so good together as Vienna sausages and sardines and rat cheese and gingersnaps. Especially if you've been up since before dawn and walked ten miles in the fresh air.

After lunch we stretched out in the shade and took a little nap. Along about two I woke up, and so did Pete and Tom, and the three of us started to skin the squirrels. It's not much trouble, if you know how. Pete and I skinned 'em and Tom cleaned and dressed 'em. I'd pick up a squirrel by the head, and Pete would take his hind feet. We'd stretch him tight, and Pete would slit him down the stomach and along the legs as far as the feet. Then he'd shuck him like an ear of corn, pulling the hide toward the head until it hung over his head like a cape and the squirrel was naked.

Then he'd just chop off the head, skin and all, and toss the carcass to Tom.

Tom made a particular point about cutting the little castor glands. Squirrel with the musk glands out is as tasty as any meat I know, but unless you take out those glands an old he-squirrel is as musky as a billy goat, and tastes like a billy goat smells. Tom cut up the carcasses and washed them clean, and I proceeded to bury the heads, hides, and guts.

The whole job didn't take forty-five minutes with the three of us working. We put the pieces of clean red meat in a covered pot, and then woke up the Old Man and Mister Howard. We were going deer hunting again.

The dogs had rested too; they had had half a can of salmon each and about three hours' snooze. It was beginning to cool off when Tom and Pete put Blue and Bell on walking leashes and we struck off for another part of the swamp, which made a Y from the main swamp and had a lot of water in it. It was a cool swamp, and Tom and Pete figured that the deer would be lying up there from the heat of the day, and about ready to start stirring out to feed a little around dusk.

I was in the process of trying to think about just how long forever was when the hounds started to holler real close. They seemed to be coming straight down the crick off to my right, and the crick's banks were very open and clear, apart from some sparkleberry and gallberry bushes. The *whoo-whooing* got louder and louder. The dogs started to growl and bark, just letting off a *woo-woo* once in a while, and I could hear a steady swishing in the bushes.

Then I could see what made the swishing. It was a buck, a big one. He was running steadily and seriously through the low bush. He had horns—my Lord, but did he have horns! It looked to me like he had a dead tree lashed to his head. I slipped off the safety catch and didn't move. The buck came straight at me, the dogs going crazy behind him.

The buck came down the water's edge, and when he got to about fifty yards I stood up and threw the gun up to my face. He kept coming and I let him come. At about twenty-five yards he suddenly saw me, snorted, and leaped to his left as if somebody had unsnapped a spring in him. I forgot he was a deer. I shot at him as you'd lead a duck or a quail on a quartering shot—plenty of lead ahead of his shoulder.

I pulled the trigger—for some odd reason shooting the choke barrel—right in the middle of a spring that had him six feet off the ground and must have been wound up to send him twenty yards, into the bush and out of my life. The gun said *boom!* but I didn't hear it. The gun kicked but I didn't feel it. All I saw was that this monster came down out of the sky like I'd shot me an airplane. He came down flat, turning completely over and landing on his back, and he never wiggled.

The dogs came up ferociously and started to grab him, but they had sense and knew he didn't need any extra grabbing. I'd grabbed him real good, with about three ounces of No. 1 buckshot in a choke barrel. I had busted his shoulder and busted his neck and dead-centered his heart. I had let him get so close that you could practically pick the wads out of his shoulder. This was *my* buck. Nobody else had shot at him. Nobody else had seen him but me. Nobody had advised or helped. This monster was mine.

And monster was right. He was huge, they told me later, for a Carolina whitetail. He had fourteen points on his rack, and must have weighed nearly 150 pounds undressed. He was beautiful gold on his top and dazzling white on his underneath, and his little black hoofs were clean. The circular tufts of hair on his legs, where the scent glands are, were bright russet and stiff and spiky. His horns were as clean as if they'd been scrubbed with a wire brush, gnarled and evenly forked and the color of planking on a good boat that's just been holystoned to where the decks sparkle.

I had him all to myself, as he lay there in the aromatic, crushed ferns—all by myself, like a boy alone in a big cathedral of oaks and cypress in a vast swamp where the doves made sobbing sounds and the late birds walked and talked in the sparkleberry bush. The dogs came up and lay down. Old Blue laid his muzzle on the big buck's back. Bell came over and licked my face and wagged her tail, like she was saying, "You did real good, boy." Then she lay down and put her face right on the deer's rump.

This was our deer, and no damn bear or anything else was going to take it away from us. We were a team, all right, me and Bell and Blue.

I couldn't know then that I was going to grow up and shoot elephants and lions and rhinos and things. All I knew then was that I was the richest boy in the world as I sat there in the crushed ferns and stroked the silky hide of my first buck deer, patting his horns and smelling how sweet he smelled and admiring how pretty he looked. I cried a little bit inside about how lovely he was and how I felt about him. I guess that was just reaction, like being sick twenty-five years later when I shot my first African buffalo.

I was still patting him and patting the dogs when Tom and Pete came up one way and the Old Man and Mister Howard came up from another way. What a wonderful thing it was, when you are a kid, to have four huge, grown men—everything is bigger when you are a boy—coming roaring up out of the woods to see you sitting by your first big triumph. "Smug" is a word I learned a lot later. Smug was modest for what I felt then,

"Well," the Old Man said, trying not to grin.

"Well," Mister Howard said.

"Boy done shot hisself a horse with horns," Pete said, as proud for me as if I had just learned how to make bootleg liquor.

"Shot him pretty good, too," Tom said. "Deer musta been standing still, boy musta been asleep, woke up, and shot him in self-defense."

"Was not, either," I started off to say, and then saw that all four men were laughing.

They had already checked the sharp scars where the buck had jumped, and they knew I had shot him on the fly. Then Pete turned the buck over and cut open his belly. He tore out the paunch and ripped it open. It as full of green stuff and awful smelly gunk. All four men let out a whoop and grabbed me. Pete held the paunch and the other men stuck my head right into—blood, guts, green gunk, and all. It smelled worse than anything I ever smelled. I was bloody and full of partly digested fodder from my head to my belt.

"That," the Old Man said as I swabbed the awful mess off me

and dived away to stick my head in the crick, "makes you a grown man. You have been blooded, boy, and any time you miss a deer from now on we cut off your shirt tail. It's a very good buck, son," he said softly, "one of which you can be very, very proud."

Tom and Pete cut a long sapling, made slits in the deer's legs behind the cartilage of his knees, stuck the sapling through the slits, and slung the deer up on their backs. They were sweating him through the swamp when suddenly the Old Man turned to Mister Howard and said, "Howard, if you feel up to it, we might just as well go get *our* deer and lug him into camp. He ain't but a quarter-mile over yonder, and I don't want the wildcats working on him in that tree."

"What deer?" I demanded. "You didn't shoot this afternoon, and you missed the one you—"

The Old Man grinned and made a show of lighting his pipe. "I didn't miss him, son," he said. "I just didn't want to give you an inferiority complex on your first deer. If you hadn't of shot this one—and he's a lot better'n mine—I was just going to leave him in the tree and say nothing about him at all. Shame to waste a deer; but it's a shame to waste a boy, too."

I reckon that's when I quit being a man. I just opened my mouth and bawled. Nobody laughed at me, either.

LOST

Burton L. Spiller

Show me a deer hunter who hunts the wild country and doesn't think about the possibility of getting lost, and I'll show you a liar or a fool—or both!

Although he is remembered and appreciated mostly for his grouse, wood-cock and trout pieces—as displayed in the books Grouse Feathers, More Grouse Feathers, *and* Fishin' Around—*Burton Spiller was no stranger to other phases of outdoor sport.*

In this selection from Firelight *(Derrydale) he takes us into the chilling spectre of an event that could happen to any of us when we leave camp and become careless.*

I HAD PARTED WITH WILSON at daybreak that morning. We had come into camp together the previous evening, riding the eleven miles in from Eustis on a springless, horse drawn vehicle which jounced and pounded over the corduroy road until we flinched at each recurrent blow of the lightly padded rest at the small or our backs.

It was snowing hard before we had completed the two hour journey: great, moist flakes which persisted in finding their way down inside our upturned collars, and left our necks cold and clammy and uncomfortable. They melted less readily, though, on the cool earth, while the cedar boughs began to bend low with the accumulation of the white burden.

Sitting between us and ever pushing his body back to wedge us more distressingly against the torturing seat, the driver flapped his reins and chirruped to the plodding horse. "You fellas are gettin' in at just the right time. First snow of the season," he said. "Oughta be good trackin' tomorrow and next day."

He proved to be a good prophet, for when we rose the next morning before the dawn, and went outside to verify his observation, we found a four inch carpet upon the ground, a moist and heavy blanket which made it possible to move soundlessly through the heavy wood. The clouds were lifting and breaking up. Occasionally a star gleamed momentarily in an opening and gave promise of a clear day.

We ate breakfast by lamplight, in the long, low kitchen of Downey's camp, to the accompaniment of the confused babel of voices of a half-score sportsmen who ate hurriedly as they formulated plans for the day's hunt.

We listened while we munched our toast, and tried to assimilate information from the scraps of conversation, for this was our first visit in that rough and rugged wilderness lying between the last frontier town in the Dead River region and the Rangeley Lakes, some thirty miles to the south.

Our gleanings were of little value, though, for these men were old timers who had spent many seasons in the locality. A group of three were going to drive the "burn." A grizzled old chap, and a black haired fellow of forty were pinning their faith in the "gap" to produce a head worth mounting. Another pair were going to work the "ridges." To the men who mentioned them so glibly these names signified a definite area, a choice preserve which was theirs by the right of discovery, and which they had located only after tramping many a weary mile, but to us they meant less than nothing. The knowledge would eventually be ours, but we must acquire it as the others had done. We built an imposing pair of sandwiches from generous slices of bread and thick and juicy venison, stuffed them in our pockets, picked up our rifles and struck out in the half light of early dawn.

The trail of the hunters who had preceded us followed a well defined path leading toward a bit of rising ground to the southwest, and this path we elected to follow. In the east the sky was already crimson with the miracle of another day, while in the west a lone star blazed and paled as it fought for supremacy over the inevitable brightness which must soon efface it.

Two hundred yards further on we came to a spot where three men had left the trail and swung off to the right. These would be the three who were going to drive the "burn." It must lie somewhere off there to the northward in that stretch of wood which extended to the Chaudiere River in Canada. Farther on a couple had turned to the left. Somewhere off to the south must lie either the "ridges" or the "gap," and these men were striking confidently toward them, with hope burning strong in their breasts that a mighty buck or a sleek doe awaited them there. Oh, well! In a few days we, too, would be familiar with the country, and strike off as unhesitatingly as they toward some spot of our own choosing, which we believed to be superior.

A splash of green attracted my attention: a dark spot among the snow laden limbs of the almost impenetrable cedar thicket which fringed our path. Something had moved beneath that limb since the snow had ceased falling. The white covering had slid earthward, leaving the bare branch to indicate the passing of an unknown forest dweller.

Stepping from the trail I scanned the newly fallen snow beside

the disturbed branch. Sure enough, there was the trail I had expected to find: the imprint of the cloven feet sharply defined. It was now light enough to distinguish the well rounded toe prints which identified the sex of the animal.

"It's a buck, and a good one," I said to Wilson. "No need to look further. Let's follow this one."

"You take him," he answered, "and I will look up one of my own. If the sun comes out this snow will be gone before night. We had better make the most of it while it lasts, and hunt separately."

Now I have always liked to have a companion when I follow a deer. I like to have one pair of eyes free to watch the country ahead, without the necessity of glancing down momentarily at the elusive trail. Then, too, I have found it is often good strategy to post a partner at some likely spot after a deer has been jumped and starts circling as they oftentimes will. More than one wily old fellow has experienced the surprise of his life, while playing hide and seek with me, because of that little coup which he had not anticipated.

Wilson, though, was more experienced than I, and I acceded to his opinion. "All right," I said, "but pick a good one if you expect to beat this fellow. If he weighs less than two hundred I am no judge of footprints."

He laughed and advised me to take my time on the trail. "The foolish ones don't live to grow so big as that." With that bit of wisdom, he left me.

The tracks led toward the south. I verified that with my compass before I started off, and checked it at frequent intervals afterward. The trail meandered back and forth as the buck chose the easier footing, but the general direction was unvarying. So fresh were the tracks that I knew he was but a short distance ahead, yet I was certain he was unaware of my presence behind him. His pace was unhurried and I could see where he had stopped occasionally to nibble a shoot of the not too common moosewood. The sun emerged from the retreating bank of snow clouds, and the trees began to drip as the already moist snow felt the warming rays.

Still the buck traveled steadily onward. At nine o'clock he detoured to a low knoll and the telltale tracks showed that a doe had joined him there. Together, and unhurriedly, they went on, still traveling southward through the wilderness as accurately as though they followed a blazed trail. An hour later they were joined by another smaller doe, but possessed with the same common purpose to learn what lay beyond the ever receding horizon to the south.

For at least another hour I followed them. Then, all at once, the trail took on an appearance of extreme freshness. It would be hard to explain why, for the footprints were not one whit more clearly defined than before, but I had a feeling they were but a few minutes' old, and knew that foolish and often laughed-at inclination to feel if they were still warm.

For the first time that morning I began moving with extreme caution, testing each step for a concealed and betraying bit of dry wood beneath my foot before I bore my weight upon it, and scanning the forest ahead with an intentness of gaze which was eye straining.

There was little wind, but, such as it was, it favored my approach, and I felt certain I would see them before they were aware of my presence. But their sense of hearing was keener than I had thought, or else some flaw in the wind carried my scent to them, for all at once there came a startled snort and the crash of leaping bodies in the tangle ahead of me. I threw the rifle to my shoulder and was made aware of the commotion ahead of me, not only by the sound, but by the violent agitation of an occasional branch or a more sturdy sapling. Of those plunging brown bodies, however, I could catch no slightest glimpse.

Then, for one fleeting instant, the buck was plainly visible; outlined as though he were engraved upon the darker background of the forest, as he leaped over some obstruction which barred his path. I tried to swing my gun on him but failed, for he was out of sight in the space of a single heartbeat.

To my ears came the sound of a few more crashing bounds, then silence descended as I pushed ahead to read the story in the snow. It was plain enough. They had detected my presence and had bounded away: the two does going straight ahead: the buck, choosing to desert them and seek safety somewhere off there to the right.

I knew that his desertion was only a temporary one, and that sooner or later he would try to rejoin the females, and I resolved to put into practice a plan whereby any such gallantry on his part might prove to be his undoing.

Calling on my already tiring legs to do double duty for a few minutes I set off on the trail of the does, and followed them for perhaps three hundred yards before I had the satisfaction of again hearing them jump before me.

A hasty examination of their tracks showed me they had not

doubled back on their former course, so I retreated some twenty yards downward from the trail, brushed the snow from a fallen log and sat down to await developments. My position, I felt, was a strategic one. The buck was separated from the does and was anxious to rejoin them. The obvious thing for him to do would be to wait until I was well out of the way, on whatever mysterious errand had brought me across his path, and then cautiously smell out the trail of the two entrancing young ladies who had so hurriedly departed. Yes, it seemed likely he would follow that plan, and it seemed equally likely he would not guess I was sitting there beside the trail, waiting for him to come along.

I glanced at my watch. It was 11:50. Almost noon. The thought reminded me of the sandwich in my pocket. I secured it and ate it slowly, meditatively, as I kept a keen eye on the trail.

The minutes dragged past; many of them. The sandwich was long since consumed and my perspiring body was beginning to know the chill of inactivity. I looked cautiously at my watch once more. 12:45! I had been sitting inert for nearly an hour. Evidently the plan was not going to work. The old fellow was either too cautious or else he had slipped around me and rejoined his companions. If I got back to camp before dark I would have to hurry. I slid the watch back in my pocket and was about to stand up when I distinctly heard the crackle of brush from down the trail whence the does had gone. I started to turn my head cautiously that way, but the motion was arrested by a louder and nearer sound from that quarter of the woods from which I had expected the buck to emerge. The significance of it dawned upon me. Each party was seeking the other, and if my luck held just a few minutes longer, were going to meet almost exactly in front of the spot I had chosen. What a nice little party we were going to have!

Their approach was cautious. At intervals I could hear the swish of a branch as a sleek body disturbed it sufficiently to relieve it of its weight of snow. Once I heard a doe emit a soft little "Ba-a," but otherwise there was silence as only a great wood can know silence.

Then, from the corner of my eye, I caught a hint of movement down the trail, and, almost instantly afterward, another from the direction from which I expected the buck to appear.

Focusing my eyes on that spot I saw him clearly as he emerged into a little opening. He carried his head low as he sniffed the path he followed, and his ears twitched alternately forward and back as he listened for a sound which would send him less cautiously forward, or one which would cause him to bound tumultuously away.

Waiting until a thicket screened him I slid the safety, brought the rifle to my shoulder and leveled it at the next opening ahead of him. He stepped into it almost at once, scarcely fifty yards away and almost broadside to. He went down as though poleaxed when I touched the trigger, and I saw him kick convulsively as I worked the action and swung about in an effort to locate the does.

A white flag became visible at once, moving in quick, erratic flashes as its owner dodged in and out through the thickly growing timber. Following that waving beacon with my rifle sight I saw her clearly for a moment, swung well toward the front of her and touched the trigger once again. Her flag went down at the report, then showed white once more as she leaped ahead in startled frenzy, and she was gone before I could shoot again.

I glanced back again at the buck. He lay where he had fallen, his head drawn stiffly back and a forefoot pawing listlessly in an ineffectual and pathetic effort to impart motion to his stricken body. That he was done for I knew, for I had held just back of his shoulder, low down for a heart shot, and the distance had been as nothing. I turned my back on him and hurried down the trail after the doe that I was certain my bullet had reached.

There was blood on her trail. Not much, but a spatter of it here and there on the watery snow. I pushed on after her with hope strong in my heart, but it died gradually as the red flecks became less frequent. My aim had been faulty and my bullet had no more than creased her skin or nicked one of her generous ears. Oh, well! It was too much to expect to kill a pair on the first day out. I would go back to my buck and perform the rather messy and disagreeable task of dressing him, and, by the time that was done, it would be necessary to make all possible haste to camp if I expected to reach it before dark.

Hastening along on my back track I came, before many minutes had passed, to the spot from whence I had done my shooting. From there I looked across the intervening space to where my prize lay. For some unknown reason I was unable to see him. With an uneasy feeling in my heart I hurried over to where he had fallen.

He was gone. There could be no denying that fact. There was the place in the snow where he had dropped, the imprint of his body enlarged and misshapen where he had twisted about in a vain effort to rise, but no tuft of hair, or most minute carmine stain, indicated that my bullet had touched any part of him. I was sure that my eyes could not have deceived me. He had gone down as though hit by a lightning bolt and I would have taken any bet that he would never regain his feet. He had accomplished the task, nevertheless. The track showed that he had risen, stumbled once to his knees, and then leaped cleanly away.

I tried to reason the thing out. I knew my aim had been accurate. I did not claim to be an expert rifle shot, but, at that distance, and shooting from a sitting position as I had been doing, I knew I could place a dozen shots in a group which my hand would span. The only possible error I could have made would have been in the manner of distance. It might have been farther than I had thought. I glanced back to the log where I had sat and knew that I had not erred. The distance was not an inch more than fifty yards.

Standing thus, with my gaze taking in the route my bullet had traveled, I became aware of an unusual white spot on a cedar sapling about half way to the fallen log. I went back and examined it. The sapling was a tiny thing, no thicker than my thumb, but my bullet had centered it accurately. The copper jacket had peeled back and was still in the ragged hole. Going over the territory carefully I found that the bullet had shattered. A grain of it had creased a larger cedar some three feet to the right of the correct line of flight. Probing a fresh wound in a white birch, some fifteen feet to the left, I dug out another goodly chunk of lead. An almost severed branch showed where a third piece had zoomed upward at an unbelievable elevation. What minute portion of it hit the buck, and at what point of his anatomy, I have never been able to determine. I followed his track for more than a mile but found no indication that he had been injured in the slightest degree. There was not so much as one fleck of blood in all that discouraging distance. His leaps were sturdy and strong, indicating that he was possessed with an irresistible yearning to occupy any other spot in the universe than the one that he was that moment vacating.

I became so absorbed with the intriguing mystery that time and place were forgotten, until a chill breath of air, and an absence of warmth in the sun's rays, brought me to myself at last. I consulted my watch. The hands pointed to three o'clock. In two hours' time it would be dark. The thought was startling. I had less than two hours in which to retrace a trail I had been eight hours making. The thing was absolutely impossible of accomplishment. The only chance was to lay a course due north by my compass, and follow it as accurately and as speedily as possible. The plan had only one drawback. Downey's camp lay at the end of the corduroy road, and the road ran north and south in an almost exact line with the route I proposed to travel. Should I err and miss it by passing to the right I would, in the course of time, come either to civilization or a road leading to it: but if I chanced to pass to the left, I might well travel to the Canadian boundary without finding so much as a lumberman's camp. The safer way would be to travel in a northeasterly direction, and then swing northward until I came to the road leading to camp, but that would occupy a longer space of time than I had at my disposal. My ultimate decision was to try, with what little woodsmanship I possess, to come out within sight of camp.

Looking back now upon the events of that entire day, I am impressed with my utter lack of common sense. The country was of a monotonous sameness, with no distinguishing landmarks to arrest the eye of a newcomer. No scarred peak thrust its spire upward as an easily read sign-board which even a novice could understand. No babbling brook or rushing river intervened to form a barrier which one would know he must not cross. The whole country was

] 279 [

uniformly flat and of an unvarying sameness until one had learned it as he learns to accurately know his own dooryard.

I was aware of these things, but I had utter confidence in my ability as a woodsman. There was no slightest doubt in my mind concerning my power to eventually reach either the camp or the adjacent road. The only disturbing thought was whether or not I would have time to do so before dark. I brushed the snow from a fallen log, leveled my compass upon it, took an accurate bearing due north and started off at the best pace possible in the loose and uneven footing.

For the first hour the way was easy. The forest was not too thick, while the land sloped almost imperceptibly in the direction I was traveling. Then I ran into difficulty. Before me stretched a cedar swamp, a thick and almost impenetrable tangle of closely set young trees whose branches touched the ground. How far the swamp extended to the right or left I had no means of knowing, and neither had I any conception of the distance it stretched before me.

There was no time left for a trip of exploration along its fringes. My way led straight ahead—and that way I went.

I believe the swamp was less than a quarter mile in width, but some distances may not be accurately measured by such standards. Occasionally one encounters a bit of terrain whose span may only be estimated by the toll it exacts of spent muscles and aching limbs. Of such nature was the cedar swamp. For untold centuries the trees had grown and died and fallen to the ground in a jackstraw confusion through which yet other trees had sprung. The only means of progress was by crawling, through spaces barely large enough to permit the passage of my body, under logs which were too high to climb, and over others which were too low to crawl under. Many of the latter lay in crisscross tangles which persisted in breaking rottenly in that moment when I had almost reached their summit: a bit of stratagem on their part which invariably threw me, with football tactics, for a loss of one or two hard won yards.

To add to my difficulties, the ground, when I did get down to it through the rotten wood, was a quagmire into which I sank almost to my knees, while the snow which still lay thickly on each hindering branch and twig, showered me and melted with the heat of my body until every thread of my clothing was saturated with it.

The sun was shining when I first pushed into the tangled mass but twilight had already fallen when I finally won through to the firm ground on the other side. I have never known a more heartbreaking hour in the wilderness.

It seemed hopeless, now, to push on. Darkness was but a half hour away and my judgment told me I was still some two or three miles from camp. If the way chanced to be open I might make it, but another tangle like the one I had just traversed would effectually bar me from further progress for the night.

I deliberated whether or not to push on or pause here and gather wood for a tiny fire which would keep me from freezing through the long hours which lay ahead. With my saturated garments, the latter plan held little of pleasurable anticipation. For that matter, the thought of forging ahead through the darkness was not conducive to merriment but there was a chance I would find an easier trail ahead. Accordingly I went on, hurrying as best I could, but ever mindful of the disaster which must inevitably follow a slip which would result in a sprained ankle or a fractured leg.

The twilight deepened and the light died in the west. Presently a star came out, winking brightly at me from the pale sky. Others followed it at intervals until the heavens were studded with them, and I welcomed their dim but friendly light.

Another hour passed and the way grew rougher. Little rolling ridges intercepted my progress. Ridges down which I had to grope with caution, and up which I climbed with an effort which took toll from my leg muscles and lifeless knees.

"Well," I thought, "here is the situation which you have visualized for more than ten years. You know what to do. Don't wait any longer. If it is necessary to spend a night in the woods, spend it as comfortably as possible. Make camp—and make it now."

That this was good advice I knew full well. Many a man has perished under similar conditions because, in his panic, he forgot that the human body weakened rapidly through cold and exposure, and that even a sleepless and supperless night spent before a rousing campfire would restore more energy than would the heaviest repast if the latter were followed by a night of aimless wandering.

I was quite confident I had not erred much in the matter of direction, but the distance to camp was still a matter of conjecture. That cedar swamp had been my undoing, and, in the darkness, I cursed the almost impregnable entanglement which had robbed me of the hour of daylight I had so sorely needed.

Then, too, the matter of selecting a camping spot was not an easy one, now that night had fallen. I needed a background of cliff or boulder or steeply cut bank to reflect the heat of my fire and cut off the freezing air which was now settling rapidly from the starlit space above me. If I could find such a spot the night would not be too uncomfortable to endure.

I slid down into another gully and began ascending the sharply rising ground before me. It seemed steeper and higher than the others I had climbed, and there was an occasional outcropping of ledge from which the snow had melted. I decided to push along to its crest and try to find an upthrust boulder which would serve my purpose.

The trees thinned as I neared the top and my hopes arose. Somewhere along this ridge which an ancient glacier had molded in its passing, I would find a friendly niche where a minimum of fuel would give me a maximum amount of heat. Swinging to the right I traveled a few yards while my eyes strained to pierce the darkness. Then, directly ahead, a square of light glowed through an opening in the trees. It was shining through a rear window in Downey's camp. No harbor light ever loomed fairer to a storm tossed mariner than did that yellow glare to me.

To reach it was a matter of minutes only. I lifted the latch and entered. A dozen faces confronted me and relief was written plainly upon them. A dozen pairs of eyes glanced questioningly at me as I closed the door behind me and strode into the room. A dozen voices lifted in simultaneous clamor for details as I searched the circle of faces for the only one I knew.

"Get lost, did you?" a grizzled old timer asked.

"Oh, no," I boasted, secretly a little vain of my success in running a course so accurately. "Only slightly delayed. Where is Wilson? Isn't he in yet?"

"Wasn't he with you?" The chorus was a general one.

"No. We separated at daylight. I followed a buck until three o'clock and then took a straight line for camp."

"This friend of yours—what's his name? Wilson? Is he a—does he know his way around in the woods?" It was Downey who spoke, and I could detect the uneasiness in his voice: a host troubled for the safety of his guests.

"Yes," I assured him. "Yes, he's a good man." I tried to extract some grain of comfort from the thought but knew a growing feeling of apprehension.

"Did he have a compass?"

"Yes."

"Well, I guess he'll be all right—if he knows how to use it—and keeps his head. You better get some dry clothes on and eat your supper. You look cold."

I had not noticed it until then, but now I could feel a tremor in my body as the sensitive nerves shrank away from my soaked garments. When I undressed I found my limbs were blue and wrinkled, and never have I known a more grateful warmth than that imparted by the feel of dry woolens against my tingling skin, and a pot of hot tea which all but blistered my tongue.

Ten minutes later I would have been physically content once more had it not been for my worry concerning Wilson's safety. Save for the natural reluctance to experience the discomfort of a night spent in the open, I had known no uneasiness concerning my own safety or my ability to speedily find camp with the coming of daylight. But now that I knew my friend was somewhere out there in the cheerless night, a score of disquieting possibilities presented themselves and added to the depressing weight which was already bearing heavily upon my soul.

Nor was the burden lifted when, warmed and refreshed, I again entered the lounging room where a crackling fire glowed in the huge fireplace, and flooded the room with both light and friendly heat.

In the face of impending disaster, man has a propensity to talk of incidents which have come under his observation where tragedy actually occurred. More than once, while riding out a howling squall in an open boat, some comforting soul has ceased his bailing long enough to observe, "This is like the blow in which Joe Doakes and his wife and three kids were drowned in Lake Suchandsuch. The motor stopped and—"

Or, while sitting with a group of friends during a severe electrical storm, how common a thing it is to hear someone say, "This reminds me of a shower we had down in Honkatonk two years ago. It came up just like this one—so dark you could hardly see across the room. It burned four stands of buildings and killed three people in that one town alone. I was standing in the doorway when the bolt came down which struck the town hall. It split three ways and—"

Evidently Downey also possessed that characteristically human trait for his voice, attuned to the open spaces, flooded the little room. "—looked like a woodsman," he was saying, "and I supposed he knew a little something. I found out afterward that he was one of them city gunners who never hunted a patch of woods that had more than two acres in it. We found him in a birch country, but he'd used up every match he had, tryin' to light a fire of green brush. Guess he didn't know that birch bark would burn. Both feet was froze, and we thought for a while they would have to come off, but he got out of it by losin' most of his toes. It beats all how a feller will go off his nut just as soon as it begins to get dark."

"There's lots of things can happen—especially when a man is alone." The seamed and wind tanned face of the speaker marked him as a man who had spent much of his life in the open. "I remember the time Folsom disappeared. He had been gathering gum before the deer season opened. We all knew he was working Black Nubble but it was weeks before we found him. I guess a dozen men had gone within twenty feet of him—but they didn't look high enough. His spurs had slipped in a bit of rotten wood.

He was sitting bolt upright, about twenty feet from the ground, and looked as though he was perched up there for fun—kinda grinning down at us. I guess he didn't laugh much, though. He had come down on a dead branch that was pointing straight up, and it was driven the whole length of his body. Made me kinda sick when we pulled him off from it."

Then someone remembered Alcide Perrault. Old Alcide had slipped on a snow covered rock and broken his leg. Dazed, bewildered and wracked with pain, he had crawled for miles and dragged that tortured limb behind him. A tough bird, Old Alcide. One of the kind who die hard. He had crawled for miles— but in the wrong direction. When they found him he was frozen stiff, while the wood mice had—

"Queer things happen," said one I had come to know as Bates. "Sometimes you can't find a reasonable explanation for them, and then again you can. Take the case of Hoffman. For a business man, who only got into the woods a few weeks each year, he was just about as good as they come. I suppose that was what made him successful in business—what I mean is that if he took an interest in anything he studied it until he knew all the angles. He certainly was a good woodsman.

"He knew this section, too. He had been coming up here for years and never asked anything of any guide but to keep out of his way. He tried to get his wife interested in hunting but I guess society appealed to her more. She was a lot younger than he, anyway. He did manage to get her up here one fall but three days of it was all she could stand.

"The next fall he brought in a sleek looking young fellow he was taking into his business. He was a smooth chap and looked like one of those collar ads you see in the magazines, but I disliked him from the first minute I saw him. That's funny, too, for when I tried to find something about him that I could object to I couldn't think of a thing, with the exception of the way he brushed back his hair and the oily look it had.

"Queer, isn't it, how we sometimes dislike a person at the first glance? Well, I didn't like him—but Hoffman did—so it was none of my business.

"They went out together the second day, and that night Stavel—the young chap—came in alone. He was scratched by branches and bruised by falls, and he said the camp certainly looked like the snake's hips to him. He had separated from Hoffman early in the morning and had become confused, he said, and had no idea where he was until he struck the tote road leading to camp.

"As darkness came on he began to worry, and suggested getting up a searching party, but we laughed at the idea. We knew Hoffman. He had a compass and he knew how to use it. If it had become damaged he still had the stars to guide him. If it was necessary for him to sleep out, why he knew how to build a leanto and how to keep it warm. Hoffman was all right.

"He didn't come in that night, so we started a search for him the next morning. The next day we sent after more help and made an organized hunt, but with no success.

"Stavel was wild. He telegraphed Mrs. Hoffman and she pulled in that night, in a big car, with a chauffeur and a private detective.

"Then the Governor got interested in the case and put a hundred men in the woods. Every possible outlet was watched, and we had a plane scouting the territory for two days, searching for a trace of smoke which might be his campfire.

"We couldn't pick up his track the first day, and after the army was turned loose on us it was impossible to follow any one man's track.

"Stavel offered a reward of five thousand dollars to any person who would find Hoffman, either dead or alive, and that brought in a lot more men. The young fellow was pretty nearly frantic but he stuck to the story he had first told, telling that and no other, and no amount of questioning could cause him to change it in the slightest degree.

"Mrs. Hoffman bore up under it remarkably well. She said she felt it would somehow come out all right. She put in quite a lot of time comforting Stavel, who was suffering the tortures of the damned, if you could judge by his looks.

"After a week the Governor called in his men, and although we hunted more or less until winter closed in, it was useless. Hoffman had vanished.

"The next spring a few of us went over the ground pretty carefully. We poled up the rivers and paddled around the lakes without finding anything. We even drained Beaver Bog, and went over every foot of it on snowshoes, with the same lack of results.

"Mrs. Hoffman waited a few months longer and then took the matter to the courts. After some deliberation they arrived at a decision. They pronounced Hoffman legally dead—at least so far as she was concerned."

He paused a moment while he selected a cigarette from its metal case. The lighter clicked, the flame flared, and he blew a cloud of smoke upward.

"I respect the court's decision," he said, then. "So far as she was concerned, I think Hoffman was dead long before that morning when he started out with Stavel. I may be wrong—but I never liked the way that guy brushed his hair. I guess she liked it, though. Anyway, she married him."

We sat silent for a moment, and, in that moment, the latch lifted and Wilson stamped in. There was blood on his hands, but the eyes which sought out mine from all those others focused upon him knew a contented look. It was good to see him and to note that a self satisfied little smile lurked at the corners of his mouth.

"Well, how big was yours?" he asked. "He'll have to be good if he beats the one I hung up just before dark. Ten points—and his head is a perfect one, too!"

JAKE'S RANGERS
HUNT THE WHITETAIL

Edmund Ware Smith

Edmund Ware Smith's name is as synonymous with New England as birch trees, brook trout, and partridge. His articles on Maine hunting, fishing, camping and backcountry life have been collected in seven books. These include tales of his most-remembered character, "The Old Poacher."

In the fifties, Field & Stream *began publishing a series of Smith's articles about a group of his cronies who called themselves "Jake's Rangers." They hunted, fished, trapped, camped, drank whiskey, ran rivers—all kinds of fun things. They even took the late Supreme Court Justice William O. Douglas down the Allagash on a canoe trip.*

This piece, collected with other Jake's Rangers adventures in the book Jake's Rangers *(Doubleday), shows the Rangers doing their thing at a deer camp.*

WHETHER YOU CALL THEM "The Trail Blazers," or "Whitetails Limited," or simply "The Old Bunch," it means the same thing when the leaves begin to fall in the little towns in the deer-hunting states of our nation. Whatever the name, and there usually is one, you are talking about a group of men, young and old, who gather each fall to hunt the whitetail deer.

The personnel of these groups is often so varied in age and walk of life that individual members rarely meet during the rest of the year. But with the first frost, and the foliage bright on the ridges, there comes a flurry of eager telephone calls. Meetings are held, the trip is planned; and, when you reach your hunting camp, you are reunited like brothers. Your rifle stands in the gun rack where it stood last year. Your sleeping bag is on your old bunk or bed. You are fraternal in the glow of lamplight, sharing the familiar warmth of the wood stove with the old bunch, and talking of just one subject—tomorrow. For tomorrow is opening day on deer.

Each fall, the phenomenon of the deer-hunting groups grows deeper into the country's grass roots. In Pennsylvania, New York, the Virginias, the Carolinas, Michigan, Maine, and perhaps other states, there are groups that were first organized well over fifty years ago. Rich in tradition, and sometimes in ritual, this annual gathering of the deer-hunting clan has become an American institution.

I suspect that my own bunch is typical of at least a hundred others. We call ourselves "Jake's Rangers"; and, in this description of the Rangers' fourteenth annual hunt, I believe you will find striking similarities to your own hunt, and perhaps a kinship between your group and ours. In fact, in what follows, you may even read words that you have actually spoken or heard spoken at night around the stove in your own hunting camp. For example:

"I was standing in a little spruce knoll, when I heard this deer coming."

That opening line, with minor variations, has been uttered at least once for every whitetail deer sighted, heard, hit or missed, since deer hunting began. It can't be copyrighted, for it is always an inspired original to the hunter who is telling his story. Certain of Jake's Rangers will be speaking the magic line presently, but first I must explain who we are and where we hunt.

Officially, there are seven Rangers. Guests bring the total to ten or more. All of us reside in, or near, the small seacoast town of Damariscotta, Maine. Typically heterogeneous, our membership includes Damariscotta's postmaster, its veterinary surgeon, its Railway Express agent, a leading physician, an insurance man, a cabinet maker, a grocer, and an artist. We have named ourselves for our leader, Maurice "Jake" Day, known to his Rangers as "the Colonel." To the rest of the world, he is Maurice Day, artist, naturalist, and authority on the woods and waters of the Pine Tree State. His nationally known watercolors of wilderness Maine are considered important regional documents, and in many of them, his favorite wild animal appears. Appropriately, it's the whitetail deer.

Every group of hunters, by tradition, has to have an old-timer, a colorful character, or highly developed curmudgeon, who is an unfailing source of camp anecdote and humor. Our candidate in this field—the man who sets Jake's Rangers apart from all other groups—is Uncle George Whitehouse, age seventy-four.

] 289 [

Uncle George, who used to be a boat builder and almost every-thing else, weighs in at around a hundred and six pounds. In build, he is virtually one-dimensional—like a canoe pole. Despite the spareness of his frame, his feats of strength and conquests of all types, as reported by himself, are without equal. He has rigged more topmasts on more four-masted schooners, felled more trees, shot more and bigger deer at greater distances, and run wilder rapids in smaller canoes—or just on logs—than any man alive. He doubts nothing that he says. His chief characteristic is his halo of invincibility.

Jake's Rangers regard Uncle George as an endowment. He is in residence the year-round in the deer-hunting camp at Sprague's Falls on the Narraguagus River, near Cherryfield in Washington County. This is fortunate, because when the camp—an old farm-house—showed signs of sagging at the sills, it was nothing for Uncle George, alone, to hold the building off the ground with one hand while he shored it up with the other.

Annually, before departing for camp and Uncle George, the Rangers go through a stage of high-octane anticipation. It has become a kind of ritual: listing and packing supplies, sighting in rifles at the local rifle range, airing sleeping bags, applying the whetstone to hunting knives, switching from white handkerchiefs to red ones.

Bentley Glidden, Damariscotta's postmaster, invariably squeezes rare juices of drama from these preliminaries. He tele-phones his fellow Rangers at odd hours. You pick up the receiver. A sepulchral voice comes over the wire:

"Is your waterproof match safe full?" Or, "Have you remem-bered your compass?" Or, "Only *you* can prevent forest fires."

Bentley is a rotund, merry, and uninhibited organizer. If you step into his Post Office in mid-October, with the opening of deer season still two weeks hence, your name is sure to be called loudly and jubilantly. Bent will snatch you into his back room, and read you the camp menu for the entire ten days:

"Friday, first night in camp: hamburg, onions, mashed potato. Saturday, opening-day night: deer liver (?) and bacon, or baked beans."

] 290 [

Sometimes, without a word, Bent will hand you a slip of paper, turn his back on you, and disappear into the darker confines of the Post Office. This year I got the paper treatment twice. The first listed the personnel of the trip as follows:

Jake (our leader), Mac (McClure Day, our veterinary surgeon, who is Jake's son), Eddie Pierce (who owns Damariscotta's Yellow Front Grocery), Dr. Sam Belknap (The Rangers' physician), Jack (Bentley's brother, our insurance man), Bud Hauglund (Railway Express agent, a newcomer), Louis Doe (Mayor of the nearby village of Sheepscott), Ed Smith (yours truly), and Bentley Glidden.

The explanatory parentheses are mine. The final words addressed to me, are Bentley's. They follow:

Please remember that you were inducted into Jake's Rangers during "Be Kind to Animals Week."

The second paper that Bentley slipped me was a command that I obeyed with pleasure. It read:

Have your station wagon in the alley back of Eddie Pierce's store at three-thirty, Thursday, October 30.
[Signed] Sgt. B. Glidden, Jake's Rangers.

The loading of grub and supplies in Eddie Pierce's back alley is always a ceremony. It's the last act in Bentley's anticipation by-play and is attended by all Rangers able to sneak a few minutes off from work. Bentley had read the camp menu to all of us, and now—passing carton by carton over the tail gate of my wagon— was the reality: a colossal turkey, an Olympian ham, a classic corned-beef brisket, enough hamburg to equip a diner, bacon, flour, canned fruits, juices, vegetables.

As the last parcel was loaded, a bystander remarked with heavy sarcasm:

"You poor guys are going to starve up there in the woods."

"Oh, no," said Bent, airily, "we'll eke this out with venison and partridge."

I locked the tail gate carefully over all this bounty, drove home, and locked the wagon in my barn as a double-security measure. I was to pick up Bentley at daylight, and we were to drive to camp ahead of the others in order to make things ready and establish peace with Uncle George.

We had had five straight days of rain, but Friday morning was as clear as a bell, with mist veils hanging low in the valleys, and the color of the last, lingering foliage painting the ridges in the sunrise.

Camden, Belfast, Bucksport, Ellsworth. The white towns flashed by, and everywhere you could see signs announcing: "Hunters' Breakfast—4 A.M. to 8 A.M." We saw other hunters heading toward their camps. Tomorrow, November first, was opening day, and the deer-hunting clans were on their way to rendezvous.

Beyond Ellsworth, the road traversed the shore of Tunk Lake, with Tunk Mountain to the north. Then the magic turnoff toward Sprague's Falls, the end of blacktop, then narrow, rutted gravel. Jake's Rangers' headquarters is the last farmhouse at the dead end of the Sprague Falls Road. There, Uncle George, in his tattered checked shirt, greeted us from thirty feet in the air. He was prancing along the ridgepole of the house, where he had been examining a chimney for smoke leaks. I held my breath while Uncle George, all the time waving at us, danced down an intricate system of ladders to the ground.

"I was scared you'd fall, Uncle George," I said.

"Five, ten years ago," he said, "I'd of jumped. Once, in a shipyard in East Boothbay, I jumped sixty feet from the topmast of a—"

"Never mind, Uncle George," Bentley said. "How's the firewood supply?"

Uncle George gave Bent an outraged look.

"Firewood? When that chimney might leak flame? Burn us all to a cinder? Would *you* of cut any?"

Uncle George was in splendid form. So was the chimney. And I had a newly filed bucksaw and an axe in the wagon. While we unloaded the supplies, Uncle George told of new enemies he had made during the past months and of his plans for disposing of them. He had done in quite a few of them, when Bentley interrupted with The Great Hardy Perennial Hunters' Question:

"Are there many deer around, Uncle George?"

"Not a one. No deer at all."

Bent and I looked at each other in a flood of relief. Uncle George's reply was a surefire omen that whitetails were plentiful. So eager were we to relay the glad tidings that we could hardly wait for the arrival of the rest of the Rangers. But the time went fast, and with the thunder of Sprague's Falls familiar in our ears, we went to work cutting wood, policing camp, and stacking supplies on the shelves.

The smell of your hunting camp, as you step across the threshold for the first time in a year, is as familiar as the palm of your hand. There's the smoke of old fires, oilcloth, coffee, kerosene, soap, gun oil, cedar kindling, and, on rainy days, the steam of damp wool and leather and rubber.

That first noon, while we were eating the lunch our wives had prepared for us at home, Bent and I noticed a new, strange odor in camp. Uncle George had loftily disdained to share our lunch and, instead, opened the door to his iceless, wooden, icebox. The box contained nothing save a fragment of dried pollock, and the new scent emanated from the pollock. I don't know how long Uncle George had been nourishing himself from this item, but it had a perfume definitely redolent of an old Model pollock. The old-timer shaved off a portion with his jackknife, chewed it with relish, and closed the icebox door, lest the remainder escape under its own power. The scent of mink bait vanished with the closing of the box, and we were at peace again—until Uncle George fired us up with the one, burning rumor that can galvanize any hunting camp.

"I hear," he said, "that there's a white buck around."

Even if the rumor was one of Uncle George's invention, the Rangers' hunt was made. All of us would be buoyant with the individual dream of at least a running shot at the white buck.

Jake Day and Mac drove into the dooryard at midafternoon. Before they had their rifles in the rack, Bent had told them of the rumored prize. They asked Uncle George if he had seen the great white creature.

At the outset, Uncle George had just heard. Now, it developed, he had seen.

"How many points?" asked Jake.

"Where was he?" asked Mac.

Uncle George waved a hand toward the wilderness stretching northward. His gesture was wide enough to include Tunk, Bog, McCabe, and Spring River Mountains, together with a fifty-degree segment of the Great Barrens—in all, roughly seventy square miles.

"Right there," said Uncle George, "is where I saw him."

By the time Jack Glidden, Eddie Pierce, Dr. Sam, and Bud Haugland arrived, it was dark. The night was still, except for the hollow rumble of Sprague's Falls—a sound that is built into the rafters of the old house. In a matter of a few hours, the white buck had ceased being a rumor. He was real. He was somewhere. He was everyone's goal, the substance of everyone's wakeful dreams that first night in camp.

Which rifle in the full gun rack would have the honor? Would any of them? I lay in my sleeping bag, wondering and visualizing the gleaming barrels. Most of the guns had names: "Cosmic Ray," a couple of "Betsys," and "Old Meat in the Pot"—and then there was Mac Day's .243, which came to be known as "Little Evil."

Bent and I cooked opening-day breakfast by lamplight, while, by custom, Dr. Sam made the toast and prepared the noonday sandwiches with his camp buddy, Eddie Pierce.

"Where you going to hunt today?"

That's the breakfast question. You hear it a dozen times every morning for the hunt's duration. A good question. If you know where your people are working, you avoid accidents. If a man gets lost, you know where to start looking.

Bent and Jack Glidden headed for the "Bowl," Bud for the "River Trail," Dr. Sam and Eddie for "Split Rock." These are landmark names first coined by Jake's Rangers. They are not on any map but our own. Other hunters range the same places, knowing them by different names.

Jake, Mac, and I took our rifles from the rack, crossed the decaying wooden bridge at the Falls, and started out toward the Barrens. This vast, boulder-strewn area is grown to scrub oak, small beech, and other hardwoods, with occasional "islands" of spruce and fir. Its high plateau fans off for miles. In the past, millions of feet of pine logs have been harvested from this reach and, latterly, millions of bushels of blueberries. An ancient tote road makes the gradual ascent to the plateau.

Mac left us and struck out alone into the woods to the westward. We watched him go. You could see his red shirt and cap, and the yellow glow of his *Fire-Glo* vest. You saw a good woodsman in action—hand instinctively fending the sharp twig and eyes focused yards ahead, channeling the way the foot would travel, estimating the slant of ledge or boulder, testing by sight and memory the traction of the trail, and the rifle—Little Evil—cradled in his elbow, a part of the man. It has a peculiar grace and is a nice thing to see.

When Jake and I reached the Barrens, the wind had picked up to a half-gale. We heard voices, and a group of four hunters emerged from a thicket—three boys, and an older man who bore the stamp of experience. His name was Grant, and he told us they hadn't seen even a track since daylight. The younger boys looked discouraged. They were pulling out for new territory.

When they had gone, Jake and I sat behind a huge boulder, out of the chill wind. Jake told of his experience of the previous year—how he was walking along the Barren's trail and a buck crossed ten yards in front of him, how he put his rifle to his shoulder, and then how a partridge boomed right up into his face between him and the deer.

"That buck should have credited the partridge with an assist," Jake said—and then we heard a shot.

Shots always fill you full of excited speculations. They have tremendous mystery—even the far ones that sound like someone whispering "Pow" in your ear. Each one can mean drama or climax or both. The shot we'd just heard sounded sharp, and there wasn't a second shot. Just that single, powerful, "Cr-rack!"

"That could be Mac and Little Evil," I said.

Jake was on his feet, and we hurried off down the trail over which we'd just come. Two minutes later, we froze in our tracks. Three or four rifles were blazing away. You couldn't count the shots. You could tell the "Bat-bat-bat—" of an automatic. The slower cadence of a lever action. Then came silence, except for the wind hollering in our ears.

We went on cautiously around a couple of bends in the trail. Ahead of us, standing in a group, we saw six hunters. Two of them were Mac Day and Dr. Sam Belknap; the other four were the Grant party—the discouraged ones. But they weren't discouraged now. They were dressing out a handsome doe. Mac had sighted the doe, and his shot had driven the animal up to the Grant boys.

When Jake and I joined the group, the tall Grant brother—the experienced one—was giving his boys a stern lecture on too much shooting. You couldn't blame the kids for their excitement. But it was a sound lecture, just the same.

"We had the doe after the first shot," said the older Grant. "All the other shots did was ruin good meat. You kids think of that, next time. You want to have some respect for your deer."

That was a good speech, and as we started back toward camp, I thought how those boys would remember it, and someday tell their own boys the same thing.

None of the other Rangers were at camp when Jake and I got back. But Uncle George was there, and he was in a cold, trembling fury, his eyes flaming like a blow-torch. The object of his wrath was a group of Connecticut hunters who had just parked their car in our dooryard and were standing around it with their rifles. Our dooryard is the customary parking place for hunters in this vicinity, simply because there is no other place. Uncle George now stated that they ought to pay a parking fee, and that the Connecticut hunters owed him for two years, besides this one. He would take it out of their hides.

We watched while Uncle George, picking up a stout cudgel,

went out to assault the army from Connecticut. This is what we saw.

Uncle George crossing the yard to the car under the apple tree, eagerly and companionably shaking hands with all four hunters; smiles of welcome and goodwill on all faces; a tall, red-coated Connecticut man handing Uncle George a bill; Uncle George waving the billed hand away in austere refusal.

And then we heard Uncle George say:

"You boys park here any time you want, day or night. Always glad to see you coming back."

I don't know whether it's more fun to hunt the daylight hours to the full or to spend an afternoon in camp looking up the trail, watching the Rangers come in one by one or two by two, and listening to their individual stories as they arrive at the door, unload their rifles, place them in the gun rack, take off their wet boots, and stretch their weary feet toward the fireplace fire. But this first afternoon after Jake and Mac left for The Big Pine, I decided to stay in and nurse a toe blister.

Bud Haugland came in about three o'clock.

"Any excitement, Bud?"

Bud grinned.

"An open, running shot—not twenty yards away. It was just now, a couple of hundred yards from camp."

"I didn't hear the shot—and I've been listening hard."

"There wasn't any shot," Bud said. "The safety was on."

The shadows got long. Bud cleaned lamp chimneys and filled lamps. Together we worked up a woodpile and stacked it on the back porch.

Mac and Jake came in. No story. Dr. Sam and Eddie Pierce came in. No story.

"You boys don't seem to be very good hunters," remarked Uncle George. "I always had my buck—a big one—hung up before seven o'clock in the morning on opening day. Sixty years running."

Bud got up and lighted the big lamp over the dining table. It was twilight outside, with full dark beginning to hover down. There was that moment of anxiety so well known to any hunting camp, that strange dread of a hunter lost, of darkness. Two men were missing.

"Where did Bentley and Jack go?" Jake asked.

"The Bowl," said Dr. Sam, who has a way of keeping track of such things.

"Maybe they got on the white buck's track," Eddie said. "That could keep them out late."

Jake began to pace up and down in front of the fireplace. Mac looked at his compass and at the framed map on the long table.

Then came the familiar voices just outside the front door. There also came a heavy thud, a groan—as in relief at dropping a heavy burden after a long, rugged haul. We grabbed flashlights and rushed outside. Bentley and Jack, their backs steaming in the chill air, stood beside the eight-pointer they had shot on the edge of the Bowl and lugged in over that rough terrain on a pole. First buck! First blood! Opening day.

"I was sitting there on a stump," said Bentley, "and Jack sitting right near me, when I saw this deer come sneaking along—"

Both the boys had fired. Both had connected. The buck had dropped instantly. Supper that night was liver and bacon.

The things you remember about the days and nights in camp—the things that keep coming back! The sounds of going to bed, the bunk springs twanging, the boots thudding on the floor; the penny-ante poker game with Uncle George standing by, telling of the times he had risked a thousand dollars on a single turn of a card; the chain-reaction coffee that Jack Glidden made; the day Bentley saw the black bear; the reshuffling of the contents of duffel bags, choosing the proper clothes against the probabilities of weather; the Sundays in camp—no hunting, but visiting with other hunters. And had anyone caught a glimpse of the white buck?

One afternoon it rained hard. That morning Uncle George had told me of two mongrel dogs belonging to a neighbor, and how he planned to do away with them. They stole his food, he said, which was why he kept his dried pollock in the iceless icebox. He had decided to pinch off the animals' heads with his own hands, but only after inflicting tortures of a surgical nature.

When the rain started that afternoon, and I came back from hunting the river, I stepped into the clearing and saw Uncle George and the dogs on the back steps. He was feeding the creatures choice scraps and speaking to them in words of endearment, all the while fondling their ears. To save Uncle George the shame and guilt of being caught red-handed in an act of tenderness, I remained hidden till the scene broke up.

That was the afternoon that Jake tagged an eight-pointer in the rain. He and Mac lugged it in and hung it alongside the Glidden boys' in the cellar under the farmhouse. It was a perfect mate for Jack's and Bentley's.

"I had just stepped over a little knoll," said Jake, "and I heard this noise, and I stopped still, and—"

A clean shot high on the backbone. No spoilage.

Through the years, Jake's Rangers have had a high of nine deer, which was one apiece for that year. The low was three. This trip was about average, with a total of four. Dr. Sam tagged a fat and highly edible spikehorn near Wasse's Beaver dam on about the fifth or sixth day.

I remember it was the day I left camp late in the morning, because I saw the Rural Delivery mailman stop at Uncle George's mailbox—the last mailbox on the Sprague Falls Road. Uncle George sprang hopefully from the front door and opened the box. Whatever was in it was for the Smith Camp across the river. The old-timer shook his head dejectedly.

"Nothing for me again," he said.

"Were you expecting a letter?" I asked.

"It's a long time," he said, with a sigh, "since I've heard from Theda Bara."

Jake's Rangers are a bunch of hardworking, resourceful hunters, and most of them are on the go from daylight till dark. I am content with a few hours. Maybe it's middle age, or a slight lameness in my back. Or maybe it's just that I can get as big a heart bump out of someone else shooting a deer as if I did it myself.

That's probably a false statement, but on this particular day it wasn't.

Mac Day and Jake came in from their hunting on "The Mountain," a wild, rocky nubble on the west side of the river. Excitement was all over them like flame, and it caught me in its contagion. Mac drew his hunting knife and showed me the blade. It had a yellow-white coating.

"What's that, Mac?"

"It's not candle wax!"

"You got the white buck!"

"Yes—me and Little Evil. We need help hauling him in."

Then Mac told it. He had been catfooting near the top of the mountain, Jake right behind him with his camera. He had stepped up on a rock, and there in a little draw, not sixty feet away, stood the white buck. The deer dropped with Mac's first shot, lifted its head once, then slowly sank back, still.

It turned out that the famous buck wasn't pure white, but calico. But it was an experience Mac and Jake will never forget, nor will I as I saw and heard them tell the story. As I write this, soon after the Rangers' return home, the four deer are hanging in the big, walk-in freezer in Eddie Pierce's grocery store. Hometown people go in for a look now and then, and anytime you happen to meet Jake, or Jack, or Bentley, or Dr. Sam, or Mac on Main Street, you can ask for the story, and it will begin with minor variations on deer hunting's immortal, and forever original opening line:

"I was standing on a little spruce knoll, when I heard this deer coming. . . ."

As for Uncle George Whitehouse, I feel it just and proper that he should have the last word. There is a moment of something like sadness when you stand at the camp door and say good-by for a year. It was particularly so when I said good-by to Uncle George. As I looked around over the land and forest, I thought of the snow that would come inevitably, the road closed in drifts that would cover the mailbox, the smoke from the chimney lonely and torn in the winter wind, and the old man huddled by the fire.

"Are you going to winter here?" I asked, as we shook hands.

"No," said Uncle George, nibbling the last of his dried pollock, "I've been thinking some of the French Riviera."

Hunters' Tracks

WHITETAILS ALONG THE BORDER

Warren Page

Warren Page's death in 1978 left a tremendous void in the world of sport-hunting.

As shooting editor for Field & Stream *and later President of the National Shooting Sports Foundation, his work was characterized by his professionalism and dedication to the sports he loved.*

In my opinion, Warren's accounts of hunting the great game fields of the world are among the finest ever written. Warren knew how to put the reader right into a story, so that he could share the action and the setting—not just receive a report on them.

Some of his most outstanding pieces have been collected in the book One Man's Wilderness (*Holt, Rinehart and Winston*), *and this fast-paced whitetail piece is taken from that volume.*

LOUD THE SONGS and long the stories about the cunning of the buck whitetail in his native habitat, the North and East. I should know. Over the years I've sung plenty of those paeans of praise. But I just quit. Heresy it may be for a Yankee raised on hunting beech-ridge whitetail, but I hereby hand the laurels for smartness and general hunter-challenge to the Coues deer, that pint-sized spook buck of the South and West.

"At least that's the way it looks right now," I said to George Parker, the Arizonan whose ranch is not named Hacienda del Cazador by accident, since George has in his time "cazadored" about every animal worth hunting. "That buck today made monkeys out of both of us."

He had, at that. We had been hunting alone, Doc Rusten of the Boone and Crockett Club Records Committee and Parker's ranching friend, Pollard, having left camp for areas more civilized than this quarter of the Santa Ritas. The terrain was typical of Arizona mountains. From the spiny point where I perched on a sharp rock, I could see both sides of the little draw George was poking out, could cover the canyon in front of me with its few cottonwoods shading the dry creek bed, and could watch the draw opposite making up into the far hills. It all looked to be wide open. Yet somehow that buck had stayed concealed from the time he first bounded out in front of George until I had finally spotted him halfway up the far draw, way out of range. Neither of us had seen him come down the draw, cross the canyon, and begin the far-side climb.

"The little sonsaguns sneak like ghosts. I'll bet that a full-sized Coues buck, big as they go at a hundred and twenty-five or so, can hide behind one pad of a prickly pear!"

"Behind one mighty small clump of grass, that's for sure," agreed Parker.

And he should know. I doubt that any living man has spent more time pursuing the Coues deer on both sides of the border than has George. Not always to hunt for himself, usually to help other people hunt. That takes even better knowledge of animal habits. George agrees with me that the Coues deer is a tough nut to crack. A buck that has fooled men for years, long enough to grow eight points and have the Boone and Crockett record-book enthusiast fumbling for his tape, the points all warty and gnarled so that the deer rates the "cactus buck" sobriquet often given him, is a worthwhile antagonist, believe you me.

Arizona's desert mountains, typical Coues country, from far away may look utterly barren, utterly empty. Closer, it becomes evident that what looked like smooth slopes are actually ravine-gashed jumbles of windworn rock, and what looked from afar like the faint green of dusty grass is actually the fuzz of palo verde, ironwood, cactus, occasional mesquite. Closer yet, actually back into the mountains, grass does grow rank enough to hide animals far larger than deer, grass not green but sun-blasted into a bone tan. The crevices between the boulders become full-sized alleys; the brush in some sections actually tangles; gladed pockets, flower-grown at certain seasons of the year, open in the canyons. When you are deepest into the jumbled mountains there is water, year-round water. It disappears now and again into the canyon sand, only to ooze up again several hundred yards below. But there's always water somewhere. Like the Apaches, the deer know where it is. What was utter emptiness from far away becomes, close up, full of surprising life. These mountains are the hideout of the Coues deer. And he *hides* in them.

"Remember those two I watched yesterday, the young buck and the doe? You screeled and squawled on that bobcat call, which you say sometimes will start deer out of a brushy pocket, but they never moved an ear no matter what horrible racket you made. Probably wouldn't have shifted until you walked right onto 'em."

"Don't your eastern whitetail do the same way?" asked George.

"Never tried scaring 'em to death with a racket like the rape and murder of two dozen rabbits—but the difference is that the whitetail back home have something to hide in, a spruce thicket

or laurel clump, or a swamp—these little gents hide out where there seems to be nothing to hide behind!"

These deer, as I came to realize, use their eyes to a far greater degree than do the timber-loving Virginia deer. They often move out so far ahead of hunters that very evidently sight, not scent or sound, alerts them.

That reliance on sight in a way handed me my first chance of the year on a Coues buck. George and I had nooned up on the peak, snoozing an hour or two out of the wind, and had actually blown the game, or so we thought, when we came over the crest and were momentarily skylined. A band of several deer had already moved out from under the rimrock, a favorite lying-up spot, for a midafternoon snack. Seeing us they had spilled off down the slope and disappeared beyond two gullies. It appeared they were going to run off the entire range.

On the way across the jagged sidehill, however, we hastened not, nor did we forget to move as quietly as Vibram-soled boots and sun-rotted granite would permit. There was no reason why an intervening Coues or two might either be staying hidden behind some eroded boulder or be lying like gray camouflage cloth in the sparse shade of an ocotillo clump. There weren't, but in Coues deer country, even when a chunk of mountain acreage seems as bare as Jimmy Durante's skull, you must continue to expect to see deer. Because you often will. Not this time, however.

We finally made out the little band of departing deer. They'd run farther than usual; had actually slipped down off the mountain into a tangle of juniper-clad sidehills, mule-deer country. But busily engaged in watching them was a fair buck, the best we'd seen in rifle range. He was so engrossed in using his eyes on the movement below that he momentarily forgot to look high and behind. This was his fatal error.

I almost missed him at that, guessing the range at three hundred when it was less than two hundred and fifty, simply because I found it hard to believe that a perfectly formed buck could be so small. The first shot went over his back, the next two were misses as he skedaddled toward better cover, but the fourth put a one-hundred-grain Nosler bullet through his chest. He still made another fifty yards, finally pitched into a sheer-sided gully where without the telltale blood I'd never have found him. A representative eight-point only, he had knocked off several sprockets in the tumble.

"And given us a merry chase, too," I said to Parker. "Let's see, now. We've been on this range for seven days of hunting, five with Doc Rusten, two more ending tonight. By my reckoning I've seen perhaps a dozen bucks, two the first evening that were in easy range, this one, and eight or ten more either on the next mountain and running or slipping out around a corner so quick as to give no shot. Yet you say this is the best Coues deer area in the state.

"Close to it," answered George. "Years back I often spotted

that many in a day. Of course the thing on Coues is not what you see but the deer you don't see!

"Come back in January, you and Russ Cutter," said George, "and we'll go down into the Sierra Madre, look up another brand of Coues deer. They run pretty far down into Mexico, you know."

I couldn't fail to agree with an excuse for another hunt as valid as that one. We'd take in the goose shooting at Babicora on the way. Meanwhile we had the job of toting out the buck. A carcass hefting only a hundred with the innards dropped and the legs off at the hock gets heavy within a quarter mile, even downhill.

When later George went to find the Jeep and drive it up the wash, there was time to think a little bit about Coues deer. Several oddities about them appeared. Their ears, for example, seemed to stick out far more than do those of the woods-loving whitetail breeds, almost as if mule-deer bucks had made a sashay or two up into Coues country. They were grayer than any northern whitetail, even the whitetail of Texas, and a mite more smooth-coated. They were obviously able to get along with little or no water, but gained needed moisture from the pulpy insides of pawed-apart barrel cactus. All the hide-and-sneak stunts of the regular whitetail were theirs, but refined and adapted to the arid Arizona terrain.

Staying put seemed to me more a trait of the Coues deer, though their cold-country cousins will often lay doggo if they think a hunter may walk on past. Parker and I had rolled tons of boulders over rimrock edges to go slamming on down slopes, blasting into noisy dust. But only once so far had this bombardment, usually so efficacious on high-country mule-deer bucks, pushed out deer lying in under us. Then a doe had moved off casually, as if rolling rocks were normal to the desert sidehills.

It struck me also that the Coues deer are more sensitive to human noise, even conversation, than are their eastern cousins, I suspect primarily because they hear less of it in the sunlit ranges. I couldn't agree with George that his beloved varmint call would surely move them out of thickets and canyon pockets because we tried that dozens of times. More often than not it produced not

deer but a boar javelina or two, trotting in to see what noisy critter was upsetting his harem of sows and piglets. But metallic
clicks, or any of those noises associated with humans rather than
with nature, would rouse instant reaction from the delicately attuned Coues deer.

When in January we rode Cutter's Cessna down into Mexico to
find the ranch far back into the Sierras where Parker's *amigos* had
promised to show us zillions of Coues deer, it looked as if hunting
them would also be tough on airplanes. The strip below us looked
impossible. It was short, though Russ and I had come in smoothly
on landings as short before. It was high, too, at seven thousand or
better, up where the air is thin and a plane's performance falls off.
But worse, a hot afternoon breeze was blowing crosswise to the
ridge of which the strip, hacked out with shovel and wheelbarrow,
scarred the side as it ran down to the edge of a two-thousand-foot
dropoff. That would create a strong down draft. We made one
pass. That was enough to see the men and mules awaiting us, but
also enough to feel the plane mushing away under us, sensitive to
the hot air and crosswind. Only an angel could land on that strip
under those conditions. If we tried it, we'd become angels.

"Not today, boys," said Cutter. "Tomorrow at dawn, mebbe.
Better we spend the night at Madera, eighty miles east."

The next morning was anticlimactic. In the heavy, cool air,
with no upsetting side wind, we put ourselves and our gear onto
the strip handily, and loaded up mules for an hour of travel to the
ranch. It, with a worked-out silver mine down near river level,
was the reason for the strip.

There was an abandoned building on the mountain *estancia*
where we could live, said the *vaqueros,* and there were many deer
in the hills surrounding it, *mucho venado.* But in two days of hard
hunting it became evident to us that though the Coues may earlier have been dwelling in the foothills, they had moved somewhere else, very likely straight up. We could see tall long-needled
pines darkening the topmost ridges.

"Maybe they just got sick of cactus and sun-blasted rocks," I
suggested, "and went home, went back to cool timber, where
whitetail ought to be anyway."

Could be, George and Russ agreed, but we'd have to change our method of operation to hunt that country. Too far from the *rancho*. Why not base on the airstrip, which was halfway up the mountain?

But even with our bedrolls laid out in an abandoned corral near the strip, it was still a long way to the crest of the sierra, four hours on bony saddle animals whose decrepit appearance belied the stamina that kept them shuffling upward. The country changed as we climbed, the brush beginning to show leaves as well as thorns. Where the trail wound back into the head of a canyon, sizable oaks proved that there was ample water underground, and in the dry stream bed a succession of low stone dams showed where some prehistoric Indian race had tried to hold back floodwaters for the drier seasons.

It was noon when we heard the faint echoes of two shots coming from the ridge series that Russ and one of the *vaqueros* had elected to climb. Two shots is usually bad news, but from the spacing the second was probably a finisher and he had his buck.

The trail we were using had been cut in centuries long past by mule trains carrying high-grade silver ore out over the mountains. It was clean but had washed away to one-hoof width in the steeper spots. There were few places to stop and glass the country.

But we didn't need glasses to see a bunch of deer moving up through the timber to the right. They had obviously been watching us, finally decided that we were coming too close even at six hundred or seven hundred yards.

"Might stop on the far side of the hogback," said George, swinging down alongside me. "If they do, they can't move left, and if we work along to the right, we might stop 'em again. One pretty good buck. He'll be staying close to his does at this season."

It seemed worth the climb. A great fault in the mountain shoulder impassably isolated that ridge from the main peak, eliminating one path of escape. We'd try it.

Beyond the knife-edge of the ridge, when we puffed up onto it, was nothing but blue mountain air. A near-cliff off a hundred yards under our feet to a narrow bench. Below that was emptiness for a thousand feet or more, the cliffs forming the rim of a vast valley accessible only if we dropped back almost off the range. The deer had disappeared completely.

Or had they? Suddenly from directly under us a doe stepped daintily away from the rock wall. Then she broke into a playful run, heading to the left, around that corner which we knew ended in a cliff impassable even by goats. Then a buck trotted purpose-fully after her, head low in the attitude typical of the rutting chase. That doe wanted to be caught!

But I was not interested in love among the *venados*. If the buck wanted to chase the doe into a cul-de-sac, that was his private business. I'd merely get set and wait for them to come back onto the bench. But both deer heard gravel slide under my boots be-fore they had turned the rock corner, stopped and looked back. Maybe there was some way for deer to get off the last cliff. Better shoot.

The 6 mm. bullet sliced neatly through the little buck's neck and he dropped, kicking, each kick carrying him nearer the cliff edge. He hung up only on the final clump of prickly pear.

"Lucky you," said George. "One wiggle more and he'd have dropped into that chasm. We never could have found him. Worst place I ever saw a critter shot in. Worse'n goat cliffs."

Maybe there is a bit of goat blood mixed into the Coues deer. The rutting buck smelled goaty and certainly the rockpile he lived on was billy heaven. But goats are a mite dumb, or at least nonsmart. And the Coues deer is smart. That is, he's smarter than a human unless there's a pretty doe to run after. Then he can be almost as dumb as a man.

FIRST BUCK

Jim Rikhoff

As readers of his book Mixed Bag *already know, the founder and honcho of Amwell Press is no slouch himself when it comes to story-telling.*

The kid gets his buck in high style and good company—something that should be every young man's birthright. This story first appeared in Field & Stream.

EVERY YEAR IN LATE SEPTEMBER or early October, the funny feeling finds its way into my body. I wake one day and the summer is over. There is a cool snap to the air, suddenly the leaves have turned and the wind is pulling them down. I find a new energy, long dormant with the summer heat, and a strange sort of nervous excitement lies just beneath the surface of my day-to-day outward demeanor. It's hunting season. As any man, from earliest pre-history until even these too modern years, I wander the fields and forests, tramping the ground in search of game. For me, it is the best of times, days to be spent with my dogs and, lately, my son.

My son was seventeen the first day of this month, November, 1978. He is about two inches taller than his liege, his hands are an inch longer and he wears a size 11½ shoe, wide and getting wider. I take a somewhat courteous approach in my corrective attitude these days than he previously enjoyed. I have also always held the opinion that firearms are like sex—an irresistible attraction to normal tads and one, that if not properly attended to at home, will certainly be experienced somewhere else, not necessarily in the best interest of all concerned. Consequently, my son has accompanied me on a number of what we tell his mother are necessary "survey" trips in the field.

He made his first Canadian fishing trip—with a motley group dubiously labeled "The Winchester Irregulars"—when he was nine. Since we had a small discussion prior to this first big expedition away from the nest, he remained reasonably quiet while the "gentlemen" were having refreshments, relating historic feats for the benefit of posterity and sharpening their skills at games of chance. He said "Yessir" and "No sir" at appropriate times, displayed passable table manners, fetched cooling fluids with a minimum of urging and kept his mouth shut upon his return home. He also caught a hellacious big bass and decided that he liked these sorts of trips better than going shopping with his sisters.

Shortly thereafter, young Jimmy found that virtue (and listening to the Old Fellow) occasionally pays off in more tangible reward than a pat on the noggin. His "Uncle" Harry Tennison launched the first Irregular's Texas deer hunt and invited both Rikhoffs the next December. Jimmy turned ten November 1, 1971 and, among other presents, there was an old cut-down .257 Roberts rifle Jack O'Connor had had made back in Arizona when he was just starting out as a gun writer. The rifle had a Sukalle barrel on a Mauser action and the woodwork, believe it or not, was by Griffin and Howe. Jack's wife Eleanor had used it for years in their early days in the Southwest and both of Jack's sons, Bradford and Jerry, had shot his first deer with it. Jack had taken a fancy to my wife Janet and, noting she was only 4′11″, had decided that .257 Roberts was just the hunting rifle for her. She agreed and carried it with some honor on a long Scottish deer stalk a little later. With Jimmy coming of age for his first deer hunt, what more appropriate rifle to carry than the O'Connor gift?

A week or so before Christmas, Gene Hill, Ed Zern and the two of us drove to Newark Airport and what we hoped would be a fast flight to San Antonio, where the troops were mustering prior to heading for the Texas Hill Country. As luck would have it, it was Jimmy's first airplane trip and it almost decided him against flying forever and hunting too, if it took airplanes to get there. Without over-reliving horrible moments, let it suffice to say we were scheduled to leave at 1:00 P.M. one afternoon and finally arrived after several plane changes, at 4:30 A.M. the next morning. After three hours sleep, we loaded into a travel lodge and headed for deer country. It was a good break-in trip for a young hunter.

Our tyro hunter had good companions with whom to identify. In addition to the aforementioned, Grits Gresham, Joe Hudson,

John Thompson, Guy Coheleach, Junior Hummel and Ben Wright were on hand to lend weighty advice and a bit of needling to keep him in line. After settling down in the bunk room and getting our gear organized, Harry took Jimmy and me out late in the afternoon so we could get the lay of the land.

As our pick-up crested a gently rolling hill, a young six-point buck popped up ahead of us and, after a cool scrutiny, leisurely took off over another adjoining ridge. Jimmy's eyes followed the buck's retreat with a great deal of interest and, I believe, a smidgen of blood lust. There was an old abandoned loafing shed for cattle in the middle of what must have been an old pasture. The fences were broken down and the shed itself had about half its roof and sides missing. It was a perfect blind from which to cover the open fields surrounding us for about half-a-mile in most directions.

We left the truck some distance away in a patch of mesquite and settled down in our shed. We cautioned Jimmy to remain quiet and motionless. There was no wind and sound carried the proverbial country mile; the shed was sufficiently open that movement was easily discernible to wild eyes on the alert. Time passed, shadows lengthened in the fading sunlight, animal noises punctuated the stillness with increasing frequency and, then, a couple of does silently glided into view. Jimmy almost had a stroke.

We watched them for minutes that stretched into timelessness. No buck. A couple of other does, one with a yearling, joined the first group. We remained quiet and immobile. Our legs cramped and we stifled nervous coughs. Then Harry slowly reached over and nudged Jimmy, silently beckoning him to look over to the far left. The six-point buck had returned. He stood still and alert on the edge of the field. After several moments, he cocked one ear and then picked his way forward toward the does.

Jimmy slowly raised his head as the buck ambled closer. Harry whispered the obvious question. Did the boy want the buck? He did. Ever so carefully he raised the rifle and inched it through the broken boards. For an eternity of time, he peered through the 4-power 'scope. The barrel was weaving from side to side in about a

three-inch arc. I looked at Harry. He was patiently holding his tongue and his breath. Finally, the boy allowed as how he couldn't see the deer. It looked like the deer could see us.

Finally the buck moved closer, but to one side, and was lost to Jimmy's view completely. There was no choice, the light was fading and we had to move out of the shed. The back wall was completely down so we crawled backward, scrunched down on our bellies until we were lying by the side rear section. Jimmy rose again, bringing the old O'Connor rifle up over a fallen timber. The gun still weaved. The buck was about 70 yards away and on the alert. We were fast losing light. Harry whispered: "The next time your 'scope passes through his shoulder, squeeze off a shot!" He was desperate. Jimmy fired seconds later. The buck leaped sidewise and took off. I jumped up with my Model 70 and was bringing it down on the buck when Harry's voice stopped me: "Don't shoot! He's going down!"

We were strangely silent as we walked to where the deer lay

about 100 or so yards away. The buck was absolutely motionless and I could see the small hole just behind his shoulder. A well-placed shot and a stone-dead deer. I looked at Harry and he answered with a quiet smile of mixed pleasure and relief. We both looked down at the young hunter.

"Is he dead? Did I do it right?" he asked.

"Yep, nailed him right through the shoulder . . . A good shot . . . Well, you've got your first deer. How about that! Congratulations . . . Must have been dead while he ran . . . They often do that . . . ," Harry's and my exclamations, once released, tumbled out in mixed excitement. The boy shivered a bit and then, suddenly, he was crying. Harry and I stopped, dumbfounded, and then Harry reached out and enveloped the boy in his arms.

"Thank God you've done that! Thank Heavens you care! I'm so glad you feel like that. Don't you know, that makes his life mean something. . . . If you hadn't cared about killing him, it would have meant that he wasn't worth anything. I always feel the same way and so does your Dad. You don't have to be ashamed of crying. I'm so glad you did. . . . It means you cared." Harry's words rushed out and around the boy, who looked up at Harry and then to me.

"That's right, son, we all feel that way the first time and, to be honest, a little bit that way *every* time. You've got to face up to what you're doing. Nobody should ever take life cheaply or else none of it is worthwhile. I think if I ever stopped being a little sad after killing an animal, I'd give up hunting."

"Pardner, it's as natural as anything in the world—both the hunting and the sorrow mixed with the satisfaction of a good hunt," Harry said, releasing the boy, but keeping an arm around his shoulder. I bent down and broke off a sprig of sage.

"Well, it's not evergreen, but this is Texas and it'll have to do." I leaned over and dipped the leaves in the spreading patch of blood on the deer's shoulder. "They have a custom in Europe called blooding. They dip a piece of evergreen in the animal's blood and smear it across the hunter's face. Then they stand silent for a minute over the animal, with the evergreen laid over the wound. That's so everyone can think about what they have just

] 317 [

done and about God's creatures, hunted and hunter, and how it's always been this way since man first crawled from a cave. The hunter doesn't wash the blood from his face for the rest of the day so he will remember." I raised my hand and gently brushed the sage across my son's cheek. His hand reached up and the fingers came away with a faint crimson staining the fingers. He was still silent but the tears had stopped. We stood by the fallen buck for a moment, heads a bit bowed, each with his own thoughts.

"You forgot," Jimmy said. He reached over, took the sage from my hand and placed it over the wound in the deer's shoulder. Harry smiled and I found that my tension slowly relaxed.

"It's getting dark," I looked up. "Now comes the other part of hunting." I rolled up my sleeves, took out my hunting knife and crouched down over the deer. Harry helped me roll him over on his back and I made the first cut down from his chest cavity, around his genitalia and anus, opening up his unpunctured stomach cavity. As with most Texas hill country, deer, he was rather small-bodied and he was easy to dress.

"You really know what you're doing," Jimmy said, seemingly surprised that his father, whom he had always secretly suspected of dimwittedness, should know something so basic as cleaning out a deer.

"Everyone has to do at least one thing well," Harry chuckled, "and it took us years to teach him that!"

We loaded the deer and drove back to camp. Jimmy had made a full recovery of both his emotions and his mouth. He kept reliving the hunt, the shot, the deer's last run and how he had dropped "like he had been axed." I looked over his head and caught Harry's eye. His wry grimace said it all. That deer was getting bigger by the minute, the shot was stretching out longer and, at the crucial moment of truth, the light had faded—even more than we realized.

We had another deer hunter on our hands.

STALKING SNOW

Walt Sandberg

The publication of Walt Sandberg's The Turn in the Trail *by Amwell Press earlier this year was a particularly happy event for me. I've been a fan of Walt's work—both as an editor and a reader—for some years and welcomed the opportunity to have his best pieces in one collection.*
"Stalking Snow" is but one of the reasons I feel that way.

THE FIRST BIG SNOWSTORM of the season swept down from Canada and into the North Country late Friday as six-hundred-thousand hunters marshaled on the highways impatient to reach their favorite stands before the opening of white-tail deer season at dawn, Saturday.

On the six o'clock news, the TV weatherman recounted the storm's advance with that sadistic delight common to media meteorologists everywhere. "It's a real Saskatchewan Screamer," he chortled, enjoying visions of atmospheric calamity. "More than six inches of snow should accumulate before morning and the temperature is expected to drop to ten degrees behind the passing cold front."

"What a jerk," Axel Abelman said as he punched the "off" switch on the TV set and turned to collect his hunting gear. "The drive north is going to be pure hell."

"Well," I said, "we'll have that tracking snow everyone has been hoping for."

"Tracking snow! What a misnomer," sputtered Axel. "A slight dusting of the stuff is all that's needed to separate a deer from its background. *Seeing* snow, I call it. Anything heavier is superfluous, redundant and absolutely unnecessary."

"Call it what you like Axel," said Hillard Selvey, "but I'll be content if it's *getting-back* snow. You won't get lost when you can backtrack your own fresh trail."

"Oh, yeah?" Hardwood Hansen questioned. "How come I found you stumbling out of the brush way over on Zinther Road last season? There was plenty of getting-back snow for you to backtrack that time."

"Ah," Hillard replied."How was I to know that some citified hunter had got himself lost while wearing boots identical to mine? Besides, the wind was blowing and covered his tracks."

I laughed, but I didn't join their banter because I had a plan for the next morning that would get me a trophy buck. And I relished the thought of the thick covering of tracking snow that would guide me to him. But that was before I learned that human hunters aren't the only creatures who will use fresh snow to stalk their quarrry.

During the night the storm subsided and daybreak brought a dull sky of tarnished silver that subdued the woods and transformed the vast expanse of North Country around Burnt Stump Lodge into a bizarrely sinister world of disquieting stillness.

Overnight, the wet snow had accumulated on the tree branches, bowing them under the load. Then, with the sudden temperature drop the TV weatherman had predicted, the weighted boughs had frozen into grotesque disarray, sprouting phantom-like through the icy mist that shrouded the forest in ghostly white gauze. The effect was enchanting, but bewildering. The landmarks that had become familiar to me while chasing grouse around these hills in October were now out of proportion and mostly unrecognizable in the billows of low-hanging, ice-crystal mists locally called a "whiteout."

I should have known better than to blunder cross country at such a time, but the trophy-taking plan had been building in me since last deer season and now I was compelled to carry it out.

After knotting a bandanna around my neck as a barrier to the frozen snow that would plop from any disturbed branches to lodge behind the collar of my hunting coat, there to send trickles of chilling meltwater down my spine, I struck off from the cabin.

First, I explored the sharp, oak ridgelines to the west that the whitetails used as a nighttime feeding area. From there, I skirted the edge cover between swamp and uplands and then I wandered toward the beaver pond along the bank of an intersecting creek.

I was looking for the track of a buck. And once a likely track was identified, I intended to follow it and walk the animal down. It's a hunting technique that sometimes pays off in a handsome trophy but it can take the better part of a day. That's why most hunters don't attempt it.

You have to get an early start, too, if you're to locate a likely track before the fresh snow becomes marred by other tracks that could divert you from the trail. Then you work the animal fast and hard until you jump it from its daytime bed. After that you ease off and doggedly pursue it until your quarry becomes confused. Usually, that will require five or six hours of methodical hounding after which the buck will become puzzled and unwary.

Then, as the animal realizes that its pursuer is a relentless cuss, it will become dazed and uncomprehending, stopping often to study its stalker. Such behavior is a signal to adjust your pace so that the deer will always be about a hundred yards away. Sooner or later, this will force the buck to stand its ground in a bold attempt to confront its tormentor. That's when you shoot.

Hardwood Hansen had indoctrinated me in this method, cautioning that its chief disadvantage is that I might have a dead animal on my hands, miles from the cabin with no clear idea of where I'd been nor where I was.

Still, my mind was made up. I would stalk a trophy buck this season and skid it back to Burnt Stump Lodge in triumph.

Now, as I wandered toward the back end of the beaver pond on the crackling new ice, I saw where deer, just minutes before, had munched on the greybeard moss that clings to the desiccated snags of tamarack and cedar that had been drowned in the rising water when the pond was formed. Evidently the moss was a delicacy, for I saw where the deer had walked directly to it over the still unsound ice.

Cautiously, keeping well away from the tree trunks, brush clumps and from the mounds of vegetation that were the muskrat's winter cache of food—all places where the ice was still dangerously thin—I studied the lacework of freshly laid deer tracks.

Although it's difficult to tell the sex and size of a deer merely by its tracks, Hardwood Hansen had shown me how careful observation will disclose a variety of clues. Taken together, the signs will help a hunter to discern the track of a trophy buck from that of a lesser deer.

Any small track, of course, can be disregarded. And a doe, even a large one, walks with a mincing daintiness. The imprint of the toe will be close to, and point forward or slightly inward of an imaginary line centered in the track. The mark of a doe's hind-foot, too, will be nearly superimposed on the impression left by the forefoot.

A large buck, however, walks purposefully, regally. Its tracks will be spread several inches to each side of the imaginary center-line, the toe will point outboard, and there will be a space be-tween the imprint of the hindfoot and the forefoot. Generally, the larger the track, the farther the impressions from the centerline, and the greater the space between hindfoot and forefoot, the larger the deer.

The single track I came upon as I walked an open area of the thickest ice left no doubt that it was that of a trophy buck. The toe of the wide, splayed hoofs pointed outboard, spread ten inches on either side of the centerline, with a gap of perhaps six inches separating the tracks.

Quickly, I moved out along the trail. By its meandering course, I could see that the buck was unconcerned. It had paused here and there to nibble on the white cedar and hemlock boughs pushed down to within feeding height by the weight of the snow. Then, a few hundred yards from the pond, I came upon a patch of urine, yellow in the snow, still steaming.

I increased my pace, sure that my trophy would be bedded down only minutes ahead, and momentarily noted the eerie si-lence that had now become pervasive. It was a quality of the out-doors that I'd encountered only twice before: once, preceding a tornado; and another time in the moments before a boar black-bear had slipped out of heavy cover to the bait below my bow-hunting stand.

A similar mood settled around me now; the soft swish of wool, the rhythmic crunch of snow, and the harsh rasping of my breathing as I walked were the only sounds. Still, I gave all of that no more than a passing thought, the image of the buck wandering about only minutes ahead firmly in my mind.

Indeed, so intent was I on the track that I was startled breathless by the flight of a snowshoe hare, mottled brown-and-white in its transition coat bounding from a brushy, snow-covered burrow at my passing.

Later, a pileated woodpecker gave me a start when it burst from a head-high hole in a gigantic dead poplar tree, brushing my cheek with a wingfeather in its haste to be away.

After a while, the buck led me on a convoluted route into country that I had never seen before; as Hardwood had warned, I had no idea of where I was.

The increasing coldness of the air working against the warmth of the moist new snow had intensified the whiteout. Visibility in the woods was down to a few dozen yards. There was thunder in the distance, too, unusual this time of year, signaling the approach of another storm.

Near noon, I realized that the buck hadn't bedded down. Either the unsettled weather was spooking it, or perhaps I was traveling so closely behind that it didn't want to chance the rest.

By now, too, I was very thirsty, and hunger sounds gurgled in my stomach—ransom for my forgetfulness in having left my canteen and lunchbag on the table back at the lodge.

About mid-afternoon, the woods around still shrouded in the whiteout, as the buck again circled and crossed an earlier track, I was startled to see a third set of imprints along our backtrail. They were large, cat-like, with traces of fresh blood in every second pawprint on what would be a quadruped's left side.

"Cripes," I muttered aloud. "I've been stalking the buck and something else is stalking me."

At the sound of my voice I heard hissing sounds from up the trail, like the periodic escape of steam from a household iron, only louder. I turned quickly, saw nothing and uneasily resumed the hunt.

Light-headed now for lack of water and from too long without food, I began to speculate about the nature of the creature that apparently prowled this territory with me.

The Indians of the area, I recalled, often told tales of the Windigo—superhuman, evil giants, cannibalistic monsters with hearts of ice whose spirits arose in the deep forests in the dead of winter. It was said of them that they hissed at every breath and that their footsteps in the snow were always soaked in blood. And they were alleged to crave human flesh and to prefer dispatching their victims by disembowelment.

The idea, I decided, was absurd. Anthropologists have established that although the ancient Indians did see strange visions hovering among the ice-locked trees, and truly believed them to be a living Windigo, the spectres were merely hallucinations brought on by dehydration and lack of sufficient carbohydrates in a sparse winter diet.

Perhaps, I reasoned, the same illusion was now being created by my own mind for the very same reasons. Perhaps I'd only imagined the bloody tracks. And if that was the case I was near my physical limit and it would be wise to end the hunt and return to the food and warmth of the cabin.

But where was I? And where was the cabin? I had no way of knowing. The compass would not help. I hadn't used it to check my progress and therefore couldn't know in which direction the cabin lay. There was only one prudent thing to do: backtrack the trail. If I pushed hard, I should reach the cabin well before dusk.

I turned, ready for the long trek back, when I heard again the hissing sounds. Then, fifty yards of plodding along the backtrail, I saw where the bloody pawprints, perhaps at the time I chose to abort my hunt, had cut away and into a thick stand of cedar well away from the trail.

Wary now, I peered into the snow-covered boughs, trying to penetrate the maze, saw nothing, but was suddenly struck with the sensation that whatever had been tracking me so diligently was watching now, awaiting my confusion, ready to pounce at the proper moment.

I squatted to examine the bloodied snow. What I saw on my fingers was blood all right. It was no illusion. The creature wasn't a phantom. It was alive, probably wounded, perhaps by a trap. And it was hungry, although patiently stalking its prey.

"Well, my friend," I called into the cedars, "here's one supper that you shall go without."

In reply the hissing sounds resumed, accompanied by a nervous rustling from deep within the screen of trees.

Then, glancing up, I saw the buck, upwind of me, pawing in the snow with a forefoot and watching me curiously from atop a small hummock not twenty yards down the trail and midway between me and the stand of cedar. He was a magnificent animal and had obviously reached the point of distraction that I'd earlier hoped would be produced by my hours of steady pursuit.

Then, beyond the distraught and unsuspecting buck, I saw something more. A huge cat-like creature leaped soundlessly from the cedars, favoring its left forepaw. And cutting in from either side, forming a phalanx that would prevent the buck's escape, two smaller cats emerged, their maltese coats glistening in the pale golden glow of diffused light passing through the icy mist.

The trio, which from my recall of all the animal books I'd read might have been outsized bobcats, converged in a few powerful and effortless bounds toward the deer. I watched, fascinated.

Too late, the buck sensed the attack. The middle cat was already on the deer's back, gripping the tawny hide with it talons, chewing at the buck's throat.

The buck, momentarily knocked off balance, screamed, reared, flailed the air with its hoofs, and whipped its antlers in a frenzied attempt to dislodge his attacker. The second cat blindsided the buck and the third cat dashed in to rip open the exposed belly with one powerful swipe of a paw.

The battle was over in seconds and the smaller cats tore into the buck's intestines, gulping the bloody, steaming tendrils with savage relish.

During the brief attack, I had remained, transfixed by the display, in my squatting position beside the trail. Now I slipped the rifle sling off my shoulder and stood to aim at the wounded cat— the largest of the three. But as I did so, the creature turned, bloody shreds of flesh clinging to its muzzle, and stared directly at me. I held the cat's gaze in my rifle sight for long moments, peering deeply into its penetrating yellow eyes, and I swear it was mocking me. For it dipped its head, curled its lips into the semblance of a conspiratorial smile, purposefully tore out the buck's heart, then tossed it skyward, catching it in midair and, swallowing the meat in a single gulp.

I should have felt revulsion, or at the very least a measure of fright. But I felt neither. It was as if some primitive signal had passed between us—predator-to-predator—that mutually acknowledged which of us was the better hunter.

I lowered my rifle, slung it on my shoulder and turned to trudge the backtrail to the cabin through the new-fallen stalking snow, as the thunder, closer now, resounded fitfully about me.

THE LADY IN GREEN

Archibald Rutledge

*Although his two best collections of hunting stories—*Hunter's Choice *(Doubleday) and* An American Hunter *(Doubleday)—contain some pieces on the Pennsylvania mountains where he taught English at Mercersburg Academy, Archibald Rutledge will probably always be remembered as the most eloquent chronicler of hunting and wildlife in the South Carolina low country—the tawny sedge flats and emerald pine woods, the black-water swamps of cypress and sweetgum.*

His famous plantation, Hampton, is only a short distance from Charleston and is virtaully on the bank of the mighty Santee River, the setting of many of his best stories.

After retiring from his teaching chores at Mercersburg in 1937, he spent the next thirty-six years at Hampton before passing away at the age of 89.

Deer and turkey hunting were his first loves of the field sports, and this piece from Hunter's Choice *is one of his best.*

FOR A VERY LONG TIME we have had on the plantation a Negro named Steve. For a generation he worked for us; and he is with me to this day. While we usually had certain Negroes who could be counted on to accomplish even difficult material tasks, in what might be termed the realm of the psychic, Steve reigned supreme. For some reason, he was at his best when something esoteric and peculiar had to be accomplished. My Colonel early recognized Steve's strange talent, and occasionally called on him to exercise it.

Thus when the lady in green came to us for a visit, and came with the hope of killing a regal buck, I felt called upon to enlist the darksome strategy of Steve.

"Steve," I asked, "have you ever seen a woman wear pants?"

"I ain't done seen it, Cap'n," he responded, a fervent fire of recollection kindling in his eyes, "but I has done seen some wimmins what act like dey wears dem."

"Has your Amnesia ever worn them?"

"When I is around home," he assured me, "she don't ever wear anything else but."

"Have you two been falling out again, Steve?"

"Cap'n," he answered solemnly, "for yeahs and yeahs we ain't never done fell in."

"I guess she doesn't like your playing around with all these young girls, and leaving her at home."

"I tole her dat woman and cat is to stay home; man and dog is to go abroad. She didn't like dat atall, atall."

"Well," I said, "this is Friday. Monday will be Christmas Day. I know just one way I can get you out of the dog-house where Amnesia has put you. Wouldn't you like to get out for Christmas?"

Steve licked his lips, a sure sign that he is about to take the bait. Besides, as I had beforehand been of assistance to him in the vital matter of domestic reconciliations, he regards me as a kind of magician.

"Tomorrow," I told him, "will be Saturday, the day before Christmas Eve. I will help you, but I expect you to help me." I was testing his loyalty in a large way.

Haunted by a sense of his own helplessness and by the mastery of his huge Amnesia, he appeared pathetically eager to do anything. In fact, such was his yielding mood that I had to be careful what I asked him to do, for he would do it. Steve can resist anything but temptation.

"I'm giving a big deer drive tomorrow," I said. "There will be twenty men and one woman—but I hear she wears pants."

"Great Gawd," was Steve's comment.

"Green ones," I went on.

"Jeedus!"

"Now, Steve, you know that old flathorn buck in the Wambaw Corner—the one that has been dodging us for about five years?"

"You mean him what hab dem yaller horns, flat same like a paddle?"

"He's the one."

"Cap'n, dat's a buck what I knows like I knows the way to another man's watermelon patch," Steve assured me grinning.

] 328 [

"What you want me to do? And how Amnesia suddenly gwine take me back because of what you is planning for me to do?"

"Well," I told him, "you've got a job, all right. I don't want to be unfair to these men, but ordinary bucks will do very well for them. Your business is to get the *buck with the palmated horns* to run to the lady in green. If you will do this, I will give you a whole haunch of venison, a ham out of my smoke-house, a dollar in cash and a dress for Amnesia. How about it?"

Steve was stunned. When he came to, he said, "Boss, when I gits to heaben, I ain't gwine ask, 'How 'bout it?' "

"Of course," I told him, "I will put her on the Crippled Oak Stand. You know that is the favorite buck run. Just how you are going to get him to run there I don't know, but you probably can figure it out. Oh," I added, "I will not hold you responsible for her killing the buck. Being a woman, she'll probably miss it anyway. But I want you to give her a chance to shoot."

I could see that Steve was already deep in his problem. Knowing the woods like an Indian, so familiar with game that he can almost talk with it, familiar also with the likelihood of big game's acting in ways unpredictable, Steve was pretty well equipped for his task. I could almost see how he would enjoy this particular job.

"One more thing," I told him: "this lady doesn't shoot a shotgun. She always uses a rifle."

"Cap'n," he sensibly asked, "does you think she knows a deer? If she don't, I mustn't get too close to dat rifle."

"I have never seen her," I told him, "and I don't know whether she is a real huntress. All I know about her is what I have been told. But she's the daughter of one of my best friends, a gentleman from Philadelphia. I want her to have a good time. Think of what it would mean if she could kill the crowned king of Wambaw Corner!"

"I sure loves to please wimmins," Steve mused, "but so far I ain't done had too much of luck."

As we parted I kept pounding home his job to him: "Drive the buck with the flat horns to the Crippled Oak Stand. Drive him there if you have to head him off. And remember the haunch and the ham that will be yours if you manage it right."

Not long after daylight the following morning the crowd of Christmas hunters assembled in my plantation yard. As the season was nearing its close, every man I had invited came. And there was the lady in green. When I saw her, I was ashamed of the way in which I had bandied words with Steve about the nature of her attire. She was slender, graceful and very lovely. She looked like Maid Marian. Clad in Lincoln green, with a jaunty feather in her Robin Hood's cap, she was the attraction of all eyes. I could see that all the men were in love with her, and I didn't feel any too emotionally normal myself. There was nothing about her of the type of huntress I had described to Steve. She appeared a strange combination of an elf, a child and a woman; and though I do not profess to know much about such matters, that particular combination seems especially alluring, perhaps dangerously so.

While my Negro drivers were getting their horses ready, and while stately deer hounds, woolly dogs and curs of low degree gathered from far and near on account of the general air of festivity and the promise of some break in the general hunger situation, I got everybody together and told them that we planned to drive the great Wambaw Corner; that we had standers enough to take care of the whole place, we had drivers and dogs, we had deer. The great, and really the only, question was: Can anybody hit anything? That is often a pertinent question in hunting.

Wambaw Corner is peculiarly situated. A tract of nearly a thousand acres, it is bounded on two sides by the wide and deep Wambaw Creek. On one side is the famous Lucas Reserve, an immense backwater, formerly used for waterpower, but now chiefly for bass and bream. In shape this place is a long and comparatively narrow peninsula, with water on three sides. On the south runs a wide road, along which I usually post my standers; but when I have enough (or too many), I post them along the creek. The chance there is excellent, for if a buck is suspicious there's nothing he'll do quicker than dodge back and swim the creek.

With the woods still sparkling with dew, and fragrant with the aromas from myrtles and pines, I posted all my standers. I had sent my drivers far down on the tip of the peninsula, to drive it out to the road. I had also had a last word with Steve.

"Only one mistake you might be can is makin', Cap'n," he told me: "I dunno how 'bout wid a gun, but with a rollin'-pin or a skillet or a hatchet a woman don't eber seem to miss. Anyhow," he particularized, "dey don't neber miss me!"

"Have you got your plan made?" I asked him. "You've got five other boys to drive. That just about sets you free to do what you want to."

"I got my plan," he said. "And," he added darkly, "if so happen it be dat I don't come out with de other drivers, you will onnerstand."

In a place like Wambaw Corner there are at times a great many deer. They love its remote quiet, its pine hills, its abundant food, its watery edges. I have seen as many as six fine bucks run out of there on a single drive, a flock of wild turkeys, and heaven knows how many does. I have likewise seen wild boars emerge from that

] 331 [

wilderness—huge hulking brutes, built like oversize hyenas, and they are ugly customers to handle.

I knew that there was sure to be a good deal of shooting on this drive, certain to be some missing, and possibly to be some killing. Everybody seemed keyed just right for the sport. I had men with me who had hunted all over the world, grizzled backwoodsmen who had never hunted more than twenty miles from their homes, pure amateurs, some insatiable hunters but rotten shots—and I had the lady in green.

After I had posted the men, there being no stand for me, or perhaps for a more romantic reason, I decided to stand with my Maid Marian. She seemed like such a child to shoot down a big buck; yet she was jaunty and serene. When I had explained to certain of the standers as I posted them just how an old stag would come up to them, I could see, from the way they began to sweat and blink, that they were in the incipient stages of nervous breakdowns. But not so my Sherwood Forest girl.

Her stand, by the famous Crippled Oak, was on a high bank in the pinelands. Before her and behind her was a dense cypress swamp, in the dark fastness of which it was almost impossible to get a shot at a deer. If the buck came, she would have to shoot him when he broke across the bank, and likely on the full run—climbing it, soaring across it, or launching himself down the farther bank. All this I carefully explained to her. She listened intently and intelligently.

She appeared concerned over my concern. "You need not worry," she assured, for my comfort. "If he comes, I will kill him."

"Have you killed deer before?" I asked.

"No," she admitted lightly but undaunted. "I never even saw one."

My heart failed me. "This one," I told her, hoping that Steve's maneuvering would be effective, "is likely to have big yellow horns. He's an old wildwood hero. I hope you get him."

About that time I heard the drivers put in, and I mean they did. A Christmas hunt on a Carolina plantation brings out everything a Negro has in the way of vocal eminence. Far back near the river they whooped and shouted, yelled and sang. Then I heard the hounds begin to tune up.

Maid Marian was listening, with her little head pertly tipped to one side. "What is all that noise?" she asked with devastating imbecility.

Tediously I explained that the deer were lying down, that the Negroes and the dogs roused them, and that by good furtune an old rough-shod stag might come our way.

"I understand," she nodded brightly. But I was sure she didn't.

Another thing disconcerted me: I could hear the voice of Prince, of Sam'l, of Will and of Precinct; Evergreen's voice was loud on the still air. But not once did I hear the hound-dog whoop of Steve. However, his silence did indicate that he was about some mysterious business.

In a few minutes a perfect bedlam in one of the deep corners showed that a stag had been roused. The wild clamor headed northward, toward the creek, and soon I heard a gun blare twice. But the pack did not stop. There was a swift veering southward. Before long I heard shots from that direction, but whoever tried must have failed.

The pack headed northeast, toward the road on which we were standing, but far from us. I somehow felt, from his wily maneuvers, that this was the buck with the palmated horns. Ordinary bucks would do no such dodging, and the fact that he had been twice missed would indicate that the standers had seen something very disconcerting.

Watching the lady in green for any tell-tale sign of a break in nerves, I could discover none. She just seemed to be taking a childish delight in all the excitement. She was enjoying it without getting excited herself.

About that time I heard the stander at the far eastern end of the road shoot; a minute later he shot again. He was a good man, a deliberate shot. Perhaps he had done what I wanted Maid Marian to do. The pack now turned toward us.

Judging from the speed of the hounds, there was nothing the matter with the deer; judging by their direction, they were running parallel to the road, at a little over a hundred yards from it. It was a favorite buck run, and at any moment he might flare across the road to one of the standers at the critical crossings. Ours was the last stand on the extreme west. It seemed very unlikely that he would pass all those crossings and come to us. Now the hounds were running closer to the road. It sounded as if the buck were about to cross.

It is now just fifty years since I shot my first buck, and I have hunted deer every year since that initial adventure. But never in all my experience as a deer hunter have I heard what I then heard on that road, on which I had twelve standers. Judging from the shots, the buck must have come within easy sight, if not within range, of every stander. The bombardment was continuous. Together with the shots, as the circus came nearer, I could hear wild and angry shouts; I thought I heard some heavy profanity, and I hoped the lady in green missed this.

She was leaning against the Crippled Oak, cool as a frosted apple. I was behind the tree, pretty nervous for her sake.

"Look out, now," I whispered. "He may cross here at any minute."

My eyes kept searching for the buck to break cover. Suddenly, directly in front of the stander next to us, I saw what I took to be the flash of a white tail. The stander fired both barrels. Then I saw him dash his hat to the ground and jump on it in a kind of frenzy that hardly indicated joy and triumph.

The next thing I knew, the little rifle of the lady in green was up. I did not even see the deer. The rifle spoke. The clamoring pack, now almost upon us, began a wild milling. Then they hushed.

"All right," said Maid Marian serenely, "I killed him."

Gentlemen, she spoke the truth, and the stag she killed was the buck with the palmated horns. At sixty yards, in a full run, he had been drilled through the heart. On several occasions I had seen his horns, but I had not dreamed that they were so fine—perfect, ten-point, golden in color, with the palmation a full two inches. A massive and beautiful trophy they were, of a kind that many a good sportsman spends a lifetime seeking, and often spends it in vain.

However, mingled with my pride and satisfaction there was a certain sense of guilt; yet I was trying to justify myself with the noble old sentiment, "Women and children first." I had told Steve to drive this buck to my lady in green. He had done it— heaven knows how. He would tell me later. But his plan had worked. But now came the critical phase of the whole proceeding. Standers and drivers began to gather, and afar off I could hear many deep oaths. These, I felt sure, would subside in the presence of Maid Marian. They did, but not the anger and the protests.

There seemed to be one general question, asked in such a way that it would be well for the person referred to to keep his distance. "Where's that driver?" I heard on all sides. "I mean the big, black, slue-footed driver. I believe you call him Steve. I had a good mind to shoot him."

"I'd have killed that buck if he hadn't got in the way."

"What was that flag he was waving? Looked to me like he was trying to turn the buck from us."

"He was coming right on me when that gorilla jumped out of a bush and started waving that flag."

"Well, after all, gentlemen," I said, "here's the buck, and I must say the lady made a grand shot. Wouldn't you rather have her kill him than do so yourselves?"

Everybody had now gathered but Steve. When questioned, the other drivers disclaimed all knowledge of his whereabouts or his peculiar behavior. But they knew perfectly of both. One artfully sidetracked the whole painful discussion by saying, "Steve ain't neber been no good deer driver nohow."

Tyler Somerset, a prince of backwoodsmen, drew me aside. "Say," he said, "I know what went on back there. You can't fool me. That's the smartest darky I ever did see. More than once he outran that buck. And he sure can dodge buckshot. I wonder where he got that red and white flag he used to turn that old buck?"

We made several other drives that day. Five more stags were

] 335 [

slain. But the buck and the shot of the lady in green remained the records. On those later drives Steve put in no appearance.

When my friends were safely gone, Steve shambled out of hiding to claim his just reward. I loaded him down with Christmas.

"By the way," I said, "some of the standers told me that you headed that buck with a red and white flag. Where did you get that?"

Steve grinned with massive shyness, as he does only when anything feminine comes to his mind. "Dat's de biggest chance I took—wusser dan dodging buckshot. Dat was Amnesia's Sunday petticoat."

"Huh," I muttered with gloomy foreboding. "If she ever finds that one out, I'll have to take you to the hospital."

"Cap'n, I done arrange it," he told me—the old schemer! "I did tore seven holes in it with all that wavin'; but I told Amnesia I was ashamed to have my gal wear a raggety petticoat, and you was gwine give me a dollar, and I was gwine give it to her to buy a new one for Christmas."

WHITE DEER ARE BAD LUCK

Arthur R. MacDougall Jr.

In his superb anthology of hunting stories, Hunting Trails (*Appleton-Century-Crofts, Inc.*) *the late writer and* The New York Times Outdoor Editor Ray Camp *introduced this piece with an eloquence that bears repeating:*

"To the sportsman who reads of hunting when he can't, Dud Dean is as real as his creator, and if you do much hunting along the margin of Maine's Kennebec you will certainly encounter the reality of MacDougall. Move along the fringe of a few Kennebec cedar swamps or drop a fly on one of its quiet pools and you are almost certain to meet someone like George, who could have lifted himself standing in a bushel basket if the handles hadn't let go. MacDougall's characters are not unreal; you just have to spend a bit of time in Maine to find them."

Although his Dud Dean tales are best remembered, MacDougall's range as a writer included engaging non-fiction accounts of hunting and fishing. All his stories are anthologized in seven books.

THE TEETH OF EARLY WINTER bit at a man's ears. The November sky was wind-blown and implacable. I was waiting on the station platform for the northbound train. That train was late.

Joseph Danner was due. There was a telegram in my pocket that said so. Danner is a man of the world, a sophisticated metropolitanite. But he was born in a story-and-a-half house that squats in forlorn abandonment beside a narrow road that long since forgot the way out. The Danners are all gone, but the little house, grim and neglected in its afteryears, is evidence that their roots go far back in the Maine soil.

I sat on my full pack and wondered how much of an alien this last of the Danners had become.

Mat Markham was with me—that is, in a detached way. He sat on the off edge of the platform and smoked a corncob pipe. And his face was as blank of emotion and expectancy as a beaver bog in the midwinter moonlight.

Mat is the only successful guide I know who is the epitome of mirthlessness. But Mat is also a crafty, careful, and skillful guide. As a cook among the old guides, he has but one equal, Dud Dean, who is his lifelong friend, although two men could not be less alike. Mat's cream of tartar biscuits are light, luscious master-pieces. And if there is time, and a suitable oven, Mat makes pies that are as good as those Mother made. And as for his bean-hole beans, are they not famous from Bingham to the border?

But Mat had come with me not as a professional guide but as a friend and fellow hunter. "I'd like to git me a deer," he had said, when I had suggested the project on a wage basis, "but I'm all done guidin' fer the year. Let folks wait on themselves."

When I had said that I was anxious that Danner have a pleasant week, and that he get his deer, Mat had said, "Thar's deer enough, but the woods is so dry that a deaf owl c'ud hear a deer mouse wiggle his ears. Can this Danner shoot?"

Danner had written me that he had not fired a rifle for ten years.

"Now, ain't that jist like them Babylonians? They hardly know which end of a gun is loaded, but they'll strike off fer the woods, expectin' all they need to do is pull a trigger, an' then all the wild things will fall out of the trees an' lay around with broken necks, er sunthin'."

So we sat there, Mat and I, waiting for the train to pull into Bingham. Down the track a whistle blew. Then we heard the engine's bell at the crossing.

There were only four passengers for Bingham, and Danner was one of them.

"Hey there, Mak," he called. "It's good to see you again. The last time was at the Lawyer's Club—a nice place for a parson! How are the prospects? Got one salted? I remember an uncle of ours who always baited them that way. He claimed that such methods expedited business."

We shook hands. Mat reached out a paw, which Danner grasped, when they were introduced.

"How do you do?" he said to Mat.

"I do jist as I dang please, part of the time," said Mat.

"What do you do the rest of the time?" asked Danner, with a

tone of levity that Mat would detect and dislike, as he had the formal. "How do you do?"

"I guide," replied Mat.

In those days the train came in to the lower station in Bingham, waited, backed out, and went on up to Kineo. By the time we had carried our duffel inside the coach, the train was leaving.

Danner and I talked. I don't think that Mat listened. At Moxie Station there was a group of men and women, and manifest excitement. Mat got off to ask questions. He came back to us when the train started.

"It was jist as I guessed," he said. "Somebody got hurt—shot in the neck."

"Dangerously hurt?" asked Danner.

"We-el, the doctor they've sent for ain't got thar' yit. It was Joe Pratt. They lugged him out from in back of Bald Mountain. If I was goin' to pass jedgment, I'd say that Joe was back from his last trip."

"How did it happen?"

"Somebudy didn't wait—took him fer a deer. An' a man on his hind legs looks erbout as much like a deer as a deer looks like a stepladder."

"Did the poor devil who did the shooting come in with him?"

"Yup. He's thar. He's takin' on like a woman with her best hat lost in the wind, but that don't do Joe no good. They've got a feller from The Forks who can stop blood, but Joe's lost a lot of it. If they don't git a doctor purty quick, it'll stop all right."

"What do you mean by a fellow who can stop blood?"

"Why, I d'know. Never knew. Some does. It's a verse in the Scripture, er sunthin'. Anyway, it's a secret amongst them that know it. A man can only pass it on to a woman. A woman can only tell a man. Them that knows it, an' has faith, can stop bleedin'. At least, so I've hear'n tell. No, dang it! They *can!*"

Danner turned to me. "There's some more of it. I remember that, too. Folks believed it when I was a small boy. My uncle did."

To my surprise, Mat made a genuine effort to lighten our mood induced by the unhappy event at Moxie.

] 339 [

"So far as Joe's consarned," he said, "that's the way of all flesh: born slow, die quick. Joe had it comin' to him."

"Coming to him!" exclaimed Danner. "What do you mean?"

"I don't mean anything against Joe." Mat made haste to say, "but last week he was foolish enough to shoot a white doe deer. That's the surest way to invite the blackest luck in the world: to shoot a white doe deer. Matter of fact, I never heard of a person who shot a white deer that didn't come to some v'ilent end, er at least to black trouble. It never fails."

"Oh," said Danner. "I remember now. The curse of the white deer. There was such a superstition when I was a boy. My uncle believed it. And there were many who shared it in those days. But as a matter of fact, superstition is common to all primitive and isolated societies."

"If ye'll excuse me," said Mat, "I want to go up front. See a feller up thar who borrowed five dollars off me last summer. He can't remember none too good."

Danner watched Mat, as the older man walked up the aisle. "My uncle," he said, "has been dead for thirty years. And I thought he was the last of men like that. Do many persons up here believe such nonsense?"

At Forsythe Siding, we left the train and shouldered our packs. A man with a packsack on his back is a symbol of other days and other ways than those of urbanity. Once out of the train, and facing the wild lands, Mat became almost cheerful. This was his country, where he was at ease and at home.

"We hain't packin' enough grub to see us through the week," he said. "So we either shoot some meat, er we go ga'nt."

"That's businesslike," said Danner.

"Better keep it in mind," said Mat.

On the way to camp—the camp Mat had chosen for our head-quarters—Danner talked as a man would want to if he had been away a long time but felt, even patronizingly, that he belonged. I answered when necessary. But Mat maintained an Abnaki silence, except for one utterance: "The deer are wilder'n hell's bells."

And they were. The ground was frozen. The leaves were dry.

We needed snow. And through the next day, and the following, we hunted without sight of a deer. But the night of the third day, Mat reported that he had seen a white deer. The incident was startling, because white deer are rare.

"Was he a big one?" asked Danner.

Mat laid aside the hot buttered biscuit that he had been lifting to his mouth. That was the sort of question Mat would answer with ponderous consideration.

"Wa-al, maybe I've seen bigger bucks—white deer don't usually live to git real big—but I never did see a bigger *white* deer 'n this 'un."

"How many points, would you guess?"

"Don't need to guess. I had plenty of time to look him over, same as he did me. All white deer are foolish, I reckon. He's got twelve p'ints, an' he w'ud dress off a hundred an' eighty pounds, maybe."

"Man!" exclaimed Danner. "That was a good one. Did you miss him?"

The question was tactless. Men like Mat fit their guns. And when they shoot, they kill. Furthermore, Mat had already made plain how he felt about the shooting of white deer.

But Mat patiently restated his position. "Young feller, I don't ever plan to shoot any *white* deer."

"Surely you do not mean that you forfeited the chance to shoot at a head like that, because the animal happened to be a sport! What is a white deer? Answer, it's a freak dropped by a normal doe. You would shoot at its dam or sire, why presume that this oddly marked offspring is attended by supernatural accruements?"

Mat's blue eyes squared away at Danner's. There was no anger in them, but a pity.

"Listen," he said ponderously. "I knew a feller by the name of George Sands. George was inclined to be sure of his own powers, an' talked erbout them. So some of the young fellers bet George a dollar that he c'udn't lift hisself in a bushel basket. An' the durn fathead tried it. He lifted until he was red in the face an' pooched. Then the ash handles let go, pulled out from the rim. 'Thar!' says

George. 'Yer see I c'ud have done it, if these danged handles had held.'

"What I mean is that a man can't lift hisself in a basket. We're mortals. A college eddication don't alter that by one hundredth of an inch. If thar's anythin' that a college sh'ud learn a man, it's that he don't come out an inch taller. But you city squirts want to come up here an' tell us folks that has learned things the hard way that what we *know* is true hain't so. An' then, like damfools, ye're surprised if we don't swallow it. Crotch!"

Danner stared at Mat. "Oh, well, heck," he said, "let it go at that. You make the best biscuits I ever ate."

It was wise to change the subject. But the incident spoiled the evening. We could feel Mat's glumness.

During the next day, when I met Mat, he said. "Do yer really think this perfessor Danner w'ud shoot that white buck if he was to see him? If yer do, thar hain't no two ways erbout it. An' I'm goin' home. Don't want no truck with unasked trouble, myself."

"Danner is a lawyer, not a professor," I said. "I don't think that you need to worry about him shooting the white buck."

"Becuz, I'll be condemned if I didn't jump that critter ag'in this forenoon," explained Mat. "Yer really don't think this per-fessor w'ud be sech a punkinhead, eh?"

"I am confident he wouldn't," I said. But I was wrong.

That day, when we were returning to camp, the white buck and a normal doe jumped from the cover of a patch of young fir.

Danner's 30-06 hit his shoulder, and he fired before Mat could bellow, "Don't do it!"

"Missed him!" said Danner, with obvious disappointment.

Mat was angry and agitated, and he did not attempt to hide those emotions. "Yer better thank God, er your own foolishness, that yer did miss him," he said. "An' I am done—goin' home. Crotch, I w'udn't even consider shootin' that natural doe, becuz of her comp'ny. An' you blaze away at the *white* buck!"

I knew that Mat had made a masterly effort not to overindulge in adjectives, and that he was profoundly moved and disturbed.

"Oh, come now," said Danner. "That was a handsome creature. Its legs and ears are standard. And there's a big brown patch on his ribs. At least, that's only half bad luck!"

"That buck," said Mat, "is as white as they usually come. I never see but one pure white deer, an' I hain't sure she warn't ancestral. [Mat meant spectral.] As fer *shootin'* this one, if ye'd hit him, it's likely that we'd all have run right plum inter bad luck. Even shootin' at him may be e-nough to bring it on."

Mat looked like an earnest if not brilliant, prophet. Even Danner sensed the man's utter concern and alarm.

"Mat," he said, "I'm sorry. Let's talk it over when we have eaten and rested. We're on edge now."

Mat grunted. "Thar's nothin' to talk," he said. "All is, if yer pro-pose to shoot at *white* deer, yer can count me out of your comp'ny, right now."

Danner looked at me. I could only shake my head. In the first place, I had been provoked at my own stupidity which had led me to stare at the departing white buck when I should have shot at the doe, for we needed meat at camp. Now, however, I was relieved that both the buck and his little doe had gone free.

The day had been cold and gray. There was the promise of snow in the sky and in the wind. The camp was pleasant with its smells of good warm food, the purring of the hardwood burning in the stove, and the lamplight, which is not so much a light as the presence of a color.

But to my disappointment, Danner provoked more talk about white deer. Taciturn Mat became evangelistically determined to convert the unimaginative and skeptical lawyer. It was the only time in all the years I have known Mat when his astringent vocabulary was overworked. Once started on the project, he told incident after incident, all illustrating the curse of the white deer.

Danner threw in words such as bosh, taboo, totemism, and the like.

I was uncomfortable, as a man always is in the presence of genuine conviction pitted against skepticism. I would cheerfully have given ten dollars for more light in that little cabin than the small oil lamp achieved. And all my efforts to change the subject were ignored by the zealot on each side of the debate.

At last, Mat grew weary of his own unaccustomed loquaciousness. "Mak," he said, "I wish this friend of your'n had more *sense.*"

Danner laughed. "I'll sleep on that," he said.

Mat pulled a cap down over his ears and went outside to inspect the weather. We heard him knock the ashes out of his pipe. When he returned to the camp, he seemed to have rid himself of the perturbed mood.

"Fellers," he said, "whatever 'it' is, it's spittin'. I sh'udn't wonder if it snowed enough to make good trackin' tomorrow."

So we went to bed—nothing settled, nothing achieved. I resolved to talk to Danner in the morning. Mat felt too profoundly about the ill omen and its aftermaths to be ignored. And if I had to choose between the friendship of Mat or Danner, the latter could go to New York. There was no doubt in my mind about that!

The next sound I heard was Mat's voice, mournfully reminding me that it was almost noon. But morning was still in obeisance, bowing the knee to the night. And the bit of earth I saw from the doorway was cold, white, and uninviting.

Breakfast waited while we washed, and Mat went after another pail of water.

"Joe," I said, "this may seem to be an unusual and even unreasonable request, but I must ask you not to shoot at that white deer again, should you see him today."

Danner gurgled in the pan of ice water, grabbed a towel, and looked up at me. He was amused.

"Why should one listen to you? After all, it seems to me that you are a neutral, not belonging to either school of thought about freakish deer."

"Mat feels this business too earnestly," I said. "After all, there are deer enough."

"Did you mean that?" demanded Danner.

"I did. And I do."

"Well, for gosh sakes. I give you my word. Far be it from me to disturb the peace of the upper Kennebec!"

I liked Danner more than ever before for that speech.

We partook of Mat's good breakfast, closed the camp for the day, and followed Mat into the shivering world. A great horned owl flew like a shadow out of a gaunt, naked tree.

Mat halted. "That is a crotchly bad sign," he said.

Danner said, "To heck with the signs and the seasons. Today, I'm out to shoot anything that comes along on all fours, except a blue ox, and that white deer of yours, Mat."

"He sartinly hain't *mine,*" said Mat, with a sober haste.

I hated that cold, sticky morning—it laid clammy hands on a fellow, and I looked back at the warm camp we had left, like the lady from Gomorrah, while I marveled at Mat and Danner, who had accepted the weather as if it were not.

Furthermore, I didn't know where we were, afer we had walked for a half hour. And I suspected that Mat did not know, because of the dull light and the rapidly falling snow.

At last we came upon the edge of a little wild meadow, a dry bog. There in the open the large, squashy snowflakes fell in an endless, whispering confusion.

Mat turned to me and whispered, "B'crotch, I can't rec'lect this place—can you?"

So we stood there watching and pondering our situation. It was Danner that heard the deer. There was a curling line of alders near the center of the meadow. And a deer was feeding there but was half concealed in the alders, and somewhat blotted out by the snow. It stood broadside to us. There was no doubt that it was a deer, or that it was a normal, brown creature.

This was our last day. We had come to it without so much as the chance to shoot a deer, unless one counted Danner's wild shot at the white buck, which Mat would not do, of course. Therefore Mat was anxious.

"Make it quick," he said to Danner.

Danner raised his heavy rifle, aimed, and fired. In spite of that dim light and the blurring snow, Danner's lead had been deadly. The deer slumped as if it had been knocked between the eyes.

"Good on your head!" said Mat. But it was only said, when we

] 345 [

saw a deer leap to its feet—no, not leap, for it seemed to rise, and to get off at top form and speed.

Danner appeared to be possessed by astonishment—unable to act. I slammed my own rifle to the shoulder, but Mat was seconds ahead of me. His .30-30 sounded like a dull thud in the snow-blanketed country. The running deer plunged forward, came up again, but went down when Mat fired a second shot.

"Thar!" said Mat, as excited as a grocer weighing out half a pound of prunes. "Thar, I reckon we got that 'un, if we did have to shoot up the whole landscape to do it."

Danner was ashamed. "I thought," he explained, "that he had gone down for keeps, after I fired."

"So did I," said Mat, as we walked out into the little opening.

And of course Mat would go first to the spot where the deer had stood, when Danner fired, for there the story began.

"Ju-das priest!" he exclaimed when he reached the spot, a few steps in front of Danner and me.

There lay a doe—dead where it fell, hit cleanly in the heart— dead beside that black ribbon of a small brook within the alders.

"Judas an' the priest," said Mat, turning from the dead doe to a spot where there was no snow on the gray-brown meadow grass. "Thar's where another one bedded down."

"Then I did get mine," said Danner.

"Yes," said Mat, "but what in the devil have I shot?"

And he left us to follow the second deer's tracks. When he came to an abrupt halt, Danner shouted, "Got him?"

Mat was slow to reply. At last, he said, "B'crotch, Mak, I've gone an' shot that *white* buck—killed him, deader'n a stun heap."

Danner stared at me. Then he sat down, or collapsed, in the slush.

"Oh, mygosh! This is comedy, Greek comedy undefiled. Oh, mygosh!"

I went to Mat, I think that I ran. Sure enough, there lay the white-buck. The last shot had smashed its heart. Mat had removed his cap. His stiff gray hair was awry, and on his face was the expression of an extrovert shipwrecked on the foam of perilous seas, in fairy lands forlorn.

"Wa-al," he said, "what's done is done, an' who in God's world can undo it? If I had only waited a min-it, but, no, I had to shoot b'fore thar was time to look it over. So I've gone an' killed that *white* buck."

With that speech finished, Mat got out a jackknife and began to dress the white buck of the Forsythe country. Once he looked up to Danner and me. "I wish you fellers w'ud unload your guns," he said, "becuz if I've got to be shot, I w'ud rather it 'ud be done by strangers."

Knowing that Mat meant what he said, I unloaded my rifle. Danner unloaded his.

"While ye're erbout it," said Mat, "unload mine."

"How would you like to have that nice, fat doe of mine?" asked Danner. "I would like to trade deer with you."

Mat was impressed. He looked searchingly at Danner. But his mind added up two and two and then stuck to it that the result was four.

"Danner," he said, "that's a handsome offer, but it w'udn't come to no good fer either of us. This is a danged deceitful world, where a feller with the best of intentions is apt to be led astray. But a man has to take his own consequences. *I* shot this white buck."

I have made my report. Now you know how it happened. Mat Markham shot a white buck—a big white buck with twelve points. Mat sold that buck for fifty dollars. An out-of-state hunter who had more money than fortune at deer hunting went home with that beautiful creature. I saw Mat pocket the money as if in a daze.

"Not that it'll ever do me any good," he said.

That was twenty years ago. I am sure that the fifty dollars have not changed hands since then. Moreover, Mat has enjoyed robust health and enough good fortune to satisfy a citizen in this good land that the Lord God gave to us. But Ecclesiastes is still the sum of Mat's conclusions concerning the lot of mortal man in this vale of tears. And to this day, he insists that it is p'ison bad luck to shoot a white deer.

THE SWAMP BUCK

Sigurd F. Olson

Sigurd Olson has spent his entire life living in and writing about the great Quetico and Boundary Waters Wilderness Area that sprawls along the Minnesota-Ontario border north and west of the outfitting center of Ely, where he lives.

Olson's six books on that area and the more-distant reaches of Canadian wilderness make a superb portrait of wilderness living and adventure and comprise, as a body of work, the most eloquent plea we have for the protection of these areas from burgeoning civilization.

Every Sigurd Olson book was published by Knopf, and they are all pure gems. "The Swamp Buck" is taken from Runes of the North.

IT WAS the last day of deer season and one of those breathless dawns that seem to come only in November. I stood outside my cabin and looked at the stars blazing against their background of blue-black sky. In the east was a hint of rose, not enough to brighten the horizon or dim the stars, merely an assurance that daybreak was near. The birds were stirring and the sounds of their cheeping filtered out of the pines. Along the shore of the lake new ice was forming on the rocks.

A partridge whirred up noisily from its burrow in a drift, lit in the top of a white birch where it fed on the frozen brown buds. The rolling tattoo of my pileated woodpecker exploring a dead aspen for grubs, reverberated again and again. Never had it seemed quite so loud, never so continuous a roll. The partridge fussed away, holding precariously to the bending, topmost branches. A pair of chickadees fluttered to the feeding tray. It was a quiet that would not last because hunters were on the trails to their watching places.

For days the hills had resounded to the rattle of rifle fire. Never an hour was it still. The kill was heavy, for the breeding season had been good and there was plenty of browse. A fresh snow had covered most of the evidence: blood-spattered trails, spots where deer had been cleaned, and the long, smooth toboggan tracks made by carcasses being dragged to the roads.

The survivors were wary now, had retreated into swamps, balsam, and jackpine thickets. Many were cripples, would stay in hiding until the furor ended. Those with superficial flesh wounds might recover, those shot through would die. The wolves would pick up some of the trails and finish what the hunters began and the cycle would be complete.

The east was brightening now, the stars fading fast. The pileated woodpecker left its tree and wickered loudly as it flew back into the timber. The partridge in the top of the birch had worked its way out to get at the terminal buds until the branch bent down sharply. Back and forth swayed the bird, and once, almost losing its balance, recovered with a furious flapping of wings.

For some time I watched and listened, then grew cold and went back to the cabin. As I reached the stoop a violent burst of rifle fire came from across the lake, five shots as fast as the hunter could reload—then, after a few minutes, one final report. It was still hardly light enough to see, but the last day of season was underway. From every point of the compass now came a staccato barrage. It was as if the initial fusilade had triggered off the rest.

Though my days of hunting were long past, I knew what that burst of fire meant, a running deer in the half-light of morning, either a final shot as it disappeared or the *coup de grâce*. The firing had come from in back of the islands near a beaver flowage almost two miles away. Not long before, I had been in there following the little creek that emptied its water into the lake, had watched a beaver bring branches of birch and aspen to a huge pile of winter food a few feet from shore and close to its house on the bank. Two birches of a fine clump of three were already down and the last would soon follow.

From the beaver house I had worked my way into a series of swamps and a morass of tangled windfalls, grass, and alders, to where the creek finally emerged as a seepage from a deep hidden pond. On that exploring trip I saw a fine buck. It was late October and I had climbed a ridge to get a view over the islands and to see the panorama of blue and gold. While standing there completely absorbed, the brush cracked and there was the buck, and a big one, working toward me. He moved leisurely along, stopping now and then to paw the leaves and scratch them away from the green and tender shoots underneath. The animal came on; the wind was in my favor, and I barely breathed for I wanted to see how close he would come. His antlers were broader and more palmate than those of ordinary deer, and I counted four points on a side. Nearer and nearer he came, then stopped to mutilate a scrubby clump of hazel. He combed the brush until it was stripped of bark and beaten down, though the antlers were cleaned of velvet long ago. Now their surfaces all but shone in the yellow light of the aspen around it.

A hundred feet, seventy-five, fifty. Suddenly the animal's eyes grew wide with suspicion, his ears swiveled slowly in my direction. The muzzle was black, nostrils distended, the diamond at the base of the throat startling in its whiteness. Then, without warning, the buck tensed, snorted in alarm, and in one beautiful motion cleared a windfall and went off twenty feet at a jump, his flag flying.

This was where the shooting had taken place. Normally a haven from hunters, the flowage, now that it was frozen, no longer offered protection. As I ate my breakfast I felt that I must know and, though I no longer carried a gun, it would seem good to get out in the hills again and cruise as I used to do. I might find my buck and perhaps see others too, but best of all would be to get the feeling of the November woods.

I took the green canoe and paddled across the lake. It was bitterly cold and though the sun was shining, ice froze on my paddle. There was no wind or spray, for which I was thankful, and I pushed the canoe swiftly across the open lake. The narrows were closing and a rock in the center was already sheathed with glistening white. As I coasted past a timbered island, a squirrel chattered at me from an overhanging pine. It was a glorious morning and with the new snow it should not be too difficult to unravel the story of the shooting.

I tried to land in a marshy bay to the right of a stream but it was frozen solid. Three buffleheads sat at the edge of the ice and fluttered off across the bay as the canoe approached. A last remnant of the migration, they would soon be far to the south. When I found I could not land, I paddled toward the mouth and, as I expected, a boat was pulled up there beside the beaver house. A man's track led from it to the ridge. The hunter was alone; he had worked his way along the creek to a high point from which he could look down into the tangle of windfalls and grass of the flowage. I followed carefully, aware that even though two hours had passed, he might be waiting and watching. Not knowing who he was, there was always danger. At last I reached the high point, looked below as he had done and remembered the day a month before when I had gone into the swamp and turned back because of the treacherous holes of muck. Some of the pools had been alive with minnows then, and in places the water ran free. I had seen northern pike in the spring during the spawning and had watched them swim around in water so shallow their dorsal fins stuck out like sails. A pair of mallards flushed that day, a gorgeous greenhead and its mate, and I watched the sun on blue and green and bronze as they climbed into the sky. Each year they chose that nesting site, for in its depths a brood was safe. Mink, weasels, and foxes prowled the edges hunting for mice and rabbits that abounded there, but few ever penetrated the inner recesses of the sanctuary. No wonder the buck had lived beyond his normal span of years.

I found where the hunter had stopped a moment, and for a hundred yards on top of the ridge his tracks went everywhere. First he had shifted to a new spot so he could look into another part of the swamp, then returned to another place overlooking the lake and examined the vantage points on either side, all this in the first light of dawn. Only an old-timer in the area, someone who knew every stick and stone could have moved like that.

At the far end of the rise, commanding a broad vista across an opening, I found empty shells. Three of them had landed against a ledge above the snow. They were bright and shiny as shells always are when carried in a pocket for some time, .30-30s, from a rifle used by most old hunters in the north. His tracks now ran into the valley. After a hundred yards he had stopped and fired again. That was the last. For a long time I did not move. He might be in there with the deer or watching for any movement in the brush. Then very cautiously I followed his trail once more.

In the open I found the first sign of blood, a thin splattering of tiny droplets, almost a spray of bright red crystals against the snow. It was a buck, and a big one. At first the jumps were long, but quickly changed to a walk. Then I found a bigger burst of blood and evidence of a dragging leg. The animal kept going, circled the second swale completely, and finally went in the direction of a little pond almost a mile away.

All afternoon I followed that trail and late in the day saw where the hunter had given up and turned back. The season was over; one lone shot echoed far beyond the ridges, someone firing at a partridge in a tree, or as a signal to a partner that he was on the way. It was still once more, still as it would be for another year.

The next morning I returned to the beaver swamps and took the trail again. It was not long before I came upon the oval, ice-encrusted bed of the wounded buck, one end stained red from the bleeding flank. He had lain there during the night, then had gone on. The bleeding had stopped and the animal was stiffened and limping. Once when crossing a small gully, he had stumbled and fallen, starting the bleeding fresh. He lay there for some time, then walked around a low windfall that normally he could have cleared with ease. His leg was dragging heavily now, making a long mark in the snow. The flank wound may have been deeper than I thought. Perhaps the hip was injured, in which case there was a little chance of recovery; but why hadn't he rested, why hadn't he gone back to his old bedding area in the first swamp? Perhaps wolves were moving in.

Far ahead, three ravens wheeled in ever tightening circles over something they had found. Lower and lower dropped the soaring birds until they disappeared among the trees. I knew the answer then. Somewhere over there I would find what I was looking for.

Old hunters have said that when they pursue a quarry for a long time, they begin to feel and think as the animal does, and Indians have told me that sometimes they become a part of the

very creatures they seek to kill. The two days I trailed the buck gave me an intimation of what they knew.

A mile or two beyond, while the buck moved in a great uneven circle, I discovered where the wolves had come close. The running was desperate now and the buck crashed brush and windfalls in its attempt to escape, leaving bits of hide and hair beside the trail. Once he had made a stand against a dense clump of balsam but was in no condition to fight. The unequal contest continued to the shore of the pond but the newly formed ice had settled his fate. Out a little way, he had broken partly through and there he lay, around him blood and a confusion of tracks.

That was the end of the long trail and the way it had always been in the wilds. True, the buck was old and beautiful, but had he escaped the wolves he would have died a lingering death or starved with the coming of the cold and deeper snows. I tried the ice but it was not strong enough to bear my weight, so retraced my steps toward the bay where I had left my canoe.

At the opening where the hunter had fired, I decided to follow the buck back into the swamp from which it had come the morning before. The trails in there were deep in moss and criss-crossed by a labyrinth of rabbit runways. A doe had been there too, and on a small dry hummock grown with long grass and hedged in by a tangle of raspberry, I found two ice-encrusted beds.

Back at the promontory above the mouth of the creek, I stopped to look over the lake once more as I had done the morning of the shooting. The long white windfalls still reached frozen fingers into the shallows and the mottled gray and green of the bush-covered slopes had not changed, but somehow I had changed and within me was a sense of loss. True, this was the way it should be, but my logic was of no help. All I seemed to remember was the beauty of an October day when those shores were blue and gold and how proudly that buck had cleared the windfall and bounded down the slope.

A metallic chuck-chuck came from one of the cabins to the east—someone was splitting wood. I paddled over there on my way back to pass the time of day.

"What luck?" I asked.

"Wounded a big one back in the beaver slough," my friend replied, "Been tryin' to get him for years, but always something happens. Hit him hard too, but couldn't catch up, followed 'til dark and quit. Wasn't bleedin' much, so figgered there was no use tryin' to find his trail again."

I told him then what I had done, how I had followed the buck just to see what happened and finally found where the wolves had dragged him down on the ice.

"Those critters," he muttered, "we'd have a lot more deer if they was all killed off. They kill a deer every few days and sometimes just for fun. They're the ones that make hunting tougher and tougher in this country."

I did not argue for I knew the attitude of many hunters regarding predators, but I could have told him about ecological balances and how wolves and deer, moose and caribou had lived together for centuries in the north; that what determined survival was not predation but the amount of winter food available; that during winters of extreme cold and heavy snow, ten to twenty per cent of the deer herd might die of starvation; that the wolves had actually done the race a favor by eliminating an aged and crippled sire and that the doe, who no doubt was bred, would replace it in the spring.

Not until mid-January did I ski across the lake to the mouth of the creek and the beaver flowage. I felt I must go into the little pond once more.

The beaver house was a smooth white mound now and the brush from the storage pile completely covered. Deer signs were everywhere again, and in the depths of the swamp where they had gone for protection and food, I counted the tracks of five. The trails were deep, the animals yarded up as they always do when the snow is deep, and feeding heavily on striped maple and dogwood; even balsam, spruce, and tamarack were eaten; and the few cedars, which they preferred, browsed as high as they could reach. If the winter continued as it had begun, only the strong would survive until spring.

On the pond the bones of the buck had been picked clean by wolves, ravens, and foxes. Even weasels and a mink had come out to the unexpected windfall of food. While I was there a whiskey jack flew from the shore and lit on one of the golden tines of the antlers. The bird warbled softly and waited while I took a sandwich out of my pocket.

A soft almost ventriloquial note emerged from its throat and its black eyes were on the bit of food.

I tossed out a piece of bread. The bird caught it swiftly and flew back to the fringe of spruces from which it had come.

SHORT SHOTS

John W. Randolph

When the late John W. Randolph was Outdoor Editor of The New York Times, *his pieces in the "Wood, Field and Stream" column broke new ground in fresh, original writing.*

Randolph knew how to write a "straight" piece of factual reporting as well as the next man. But he shined best as a writer when he moved the column into the area of wit and fun. He loved poking humorous barbs into sacred cows who took their sport too seriously.

Randolph never forgot that hunting and fishing were for fun—or were supposed to be.

These three separate columns, collected in the anthology of his columns, The World of Wood, Field and Stream, *published by Holt, Rinehart and Winston, show Randolph at his best.*

COLRAIN, MASSACHUSETTS—Three or four inches of new snow are a great help to a deer hunter, especially when the snow keeps coming. It is a new page on which everything is written clearly.

So everybody saw deer tracks today; clear, new tracks. Clear, new tracks in fresh snow are a fine thing to look at, and very interesting to look at, and very exciting. But they are not deer, and cannot be hung in the barn. Fourteen anathemas on them.

Three of us started the day in just such snow by taking stands in the neighborhood of an old sugar house on Colrain Mountain. My own stand was against a great maple on the edge of an old field backed by thick pines in which deer love to hang around.

They were hanging around there, all right. Joe Jurek, who stood at the head of an old apple orchard a quarter of a mile away, had tired of cold feet when he put a good buck out of those pines a couple of hours later. But it didn't go past me, and it didn't go past Jurek's brother, Bill. It went over a little hardwood ridge, through a swamp, and over a pine ridge, and probably it is still going.

Somewhat later I had sense enough to move my frozen feet, and Bill Jurek elected to move his at the same time.

The three of us prowled that part of the mountain, which spread for miles, for several hours and saw plenty of fresh, clear, exciting deer tracks. Nobody caught sight of a flag.

There was shooting from every part of the compass, but none of it within a thousand yards of us. We met other hunters following fresh, clear tracks and did not shoot any of them. Others met us following fresh, clear tracks and did not shoot us. From this vital point of view, it was a successful day.

Late in the afternoon, when we had started toward the road, we found where five deer had dawdled out through a sheep pasture, wandering aimlessly through the hardhack in plain sight for a quarter of a mile with nobody present to see them. Their course took them past several places where one or the other of us had stood or walked.

Less than twenty minutes after I had left that maple tree of freezing memory, a buck walked within thirty yards of it, with Lawrence Shearer, Jr., walking a few minutes behind it. He never caught up.

Another deer walked straight through Bill Jurek's former stand at about the same time.

The shooting went on all day long, and the Jureks and I listened to it with calm detachment. Strong, hardy outdoorsmen are never envious. They are just tired and half frozen.

Meanwhile, back at the ranch, three high-school seniors, all football players of local renown, set out to pit their inexperience against the cagey deer.

They are all eighteen years old and weigh in the neighborhood of two hundred pounds apiece, but they are only youths, after all. They could hardly be expected to outwit the trickiest game of the forest.

In time, as they garner the "Lore of the Wildwood," they may become journeymen deer hunters. But they are boys now, mere boys. They must observe, and learn.

They did not even hunt on Colrain Mountain but went to a nameless hill of no particular repute as a deer hangout, wandered to the top of it, sat down awhile, wandered about for awhile, sat

] 359 [

down again, and then went home. They went home with three deer. It was about noon.

But that is not the worst. A high-school *girl* killed her deer by 9:30 A.M. and was back in school before noon to receive the plaudits of the academic multitude. It was reported that she was overwhelmingly modest about the thing, but her classmates could think of nothing to do about it.

* * *

Never has there been a time since men hunted with pointed sticks when the strong, hardy outdoorsman could be strong and hardy with so little inconvenience. The vast resources of modern technology are at the instant call of the modern gadget-master, whose equipment sees all, hears all, shelters all, warms and cools all, guides all, lures all, and, in theory, kills all.

Consider the modern deer hunter who rises from under his electric blanket in a centrally heated lodge to the chimes of an electric alarm clock, and begins the ceremony of dressing, which he often is able to do without help.

He dons his cotton-and-wool insulated underwear, and draws over that his insulated quilted underwear. His feet he clads in plastic insulated socks and either insulated rubber or insulated leather boots. His pants are not insulated, but they are made of fine wool with leather pockets and they cost enough to satisfy him, anyway.

His jacket is an architectural triumph of various layers, with rubber game-pockets, special pockets for shells (which he does not need, since he also is wearing a special shell-belt), and a drop-flap that he may lower in order to sit dry on wet stumps. His cap is a lustrous yellow or red and it has ear-flaps, which he may need, although his jacket has a hood.

In the dining room, he lights four hand-warmers, two for his hand-pockets and two to stuff inside his shirt against his kidneys. He also fills a couple of cigarette-lighters. Into his pockets with these go a hand-compass, to use in case his wrist-compass goes wrong (his car-compass will guide him along the road) and a handful of fire-lighters in case he has to build a fire in the woods.

Around his neck he hangs a pair of powerful binoculars, to use when he doesn't care to lift his rifle in order to scan through its two-and-a-half- to eight-power compensating lenses.

It is time to put his ready-lunch into his game-pocket, along with a Thermos bottle of coffee (his full lunch will be in a thermal container in the car along with beer in a cooler and more hot coffee). Into the game-pocket with them may go his cushion, for sitting soft as well as dry.

Before stepping into the chill morning, he sprinkles deer-lure, made perhaps of apple essence, delicately on the lapel of his jacket, and puts his deer-call, made of plastic and a rubber band, into his pocket.

He now is almost ready to go sit down in the woods and wait for his guide to drive a deer his way. Of course, he takes his rifle, an auto-loader bearing the scope that does everything except cook the game.

He may want to take along a few other things, such as thermal gloves or mittens, a good mirror to enable him to see deer coming behind him, a pocket stove with canned fuel, a knife with blades on it for getting stones out of horses' hoofs, together with a German belt-knife for looks, a patent deer-pulling rope, a gun-cleaning kit in case he rams his rifle barrel trigger-deep into a swamp, and a silver flask full of whiskey in case of faintness or freezing. And a bottle of chemical to keep fog off his spectacles, and a few vitamin pills.

But on the whole he is ready, prepared to stalk the woods with iron, impassive face, meeting all hardships like the stoic that he is. Hiawatha never had it so good.

* * *

It is a dirty trick to assemble and make public a table by which a deerslayer may determine the live weight of a deer he has slain simply by looking it up opposite the dressed weight in the table. But the thing has been done now, and nothing can diminish the harm that is bound to ensue.

Hunters have little enough imagination and invention to adorn their poor stories about the wildwood, though they are not quite so mentally torpid as fishermen. This sneaky table robs them of one of the best of their threadbare resources: the right to overestimate honestly the live weight of any deer they may accidentally kill.

It is odd that the blow should be delivered by Winchester Arms, which depends largely upon hunters for its existence. How can Winchester hope to sell arms and ammunition by low-grading the prizes of its customers?

The table, published in *Winchester Proof,* a publicity sheet, nails the deer hunter to a cross of paper. If it is correct, and it almost certainly is, the deerslayer will know without doubt that the fawn that he had downed and that weighs 60 pounds dressed weighed only 80 pounds when it was alive.

Without the incriminating table, he could honestly guess that live weight as maybe 110, 115, and thereby promote his prize from fawn to young adult. But he cannot do this honestly now, and every red-blooded American outdoorsman considers himself a man of rugged honesty.

There is no use trying to cover the matter up, or slur it over. A fawn that weighs forty pounds dressed weighed fifty-five alive. These are the dressed weights followed by the live weights: 50–65, 70–90, 80–105, 100–130, 110–140, 120–155, 130–165, 140–180, 150–190, 160–205, 170–215, 180–230, 190–240, 200–255, and 210–265.

This leaves little hope for the average hunter except the brassy lie, which is the most valued resource of the trained operator but a dangerous boomerang in the hands of the witless. Average hunters either bluster or cringe when attempting to use it.

But one hope is left. A man with the right kind of memory can throw the table away and remember only that there is a difference of 55 pounds between the dressed and live weight of a deer, forgetting as immaterial that this applies only to a deer that weighs 200 pounds dressed. By applying this to the scrawny 50-pounder he can arrive at a respectable 105 pounds.

He can reverse this, too. Since a deer weighing 60 pounds dressed weighed 80 alive, it is plain that by adding a third to the dressed weight he can arrive at the real live weight. Therefore, his big 210-pounder weighed 280 alive, instead of 265, and he can honestly say that he slew a 280-pound deer.

The important thing is to get rid of the table. Why should anybody let Winchester make him carry an anvil around on his back?

* * *

A couple of western Massachusetts deer hunters have been in a dilemma for a couple of years over what their attitude should be toward the game laws. They have concluded that every decent hunter should obey every law, but that he is not obliged to brag about it or even to make claims that he obeys.

Their wives were the subversive influences. These two men, whose names were not Smith and Jones, had hunted bucks in Vermont for a week without getting a shot. Every evening they endured torrents of contempt from their wives, who love venison.

At the end of the seventh shotless day they were returning home when Smith, a cow trader, stopped to see a farmer and found him taking down the carcass of a young goat, which had hung for a week. It struck Smith and Jones that a goat with its lower legs cut off looked much like a young deer.

They bought the goat, took it to Smith's home, where both women were waiting, hung it in the garage, and announced that they had killed a deer. But they said Smith had shot it by mistake; it was a small, illegal doe. They said they had been afraid to report it but hadn't wanted to leave it in the woods, so had brought it home illegally.

Women as a whole probably cannot be classified as criminals, but they are never so happy as when they have run a red light without getting caught. These women were enchanted. They had venison, and quickly brushed aside legal questions as irrelevant and incompetent.

Small steaks were quickly carved from the goat, broiled, and eaten on the spot.

"Oh, divine!" Mrs. Smith trilled. "The best venison I ever tasted!"

"Not too much wild taste!" Mrs. Jones exulted. "Just exactly the right amount!"

Both families ate from that goat for a month, off and on, and both wives were delighted. Smith and Jones, though, of course, they could not be heroes to their wives, were cordially tolerated for as much as a week.

Nobody ever questioned that the goat was venison and nobody ever mentioned any laws.

The following October, Jones went pheasant hunting with a friend and told him the story, swearing him to secrecy. But the friend came to dinner that night, drank several milk shakes, and could not hold his tongue. He spilled it.

Jones, struck dumb by terror, awaited the blow. But it did not fall. His wife reacted with inexplicable serenity, laughing mildly and playing the gracious hostess with determined charm. It was only when the friend left that Jones got his explanation. His wife began immediately to laugh ungovernably.

"It was all I could do not to laugh in his face," she shrieked. "I knew you had told him the story so he couldn't spread it around that you and Louis had shot a doe in Vermont. And, golly, he *believed* it!"

But that is not the end. Somebody else told them the goat story and they did believe it. Smith and Jones were reminded angrily for months that they were phonies. And Mrs. Smith and Mrs. Jones didn't want to hear anything about laws. They still don't.

Moral: Obey the hunting laws and keep your mouth shut.

* * *

The marvels of modern technology are in truth a great aid to the modern hunter, but sometimes it seems as if a man might do better to stay at home in an old-fashioned rocker reading a good old-fashioned comic book. Look at the record of a very recent deer and bobcat hunting trip to New Hampshire.

A party of four started in a two-year-old car owned by one of them. He had traded it in, but the modern technologists of Detroit were three weeks late in delivering the new car. After about a hundred and fifty miles, the one in use developed a steering-wheel shudder.

A modern technologist in a Massachusetts garage diagnosed the trouble with instant authority as something to do with bushings in the steering box. It sounded like he said bushings, anyway; might have said camshaft or eccentric or worm gear or something technological like that.

In any case, he fixed it and it shuddered worse. Another modern technologist in a New Hampshire garage stated with instant authority that the first modern technologist was a bum and that the trouble was in the wheels. Nobody caught the specific detail of this, but it was pretty technological. The car was fixed again.

The party had been scheduled to start deer hunting at 10 A.M. and it was now 2 P.M. There was fine deer hunting all around, and it would have been nice to start then, but the car began to shudder so violently that it could be driven no more than ten miles an hour.

Somehow the car was nursed to a bigger town, which cherished a dealer in that make of car. This modern technologist stated with instant authority that the trouble was in the differential and that it would take about four days to fix it. The car was left there, and its owner called his home in White Plains to explain his predicament to his family. He was cordially informed that his new car was ready.

A second member of the party had a car in the New Hampshire area where the party had intended to hunt. It had been left there with a friend. The party went to get it, although the deer-hunting project was by now dead.

It had a flat tire, and the trunk containing the spare was locked. Its owner took the tire off and toted it to a local garage, which was closed. The garage operator was phoned and showed up to fix the tire. He also provided four quarts of antifreeze.

The tire was replaced and the car started. A half hour later its owner lighted a match to see whether the radiator was still full, and the antifreeze caught fire. The fire was extinguished with snow. A little later both antifreeze and water boiled out.

It was then 1 A.M. and bobcat hunting was slated for 7 A.M. The hunters got something to eat, drained the radiator and block, and went to bed at 2 A.M. At 6 A.M. a modern technologist who had been called in advance by telephone opened his filling station and with instant authority diagnosed the trouble: the freeze-plug had rusted through. He did not have another. The car was left there for the day, and the hunters proceeded in a rented car and vainly hunted bobcats. The car was ready that evening, and held water.

Nobody got shot. Nobody broke a leg. One member of the party changed a diaper for a young mother who had to leave her baby for a few minutes. That was a marvel of old-time technology.

* * *

Township 24, Washington County, Maine—These Maine deer are about as unaccountable as the tough and intrepid outdoorsmen who pursue them, and that at times is very unaccountable.

On our first drive today through a swamp lying between blueberry barrens, we saw two hunters sitting on a large boulder on a slope far away fire a dozen times at a buck at least a quarter of a mile from them. The buck did not seem disturbed; just ambled away into some maple sprouts.

In the next couple of hours we drove through two or three of those swamps, all of them places that have produced deer in the past. There were no deer in any of them, or in the thickets of sprouts through which we frequently passed.

Six of us were returning to the truck that had brought us as near as possible to the swamps we had just investigated. Stillman Look, the big, sharp-eyed guide who runs Dan Hartford's Camp with George Drisko, was in the lead a step or two ahead of me.

We were no more than a hundred yards from the truck, in open blueberry barren, when a buck burst from a little rick hole no bigger than a medium-sized Second Avenue bar. A rick hole, in the parlance of this region, is a shallow cup of damp land containing a few sprouts and maybe a dead birch or so.

Look was carrying no rifle. I had a Winchester Model 88, lever action, .243 caliber, with a four-power Weaver telescope on a slide

] 367 [

mount. It is possible to dismount the scope quickly in thick brush and mount it again quickly in the open. At the moment, it was mounted.

The buck jumped out across the barrens, running across our path. When the rifle came up, he seemed to jump into the scope. I aimed behind his left shoulder, but I must have stepped into a hole or something, because the bullet caught him behind the left shoulder. He piled up there, dragged himself a few yards, and was dispatched with the next shot.

Hunters and guides gathered around the buck, an eleven-pointer that later weighed two hundred and eight pounds field-dressed. Bud Leavitt, sports editor and columnist of the Bangor *Daily News,* carefully unloaded his rifle. He doesn't like loaded rifles when people are standing around.

A few minutes later Leavitt was returning to the truck when a large doe jumped from the same litle rick hole. She had stayed there quietly in all the doings of the last half hour. Leavitt was caught without a clip in his rifle.

But four strangers who had come up to the truck and were standing there were not caught that way. All for started firing at the doe, and they fired past Leavitt, their bullets coming within a dozen feet of him. Leavitt ducked and forgot about getting a clip into his rifle. None of the four touched the doe.

Leavitt killed a doe a little later in the day but didn't feel much like hunting anyway. He seemed abstracted during the afternoon. Not even Mrs. Gladys Mace, the amiable storekeeper at Aurora who tags five hundred deer a year, could tease him into teasing her. This is a record that will stand for years.

The End

RACE AT MORNING

William Faulkner

If you don't know Mr. Faulkner and his work, then go back to school.

All I can tell you is that it's great to have a Nobel Prize winner in The Deer Book.

The piece originally appeared in The Saturday Evening Post *and later was anthologized in Faulkner's* The Big Woods, *published by Random House.*

I WAS IN THE BOAT when I seen him. It was jest dust-dark; I had jest fed the horses and clumb back down the bank to the boat and shoved off to cross back to camp when I seen him, about half a quarter up the river, swimming; jest his head above the water, and it no more than a dot in that light. But I could see that rocking chair he toted on it and I knowed it was him, going right back to that canebrake in the fork of the bayou where he lived all year until the day before the season opened, like the game wardens had give him a calendar, when he would clear out and disappear, nobody knowed where, until the day after the season closed. But here he was, coming back a day ahead of time, like maybe he had got mixed up and was using last year's calendar by mistake. Which was jest too bad for him, because me and Mister Ernest would be setting on the horse right over him when the sun rose tomorrow morning.

So I told Mister Ernest and we et supper and fed the dogs, and then I help Mister Ernest in the poker game, standing behind his chair until about ten o'clock, when Roth Edmonds said, "Why don't you go to bed, boy?"

"Or if you're going to set up," Willy Legate said, "why don't you take a spelling book to set up over? He knows every cuss word in the dictionary, every poker hand in the deck and every whiskey label in the distillery, but he can't even write his name. Can you?" he says to me.

"I don't need to write my name down," I said. "I can remember in my mind who I am."

"You're twelve years old," Walter Ewell said. "Man to man now, how many days in your life did you ever spend in school?"

"He ain't got time to go to school," Willy Legate said. "What's the use in going to school from September to middle of November, when he'll have to quit then to come in here and do Ernest's hearing for him? And what's the use in going back to school in January, when in jest eleven months it will be November fifteenth again and he'll have to start all over telling Ernest which way the dogs went?"

"Well, stop looking into my hand, anyway," Roth Edmonds said.

"What's that? What's that?" Mister Ernest said. He wore his listening button in his ear all the time, but he never brought the battery to camp with him because the cord would bound to get snagged ever time we run through a thicket.

"Willy says for me to go to bed!" I hollered.

"Don't you never call nobody 'mister'?" Willy said.

"I call Mister Ernest 'mister,' " I said.

"All right," Mister Ernest said. "Go to bed then. I don't need you."

"That ain't no lie," Willy said. "Deaf or no deaf, he can hear a fifty-dollar raise if you don't even move your lips."

So I went to bed, and after a while Mister Ernest come in and I wanted to tell him again how big them horns looked even half a quarter away in the river. Only I would 'a' had to holler, and the only time Mister Ernest agreed he couldn't hear was when we would be setting on Dan, waiting for me to point which way the dogs was going. So we jest laid down, and it wasn't no time Simon was beating the bottom of the dishpan with the spoon, hollering, "Raise up and get your four-o'clock coffee!" and I crossed the river in the dark this time, with the lantern, and fed Dan and Roth Edmondziz horse. It was going to be a fine day, cold and bright; even in the dark I could see the white frost on the leaves and bushes—jest exactly the kind of day that big old son of a gun laying up there in that brake would like to run.

Then we et, and set the stand-holder across for Uncle Ike McCaslin to put them on the stands where he thought they ought

to be, because he was the oldest one in camp. He had been hunting deer in these woods for about a hundred years, I reckon, and if anybody would know where a buck would pass, it would be him. Maybe with a big old buck like this one, that had been running the woods for what would amount to a hundred years in a deer's life, too, him and Uncle Ike would sholy manage to be at the same place at the same time this morning—provided, of course, he managed to git away from me and Mister Ernest on the jump. Because me and Mister Ernest was gong to git him.

Then me and Mister Ernest and Roth Edmonds sent the dogs over, with Simon holding Eagle and the other old dogs on leash because the young ones, the puppies, wasn't going nowhere until Eagle let them, nohow. Then me and Mister Ernest and Roth saddled up, and Mister Ernest got up and I handed him up his pump gun and let Dan's bridle go for him to git rid of the spell of bucking he had to git shut of ever morning until Mister Ernest hit him between the ears with the gun barrel. Then Mister Ernest loaded the gun and give me the stirrup, and I got up behind him and we taken the fire road up toward the bayou, the four big dogs dragging Simon along in front with his single-barrel britchloader slung on a piece of plow line across his back, and the puppies moiling along in ever'body's way. It was light now and it was going to be jest fine; the east already yellow for the sun and our breaths smoking in the cold still bright air until the sun would come up and warm it, and a little skim of ice in the ruts, and ever leaf and twig and switch and even the frozen clods frosted over, waiting to sparkle like a rainbow when the sun finally come up

and hit them. Until all my insides felt light and strong as a bal-
loon, full of that light cold strong air, so that it seemed to me like I
couldn't even feel the horse's back I was straddle of—jest the hot
strong muscles moving under the hot strong skin, setting up there
without no weight atall, so that when old Eagle struck and
jumped, me and Dan and Mister Ernest would go jest like a bird,
not even touching the ground. It as jest fine. When that big old
buck got killed today, I knowed that even if he had put it off another ten years, he couldn't 'a' picked a better one.

And sho enough, as soon as we come to the bayou we seen his
foot in the mud where he had come up out of the river last night,
spread in the soft mud like a cow's foot, big as a cow's, big as a
mule's, with Eagle and the other dogs laying into the leash rope
now until Mister Ernest told me to jump down and help Simon
hold them. Because me and Mister Ernest knowed exactly where
he would be—a little canebrake island in the middle of the bayou,
where he could lay up until whatever doe or little deer the dogs
had happened to jump could go up or down the bayou in either
direction and take the dogs on away, so he could steal out and
creep back down the bayou to the river and swim it, and leave the
country like he always done the day the season opened.

Which is jest what we never aimed for him to do this time. So
we left Roth on his horse to cut him off and turn him over Uncle
Ike's standers if he tried to slip back down the bayou, and me and
Simon, with the leashed dogs, walked on up the bayou until Mister Ernest on the horse said it was fur enough; then turned up into
the woods about half a quarter above the brake because the wind
was going to be south this morning when it riz, and turned down
toward the brake, and Mister Ernest give the word to cast them,
and we slipped the leash and Mister Ernest give me the stirrup
again and I got up.

Old Eagle had done already took off because he knowed where
that old son of a gun would be laying as good as we did, not making no racket atall yet, but jest boring on through the buck vines
with the other dogs trailing along behind him, and even Dan
seemed to know about that buck, too, beginning to souple up and
jump a little through the vines, so that I taken my holt on Mister

Ernest's belt already before the time had come for Mister Ernest to touch him. Because when we got strung out, going fast behind a deer, I wasn't on Dan's back much of the time nohow, but mostly jest strung out from my holt on Mister Ernest's belt, so that Willy Legate said that when we was going through the woods fast, it looked like Mister Ernest had a boy-size pair of empty overalls blowing out of his hind pocket.

So it wasn't even a strike, it was a jump. Eagle must 'a' walked right up behind him or maybe even stepped on him while he was laying there still thinking it was day after tomorrow. Eagle jest throwed his head back and up and said, "There he goes," and we even heard the buck crashing through the first of the cane. Then all the other dogs was hollering behind him, and Dan give a squat to jump, but it was against the curb this time, not jest the snaffle, and Mister Ernest let him down into the bayou and swung him around the brake and up the other bank. Only he never had to say, "Which way?" because I was already pointing past his shoulder, freshening my holt on the belt jest as Mister Ernest touched Dan with that big old rusty spur on his nigh heel, because when Dan felt it he would go off jest like a stick of dynamite, straight through whatever he could bust and over or under what he couldn't, over it like a bird or under it crawling on his knees like a mole or a big coon, with Mister Ernest still on him because he had the saddle to hold on to, and me still there because I had Mister Ernest to hold on to; me and Mister Ernest not riding him, but jest going along with him, provided we held on. Because when the jump come, Dan never cared who else was there neither; I believe to my soul he could 'a' cast and run them dogs by hisself, without me or Mister Ernest or Simon or nobody.

That's what he done. He had to; the dogs was already almost out of hearing. Eagle must 'a' been looking right up that big son of a gun's tail until he finally decided he better git on out of there. And now they must 'a' been getting pretty close to Uncle Ike's standers, and Mister Ernest reined Dan back and held him, squatting and bouncing and trembling like a mule having his tail roached, while we listened for the shots. But never none come, and I hollered to Mister Ernest we better go on while I could still hear the dogs, and he let Dan off, but still there wasn't no shots, and now we knowed the race had done already passed the standers, like that old son of a gun actually was a hant, like Simon and the other field hands said he was, and we busted out of a thicket, and sho enough there was Uncle Ike and Willy standing beside his foot in a soft patch.

"He got through us all," Uncle Ike said. "I don't know how he done it. I just had a glimpse of him. He looked big as a elephant, with a rack on his head you could cradle a yellin' calf in. He went right on down the ridge. You better get on, too; that Hog Bayou camp might not miss him."

So I freshened my holt and Mister Ernest touched Dan again. The ridge run due south; it was clear of vines and bushes so we could go fast, into the wind, too, because it had riz now, and now the sun was up, too; though I hadn't had time to notice it, bright and strong and level through the woods, shining and sparking like a rainbow on the frosted leaves. So we would hear the dogs again any time now as the wind got up; we could make time now, but still holding Dan back to a canter, because it was either going to be quick, when he got down to the standers from that Hog Bayou camp eight miles below ourn, or a long time, in case he got by them, too. And sho enough, after a while we heard the dogs; we was walking Dan now to let him blow a while, and we heard them, the sound coming faint up the wind, not running now, but trailing because the big son of a gun had decided a good piece of back, probably, to put a end to this foolishness, and picked hisself up and soupled out and put about a mile between hisself and the dogs—until he run up on them other standers from that camp below. I could almost see him stopped behind a bush, peeping out and saying, "What's this? What's this? Is this whole durn country full of folks this morning?" Then looking back over his shoulder at where old Eagle and the others was hollering along after him while he decided how much time he had to decide what to do next.

Except he almost shaved it too fine. We heard the shots; it sounded like a war. Old Eagle must 'a' been looking right up his tail again and he had to bust on through the best way he could.

"Pow, pow, pow, pow" and then "Pow, pow, pow, pow," like it must 'a' been three or four ganged right up on him before he had time even to swerve, and me hollering, "No! No! No! No!" because he was ourn. It was our beans and oats he et and our brake he laid in; we had been watching him every year, and it was like we had raised him, to be killed at last on our jump, in front of our dogs, by some strangers that would probably try to beat the dogs off and drag him away before we could even git a piece of the meat.

"Shut up and listen," Mister Ernest said. So I done it and we could hear the dogs; not just the others, but Eagle, too, not trailing no scent now and not baying no downed meat neither, but running hot on sight long after the shooting was over. I jest had time to freshen my holt. Yes, sir, they was running on sight. Like Willy Legate would say, if Eagle jest had a drink of whisky he would ketch that deer; going on, done already gone when we broke out of the thicket and seen the fellers that had done the shooting, five or six of them, squatting and crawling around, looking at the ground and the bushes, like maybe if they looked hard enough, spots of blood would bloom out on the stalks and leaves like frogstools or hawberries, with old Eagle still in hearing and still telling them that what blood they found wasn't coming out of nothing in front of him.

"Have any luck, boys?" Mister Ernest said.

"I think I hit him," one of them said. "I know I did. We're hunting blood now."

"Well, when you find him, blow your horn and I'll come back and tote him in to camp for you," Mister Ernest said.

So we went on, going fast now because the race was almost out of hearing again, going fast, too, like not jest the buck, but the dogs, too, had took a new lease on life from all the excitement and shooting.

We was in strange country now because we never had to run this fur before, we had always killed before now; now we had come to Hog Bayou that runs into the river a good fifteen miles below our camp. It had water in it, not to mention a mess of down trees and logs and such, and Mister Ernest checked Dan again, saying, "Which way?" I could just barely hear them, off to the east a little, like the old son of gun had give up the idea of Vicksburg or New Orleans, like he first seemed to have, and had decided to have a look at Alabama, maybe, since he was already up and moving; so I pointed and we turned up the bayou hunting for a crossing, and maybe we could 'a' found one, except that I reckon Mister Ernest decided we never had time to wait.

We come to a place where the bayou had narrowed down to about twelve or fifteen feet, and Mister Ernest said, "Look out, I'm going to touch him" and done it; I didn't even have time to freshen my holt when we was already in the air, and then I seen the vine—it was a loop of grapevine nigh as big as my wrist, looping down right across the middle of the bayou—and I thought he seen it, too, and was jest waiting to grab it and fling it up over our heads to go under it, and I know Dan seen it because he even ducked his head to jump under it. But Mister Ernest never seen it atall until it skun back along Dan's neck and hooked under the head of the saddle horn, us flying on through the air, the loop of the vine gitting tighter and tighter until something somewhere was going to have to give. It was the saddle girth. It broke, and Dan going on and scrabbling up the other bank bare nekkid except for the bridle, and me and Mister Ernest and the saddle, Mister Ernest still setting in the saddle holding the gun, and me still holding onto Mister Ernest's belt, hanging in the air over the bayou in the tightened loop of that vine like in the drawed-back loop of a big rubber-banded slingshot, until it snapped back and shot us back across the bayou and flang us clear, me still holding onto Mister Ernest's belt and on the bottom now, so that when we lit I would 'a' had Mister Ernest and the saddle both on top of me if I hadn't clumb fast around the saddle and up Mister Ernest's side, so that when we landed, it was the saddle first, then Mister Ernest, and me on top, until I jumped up, and Mister Ernest still laying there with jest the white rim of his eyes showing.

"Mister Ernest!" I hollered, and then clumb down to the bayou and scooped my cap full of water and clumb back and throwed it in his face, and he opened his eyes and laid there on the saddle cussing me.

"God dawg it," he said, "why didn't you stay behind where you started out?"

"You was the biggest!" I said. "You would 'a' mashed me flat!"

"What do you think you done to me?" Mister Ernest said. "Next time, if you can't stay where you start out, jump clear. Don't climb up on top of me no more. You hear?"

"Yes, sir," I said.

So he got up then, still cussing and holding his back, and clumb down to the water and dipped some in his hand onto his face and neck and dipped some more up and drunk it, and I drunk some, too, and clumb back and got the saddle and the gun, and we crossed the bayou on the down logs. If we could jest ketch Dan; not that he would have went them fifteen miles back to camp, because, if anything, he would have went on by hisself to try to help Eagle ketch that buck. But he was about fifty yards away, eating buck vines, so I brought him back, and we taken Mister Ernest's galluses and my belt and the whang leather loop off Mister Ernest's horn and tied the saddle back on Dan. It didn't look like much, but maybe it would hold.

"Provided you don't let me jump him through no more grapevines without hollering first," Mister Ernest said.

"Yes, sir," I said. "I'll holler first next time—provided you'll holler a little quicker when you touch him next time, too." But it was all right; we jest had to be a little easy getting up. "Now which-a-way?" I said. Because we couldn't hear nothing now, after wasting all this time. And this was new country, sho enough. It had been cut over and growed up in thickets we couldn't 'a' seen over even standing up on Dan.

But Mister Ernest never even answered. He jest turned Dan along the bank of the bayou where it was a little more open and we could move faster again, soon as Dan and us got used to that homemade cinch strop and got a little confidence in it. Which jest happened to be east, or so I thought then, because I never paid no particular attention to east then because the sun—I don't know where the morning had went, but it was gone, the morning and the frost, too—was up high now, even if my insides had told me it was past dinnertime.

And then we heard him. No, that's wrong; what we heard was shots. And that was when we realized how fur we had come, because the only camp we knowed about in that direction was the Hollyknowe camp, and Hollyknowe was exactly twenty-eight miles from Van Dorn, where me and Mister Ernest lived—jest the shots, no dogs nor nothing. If old Eagle was still behind him and the buck was still alive, he was too wore out now to even say, "Here he comes."

"Don't touch him!" I hollered. But Mister Ernest remembered that cinch strop, too, and he jest let Dan off the snaffle. And Dan heard them shots, too, picking his way through the thickets, hopping the vines and logs when he could and going under them when he couldn't. And sho enough, it was jest like before—two or three men squatting and creeping among the bushes, looking for blood that Eagle had done already told them wasn't there. But we never stopped this time, jest trotting on by with Dan hopping and dodging among the brush and vines dainty as a dancer. Then Mister Ernest swung Dan until we was going due north.

"Wait!" I hollered. "Not this way."

But Mister Ernest jest turned his face back over his shoulder. It looked tired, too, and there was a smear of mud on it where that ere grapevine had snatched him off the horse.

"Don't you know where he's heading?" he said. "He's done done his part, give everybody a fair open shot at him, and now he's going home, back to that brake in our bayou. He ought to make it exactly at dark."

And that's what he was doing. We went on. It didn't matter to hurry now. There wasn't no sound nowhere; it was that time in the early afternoon in November when don't nothing move or cry, not even birds, the peckerwoods and yellowhammers and jays, and it seemed to me like I could see all three of us—me and Mister Ernest and Dan—and Eagle, and the other dogs, and that big old buck, moving through the quiet woods in the same direction, headed for the same place, not running now but walking, that had all run the fine race the best we knowed how, and all three of us now turned like on a agreement to walk back home, not together in a bunch because we didn't want to worry or tempt one another, because what we had all three spent this morning doing was no play-acting jest for fun, but was serious, and all three of us was still what we was—that old buck that had to run, not because he was skeered, but because running was what he done the best and was proudest at; and Eagle and the dogs that chased him, not because they hated or feared him, but because that was the thing they done the best and was proudest at, and me and Mister Ernest and Dan, that run him not because we wanted his meat, which would be too tough to eat anyhow, or his head to hang on a wall, but because now we could go back and work hard for eleven months making a crop, so we would have the right to come back here next November—all three of us going back home now, peaceful and separate, but still side by side, until next year, next time.

Then we seen him for the first time. We was out of the cut-over now; we could even 'a' cantered, except that all three of us was long past that, and now you could tell where west was because the sun was already halfway down it. So we was walking, too, when we come on the dogs—the puppies and one of the old ones— played out, laying in a little wet swag, panting, jest looking up at us when we passed, but not moving when we went on. Then we come to a long open glade, you could see about half a quarter, and we seen the three other old dogs and about a hundred yards ahead of them Eagle, all walking, not making no sound; and then suddenly, at the fur end of the glade, the buck hisself getting up from where he had been resting for the dogs to come up, getting up without no hurry, big, big as a mule, tall as a mule, and turned without no hurry still; and the white underside of his tail for a second or two more before the thicket taken him.

It might 'a' been a signal, a good-bye, a farewell. Still walking, we passed the other three old dogs in the middle of the glade, laying down, too, now jest where they was when the buck vanished, and not trying to get up neither when we passed; and still that hundred yards ahead of them, Eagle, too, not laying down, because he was still on his feet, but his legs was spraddled and his

] 379 [

head was down; maybe jest waiting until we was out of sight of his shame, his eyes saying plain as talk when we passed, "I'm sorry, boys, but this here is all."

Mister Ernest stopped Dan. "Jump down and look at his feet," he said.

"Ain't nothing wrong with his feet," I said. "It's his wind has done give out."

"Jump down and look at his feet," Mister Ernest said.

So I done it, and while I was stooping over Eagle I could hear the pump gun go, "Snick-cluck. Snick-cluck. Snick-cluck" three times, except that I never thought nothing then. Maybe he was jest running the shells through to be sho it would work when we seen him again or maybe to make sho they was all buckshot. Then I got up again, and we went on, still walking; a little west of north now, because when we seen his white flag that second or two before the thicket hid it, it was on a beeline for that notch in the bayou. And it was evening, too, now. The wind had done dropped and there was a edge to the air and the sun jest touched the tops of the trees now, except jest now and then, when it found a hole to come almost level through onto the ground. And he was taking the easiest way, too, now, going straight as he could. When we seen his foot in the soft places he was running for a while at first after his rest. But soon he was walking, too, like he knowed, too, where Eagle and the dogs was.

And then we seen him again. It was the last time—a thicket, with the sun coming through a hole onto it like a searchlight. He crashed jest once; then he was standing there broadside to us, not twenty yards away, big as a statue and red as gold in the sun, and the sun sparking on the tips of his horns—they was twelve of them—so that he looked like he had twelve lighted candles branched around his head, standing there looking at us while Mister Ernest raised the gun and aimed at his neck, and the gun went. "Click. Snick-cluck. Click. Snick-cluck. Click. Snick-cluck" three times, and Mister Ernest still holding the gun aimed while the buck turned and give one long bound, the white underside of his tail like a blaze of fire, too, until the thicket and the shadows put it out; and Mister Ernest laid the gun slow and gentle back across the saddle in front of him, saying quiet and peaceful, and not much louder than jest breathing, "God dawg. God dawg."

Then he jogged me with his elbow and we got down, easy and careful because of that ere cinch strop, and he reached into his vest and taken out one of the cigars. It was busted where I had fell on it, I reckon, when we hit the ground. He throwed it away and taken out the other one. It was busted, too, so he bit off a hunk of it to chew and throwed the rest away. And now the sun was gone even from the tops of the trees and there wasn't nothing left but a big red glare in the west.

"Don't worry," I said. "I ain't going to tell them you forgot to load your gun. For that matter, they don't need to know we ever seed him."

"Much oblige," Mister Ernest said. There wasn't going to be no moon tonight neither, so he taken the compass off the whang leather loop in his buttonhole and handed me the gun and set the compass on a stump and stepped back and looked at it. "Jest about the way we're headed now," he said, and taken the gun from me and opened it and put one shell in the britch and taken up the compass, and I taken Dan's reins and we started, with him in front with the compass in his hand.

And after a while it was full dark; Mister Ernest would have to strike a match ever now and then to read the compass, until the stars come out good and we could pick out one to follow, because I said, "How fur do you reckon it is?" and he said, "A little more than one box of matches." So we used a star when we could, only we couldn't see it all the time because the woods was too dense and we would git a little off until he would have to spend another match. And now it was good and late, and he stopped and said, "Get on the horse."

"I ain't tired," I said.

"Get on the horse," he said. "We don't want to spoil him."

Because he had been a good feller ever since I had knowed him, which was even before that day two years ago when maw went off with the Vicksburg roadhouse feller and the next day pap didn't come home neither, and on the third one Mister Ernest rid Dan up to the door of the cabin on the river he let us live in, so pap could work his piece of land and run his fish line, too, and said, "Put that gun down and come on here and climb up behind."

So I got in the saddle even if I couldn't reach the stirrups, and Mister Ernest taken the reins and I must 'a' went to sleep, because the next thing I knowed a buttonhole of my lumberjack was tied to the saddle horn with that ere whang cord off the compass, and it was good and late now and we wasn't fur, because Dan was already smelling water, the river. Or maybe it was the feed lot itself he smelled, because we struck the fire road not a quarter below it, and soon I could see the river, too, with the white mist laying on it soft and still as cotton. Then the lot, home; and up yonder in the dark, not no piece akchully, close enough to hear us unsaddling and shucking corn prob'ly, and sholy close enough to hear Mister Ernest blowing his horn at the dark camp for Simon to come in the boat and git us, that old buck in his brake in the bayou; home, too, resting, too, after the hard run, waking hisself now and then, dreaming of dogs behind him or maybe it was the racket we was making would wake him, but not neither of them for more than jest a little while before sleeping again.

Then Mister Ernest stood on the bank blowing until Simon's lantern went bobbing down into the mist; then we clumb down to the landing and Mister Ernest blowed again now and then to guide Simon, until we seen the lantern in the mist, and then Simon and the boat; only it looked like ever time I set down and got still, I went back to sleep, because Mister Ernest was shaking me again to git out and climb the bank into the dark camp, until I felt a bed against my knees and tumbled into it.

Then it was morning, tomorrow; it was all over now until next November, next year, and we could come back. Uncle Ike and Willy and Walter and Roth and the rest of them had come in yestiddy, soon as Eagle taken the buck out of hearing and they knowed that deer was gone, to pack up and be ready to leave this morning for Yoknapatawpha, where they lived, until it would be November again and they could come back again.

So, as soon as we et breakfast, Simon run them back up the river in the big boat to where they left their cars and pickups, and now it wasn't nobody but jest me and Mister Ernest setting on the bench against the kitchen wall in the sun; Mister Ernest smoking a cigar—a whole one this time that Dan hadn't had no chance to jump him through a grapevine and bust. He hadn't washed his face neither where that vine had throwed him into the mud. But that was all right, too; his face usually did have a smudge of mud or tractor grease or beard stubble on it, because he wasn't jest a planter; he was a farmer, he worked as hard as ara one of his hands and tenants—which is why I knowed from the very first that we would git along, that I wouldn't have no trouble with him and he wouldn't have no trouble with me, from that very first day when I woke up and maw had done gone off with that Vicksburg roadhouse feller without even waiting to cook breakfast, and the next morning pap was gone, too, and it was almost night the next day when I heard a horse coming up and I taken the gun that I had already throwed a shell into the britch when pap never come home last night, and stood in the door while Mister Ernest rid up and said, "Come on. Your paw ain't coming back neither."

"You mean he give me to you?" I said.

"Who cares?" he said. "Come on. I brought a lock for the door. We'll send the pickup back tomorrow for whatever you want."

So I come home with him and it was all right, it was jest fine—his wife had died about three years ago—without no women to worry us or take off in the middle of the night with a durn Vicksburg roadhouse jake without even waiting to cook breakfast. And we would go home this afternoon, too, but not jest yet; we always stayed one more day after the others left because Uncle Ike always left what grub they hadn't et, and the rest of the homemade corn whiskey he drunk and that town whiskey of Roth Edmondziz he called Scotch that smelled like it come out of a old bucket of roof paint; setting in the sun for one more day before we went back home to git ready to put in next year's crop of cotton and oats and beans and hay; and across the river yonder, behind the wall of trees where the big woods started, that old buck laying up today in the sun, too—resting today, too, without nobody to bother him until next November.

So at least one of us was glad it would be eleven months and two weeks before he would have to run that fur that fast again. So he was glad of the very same thing we was sorry of, and so all of a sudden I thought about how maybe planting and working and then harvesting oats and cotton and beans and hay wasn't jest something me and Mister Ernest done three hundred and fifty-one days to fill in the time until we could come back hunting again, but it was something we had to do, and do honest and good during the three hundred and fifty-one days, to have the right to come back into the big woods and hunt for the other fourteen; and the fourteen days that old buck run in front of dogs wasn't jest something to fill his time until the three hundred and fifty-one when he didn't have to, but the running and the risking in front of guns and dogs was something he had to do for fourteen days to have the right not to be bothered for the other three hundred and fifty-one. And so the hunting and the farming wasn't two different things atall—they was jest the other side of each other.

"Yes," I said. "All we got to do now is put in that next year's crop. Then November won't be no time away atall."

"You ain't going to put in the crop next year," Mister Ernest said. "You're going to school."

So at first I didn't even believe I had heard him. "What?" I said. "Me? Go to school?"

"Yes," Mister Ernest said. "You must make something out of yourself."

"I am," I said. "I'm doing it now. I'm going to be a hunter and a farmer like you."

"No," Mister Ernest said. "That ain't enough any more. Time was when all a man had to do was just farm eleven and a half months, and hunt the other half. But not now. Now just to belong to the farming business and the hunting business ain't enough. You got to belong to the business of mankind."

"Mankind?" I said.

"Yes," Mister Ernest said. "So you're going to school. Because you got to know why. You can belong to the farming and hunting business and you can learn the difference between what's right and what's wrong, and do right. And that used to be enough—just to do right. But not now. You got to know why it's right and

] 384 [

why it's wrong, and be able to tell the folks that never had no chance to learn it; teach them how to do what's right, not just because they know it's right, but because they know now why it's right because you just showed them, told them, taught them why. So you're going to school."

"It's because you been listening to that durn Will Legate and Walter Ewell!" I said.

"No," Mister Ernest said.

"Yes!" I said. "No wonder you missed that buck yestiddy, taking ideas from the very fellers that let him git away, after me and you had run Dan and the dogs durn night clean to death! Because you never even missed him! You never forgot to load that gun! You had done already unloaded it a purpose! I heard you!"

"All right, all right," Mister Ernest said. "Which would you rather have? His bloody head and hide on the kitchen floor yonder and half his meat in a pickup truck on the way to Yoknapatawpha County, or him with his head and hide and meat still together over yonder in that brake, waiting for next November for us to run him gain?"

"And git him, too," I said. "We won't even fool with no Willy Legate and Walter Ewell next time."

"Maybe," Mister Ernest said.

"Yes," I said.

"Maybe," Mister Ernest said. "The best word in our language, the best of all. That's what mankind keeps going on: Maybe. The best days of his life ain't the ones when he said 'Yes' beforehand: they're the ones when all he knew to say was 'Maybe.' He can't say 'Yes' until afterward because he not only don't know it until then, he don't want to know 'Yes' until then. . . . Step in the kitchen and make me a toddy. Then we'll see about dinner."

"All right," I said. I got up. "You want some of Uncle Ike's corn or that town whiskey of Roth Edmondziz?"

"Can't you say Mister Roth or Mister Edmonds?" Mister Ernest said.

"Yes, sir," I said. "Well, which do you want? Uncle Ike's corn or that ere stuff of Roth Edmondziz?"

THE CLEARING BUCK

John S. Martin

I've always loved this piece, even though I am not familiar with other works by its author.

The story originally appeared in Field & Stream *and was later anthologized in the story collection* Outdoors Unlimited *published by A. S. Barnes and Company in 1947.*

THE MOONS THAT RIDE over the Adirondacks look, I suppose, just as they always did—soft and warm when the brook trout are rising to an evening hatch of May-flies, cold and hard when the bucks' necks are swelling and the shadows are like fine black lace along the silvery beech ridges. The people who move around in the Adirondacks have not changed so much, either. Vacationists escaping the grind of their cities are motivated not much differently from the first trappers and settlers who came there to escape the grind of colonial poverty; to consume the wilderness and, by taming it, to quench the ache that its savagery put in their hearts.

But I think the Adirondack deer have changed. When the Indians were there, deer were only deer, for then there were elk, too, and moose, and the little fellows with white tails were minor characters. Today they are the region's biggest wild creatures, barring a few bear.

I know one deer that stood for something eternal in the Adirondacks. He lived at a time when Lake Placid was already loud with college kids and Lake George and Schroon and Long Lakes were already lined, on one side, with hot-dog stands and gents' clothing stores. He lived back in a sheltered country, west and a little north of Brandreth Lake, ranging between North Pond Flow and Deer Pond in the section drained by Shingle Shanty Stream. Folks used to see him or find his track around the long clearing that lies two-thirds of the way in to the lake from Brandreth Station. The clearing was made for a logging camp when they cut the soft wood off that section for the first time, more than a generation ago. This clearing was grown with hay, sparse but sweet, and across that long forest meadow at dusk sometimes people traveling the wagon road would see a huge deer, gray with age, feeding in the open at the far edge.

If the traveler stopped to watch, this buck—a true stag in size and dignity—would not flounce away like the young bucks and the does and fawns. He would just raise his head, which was crowned with what looked like the top of a dead chestnut tree, and gaze back majestically. Then he would move slowly off into the timber—royalty whose privacy had been invaded. A true monarch of the wilds.

They called him the Clearing Buck. Jim Hall, the head guide, used to call his track "as big as a bull's." Reuben Cary, who had been at the camp ever since the late General Brandreth got the township as his bonus after the Civil War, used to say gently, into his snowy whiskers, "He's been around there a number of years." That was going some, from old Reuben.

No one had ever had a shot at him.

Our guess was that the Clearing Buck nooned on the high, steep beech ridges that ran southwest of the old logging track. He was so wise and alert that he probably picked spots to spend the day, even in rutting season, where he could hear or smell a man coming for half a mile. Then he would just slip over a ridge and move away unseen without your knowing he had even been there.

Maybe, too, he had a much wider range than most deer—all the way to the foot of the big lake and 'way out to Panther Pond. Anyway, we used to drive his section every now and then and never see anything more of him than that enormous deep hoofprint, more than four inches long and splayed in front as wide as your rifle butt. In soft ground you could see where his fetlocks had pressed in. Two hundred pounds, dressed, is heavy for an Adirondack buck. The Clearing Buck would go nearer three hundred. Even old Reuben thought so.

But we never saw him except when he showed himself at the clearing. We felt about him as you feel about the spirit of a place, a spirit too shy to be conjured. Nor could you lie in wait for this spirit to appear. We tried that many an evening at the clearing, and he never showed. Either he knew we were there, or he came and stayed invisible. We had this feeling about him: that he was just a little bit supernatural.

Some people get sentimental about wild things. They think you should leave them entirely alone, let them live out the lives they were born to, even though you know they won't live so long and though man, when he hunts them, is only reverting to whatever wild is left in him.

We were pretty lusty young animals in the Clearing Buck's day, and fancied that our killing was more aboriginal than most hunters'. We stalked our game ourselves and dressed it out and carried it in with only a little help from the guides, or so we thought. But

about the Clearing Buck even we had something of that soft feeling, almost a reverence. He was so superior to all other deer that it would be a crime to shoot him if you did get the chance, so mysterious and patriarchal that to kill him would be to rob Brandreth of its most important unseen presence.

And yet, we realized, he could not live forever. He must be so old that, any season now, he would lay his great body down in some deep tamarack swamp and go to sleep for always; leaving behind him nothing but his legend. And even that would become thin and unbelieved as the people who knew it stopped coming to Brandreth. The Clearing Buck's head belonged in the Colonel's big game room at the main camp, up on the stones over the ten-foot fireplace, to stare proudly across at the long rows of lesser bucks which Brandreths and McAlpins and Potters and Pyles had shot through the generations. At least, that was our way of rationalizing the challenge, almost the scare, that the Clearing Buck's shadowy existence put into our predatory young hearts. We didn't hunt him often, but every once in a while some one of us would say, "Let's go out to the clearing and see if we can get a crack at him." And then two or three of us boys would go out there together, talking very little and only in whispers, because going for the Clearing Buck was really awesome.

I lately flew over the Adirondacks and didn't see much of them. The overcast was thick, and the Montreal plane went high above it. We flew far east of Brandreth, but I knew about where it lay as we passed, and I thought how different it all looked from up there. The autumn sun was hot on the clouds below us and through the cabin window. Down under the clouds I knew it was drizzling through the Adirondacks, the way it drizzled and then froze and sleeted and finally snowed the day Don and I hunted the Clearing Buck, and saw him close to, and fired lead into him.

That was one of those days when it rained so hard just before dawn that it wakes you up, and you turn the other ear to it and forget about hunting. But something got me up, and I made breakfast before rousting Don out.

Then I broached the idea of going out the track past the clearing as far as the old Potter camp, rain or no rain, if only to pick up a few partridges. We were due to go home in two days, and he hadn't killed his buck yet; so he would carry a rifle, I a shotgun, or, rather, old Reuben's three-barreled gun with buckshot in the left side and a .30-30 bullet underneath, just in case. The weather ought to fair off about eleven o'clock, I figured, and we could hunt a buck for him coming back.

Don went, but he grumbled a lot and said I was crazy, and he was right. It certainly didn't fair off. We were soaked through by the time we reached Potter's. But the wind died out and the rain became a fine drizzle and the woods went dead. They had that damp, dark silence that makes the trees sound as though they were mourning when a breath does stir them. Even their steady dripping stopped as the air turned colder and the drizzle congealed into fine sleet. No bird or squirrel moved. The only thing alive in the woods was Shingle Shanty Stream, raised by the rain, pouring down its course into the ghostly swampland below the ridges.

Wet as we were, we might as well make a swing along the ridges, for now stalking conditions were perfect. Under our feet the dead leaves lay limp, turning to forest mold. You could move like a wraith, and in the still air all scents carried nowhere, but hung heavily where they were—our tobacco, our sweat, our guns' oil and our wet wool and leather. We worked up over one ridge and found the big trees on its top groaning softly like an organ. Down in the next hollow all was still again, and entering a blue-spruce thicket was like pushing through damp velvet curtains. The sodden carpet of needles was centuries deep.

Don and I had hunted together so often this way, one ahead with birdshot, the other behind with a rifle, that ordinarily we scarcely exchanged glances. But today was somehow ominous. We knew we would likely be right on top of deer before seeing them, and just lately one of the guides had been charged by a rutty buck when he surprised it with a doe. I kept looking back at Don to see if he saw in the trail what I saw—old prints of the Clearing Buck. After so much rain it was hard to tell how old they were. But we were on his range, all right.

I remember I had on a red worsted hockey cap which got brushed off on to my knees by a twig as I crouched suddenly at an exclamation behind me from Don. I looked around and saw him staring pop-eyed, his gun half raised, after a fawn which had jumped up right beside him and was bounding away without a sound through the thicket. I must have passed its bed within two paces without its stirring. It startled Don so badly that he was panting as he lowered his rifle and grinned at me sheepishly. I grinned, too, pulled on my sopping red cap, straightened up, and started along the trail again toward where it climbed a small hummock. I had to chuckle at Don, letting a fawn panic him.

When I was halfway up the little rise, I squatted suddenly a second time, and now it was my turn to pant. Every bit of breath had gone out of me, every nerve and muscle had gone instantly taut, at what I had seen just beyond the blue-spruce hummock, I had seen, without his seeing or hearing me, the biggest, grayest deer in the world, with a head of horns like chestnut rampikes. He was lying right beside the trail, not twenty paces away, broadside to, with his head turned away. It could only be—it was without any question—the Clearing Buck!

I have never had such a moment in the woods, before or since. There lay the fabled monster, and there crouched I, with his certain death in my hands. All I had to do was cock the gun, rise, aim and fire. But I didn't do any of those things. I crouched there frozen, getting my breath in and out in gulps as silently as I could.

I knew the buck was absolutely unaware, undisturbed. But Don hadn't seen me yet, either. He was feeling in his breast pocket for a cigarette, after the fawn episode, coming along slowly behind me without looking. The great buck was right there for him to shoot, but I had to get Don's eye to make him crouch and creep to where I was. The seconds were torture until he looked up, saw me gesturing, grinned again and said right out loud: "Damn that little critter! He made me jump almost out of my skin."

Then he caught my excitement, put his hand over his mouth and hunched down where he was. But he stage-whispered, "What's the matter?" still smiling. He still had that fawn on his mind.

I made the words "Clearing Buck" with my lips and pointed to the hummock. He didn't understand, but began stealing toward me; so I turned to cover that astonishing quarry, sure now that he was ours. I stayed down until Don reached my shoulder, and by the time I could whisper to him I was cold calm once more.

I know now that I should never have named that awful name to him just then, "The Clearing Buck." For those words shook him apart again, into the state the fawn had started, and as we both straightened up—much too fast—for Don to let him have it the great animal sprang to his feet and whirled away in one incredible blur of motion. Don, who is a crack rifleman, missed him cleanly with one, two, three shots as he crashed off to our right. I cut loose with the buckshot charge and never even slowed him up.

Then he was gone, and we stood looking at each other as though the world had come to an end. The silence of the dead forest closed in around us. We just looked at each other, trembling, and then one of us said, "My God!" We sank down on the spruce needles to whisper it over.

He may not run too far, we said, and in these wet woods we can follow his track easily. The thing will be to see him first, because he is as old as these hills and twice as wise. He will stop and look back, listening, smelling. It's dark enough today so that maybe we can get up on him, with no wind and such quiet going. But now Don had better go first, for a snap shot. And we'll both move mighty slowly.

I took off the red cap. We gave the buck the time it takes to smoke one cigarette. Then we took his trail.

Up the beech ridge it led, in bounds so far apart you wouldn't have believed an animal his size and weight and make them through thick timber. We followed stealthily for a mile before we came to the place he had stopped for the first time. That made us feel better. Beyond this spot, on a high knoll, the broad, heart-shaped hoofmarks fell into line where he had walked off instead of running. They led to and around a brush pile which he had skirted instead of leaping. They paired again and lengthened out where he had bounded across an opening, but on the far side he had stopped for a second look back. From there on the tracks were a stately march, ever toward higher ground. He was over his first fright, but an old-timer like this would be extra alert for days to come.

On the higher ground, the sleet turned to wet snow. Big flakes swirling down so densely they made you feel they had pressure. This would be a help, if we hurried, because we could go forward farther apart, and still keep the buck's trail in sight between us. But it cut down the visibility, and the motion of the snowflakes sometimes imparted itself to rocks and stumps, so that we paused more often, peering breathlessly ahead at nothing.

When I did see the Clearing Buck again, Don wouldn't believe me. He was halted a good hundred yards away, with head and horns concealed from us, behind a thick beech butt. My eye must have caught one twitch of his tail, which he did not repeat for the longest time after I got Don to see what otherwise looked like a tall gray boulder coated with snow. We stood together, straining for verification. I was on the point of agreeing with Don that I was "seeing things," that no deer's body could possibly stand high and massive. Then that tail twitched again. Don drew a long breath and laid his wet cheek against the stock of his rifle.

Lots of bucks spring into the air when you hit them, or crumple right to the ground. This one just sagged a bit, then straightened, moved out beyond the beech trunk and sank deliberately to his knees, as though lying down by choice. But his incredible head went on down too and he rolled over on his side, and when we saw that we started walking in.

You always see afterward how easy it would have been to do the right thing, and how that hurts! We hadn't gone five steps before that buck was up and away over the next knoll as though nothing in the world had happened.

How badly he was shot, how strong a beast he must be to run at all, we could only judge by a two-foot splatter of dark blood where his side had been and by more splotches on the underbrush for fifty yards.

Old Reuben, of course, later rubbed it into us cruelly about what we should have done then: hold still for an hour and let the buck lie down wherever he would, until the wound stiffened. Then trail him; he would never get up again. But I doubt if anyone who had seen and shot that magnificent, ghostly animal, and judged from the sign how deeply he was wounded, could have exercised such patience. Besides, it was snowing hard, and it was getting late. In a few minutes the trail would be blanketed, first by those cascading snowflakes, then by evening gloom.

We pushed ahead feverishly, both of us ready to fire the finishing shot when the Clearing Buck should surge up, as we were sure he would, from a windfall or rocky pocket or clump of beech switches. We pursued those tremendous leaping hoofmarks, now punctuated on the off side by splotches of blood, just as hard as we could, without caution. Instead of uphill, the tracks now led down—another sign that the buck was mortally hurt. He was heading for water to kill his scent, and a swampy tangle to hide in.

Twice we heard him start up just ahead of us, both times out of sight. He blew furiously when he winded us and crashed off into the gathering dusk. We hurried on faster, stumbling and slithering on rocks and down timber.

Where a rivulet cut under the hill's shoulder, we found that he had slid down a long, steep gravel bank, too steep for us to take

] 393 [

without risk of grit in our guns. We had to descend a longer way. At the bottom we knew he had followed the stream bed, undoubtedly downward toward the fastnesses of Shingle Shanty Swamp.

We splashed down the watercourse after him, and dismay got its first clutch on us when we came to a long pool, too deep to wade, that beavers had backed up with many yards of wabbly bog on either side. We were twenty precious minutes floundering through and around that obstacle. Meantime, somewhere ahead of us, into the wilderness and the night, struggled the greatest buck we had ever heard of, the high-headed monarch of these mountains, wounded, dying, never more to be seen.

Don and I didn't get into camp that night until long after the rest had finished dinner. Finding our way back to the logging track was a job in itself, after our matches gave out and we had to admit we would never find that deer in the dark. We told everyone in camp our story, over and over, suffering intensely when old Reuben poured on us his gentle scorn.

But I think we suffered even more lying in bed that night with the awful thought that the Clearing Buck lay dead somewhere and that we who had killed him had done it clumsily, ignobly. Unless we found him the next day that shaggy, hoary hide would never be tanned soft and spread across a gun room table for hunters to admire. Those magnificently spiked and palmated antlers would be meanly nibbled by mice, or would just rot in the swamp muck, instead of gleaming in a place of honor for years to come.

We never did find him. The whole camp turned out next day and combed that run, right down into Shingle Shanty, until sundown. It had stopped snowing in the night, so that everyone saw the deep blood stains. Old Reuben said we had simply "hit him in the short guts," which would let him travel a long way, until he lay down and stiffened. But it must surely be fatal.

Maybe it was, for he was never seen alive again, and his great track was gone from the Brandreth region. But I like to hope that somehow he survived, to live out his days in some distant range, and I almost wish that I had never seen him alive at all. It's a fearful thing to know that the wild held something so splendid, and that you spoiled it.

OLD KING PIN

Harry H. Sheldon

Here's one of those classic, fun-reading tales the outdoor magazines seldom seem to have room for any more. It's taken from the Field & Stream Treasury, *published by Henry Holt and Company in 1955.*

ROCKS RATTLING DOWN THE BIG MOUNTAIN diverted my attention from the picture I had been enjoying through my binoculars. I looked up and saw three mule deer making their way down the mountain in stiff-legged jumps. A whale of a big buck was in the lead, with two does bringing up the rear in follow-the-leader fashion.

Neatly they sprang over logs, boulders and brush, down the face of the mountain, which for steepness seemed a more likely habitat of mountain sheep. It mattered not how rough the country, these blacktails were in their summer home, and Rocky Mountain environment was as natural to their requirements as the low, brushy river bottoms was home to their white-tailed cousins.

The buck was a perfect specimen, a ten-point head of wide dimensions. A shotgun was the only weapon I had with me; so the picture was undisturbed. I watched them trot along the shore of a small lake far below me, without stopping to drink, then disappear over a ridge. They were headed for the low country, where they would have a change of climate and food among the juniper hills—a downward migration that commences with the first hint of winter.

Resolved to follow this big fellow next day, I stretched myself and settled down again to enjoy the wilderness movie I had been viewing through my glasses. Some mallards and redhead ducks, a thousand feet below me, were feeding among golden-colored water lilies, diving and bobbing among the big green leaves which lay so flat on this crystal clear alpine lake that they seemed to be painted on its tranquil surface. Here was a hidden lake in the Rockies—a mecca where many varieties of birds and animal life congregated. From my balcony seat aloft, among some granite boulders as large as city bungalows, I watched the actors play their parts. Up the center of this smooth sheet of water spread a V-shaped line; at the apex was the artist, and his course through the water was marked by the ripples that spread on either side of his nose. His identity was revealed when he climbed on to an old spruce log that extended well into the lake.

A beaver had come to his afternoon rendezvous. He sat on his haunches, scratched his sides and frisked his furry coat with his deft paws, then waddled up the log and disappeared in a jungle of aspens along the lake shore. The little conies living among the boulders where I was sitting had ceased to squawk their disapproval of my intrusion into their habitat, which caused me to realize that the curtain of dusk had cast its shadow on my wilderness movie. Then, as if to emphasize its grandeur, the snowy crest of the Rockies, playing the role of Narcissus, looked over the spruces into this exquisite mirror of Dame Nature, where the mallards and the beaver and the golden-hued water lilies had added their quota of charm.

I had been making a biological survey of the country about Bill Latham's ranch in the Medicine Bow Range. Bill had lived on this ranch since the time when he could watch a herd of elk migrating across a section of the valley without seeing either end of the line, and when it was a common occurrence to go on a grizzly hunt which usually ended in success. Many a tale that rang true was listened to by a naturalist and Bill's gang of cowpunchers as they sat about a roaring stove in the bunk house of the Circle H.T. Ranch.

But that night when I told Bill about the big king-pin buck I had seen, he got out his old .30-30 and prepared to join me in a hunt. Bill was just about fed up on cattle and ranch stuff, and he joined in my enthusiasm for a hunt to the finish. He well knew the country I described and confidently prophesied with a chuckle that we would have venison steaks ere long.

Next day a couple of the boys drove Bill and me up the valley several miles to the base of a lofty range. The plan was to work up to a certain point on the range and return to the ranch down a long spur. After climbing for half an hour we reached a place where the formation had faulted and flattened out for a few hundred yards. Strange as it was, though we were in the mule deer country, we had been tramping along a used trail of a band of mountain sheep. Their shedding summer coats had caught in the gnarled and windswept growth along this knife-blade ridge, and as much as a handful of the long, crinkly hair could be seen hanging on the brush.

We rested while Bill related a hunt that netted two bighorns from the very ridge we were on. Then, to add color to his story, he pointed at the crest of the range almost a mile above to a band of bighorns, all ewes and lambs, crossing one of the big snowbanks atop the world.

Some miles away and far below lay the big valley—seventy-five miles of sagebrush and wild hay meadows. Many wonderful trout streams issued from the big continental divide and the Medicine Bow Ranges that bounded the big park. From our viewpoint they appeared like silver ribbons winding through the purple sage. A puff of dust several miles down the valley marked the boys with the mules and buckboard, returning to the ranch.

"Well, we must gain some more altitude," said Bill, "and then work down to the cedars."

Soon we struck a patch of brush that showed an abundance of sign and I began to think Bill's deer lore was O.K. Then we came to a big snowbank—hard snow that seldom disappears on the north exposure of the mountain. This we had to cross. A slip, and down we would go for a thousand feet or more at an angle of 50 degrees. We cut each step in with our heels and used the butt of our rifles for balance.

We crossed several of these snowbanks and it is quite obvious that we never did slip. Finally we came into a beautiful alpine meadow, a half mile long and about a quarter wide. A lot of down timber and some fine browse covered the gentle slope approaching the meadow. What a typical resort for mule deer, I thought, and Bill whispered to me while we silently gazed, "What d'you think of it?"

My approval was apparent to Bill without words.

Then we outlined a little hunt in this choice bit of deer land. Bill left me and worked down to the far end of the meadow. I took the opposite course. Before I had reached the head of the little valley, Bill's rifle cracked with a roar that seemed to echo over the entire range. Twice he let go.

I figured that if Bill failed to get him down, the deer would take to the country which I was headed rather than the slope to the valley. So I ran to the ridge beyond, across freshets of snow water and into mountain bogs and over down timber, whacking my shins and getting bruised and scratched, though without being aware of it at the time.

I gained a good outlook on the ridge and at once spotted a big buck, about two hundred yards distant, working his way through the brush and timber on the opposite side of a deep canyon. It was plain that he was badly hit, but I did not hesitate to finish him and he dropped dead with the second shot through the back and vitals.

Then another buck appeared from the ridge above, the running mate of the dead one. Completely fooled by the echo of my shots, he ran down the slope, passed within ten yards of the dead buck, crossed the canyon and came up my side of the mountain on the jump. I froze until he got within twenty yards of me. He dropped with one fatal shot—an eight-point buck. I could see he was much smaller than the one Bill had crippled.

I enjoyed a smoke and waited for Bill, who soon came along breathing hard. Here's about the way the conversation went. "Did you get him?" "Sure! There he is." And Bill followed my wave of the hand to the buck that lay a few yards below. He was on the point of congratulating me, and then sadly advised me that we lost the granddaddy of them all.

"Oh," I kidded, "you just imagined when you saw this deer capering through that down timber that he carried the proverbial rocking chair on his head."

"Say, young fellow, I been huntin' these mule ears too long to be fooled for size. The buck I was a shootin' at was big as an elk."

"Well, do you think you hit him, Bill?"

"Couldn't tell. Slammed it to him as he cleared some down timber and just got to the spot where I limbered up on him when you banged away. Had no chance to look for blood. Thought you had him, and came a-runnin'. Come on 'fore it gets too dark. We'll see if I did mark the gentleman."

"No, Bill, no use to look for blood. See that little green sapling the other side of the canyon, fifty feet from the bottom?"

"Yep."

"Well, ten feet this side you'll see a white spot."

"Yep."

"Well, that's the rump patch of your big buck."

"You sun-of-a-gun," was all he said, but his eyes twinkled with warmth as he chuckled merrily for the great luck.

As we scrambled down to get a close-up of the big deer I told Bill how it all happened and he was indeed happy to find that his old .30-30 hadn't failed him. The head was identical to the one I had seen the day before and we were content to believe it was old King Pin. He weighed 230 pounds dressed, measured thirty inches across beams and had a perfect development of horns, five points to an antler. The smaller deer was sixty pounds lighter.

An hour later the two fine bucks were hanging to a spruce bough in a camp that has never been surpassed for its memories of a perfect retreat in the wilderness. Here two tired men, fatigued yet content with the rest that follows a successful end to a day's hunt, satisfied their appetites with venison tenderloins. Then we built a shelter against two mighty spruce trees and rolled up in a blanket, with feet to a glowing fire, to sleep. While we slept as only tired men can, old man Winter came along and covered us up with a beautiful white blanket of snow.

Next morning we stepped out lively for ten miles, on empty stomachs, to the ranch. The detail most vivid in my memory in connection with that hike is the breakfast that Bill and I put away when we reached the ranch. Never had an appetite been more thoroughly seasoned with fresh air, exercise and mental pictures of food. Bill had most of the ranch help cooking for us that morning. Then the boys hooked the mules to the buckboard and the deer were brought back.

That night a hunting story fresh from the haunts of the mule deer was listened to by all hands as we sat around the stove in the bunk house of the Circle H.T. Ranch.

THREE MEN AND A BUCK

William A. Miles

Another selection from Ray Camp's anthology, Hunting Trails *(Apple-ton-Century-Crofts, Inc.). If the farm-fringe deer hunter felt I was leaving him out, he'll be in for a pleasant surprise when he reads this one.*

THE WHOLE THING HAPPENED because Doc had a friend who owned a farm in upstate New York, in the foothills of the Adirondacks. Here he had retired to the placid life of reading and checker playing. That is, most of his time was spent that way. The rest of the day was spent chasing deer out of his young orchard. That's the way the story came to us.

Now the mere mention of venison seems to rouse the sporting instinct. The pulse quickens; the fountain of youth starts bubbling. Even the most serene individual will prick up his ears. It's like a bugle call to an old war horse. Must be a throwback to our pioneer forbears.

Anyway, it was the origin of the most incongruous foursome that ever responded to the call of the wild. There was Jim, a surgeon of great repute in the greatest city; Joe, a dentist who asked and received better than ten dollars an hour for his labors; Sam, an undertaker, who, contrary to tradition, was fat and jolly and as full of jokes as a hound dog is of ticks. And a magazine publisher. I was the publisher.

How we ever got together for a deer hunt remains a mystery to this day. We had nothing in common. We were, indeed, members of the same club—but all for different reasons. However, just the suggestion of venison seems to make strange bedfellows.

Jim started it all at the round-table lunch at the club when he passed around a letter from his retired friend in the Adirondacks. It wasn't much of a letter, as I recall. Merely the suggestion that Jim come up and help dispose of some of the deer that were chewing up the young fruit trees. So the four of us looked at one another and asked: "Why not?" Sam, the undertaker, was more candid. He still maintains that he went along solely for business reasons.

] 401 [

The outfits that were lugged aboard the Adirondacks Special at Grand Central Terminal a couple of weeks later were just as much mismated as we were. That is, all but Sam's. All he brought was an overnight bag, which held a gallon jug and a change of underwear. Sam said the jug contained embalming fluid. It did. It was four-year-old applejack—also known as Jersey lightning. It has other names too, that are just as apt as the drink is effective.

The treasure in Jim's outfit was a sheep-lined trench coat that reached below his knees—just the right length to entangle the leg action. Joe simply brought his oldest clothes and a borrowed Winchester. My rig was fairly complete, with duffel bag, hunting togs, shoepacs with no heels. The shoepacs were a mistake. My gun was an 8 mm. Sauer-Mauser that immediately got a lot of examining and required a lot of explaining.

When we tumbled out of the sleeper on a cold November morning, the temperature was well below freezing. There was nothing in sight but the platform and a horse-drawn stagecoach. Funny how some Adirondack villages are located so many miles away from the railroad, and use train stops in the wilds. The ten-mile ride before breakfast over slippery mountain roads took a couple of hours, and during the ride Sam's supply of embalming fluid was appreciably lowered. State troopers stopped us en route to check our licenses, which luckily were in order, though one of the troopers took plenty of time to examine the Sauer-Mauser.

It was still early in the morning, according to city standards, when we arrived at the farm. Just seven o'clock. Breakfast was waiting, for we were expected. Now, if you've never sat down to an Adirondack farm breakfast on a cold November morning after a two-hour ride—man, you've missed something. That meal alone was worth the price of the whole trip. Fried cakes (flapjacks to you), real maple syrup, country sausage homemade from home-grown pigs, fried eggs by the dozen, sizzling bacon, fried ham, and country-fried potatoes—and coffee in what looked like a lumber-camp coffeepot.

That was the assortment. The quantity was even larger. But it wasn't too much. Four healthy appetites can do wonders to such a meal. But what a far cry it was from our usual orange juice, toast, and coffee, with which we started the day's work back in the city!

] 402 [

Even the irrepressible Sam finally called quits, though he did try to kiss Sally, the dusky cook, from sheer gratitude. He stopped only when she said: "Ah declares, Mistuh Sam, ef yuh don't quit dat monkeyin', Ise gonna souse yuh with dis yere dishwater." But she was pleased by his enthusiasm just the same. From then on, he was her favored "chile."

The two natives who were to do the "guidin" arrived shortly after breakfast. They were an odd pair. Lou was about six feet four, looking a lot as Lincoln must have in his rail-splitting days, and with just as dour a countenance. Jules, his partner, a French-Canadian, was at least a foot shorter, and as round and chubby as Lou was tall and lean.

We were late in getting started. Much too late, as we found out afterward. But then we found out lots of other things too. Sam decided that he would stay at the farm, and no amount of persuasion would make him change his mind. "Nope," he said, "I'm tired already, and it's too soon after eating. I'll just wait here until you fellows get back—one way or another. You may need me. Besides, Sally's going to bake me an apple pie."

That was that. The three of us got off finally, sometime after nine o'clock, with the two guides leading the way. There was a bit of misgiving, however, for Sam's remarks, jokingly made as they were, stuck in our minds. The pace set by Lou and Jules should have been warning enough. But we were all mature men in fair physical trim. We had knocked around plenty—and had taken plenty of knocks. So the pace was a challenge which we accepted. It never occurred to any of us then that we were getting the works. But we were. The snow was just a couple of inches deep—just a fine tracking snow, according to Lou. The first mile or so across the pasture that led to the edge of the woods, passed without any particular discomfort, though it wasn't exactly a Sunday stroll.

It was not until we were in the woods, headed up the mountain, that the first sign of trouble appeared. Jim's knee-length sheep-lined coat began to get in its fine work. If there was any trail, it had been carefully avoided. Climbing through down timber is a tough job at the best. In such a rig, Jim had trouble aplenty. He was sweating profusely and cussing more profusely—when he had breath enough to cuss. I offered to take his gun, but he wouldn't hear of it. It was just as well. My heel-less shoepacs worked satisfactorily crossing the flat pasture land. Upgrade in the woods was another story, and I found myself slipping back two steps for every one I advanced. They were of no help climbing in and out of ravines, of which there seemed to be plenty.

Somewhere up ahead, Lou and Jules had disappeared. It was an easy matter to follow their trail, but we were falling far behind the pace. I lost count of the number of times we stopped for a breather, but there were many of them. Joe, the dentist, wasn't doing so badly in his outfit of old clothes. His footgear was most unorthodox, for a well-rigged Nimrod—just a pair of overshoes or arctics over his city shoes—but they were mighty effective and I would gladly have swapped my shoepacs for them.

It was nearly noon when we reached the ridge from which we were to hunt. It wasn't much of a mountain, according to Western standards—just a mere three or four thousand feet. For us it was too much, particularly as we had found every ravine and had climbed over or under every piece of fallen timber on the way up. Lou and Jules were waiting for us, calmly smoking their pipes, their backs resting comfortably against a tree trunk. Apparently it had been just a nice morning jaunt to them. They eyed us speculatively but said nothing. We gave it right back to them with suspicion added, but we too, said nothing. We couldn't. There wasn't breath enough.

Maybe fifteen minutes passed in silence. Darn taciturn, these natives. Then Lou outlined the plan of campaign. It was simple enough, and sounded logical. The three of us were to be placed on separate stations or posts about a quarter of a mile apart, where each of us could get a good view down each side of the ridge. Lou and Jules were to separate, each taking a side of the mountain and working up again from the bottom. The idea was, that any deer lurking in the thickets would be jumped by one or the other of them and would head up the mountain, crossing our line of posts, so that one of us might get a shot. Yes, it seemed logical enough then. None of us figured that the noise we'd made coming up the ridge had probably scared every deer—if there ever were any—clear into the next county. All we had to worry about was not to take a shot at each other.

So off we went with Lou to take our respective posts. Joe was dropped first, by a nice round stump, and with a clear view in all directions. Jim was next. He drew an outcrop of rock that also gave him an unbroken view. On we went up the ridge to the very end. Below was an almost sheer drop of several hundred feet. This was my station—also with a nice rock outcrop. South of me were my two companions, perhaps a quarter and half a mile away respectively. They were in plain sight when they stood up. If they sat down there was nothing but the mountain ridge with its sparse covering. Off in the distance were more ridges, more ravines, and more mountains.

Lou left me without a word and departed down the mountain. No final word of instruction. No warning of any kind. No suggestion of when he'd be back. He just went. And then silence. Nothing moved or made a noise except as a vagrant breeze occasionally rustled a dead leaf. I slipped the cartridge clip into the Mauser and waited. Fifteen minutes passed—then a half hour. Nothing happened. Nothing stirred.

To the south, I could see Jim and Joe, equally alert, like two sturdy outposts ready to go into action at the first opportunity. And so we passed the first hour. That was about as long as the alertness lasted. I found a sheltered nook against the rock outcrop and settled down with my back against it. I wanted to smoke, but didn't dare, for fear the tobacco aroma would reach the keen nostrils of some soft-footed deer. That was all I remembered for some time. The utter stillness covered me like a blanket—and I slept.

When I awoke the sun was well down in the southwest. My wristwatch said three-thirty, so I got up and stretched. Not a sign of Jim or Joe. I tried a cautious yell to attract Jim's attention. No response. That was too much. Picking up my rifle, I made my way to Jim's post. He was there right enough but sound asleep. The

snow was littered with cigarette butts. If he had thought the tobacco odor might reach the deer, he didn't care about it. I stirred
him with my foot. He roused with a sleepy "Hello—what's up?"

Joe popped up on his stump and we waved for him to join us.
He hadn't been asleep, he said, and produced a nicely carved
cane whittled from a handy bush as proof. So we held a council of
war. The sky was thickening fast. Clouds had come up from nowhere, and the sun had disappeared. It was colder. There was a
distinct smell of snow in the air.

Whatever decision we might have reached eventually was post-
poned by a bedlam of noise from down the mountain—loud yells
and much baying of hounds. Lou and Jules had jumped a deer.
Jim lost his lethargy immediately, as Joe and I sprinted for our
opposite posts. At last we were to get some action. Back at the
rock outcrop I waited. If I examined the action of my Mauser
once, I did a dozen times. I wondered if I would get buck fever.

The noise was getting closer, but the baying of the hounds had
stopped except for an occasional yelp. It was beginning to get
dark, and the snow started—big flakes, they were, that made for
poor visibility. But I was all set for a quick snap shot if necessary.

Suddenly all noise stopped; then from out of the silence came
the single sharp crack of a rifle. I looked toward Jim and Joe.
They were alert but barely visible. Neither of them had shot—the
report was more to the west of them. Lou or Jules. Maybe they
had missed, and I might get a running shot. I knew that the deer
would be getting away fast, if he could get away at all. So I
waited, nerves tense. Nothing appeared. A crashing in the underbrush at my right focused my attention there. It was followed by a
loud "hello, thar" that brought my rifle down. Out from the
brush came Lou, followed by Jules, who let out a loud bay as he
appeared. So Jules was the baying hound. Jules carried a nice
plump snowshoe rabbit. So that was the deer!

"Well, too bad you boys didn't get no shootin'. Guess they ain't
no deer amovin' today." It was Lou. "Well, we might git one in
the swamp on the way out," he continued, "but we gotta git
agoin'. It's gittin' dark, and acomin' on to snow." And with no
further word he and Jules started off. If the pace had been fast for
us coming up the mountain, it was as nothing at all to the rate

going down. Lou's long legs just reached out in four-foot strides. Jules, shorter geared, with legs fairly twinkling, looked like a small boy being led to the woodshed by an irate father. We picked up Jim and Joe with a curt "Come on, we gotta git." We did—and how!

But lo—a miracle. Going up that darn mountain we had the toughest kind of going. In and out of ravines, over and under logs and down timber that had pulled our corks. Now Lou had found a perfectly good wood or tote road that was a boulevard by comparison, and down which he fairly flew.

If my shoepacs had given me trouble going up, that trouble was doubled on the way back. I had absolutely no traction. I lost count of the number of times that I sat down, sometimes gracefully like an adagio dancer, but more often suddenly, and with a jar that shook my back teeth. The fast pace set by the guides, the snow, and fast-approaching darkness made it worse. We had been jobbed. I was sure of it. Somehow we reached the bottom.

The ground flattened out and I greeted it with a welcome sigh. Too soon. A little farther along, just as I'd begun to hit my stride, one foot sank down about six inches, and I nearly pitched on my face. A swamp. The rest was nightmare. Every few steps, one foot or the other would sink into the half-frozen bog until it seemed there would be no ending. There was. I fetched up suddenly against the man ahead. Forward progress had ceased. What now? Just a beaver dam to be crossed!

If you've ever crossed a beaver dam in shoepacs, in snow and darkness, carrying a rifle like a balancing pole, it's an experience you won't ever want to repeat. On one side, a pond covered with slush ice and deeper than you cared to think about; on the other side, rocks, and darkness with somewhere a brook trickling. There was little choice. Just a thorough wetting one way, and a broken leg the other. If I had any leaning at all, it was definitely toward the wetting.

Somehow we all made it safely. Lou led the way. He can have that credit for what it's worth. Jules brought up the rear—to fish us out from one side or the other, I suppose. Yes, we made it, but I wouldn't tackle it again for all the deer in the woods.

"You boys did all right," said Lou from somewhere out of the darkness ahead, as we trudged down the road toward the farm-house, whose lights faintly shone in the distance. Nobody answered. What was there to say? What we thought was something else again. And so we got back to the farm—silently and in single file.

Our entrance into the farmhouse was made with no exuberation. Sam was playing checkers with our host. The half-emptied jug of applejack sat conveniently on the floor by his chair. "All back safe, eh? That's good," he said, as if he didn't mean it. "Any luck?"

Our silence gave him the answer. "Too bad," he continued. "Here, take a shot of apple and you'll feel better."

There was a smirk on his face that I didn't fancy. He had a look like the cat that ate the canary. Was he responsible for our ragging? I wondered, as I reached for the extended glass. But no. That couldn't be. Sam didn't know either Lou or Jules. He'd never seen them before. What was it? Something was in the air.

Then Sally stuck her head in through the kitchen doorway and announced: "Supper's gwine be ready in a shake, gemmun. Yo better git yosef cleaned up." And back she went into the kitchen with a chuckle.

The wash bench was out back of the kitchen. Jim was the first to reach it . . . a wild yell from him brought us all running.

Out back of the woodshed, strung up by his horns, was a nice plump spike-horn buck. So that was the Ethiopian.

Then the story came out. Sally had spied the young buck in the orchard behind the barn. She had told Sam, who quit his checkers and applejack long enough to borrow a rifle from our host, then meandered out and shot the buck—not a hundred yards from the house.

That's all there was to it. But it was too much for Lou and Jules. They disappeared into the darkness with a well-emphasized "GOOD NIGHT!"

Some day, though, I'm going on another deer hunt. And when I do, there'll be no climbing mountains, clambering through ravines, or crossing beaver dams. I'm just going to get a bag, and a jug—and follow Sam's system.

YOU'VE GOT TO SUFFER!

Gordon MacQuarrie

Gordon MacQuarrie was Outdoor Editor of the Milwaukee Journal *for
20 years before his death in 1956, and during that time he created one of the
most colorful, entertaining and warm series of articles outdoor literature has
ever known—"The Old Duck Hunters."*

*Built around his father-in-law and himself, MacQuarrie's pieces were a
collection of fact and fantasy, all based upon his tremendous knowledge and
field experience.*

Almost all appeared in Sports Afield *and* Field & Stream *and were
never anthologized until 1967, when Zack Taylor,* Sports Afield's *Boats
Editor and a MacQuarrie fan all his life, assembled the finest MacQuarrie
pieces for Stackpole Books:* Stories of the Old Duck Hunters And
Other Drivel. *The book has subsequently been republished in soft-cover.*

*"You've Got to Suffer" is the only deer piece in the anthology, but that
doesn't exclude it from being among the best ever written.*

*MacQuarrie's words never seem old and tired to me. The man really had
something as a writer, and I would* re-read *him than read most new stuff.*

THE PRESIDENT OF THE Old Duck Hunters' Association, Inc., was
waiting for me; so I had to get in there, even if the snow was a foot
deep on the level and heavily drifted. I lay on my back in city
clothes to jack up the rear wheels for tire chains, wishing that the
guy who had designed those petticoat fenders was properly pun-
ished for his sins against a humanity which at some time or other
simply must use auto chains.

The chains, momentum and good luck took me into a solid
three-foot drift. Well, I got halfway through it. A half hour of
shoveling ensued, and then I turned off the back road on the narrow, twisting by-road.

It was a shambles of drooping pine trees. Jack-pines thirty feet
tall and up to five inches thick were arched over the road,
weighted down under tons of damp snow. A few clips with the
pocket-ax which I always carried in the car snapped them; then
it was necessary to shake the clinging snow from them and drag
them off the road.

] 409 [

There would be no deer hunting the next day—I was sure of that. Getting about in that snow would be impossible. But I had said I would get in there. The Old Man was waiting. It is amazing what a man will do to keep a date with the President of the Old Duck Hunters.

I was six hours behind schedule when I stopped the car beside Mister President's snow-shrouded car. I was sweating and unsteady afoot. There had been almost a whole day of nerve-racking driving in the storm before the final climactic effort to get over that last half mile. I grabbed pack-sack and rifle and wallowed to the door of the place.

The Old Man was asleep, with his feet stretched toward the fireplace. I moved quietly. I put new wood on his fire, broke out duffel and had the teakettle going in the kitchen before he awoke. He called from the big room, "That you, Tom?"

"Yep," I answered, sounding as much like Tom as I could.

"When did you get here?"

"Minute ago."

Tom is a neighbor who is likely to appear at the abode of the Old Duck Hunters almost any time. The Old Man continued, still unsuspecting:

"Where do you suppose that whelp of a boy is? Said he'd be here for supper, and it's midnight."

I heard him yawn and heard him wind his watch. Then he said: "Dammit, Tom, I'm worried. He might try to make it here in this storm, and he doesn't know the first thing about driving a car in snow."

"And never will. Don't worry about him. He'll hole up in some luxurious hotel down the line and wait for the snow-plows."

That speech was too long. The Old Man's feet hit the floor, and he stamped to the kitchen, all sympathy vanished.

"You pup of a boy!" he snorted. "You lame-brained rooster!" He carried on over a snack of tea and toast. "Cars stuck all over the country. This is the worst storm ever hit this country before a deer season opening."

I looked around. He had brought in enough wood to last for several days. I said, "We'll just hole up, as long as we can't hunt."

] 410 [

"Not hunt!"

He had it all figured out. He'd looked over the near-by thoroughfare country in the storm and had found deer working down into it, out of the more open jack-pine on higher ground.

"We'll hunt, all right!"

That was the last thing I heard before dropping off to sleep. I think I did not change my position once, and slept until noon, right around the clock.

"I'm saving you," he explained. "Had to get you in shape. You're going to make one little drive to me."

"I'm not mooching in this snow."

The Old Man pointed to the wall at the end of the room. "See

those snowshoes? All you've done to them the last two years is varnish 'em. Today you're going to wear off some varnish."

It was bitter cold, near zero, after the snow had ceased and the clouds passed. All right, if the Old Man was going to sit on a stump in that weather, he was going to put on some clothing. I persuaded him, over his objections, to pile on plenty of underwear, a wool sweatshirt and a heavy outer shirt. He bulged rather ridiculously, I had to admit, with all that clothing, but for good measure I made him carry along my huge, ungainly but wonderfully warm sheep-lined aviation boots.

He hated the clothes that bore him down. I knew what he wanted to wear—just his regular duck or deer-season gear, which is not too much, topped off with the old brown mackinaw. He vowed that the only way a man could wait out a deer was to do a little personal freezing.

I had to laugh when he started out. He was so swaddled in clothes that he could hardly turn his neck above the shawl collar of the ancient mackinaw. But I did not laugh, for I was afraid he'd go back into the house and shed some of the garments, and in that searching cold I could not see him suffering while I took what is really the easier course, moving and so keeping warm.

South of us lay the Norway pine hill facing the thoroughfare, or river, between two lakes. Mister President had it all figured out. He would take an old stand at the top of the Norway hill. I would circle to the south and west of him, then drive up through the thick cover lying at the edge of the thoroughfare. If anything with horns came through, he would have shooting as it hit the open Norway grove.

Northwest Wisconsin, in twenty years, never saw a storm like that one at that season. Nor did it, in that time, see cold like that so early, combined with deep snow. The freak storm kept hundreds out of the bush. It was the first day of the four-day buck season. We had the country practically to ourselves. Most of the army of hunters was waiting for the snow to settle or thaw. And a four-day doe season was coming up in seven days.

Mister President's self-imposed assignment was to mush through the snow for about a mile, hard going without snowshoes, which he does not like. I left him plodding through the stuff toward his stand and began the great circle which would bring me below him.

At any rate, that snow was good for snowshoeing. It had the solid permanence of snow that has lain and settled and proposes to stay until spring—which it most certainly did.

It felt good to be on snowshoes again, carrying a rifle. I went through a long pulpwood slashing. All the tracks in that slashing confirmed what Mister President had said—that deer were moving into the denser cover, away from the open pinelands. Down there along the thoroughfare's edge they could find protection and browse, even some white cedar—champion of all winter deer browse.

The slashing was lovely. A bluejay yammered at me. Chickadees hung upside down on branches. Will someone tell me how these minute wisps of down maintain their high spirits in the face of any weather? A red squirrel in a jackpine cussed me roundly: "Bad enough for this storm to come so early without you moving in on my property!"

Snow-bent jacks lopped to the southwest, for the snow had come from the northeast, off Lake Superior. That storm gave the North a wonderful pruning. Old Lady Nature every so often throws one like that over her wild garden to nip off old branches, weed out the weak ones and compel the strong ones to prove it.

There was plenty of snow down my neck. Charlie Garvey, the forest ranger at Gordon, had warned me the evening before: "Stuff is down so much the rabbits can't get through." He knew, too, that the impact of this storm had pushed vast supplies of browse within reach of hungry deer. Incidentally, before winter was finished in the North, the sly dame did the same thing on two more occasions. So that deer got plenty to eat and the forests had a splendid pruning.

When I got to the thoroughfare where I was to turn back and drive north, I sat down a minute. At this place the thoroughfare drops three feet. There were wings overhead, belated bluebills and early golden-eyes hunting water in the frozen lake country.

The sun was varnishing the jack-pine tops as I began the drive. In the shadows the snow as turning lavender. Downy and hairy woodpeckers hid behind tree trunks as I went along. The snowshoes creaked. I followed the thoroughfare edge. There was ice out from shore forty yards at my right. At my left and ahead of me was thick cover.

There were many tracks, all old ones. Deer had certainly come down here out of the pinelands in the night. But where were they now? Then I saw a fresh track. You know how it is—that virgin white scar of a hoof in snow, so unlike the settled, stiffened track of twelve hours before.

The deer was moving ahead of me. Buck or doe? I do not know. Even in fresh mud I do not know, and I think that no one else can tell for certain. That track was big and brand-new. It was a mark left by a critter moving exactly the way the Old Duck Hunters wanted it to move—straight north toward the Old Man.

This deer was not plunging. It seemed to know my pace and kept just ahead of me. Likely it had heard me when I was a hundred yards away from it, had got up quietly and just sneaked away from me. You wonder at such times where the rascals get the wisdom to know that a man in snow cannot move rapidly. Deer can be very contemptuous of a man.

The wind was not a factor. There was a little drift from the northwest. Up in the open slashings it could be felt. Down along the thoroughfare bottoms, however, pipe smoke went straight up.

Sometimes this deer stayed on the beaten trails which had been worked in the night before. Sometimes it cut across lots through fresh snow. Contemptuous of me? Indeed, and then some.

I saw where, during the night of the storm, deer had come into the thoroughfare bottoms and nibbled on cedar. Even the little fellows could live off a storm like that. Everything was caved in, trees formed solid white wigwams, branches drooped—as inviting a deer cafeteria as you might wish to see.

Why hadn't this big one moved out of the bottom with the others? Was it an old grandfather or a grandmother that chose the easy living of this place to getting out of there and seeing country? Once I thought I saw it a hundred yards ahead, but that turned out to be mere flipping of white snow from a branch released from pressure—not a flag.

My deer had passed the place where the snow slid off the tree, a full twenty yards to the west. A calculating beggar, that animal. Just so far ahead of me—no farther.

Well, if a buck, it was venison on the pole. It went dead on toward a rendezvous with a .30-30 carbine held by a very steady old gentleman in an old brown mackinaw.

That critter had me figured out so well that sometimes it even stopped to browse. It would pay for that—if it was what Mister President called "a rooster deer." Contempt of court, that's what it was! Just wait until that old goat moved out from the thick stuff and started ambling through those open Norways! The Old Man has killed a half dozen bucks from that stand. Most of them have dropped within an area not larger than a baseball diamond.

Good, I thought. Whatever it was, it was right on the beam going in. The darkness drew down. Purple worked up to the zenith from the eastern sky. I moved that deer along the way a farm collie brings home the cows. Finally I saw him.

He was across an opening, perhaps a hundred yards off. He was big and dim. No question now what he was. He was "he." His rack went up and back like branches on an old oak. I might have had one quick fling at him, but why chance it? The Old Man was waiting, and it was better to move that deer into the open Norway grove. Then, if the first one didn't clip him, there would be other chances.

I went along. I know that terrain as well as the buck knew it— almost as well as the Old Man knows it. Pretty soon, up ahead, there would be a shot. Just one shot, it ought to be. That would be the Old Man's 150 grains of lead and copper going to its destination. Then silence—the sort of quiet after one shot that means so much to a deer hunter.

It was working out perfectly. In my mind's eye I pictured the Old Man, alert on his hillside. I saw him scan the cover, saw the buck walk out and turn to listen along its back trail. I saw Mister President draw down on the buck, wait until the buck stood with cupped ears, raise the little rifle and squeeze it off. Yes, I even pictured him setting down the rifle and reaching for the big, bone-handled clasp-knife in his right hip pocket.

It was as easy as falling off a log. Mister President's formula had been right. If the ground had been bare, that buck might have busted through the Norway grove with his foot to the floorboard.

I wondered if we should drag him the mile home. Or if we should borrow Hank's toboggan, or just commandeer his truck, which has high wheels and is at home in deep snow. I decided that with the weather cold as it was we could dress him, hang him, cool him and have decent steaks by supper-time tomorrow.

Minutes passed. The Old Man would let him have it now.... Or now.... Now, then! The buck must be in the Norways at the foot of the hillside. Heavens above, he must be halfway up the hillside! I could see the big Norways ahead of me. The only sound was the creak of the snowshoes and the "kra-a-a-ak" of a raven.

I broke through the bottomland cover and faced the hillside. Over the hilltop in back of the old man I saw the buck the second time, slowly and contemptuously effacing himself from me.

I took one quick shot. It was just a shot at a skulking shadow, and I knew as I pulled the trigger in the instant I had for shooting that I was over him a good two or three feet.

At the shot Mister President waved to me from his stand. I trudged up the hill to him. He looked guilty.

"You git 'im?"

"Mister President, do not speak to me ever again."

He made a clean breast of it, then and there. "All right, I fell asleep. Your shot woke me."

It was plain as sin what had happened. Mister President had brushed the snow off a fallen Norway and sat there a while. He had lit a fire. He had banked browse against that two-foot-thick down log so that he could stretch out. Then—oh, my brethren!—he had fallen asleep. "Dammit, I had too many clothes on," he said.

And then I just had to laugh. He wasn't the Mister President of other deer drives, chilled and lean and ready, with a drop on the end of his nose. He was swathed and cluttered in sleep-producing items—those huge aviator's boots, which are with clothes and over his swampers, comparable to separate steam-heating systems.

We went home, boiled the kettle, and ate pork chops and boiled potatoes. We drank quarts of tea. At bedtime, the Old Man announced: "If anyone tries to tell me what to wear tomorrow, I will resign the presidency of the Old Duck Hunters. I must have dozed there for two hours."

The next day we did it again. The weather had moderated. He went to the same stand. I made the long-swing south and west on the snowshoes and drove up through the thoroughfare bottoms.

Making the drive, I knew that now the Old Man was standing there by his down log, in his thin swampers. I knew that sometimes he shivered, and sometimes he whapped his arms across his breast to get circulation going. I knew that he'd move up and down on his feet and wriggle his toes, and that he was standing there with his earlaps up, so that he could hear better.

The drive was easy. There were more deer in the bottoms along the thoroughfare. Driving up through and watching the tracks ahead of me, I felt that I was pushing a whole herd into that Norway grove. One of them might be Old Horny, might be the same old fellow who beat the Old Duck Hunters yesterday, hands down.

Pow! He had shot just once. I came into the grove at the foot of the hillside, and Mister President called down to me: "He's lying over to your left. Four hens came out, and the rooster after them."

I do not know whether it was the same buck. I think it was another. The one of the day before seemed a larger animal. There he was, a good ten-pointer. I called up the hill: "Bring your knife down here, and I'll dress him out."

He came sliding down the hill in the snow. "I'll dress him out myself. Maybe I can get warmed up that way."

Mister President was certainly a sight. His nose was red and his lips were blue. He was hunched and shivering beneath the old brown mackinaw. The wait in the cold had been a long one, but worth it. He went to work, and I went off to fetch Hank with his truck. When we got back, the Old Man had finished the job—had even dragged the buck up his hillside and out to the road to meet the truck.

"Well, you sure got warmed up," I said.

"I did," he agreed. "But you got to suffer first."

MISSISSIPPI BACKWOODS BUCK

Charles Elliott

The venerable and peripatetic southeastern field editor of Outdoor Life *has informed and entertained millions of readers with hundreds of magazine articles and two of the best books in outdoor literature,* Gone Fishin' *and* Gone Huntin' (*both Stackpole*).

If you've never had the chance for a southern-style deer hunt, then join Charley for this one. It's from Outdoor Life's *Deer Hunting Book, published by Outdoor Life and Harper & Row.*

I DECIDED, after a total of twenty-four hours perched in a tree, that making like a bird was for the birds and not for me. The wooden platform that John Jared, my old hunting partner, had nailed to the trunk of a massive beech had both advantages and disadvantages. It definitely had not been designed to fit my anatomy, yet it was high enough above the swamp so that I could occasionally shift from one aching muscle to another without disturbing the creatures at ground level. Not many forest inhabitants expect to find a man sitting serenely in a tree, especially when the woods is saturated with rain.

I had proved that point on the first morning of our hunt when an old turkey gobbler flew off his roost after daylight and landed 100 yards behind me in the swamp. Since turkey season was not in and I'd left my yelper at home, I cautiously fingered the yellowing beech leaves around the platform until I found one soft enough to simulate the gentle notes of a hen. The gobbler answered immediately. Then, craning his long neck from side to side, he made a wide circle around my tree.

When he started to move away, I again clucked softly, and he came back to the beech, apparently never thinking to look up until my third attempt with the leaf hit a sour note. Then he simply stepped behind a bush and vanished.

On that first day of perching in the branches, I had seen one deer, and later a second, trail through the swamp just at the limit of my vision. In the downpour, and through a screen of colorful foliage, I could not identify either animal as a buck, even through my 4X scope; so passed them up.

For two and a half days I'd scoured the platform and dripping branches around it with the seat of my pants and associated intimately with gray squirrels, woodpeckers, and a host of tiny birds.

We were hunting a corner of the 45,000-acre Noxubee National Wildlife Refuge below Starkville, Mississippi. This is primarily a waterfowl wintering area. On its lakes, rivers, and flooded, green-timber swamps, the Noxubee claims a winter population of 70,000 ducks and geese, with a peak year of almost 120,000 birds. No shooting of these migrants is permitted, but seasons have been established to allow the harvesting of surplus deer, turkeys, and squirrels. A split deer season is usually set up for Thanksgiving and Christmas weeks, and we were there for the early hunt.

"It's one of the fine deer areas in Mississippi," I'd been told by long-time hunting partner John Jared, who was then with a construction outfit of Meridian, Mississippi. "Whitetails were first stocked on the refuge in the early 1940's and the first hunt held in 1958, with only seven bucks taken. The high kill was in 1961, with two hundred animals brought out of the area, and a great many more were taken on adjoining private lands. This fall should be a dilly."

So far it hadn't panned out that way.

Before the middle of November, John had scouted the region and built tree stands where he found a concentration of trails and tracks. On the afternoon before the season opened, we had gone into the swamp with W. M. (Doody) Callahan, who operates a tonsorial and beauty salon with his wife in Starkville, Mississippi, and Henry Beattie, who runs a feed mill in Starkville. We established quarters in Henry's comfortable cabin in a hairpin bend of the Noxubee River.

By way of a high, swinging bridge which spanned the river between cabin and hunting area, we crossed before daylight on opening morning and worked our way through the rain-soaked forest to the burly beech in which John had nailed his first tree stand. He disappeared into the gray light, and I eagerly arranged my carcass on the wooden platform.

To a casual observer, the swamp might have been virgin woods, columned with the massive trunks of beeches, oaks, and hickories. Burton Webster, refuge manager, told me later that a small amount of logging had been done on the Noxubee, mostly for the outsize ash, which has a high market value but does not furnish food for any of the game species. Into these logging gaps have sprouted seedlings to provide low-growing browse for the deer.

I'll admit that as a stander I belong close to the foot of the class, but except for a few noonday hours when the deer are supposed to be curled up in thickets for the midday siesta, I stayed with the beech-tree platform for two and a half days. I had little choice in that country, with the flat, open woods, there's slight chance of walking up on a whitetail.

Before noon on Thanksgiving day, however, I decided that if the refuge supported the alleged deer population, then the animals were in some other neck of the swamp. If we were to hang a buck on the front porch of the cabin, we'd have to search out a lot more territory than I could see from my platform.

We drove to the Callahan home in Starkville for a delightful Thanksgiving dinner which more than helped to supplement the cabin fare. With our paunches rather uncomfortably stuffed, Doody, John, and I were nervously watching one of the Thanksgiving Day football games on television, when Travis, Doody's wife, came in from the kitchen. She glanced from one to the other of us and laughed.

"By the looks of you, I doubt if you even know who's playing. You've been here long enough after dinner to prove you are gentlemen. I know how badly you want to get back to the swamp, so I'll forgive you if you make a mad rush for the door."

Back at the cabin, we discovered that our hunting crew had been augmented by Doody's three grown sons: Ramon, working on his master's degree in wildlife management at Mississippi State; Billy, a forester for Sears, Roebuck, and Joel, a resident of Jackson who was at work on his medical degree. Also included was nine-year-old Henry Beattie Jr., who had driven in with his father. It was midafternoon when we held a caucus in front of the cabin fireplace.

"We've got enough hunters to spread out now and do some good," I said. "I'd already planned to make a big circle at the head of the lake to look for more sign than John and I have found in the last two days. If you fellows will take stands at all the crossings and trails between the upper corner of the lake and the river, I might run a buck over one of you."

"That's a good deal," John Jared speculated. "And since you won't see any deer while you're moving around like that, why don't you take your .22 rifle, angle through some of the private property next to the refuge, and collect a few squirrels for the pot."

While I'd been sitting quietly in the beech tree with my deer rifle, the grays had trooped around me. So I guess it was only natural that when I replaced the .308 Kennon custom-built rifle with my .22 Marlin repeater, the squirrels should prove as elusive as had the bucks.

That section of forest was open and studded with magnificent oaks and hickories. Among them were huge holly trees, thick as a man's body and mingling their emerald crowns with the colorful fall foliage of the other hardwoods. Both Ramon and Billy had told me that many of the squirrels they'd killed earlier in the season had been feeding on the bright masses of holly berries.

With my standers spread in a wide semicircle to cover that corner of the swamp, I cut a circle along a shallow slough, tiptoeing very slowly and as quietly as possible, listening for a squirrel to bark or for the patter of shell fragments where the animals were cutting in one of the hickory trees. The late-afternoon woods were bright, but so still they seemed uninhabited. I squatted on my heels beside a hickory for five minutes before I heard the churr of a gray 100 yards away. I stalked him—one cautious step after another—until I got close enough to see the flicker of his tail through the lofty foliage.

I didn't know it then, but there was another hunter in the woods. I had not disturbed the squirrel and was working into position for a shot with the Long-Rifle cartridge, when a small Cooper's hawk flashed through the tree crowns. Just as I got a glimpse of the winged predator, the squirrel vanished into a knothole.

To my left sprawled a dense honeysuckle thicket in an open glade. I was moving stealthily toward it when the vines suddenly crashed and a whitetail buck, his rack a little larger than average, bounded out of the copse and stopped a few yards away to look back over his shoulder. With the inadequate .22 rifle, all I could do was mutter under my breath. Two more bounds and he disappeared in the direction of the river where I was certain one of the standers would get him. So I squatted on my heels for ten minutes, waiting for the sound of the shot. All we could figure later was that the buck had seen or winded the hunters and turned back into the swamp.

After that, I forgot all about squirrels. An examination of the honeysuckle patch showed it had been heavily browsed, and there were signs where a few deer had bedded in the thicket.

From the honeysuckle, I made a wide circle along the extreme northwest corner of the lake. Here I found the swamp crisscrossed with deer trails and fresh track impressions in the soft earth. Two of the trails showed imprints I was sure had been left by large bucks.

Not knowing whether I had spooked other deer in addition to the one I'd jumped, I sat down to wait out the fading light, with no intention of further disturbing this portion of the swamp where the whitetails seemed to be concentrated. In the last minutes of the afternoon, I discovered why at least some of the squirrels had deserted the holly trees. They were cutting on the thin-shelled, scalybark hickory nuts. Two trees near me were full of grays, and they were running out to the ends of the limbs, clipping nuts, and scampering back to more substantial perches to rain cuttings on the forest floor. In the two trees, I counted at least a dozen busy bushy-tails.

It was after dark when our group slipped out of the woods and followed a dim logging road to the swinging bridge over the river. Even before we put on the charcoal for steaks, we held a council of war and decided that next morning each gunner would occupy the same stand where he had sat out the twilight hours. I was to watch over the corner of the lake near the honeysuckle patch where I had jumped the buck.

We were in the swamp woods before daylight. Though the temperature was a few degrees above freezing, the leaves were covered with frost. Henry, Doody, and John took their same stands along the remains of an ancient road which Henry said was one of the first thoroughfares through that country. A small stream drained this end of the lake and followed the road from the lake to the river. Well-used deer trails crossed the rivulet in half a dozen places. Instead of stopping at the river, however, Billy and Ramon walked the extra half a mile with me to the corner of the lake and then went on deeper into the woods to a high finger of brushy land that crossed the upper end of the swamp and paralleled a man-made dike which had been thrown up along the northern border of the lake.

A hundred yards from where I had seen the buck, I cut an armload of low, bushy, water-oak sprouts and arranged the crowns of green leaves in a semi-circular blind around the base of a big white oak. I zipped up my camouflage jacket, made myself as comfortable as possible, and settled down to wait for dawn.

Shortly after first light, leaves crackled off to my left. I froze, my rifle ready, and two does came into sight. They were on the upwind side and so close I could have touched them with a cane pole. They spotted rather than winded me, paused momentarily to look me over, then moved unhurriedly along, browsing as they went.

Following at a good 100 feet was a small buck with spikes so short I knew I'd have to measure to determine whether they were legal. I let him pass, which he did without seeing me. I fully expected the three deer to be trailed by the buck I'd passed up when I'd had the .22. But if he was a part of that group, he remained out of sight in the brush.

Twenty minutes later three more does and a fawn passed just at the limit of my vision. They were within range of the .308, and again I was cocked on hair-trigger ready, when the dawn woods were blasted by a single rifle shot, which rang like the report of a .30/30. The reverberations rolled around me in such a way that I couldn't tell whether it had come from 200 yards or half a mile away.

For another half an hour I sat perfectly still, hoping the sound of the shot might have started a buck tiptoeing toward my stand. Then curiosity got the best of me, and I angled through the woods to where Billy had perched on a tree limb and downed a small forkhorn walking almost under him.

When Ramon appeared from the other direction a few minutes

later, we dressed out the buck, tied it on a pole, and marched back to the cabin.

We had only that afternoon and one more day left in the first week of the split season. Henry suggested that, since we might have disturbed that corner of the swamp, we save it until the next morning and scatter out on both sides of the Noxubee River for our afternoon hunt.

The area assigned to me lay between the northeast dike of Buff Lake and the river. I spent an enjoyable but unproductive afternoon in the radiant fall woods and got a glimpse of one doe. I met her in the trail on my way to the cabin when the light was almost too dim to see the crosshairs in my scope.

Saturday was the last day of our hunt. Billy's buck, hanging on the wide porch of the cabin, had put new enthusiasm into the party. Long before dawn, fortified with ham and eggs, biscuits, and mugs of hot coffee, we crossed the swinging bridge, and felt our way through the black swamp forest.

I intended to find the blind I'd built around the white oak but in the darkness missed it by a couple of hundred yards. With mallards cackling out on the lake, squirrels purring around me in the swamp, and light filtering into the tree crowns, I gave up my search for the oak and built another blind where I could make out the crossing of a couple of fresh deer trails.

The dawn was still and crisp enough to work its icy fingers under my hunting coat and rub a patch of goose bumps here and there, but somehow I didn't mind. It was the sort of morning that keeps a whitetail on the move.

Two rifle shots somewhere in the distance quickened my anticipation, and minutes later a report rang out from the rise about half a mile in front of me. I knew it had to be Ramon, who had gone back to the same tree he'd occupied Friday.

At the report, a flock of mallards, feeding in the shallow rim of the lake, took wing, and the busy squirrels froze into gray knots. A doe appeared out of the brush ahead, stopped, and looked back. Then she walked on toward the upper end of the lake. I put up my rifle, half expecting a buck to follow her, but the next deer was also a doe. For fully a dozen minutes after the whitetails had moved beyond my vision, I sat tense and expectant and then felt a growing sense of disappointment. I could only guess that the single shot accounted for a buck which had been following the two does.

A patch of gold appeared in the forest top, and I knew that the sun had cleared the horizon. For minutes after that, I struggled with the indecision of whether to find Ramon and help him with his buck or remain on my stand and hope the shot hadn't spooked the deer out of this corner of the refuge.

I felt the first sunlight on my face and had about decided to look for Ramon when the brush crashed off to my left, and a small buck dodged into sight. He had a rather odd gait, which gave the impression he'd been wounded. I watched him across 20 or 30 yards of swamp and then was not certain that my first appraisal had been correct. He passed not more than 40 yards away, but instead of going around a corner of the long slough, he waded directly into it, another indication that he might have been hurt.

I don't know what I'd have done if a granddaddy buck had broken out of the brush behind the forkhorn. Normally I will take a wounded animal over a healthy one, regardless of size. Nor do I know whether I would have passed up the small buck if he had appeared completely healthy. Those things race through a fellow's mind in much less time than it takes to tell them. This particular chain of thought ended with the decision to kill the loping whitetail.

How I missed that first shot, I don't know; the .308 had been sighted in so accurately that it would drive a nail at forty paces. My next shot broke his neck.

I waded in over my boot tops to skid the buck to semidry swamp where I could dress him out. He appeared not to have a bullet mark on him, other than the one I had made. My decision then was whether I should try to locate Ramon and help him with the buck I was sure he had killed or wait for help in getting my own deer out of the woods. Apparently the best solution was to carry the buck half a mile through the swamp to the ancient road where John, Joel, and the two Henrys kept watch, and make further plans from that point.

After the small buck had drained properly, I worked him onto my shoulders for the trip to the old road. That, of course, is something I never would have done in ordinary deer woods, but I knew

that only our hunting crew occupied this corner of the swamp, and I knew my companions well enough to be sure they wouldn't pot a deer on the shoulders of a hunter.

I waited an hour at the foot log over the creek which parallels the forgotten road before Ramon arrived with his account of the morning. A small buck had gone under his tree, and just as he decided to kill it, a deer with a massive rack passed through the brush just at the limit of his vision. At 150 yards, he had only one quick look over the open sights of his .30/30. He made the shot but could not find signs to indicate that he'd scored. He climbed into a tree much farther up on the ridge but had not seen another legal deer. The others in our party had drawn blanks.

"We've got Christmas week to finish our our job." Doody pointed out.

"By then." Henry put in, "those big bucks will be running all over one another on this end of the refuge."

From the sign I saw, I was certain they would be, but since I'd already made my legal kill, I could only look forward to another season in this picturesque backwoods swamp.

DAY OF STEALTH AND GRAPPLING

Ken Crandall

The rousing tale of a western hunt, it originally appeared in Outdoor Life *under the title "A Stalk to Remember" and was anthologized in the book* Outdoor Life's Deer Hunting Book, *published by Outdoor Life and Harper & Row.*

I WAS SITTING in a fresh deer bed that was big enough to couch a yearling steer. It had rained all night, but the ground was gouged with big splayed tracks, some of them made by animals so heavy that the dewclaws had been driven right into the sand. The willow clumps had been hooked and horned beyond belief. Little piles of shredded bark lay beside deeply scored trunks. Heavy antlers had torn and broken large branches.

I was certain my two days of hard scouting was going to pay off, but I sat there for over an hour without hearing a sound. Then I heard an explosive, heaving cough. From its deep tone, I knew it was a big deer. That deer was probably lying in its bed, and it was only about forty yards away. From the evidence around me, the odds were that it was a buck. My problem was to stalk the deer in brush so thick I couldn't see more than fifty feet.

Such problems are hereditary in my family. I was born in Okanogan County, Washington, which is noted for its fine mule-deer hunting, and I grew up in a deer-hunting family. At the age of four, I was posed for the camera with my dad's rifle in front of a row of heavy-horned bucks hanging from a meatpole. I nearly blew it at the age of nine when a fat forkhorn walked out in front of my dad and me. Dad wouldn't let me carry a rifle at that age, but watching him bag that deer is one of my treasured memories.

When I was ten, an uncle gave me an old Model 1886 Winchester lever action in .45/70 caliber, and I was the happiest kid in town. I had just turned eleven when I stood beside my dad on another quiet mountainside. He was looking at a bunch of deer through his rifle-scope. They were only about 80 yards away, but they were in the brush. Finally they moved out.

"The deer on the left," Dad whispered, "is a buck. Shoot!"

I've never had buck fever, but I'll never be able to explain that shot. I had the bead right in the middle of that forkhorn when I pulled the trigger, but the big slug hit him right behind the ear.

From that day on, nothing could keep me out of the mountains during deer season. With a lot of hard work and a lot more luck, I hung up twenty-three sets of antlers in twenty-three seasons. I learned that there is a lot more to hunting mule deer than wandering around hoping to blunder into one. A big mule-deer is sophisticatedly programmed by weather, feed, water, cover, hunting pressure, and instinct.

I once bet a friend that I could show him a buck by eight o'clock in the morning. He had hunted most of the season without seeing so much as a spike. I was pushing my luck, but there had been a heavy snowstorm, and I knew just where to take him. I was back in my office by 8:30 A.M., and my friend had a dandy fourpointer to brag about. Knowing when and where to hunt are major factors. I'm reasonably certain that before that snowstorm there hadn't been a buck within five miles of the spot I selected.

As time went by, I kept trying for bigger and bigger bucks. When the Game Department opened a special High Cascade deer season in September of 1958, I didn't pay much attention, but a friend went and came back with glowing tales of bucks all over the place. That friend was John R. (Bob) Duncan, who is now a neighbor of mine at Malott, Washington. Bob works in the supervisor's office of the Okanogan National Forest. We passed the word to Art Lucas, who is a shop foreman for the state Department of Highways and lives in Okanogan. I work for the Okanogan County Agricultural Stabilization and Conservation Committee as county executive director for their facility in Okanogan.

The three of us eventually packed into the High Cascades for the special hunt. We hunted in an area near the Spanish Camp fireguard station, which we reached via the Andrews Creek trail north of Winthrop, Washington. We saw big mule-deer bucks everywhere—sometimes in bunches—and took three fine trophy heads.

I wrote about our adventure in *Outdoor Life*. As a result of that story and other publicity, a horde of hunters hit the high deer area that fall. Some got deer, but very few really good bucks were taken, and many hunters came back empty-handed. The word was that all the big bucks had been killed in the previous hunts or had been driven into Canada. We didn't believe it.

The high area we had hunted consisted of beautiful open-meadowed ridges surrounded by miles of thick second-growth lodgepole pines. We had set up our camp with little disturbance. We even ruled out woodchopping and campfires. Yet those deer were extremely timid, and after only a few days of light hunting pressure they seemed to vanish.

We were convinced that the heavy influx of hunters had sent those bucks scooting into the dense brush just before the season opened. To test our theory, we decided to go into the High Cascade area a week before the next deer season. We had heard about some fine fishing in Sheep and Ramon lakes, which are about seven miles due west of the Spanish Camp cabin. We planned a two-week trip—a week to fish and look for deer, and a week for deer hunting. Bob and I had horses of our own, and we begged and borrowed a few more. We even included my contrary burro, Cactus Jack, in our packstring.

We had such a heavy load of supplies for the two-week stay that we made only the fifteen miles to the Spanish Camp cabin the first day. We stayed overnight nearby and left the next morning. It may have been only seven miles in a straight line, but it took us all day to battle the gruelling switchback trail that led to Sheep Mountain. But it was worth the effort. Sheep Lake, cradled in the bosom of that mighty 8,300-foot-high mountain, is breathtakingly beautiful. The two little Ramon lakes nearby were dazzling.

The lakes were full of cutthroat trout, the weather was perfect, and deer were so thick that we gave up trying to count them. We did count up to forty-five of them in a big meadow and on an adjoining hillside one evening.

We saw innumerable bucks, but they didn't behave as mule deer are supposed to behave. They rarely came out into the open. They lurked along the edges of the timber and came out when it was difficult to see them even with the aid of big binoculars. One night we saw two old monarchs against the skyline; they had racks we couldn't believe. Our suspicions were confirmed. Those high-country bucks hadn't been eliminated, but they were educated.

Our other suspicions were also confirmed. We set up our deer camp the day before the season was to open, and hunters were everywhere. By opening morning nearly every deer on the ridge had plunged into the heavy brush. I did see two small four-pointers just at dawn, and I watched to see what they would do. They headed down off the ridge and zipped into the brush as fast as a nightcrawler going down its hole.

I didn't really try to hunt the first day, because I knew things would soon quiet down. I was reasonably certain I could find some of those wise old bucks, so I spent two days scouting the country. I beat my way through miles of lodgepole tangles and climbed to every vantage point I could find.

On the third day I found what I was looking for. It was a high and steep mountainside, almost completely covered with dense second-growth lodgepole pine, interlaced with fallen trees and standing snags. A brook started near the top and coursed almost straight down the mountain. There were other places almost identical to the one I picked, with one very important exception. Right in the middle of that almost impenetrable mass of brush was a patch of willows next to the stream. It wasn't more than an acre in size, but the heavy willow cover made it an ideal place for big mule-deer bucks. They are plain lazy and like nothing better than a place where they can get up out of their beds and walk a few yards to eat and drink. If you subject the big bucks to hunting pressure, hiding becomes their first consideration. They will go several miles between good feed and a secure hiding place, but they don't like it. If a big lazy buck can have his cover and eat it too, he will usually stay put.

I liked something else about that little patch of willows. A buck mule deer wants to hide in dense cover, but he also wants to be able to see out. The patch of willows was on a little flat on the mountainside, but a small fingertip ridge ran right up to the creek where it bordered the willows. I inspected it with binoculars from a vantage point about a mile away and saw quite a few openings in the willows around the end of that point. It was a perfect place for a buck to lie in the sun and gaze out.

For over an hour I surveyed the mountainside with my binoculars. I had to plot a course through dense lodgepole timber. I wanted to hit the stream about 300 yards above the patch of willows. In that lodgepole jungle, the only way to see any distance was up. So I carefully memorized the tops of the standing snags along my route.

Bob and Art were a little discouraged when I reached camp that night, but I didn't tell them of my plan. I'm not selfish, but I did know of the odds against nailing a buck in such dense cover, and I also knew that one man can hunt more quietly than two or three.

I was well equipped for that kind of hunting. In the previous week I had developed a slight growth of beard. I'm firmly convinced that one look at a pale face often sends hayrack bucks rocketing for cover.

That was clearly demonstrated once when I was mincing along a deer trail in the middle of a dense thicket. I was moving only one step every two or three minutes because I wanted to see the deer before they saw me. I crouched down to get a better look under the tree limbs and found myself looking a big buck in the eye at fifty feet. He too had his head down to peek under the limbs. It took him about three seonds to hit the panic button, and I heard him shredding brush for half a mile. I am sure he had already seen my legs, but he didn't sense danger until he saw my face. I often rub my face with mud or dirt when I'm hunting in close cover.

My broad-brimmed hat helps because it shades the upper part of my head and makes it harder for deer to see my face. I go one step further. I carry a loop of narrow elastic that I wrap about four times around the crown of my cowboy hat. In hunting where there are a lot of hunters, I use the elastic to hold a piece of bright fluorescent plastic around my hat. When I get away from the crowd on a hunt, I remove the plastic and jam four or five small evergreen branches into the loops to break up the outline of my head. The Game Department doesn't like deer hunters in camouflage, but it's legal. Nevertheless, I never dispense with my fluorescent plastic unless I'm alone in a very isolated area.

I wear crepe-soled hunting boots, an old pair of wool army

pants, and a lightweight wool jack shirt. Soft, fuzzy clothing doesn't make scraping noises as you move through heavy brush.

I was carrying an old Model 95 in 7 mm. It's short and light, and it's equipped with a peep sight. I had removed the small aperture insert so that I had the large, fast rear ring for shooting at close range in poor light. Trying to use a scope in heavy brush is one of man's most confounding experiences.

The wet underbrush made movement quieter, but I also wanted to use thermal currents. From about noon on, the mountainsides get well heated under the September sun. The rising air would help me during my approach toward that willow patch from above. If the air stayed wet and heavy, however, my scent would spread all over the willow grove as soon as I got near it. I was really tickled when the air started to clear at about nine o'clock.

I had to walk a long distance to my preplanned starting place, and the brush was still wet when I started down the mountain. In ten minutes I was soaked to the skin as I crawled, rolled, and wriggled through that lodgepole jungle. I hit the little stream on the nose and disguised my hat with lodgepole twigs, swabbed my face with mud, and started Stage 2.

If a wise old buck was bedded down in or near the willows, I knew that I would need every trick in my book and a lot of luck besides to get a shot. That splashing, gurgling brook would help. It would drown out the slight noises I knew I would make. Those big ears mule deer have aren't for decoration.

Their hearing is fantastic. Sit quietly in the forest for half an hour; it comes alive. Squirrels chase each other, woodpeckers hammer, small birds tap, scratch, and flutter. Yet a wise old buck seems to have the uncanny ability to lie right in the middle of this subdued clamor and single out sounds made by a cautious hunter 100 yards away.

It took me an hour and fifteen minutes to cover the 300 yards to the willow clump. The sun came out bright and warm, and I was reasonably confident that my scent wouldn't give me away. I was completely drenched when I finally sat down in that deer bed I described at the start of this narrative. I felt as though I had swum to the spot. I slipped off my boots, wrung the water out of my socks, and hung them up to dry. Then I broke out a somewhat sodden lunch and ate it slowly. If deer were bedded nearby, they might have heard me moving. I had to give them plenty of time to forget the suspicious sounds. I was hoping that the deer would move or make some sound so that I would know where to look. That's just what happened when I heard that explosive cough.

I put on my boots and started edging down through the willows in what I could call a kneeling hitchalong. I got into the rifleman's kneeling position and inched forward on one knee. You must move slowly on a stalk, but if you try to crawl, you are at a disadvantage. Your hind end bounces up and down like a crippled camel's back, and you must drag your rifle. If a deer spots you, you can't get off a quick shot. You would also have to be superhuman to crawl along for any great length of time. I can hitchalong in a kneeling position and have many advantages. I hold my rifle in a natural shooting position and I can therefore shoot almost instantly. My eyes are high enough to see over low shrubs, but they are low enough to see under most trees. When a deer spots me, I can sit back, duck my head, and stay still as long as I need to, but I can stand up to shoot quick as a flash.

I moved a few inches at a time, and then sat on my heel to inspect every opening in the underbrush. I had to spot that deer before it spotted me! I finally reached the middle of the flat and found I could see a little farther because of wider spacing between the willow clumps. I was about ten yards from the creek and directly opposite the end of the little ridge I described earlier. The creek had washed away the end of the ridge, making a cutbank about thirty feet high. Willows growing along the creek screened most of the lower half of the bank. I was peering intently into the brush directly below me when a slight movement across the creek caught my eye. I turned my head very slowly, and sucked in a gasp of air that should have gone clear to my toes. An oversize buck with blood-red horns and flapping, bloody tatters hanging from them around his eyes and ears was rising like a devilish apparition right out of the willows.

It was at least thirty seconds before I could collect my wits. The buck had started to work the velvet from his antlers but had only succeeded in tearing it loose from the long, high tines on each side. His antlers were large but strange. They stood almost straight up from his head. The red tips and flapping velvet made a sight seldom viewed by sober eyes. He was only fifteen yards away, and now he was climbing the cutbank, nibbling at a few dwarfed willows growing on the slope. He didn't have the slightest idea that I was there.

He was such an amazing sight that I simply sat there and watched him until he turned abruptly and walked back down the bank. When I finally tried for a shot, he was completely screened by the willows and I couldn't see well enough to sight. He was feeding farther and farther upstream, and I knew those helpful thermals would soon carry my scent to him.

He finally moved his head and neck behind a few small openings. I pulled down on the thickest part of his neck and squeezed the trigger.

The buck hit the ground with a shuddering crash and slid rear-end-first down the bank and through a small hole between two willow clumps. He landed right in the creek.

I walked to a spot right above him and watched him carefully for about two minutes. It was steep and brushy down to where he lay, so I leaned my rifle against a log and climbed down through a bunch of downed poles. He had landed with his rear hanging down over a two-foot waterfall. His front feet and head were lying out in the creek on top of the little ledge.

A few small downed lodgepoles were directly in front of him, the top one about two feet above the rocks and water. I got out my sheath knife, knelt down behind that pole, and grabbed an antler. The buck gave a low moan and jerked his head away from me. I was so sure his neck was broken that I put my knife down, reached out, and grabbed his antlers with both hands. I wanted to pull his head back so I could get at him.

That buck let go with an explosive snort, rolled his eyes, and started to get up. Then he let loose with a bawl that could have been heard for miles. I was amazed, but I slammed his head against that pole and hung on. If he got to his feet, I would be in plenty of trouble.

I was right in the middle of the only place he could go if he got up, but he couldn't get good footing in the creek. Mud and water were flying as though someone had started a giant eggbeater. He never quit bawling. Every time he tried to lunge to this feet, I gave a mighty yank to throw him off balance. If it hadn't been for his long, high antlers I would have been cut to ribbons. I gained a tremendous leverage by jamming the base of one horn against that lodgepole and hauling for all I was worth against the tips.

I could feel the blood pounding in my head, and I knew I had to do something fast or lose the battle. He was getting stronger, and I was getting weaker. In sheer desperation, I released the antler in my right hand and hooked my elbow around his nose. Then I hooked my knees under the pole and gave a heave that would have ruptured a grizzly bear. I threw him clear over on his back and jammed his antlers down behind the pole while I hauled his nose straight up. For some reason this seemed to nearly paralyze him.

Then I couldn't find my knife! I sat there like an idiot, covered with mud and soaked with water and sweat, my blood pounding in my head so wildly that everything I looked at was red and fuzzy. I stupidly hung onto a very large and very strong mule-deer buck. One phrase kept running through my mind: "Fools rush in where angels fear to tread!"

I finally twisted his head clear back over the pole until I could hold his chin still with my chest. Then I reached into my pocket and dug out a very dull pocket knife. I will spare the grisly details, but I dispatched that poor buck as quickly as the situation allowed.

When I finally regained my breath, I examined the deer closely. My bullet had gone through his neck just above the spine and had only stunned him. I've often thought just how serious it might have been. No one knew where I was, and if I had been badly hurt, I could never have gotten out of that jungle by myself.

I dragged the buck out of the creek and dressed him out after I found my sheath knife in the creek. Then I backtracked to see where the deer had come from. His tracks led me down to the creek and then right out around to the sunny side of that little finger ridge. His bed was there, and it appeared that he had lain there for some time. A few yards away was an equally large and freshly used bed with great splayed tracks leading away from it.

My buck's companion apparently had lain there until the ruckus started. Then he had leaped into the brush. I'm reasonably sure that the second buck was the one I had heard coughing. From the beds, droppings, and horned brush I found, it seemed two more old bucks were using that grove regularly.

My buck wasn't an old deer, but he was just plain big. We became a little more convinced of that fact the next day. It took all three of us most of the day to get him out to the closest point we could reach with the horses. We skinned him out and found him amazingly fat, with over an inch of tallow down his back and on his rump. The four quarters weighed out at 218 pounds later on a creamery scales. Allowing for the head and neck, the hide and lower legs, and all that tallow, which we cut away, I'm reasonably certain that the buck field-dressed in the neighborhood of 280 pounds. That's much heavier than the average in the area.

Two days later, we hunted another steep hillside where a stream ran down through willows and other leafy brush. The willow patch was too big and too open for stillhunting, so we set up a drive with me as the dog. The drive was well planned, but it turned out to be a complete flop because I got mixed up in the adjoining heavy timber and went through in the wrong place.

Art finally tired of waiting for my dog act and walked out onto the edge of a small cliff to look at the scenery. An old buster buck was bedded at the base of that cliff and went out of there fast. Bob was coming out of the timber about eighty yards away, and the buck was headed right at him. Bob had no idea Art was up on the cliff, and he held his fire, figuring to drop the buck at point-blank range.

Bob didn't take into account the fact that Art grew up in Nebraska and cut his shooting teeth on running jackrabbits. Art was using a Model 720 Remington .30/06 equipped with a Weaver 3X scope. He nailed that old buck through the neck while it was running flat out.

Bob was completely flabbergasted when the buck dropped out of his riflescope's field, skidded, and rolled to within thirty feet of him, stone dead. The buck's antlers were large, three points on one side and four on the other.

After helping Art dress out his deer, Bob climbed clear to the top and started hunting down through the timber at the edge of the brushy area. He jumped a big buck and got a fleeting shot as it tore through a small opening in the timber. He heard his bullet hit, but the buck kept going.

It was extremely difficult tracking because there were so many other fresh deer tracks, but Bob stuck it out and jumped the buck far down the mountain. His second shot knocked the buck down for good. His rifle was a Model 720 Remington .30/06 equipped with a 2½X Lyman Alaskan scope. The buck also had a fine rack with three points on one side and four on the other.

We were a jubilant bunch of deer hunters, but we had quite a time getting all that meat to camp. I figured it was worth every minute. We had found those vanishing high-country bucks, and I had pulled off a stalk I'll never forget.

NORTHWESTERN WHITETAIL TROPHY

Jack O'Connor

When I read O'Connor pieces like this one, I tend to find myself agreeing with his devoted army of fans: On actually giving the reader the sense of being in the hunt, he was the greatest of them all. The piece originally appeared in Outdoor Life.

THE NORTHERN VARIETY of the whitetail deer in its various forms is the most widely distributed big-game animal in the United States. Found from Maine to Oregon, it furnishes more sport to hunters than any other big-game animal and is responsible for the sale of more rifles and ammunition for the manufacturers and more telescope sights for the scope makers. And, because sportsmen buy licenses to hunt it, the money it brings in keeps most game departments functioning.

But until recently the Northern whitetail was to me as strange a trophy as the greater kudu, the desert bighorn, and the ibex are to most hunters. I have hunted all of these fine animals and others just as exotic, but the Northern whitetail had always eluded me.

Of all the varieties of Northern whitetails the one least known is the one found in the Northwest. The more plentiful mule deer and the elk sell the out-of-state licenses and get the publicity. In fact, many hunters do not even realize that some of the largest whitetail deer in North America and some of the best trophies come from the Northwestern states of Idaho, Washington, Montana, and Oregon, and from the Canadian province of British Columbia. These Northwestern whitetails are probably just about as heavy as the famous whitetails of Maine, and their heads compare favorably with those of whitetails shot anywhere. The Number 4 listing in the 1964 edition of *Records of North American Big Game* is a whitetail shot in Flathead County, Montana, in 1963, and I have seen handsome and very large antlers nailed to barns and garages and poorly mounted on walls of backwoods bars and country stores. Mostly these big whitetails are taken not by trophy hunters but by backwoodsmen and farmers who are after meat.

These whitetails of the Northwest are classified *Odocoileus virginianus ochrourus.*

I grew up in the country of the Northern whitetail's little Southwestern cousin in the Sonora, Arizona, or Coues whitetail. I have hunted these fine deer in Arizona, in Sonora, and in the Big Bend of Texas, and I have taken many handsome bucks of this diminutive species. Such small skill as I have at hitting running game I owe to the Arizona jackrabbit and the Arizona whitetail. I have also shot the small but quite different Texas whitetail found around San Antonio. But a good Northern whitetail was one of the few major North American trophies I did not have.

I had never laid eyes on a Northern whitetail until I moved from Arizona to Idaho more than twenty years ago, and then it took me about three years to see one. I'll never forget the first one I saw. I was hunting pheasants with a wonderful Brittany spaniel named Mike. He had been cruising through a field of rich golden wheat stubble when he went on point at the edge of a grassy swale. I thought he had pinned a cock pheasant, but when I got up to him he looked at me out of the corner of his eyes and wore the sneaky expression he assumed when he was doing something he knew he should not do.

I picked up a stone to flush whatever it was, and threw it at the spot in the grass where Mike's nose was pointed. Out burst a little whitetail doe. Most dogs are convinced that they have been born to be deer and rabbit hounds, but Mike almost fell backward in surprise.

Another time Mike hauled up on the edge of a brushy draw on solid point. I walked in, kicked the brush. A pair of cackling roosters came barreling out. I shot, dropped one of them, was about to take the other when a big whitetail buck sailed out of the brush and headed across the stubble toward a patch of woods. For the rest of the bird season, which mostly at the time ran concurrently with the deer season, I carried a couple of rifled slugs in my pants pocket so that if I jumped another whitetail I could jerk out a shot shell and slam a shell loaded with a slug into the chamber. But the news must have got around; I never saw a buck.

A farmer I knew told me he just about had a big whitetail buck tied up for me. He said that the old boy lived in a canyon that bounded one of his wheatfields. That buck fed on wheat all summer and in the fall feasted on the sweet, stunted little apples that fell in an abandoned orchard in one corner of his place.

So I spent about ten days hunting him off and on during the season. His tracks were everywhere—in the orchard, in the wheat stubble, along the deer and cattle trails among the brush and trees, and on the bank of the little trout stream that ran through the bottom of the canyon.

Keeping the wind in my favor, I still-hunted cautiously and quietly along the trails, taking a few steps, stopping, listening, watching. Once I heard something moving quietly off through thick brush, and I found his bed below a ledge in a warm spot where the sun had melted the frost off the grass. Another time I heard a crash below me and caught a glimpse of his white flag flying. I sat for hours with my back to a tree waiting for him to show up. He didn't

"I can't understand why you can't see that buck," my farmer friend said. "I seen him yesterday when I was looking for a stray cow, and Bill Jones seen him from his pickup when he was coming back from getting the mail four or five days ago. Said he wasn't a danged bit wild; stood there looking at him. He could have hit him with a slingshot."

Another year, while scouting for good pheasant areas in eastern Washington, I found a pretty little valley full of trees and brush and with a clear brook wandering through it. It lay between two grassy hillsides that ran down from rolling wheatfields. The valley was full of pheasants. The hillsides supported several coveys of Huns. Quail roosted in the trees. And the valley also contained a herd of whitetails. I saw a doe, a fawn, one small buck, and also the tracks of a big buck.

I made up my mind to be in a strategic spot in the valley as soon as it was light enough to shoot on opening day. So when the day came I parked my station wagon along the road half a mile from the valley and left my Model 21 Winchester 12 gauge and my puzzled, whining Brittany spaniel locked up. Wearing a pair of binoculars around my neck and carrying a light 7 x 57, I walked through a wheatfield toward the head of the valley. I was almost at the spot I had in mind when I heard the crash of rifle fire. A startled doe streaked by me. Running along the grassy hillside and up into the wheat stubble were the dim forms of about a dozen deer flaunting white tails. I sat down and got them in the field of the binoculars. All were does and fawns. Then something caught my attention just under the skyline about a quarter of a mile away. I put the glasses on whatever it was. It was a big buck sneaking along. When he topped out I saw heavy antlers.

About twenty shots had been fired, but now the last deer was out of sight. I could hear voices coming from the valley. It was quite light now. I walked a little farther. Then I saw four men gathered around a small and very dead buck. One was gutting him. I talked to the men a few minutes. Before long they departed in triumph, each holding a leg of the buck. I went back to my car and stowed the rifle and the binoculars. Then I let my joyful dog out and set off to see if I could have any luck on birds.

In Arizona and Sonora the Coues deer are found high. In southern Arizona they are seldom lower than the altitude where the evergreen oaks the Mexicans call encinos grow—about 4,000 to 4,500 feet. The desert variety of mule deer are out in the mesquite and cactus of the flats and the low rolling hills. Out on the flat Sonoran desert west of the railroad that runs south from Nogales, Arizona, the mule deer are on the perfectly flat sandy aboreal desert where they range among the mesquites, ironwoods, and chollas. Low hills and little ranges rise from the desert floor, and on all of them are (or used to be) whitetails. Sometimes the whitetails are in easily navigable foothills of the tall, rocky, desert-sheep mountains.

But in the Northwest, at least in areas with which I am familiar, whitetails are found lower than the mule deer, on the brushy hillsides near wheatfields, and in the wooded riverbottoms back in the elk mountains. They are bold but furtive, and they'll live all summer in a farmer's woodlot.

Some of them grow to be very large. I once knew a man who ran a meat locker in Lewiston, Idaho, my home town. He told me that the heaviest buck ever weighed at his plant was a whitetail. As I now remember he said its field-dressed weight was around 335 pounds. I have heard of Northwest whitetails in Washington as well as Idaho that were about as heavy. I have never seen a deer of any sort that I thought would dress out at anything like 300 pounds, but now and then one undoubtedly turns out to be that heavy.

I started closing in on my first Northwestern whitetail in the fall of 1969 when my wife and I drove to the ranch of our friend Dave Christensen on the Salmon River downstream from Riggins, Idaho. Dave operates an elk hunting camp on Moose Creek in the Selway Wilderness Area and lives most of the year on the beautiful Salmon River ranch. When I first knew the elk-hunting camp it was Moose Creek Lodge, a luxurious bit of civilization out in the wilderness. A hunter could go out after elk all day and return at night to a drink around a fireplace, a good meal served with silver and linen, a hot shower, and a sound sleep on an inner-spring mattress. But the area was declared a wilderness. The federal government bought the lodge and burned it down. Now in the fall Dave's dudes fly in to a U.S. Forest Service landing strip a few miles away and hunt elk from a comfortable tent camp near the spot where the lodge used to be. I have shot five, six, and seven-point elk out of Moose Creek. Dave and his father, Ken, took the money they got from the sale of the lodge and their land and put it into the Salmon River ranch.

As my wife and I drove in that November day in '69 we saw a whitetail buck in a field a mile or so from the ranchhouse. Not long afterward we saw some whitetail does and fawns.

"You must have a lot of whitetails around here." I said when Dave came out to meet us.

"Plenty," he told me. "The whitetails are mostly low down along the creek and in the brushy draws that run into it. The mule deer are higher."

The season around Dave's place was closed then, so my wife and I had to forgo the whitetails. We hunted mule deer in another management area about twenty miles away. But we made a promise to take a run at the whitetails.

] 442 [

Along in August, 1971, Dave called me.

"You haven't forgotten our date to hunt whitetails?" he asked. "No? Well, the season opens October second. Drive down the afternoon of the first and we'll have at them."

My son Bradford, who is outdoor editor of the Seattle Times and who is a long-time pal of Dave Christensen and his wife Ann, flew from Seattle and joined us on the drive to the ranch.

One of Dave's successful elk hunters from Moose Creek had come down to the Salmon to try for a deer, and three other hunters who were on their way into Moose Creek for elk were camped down the creek a mile or so from the ranchhouse.

The strategy was simple. Eleanor, Bradford, and I, accompanied by a guide named Stan Rock, would climb about 1,000 feet above the ranch near the head of a canyon that carried a little stream that ran into Dave's creek. After giving us time to get into position, Dave would walk up the canyon on a deer-and-cattle trail that ran along the bottom. There were whitetails and mule deer in those canyons, and with luck we should get some shooting.

It was dark and chilly when we started out, and the sun was not up when we arrived near the head of the canyon. We were high on a grassy ridge. The canyon dropped sharply below us, and the bottom was a tangle of trees and brush. The far side of the canyon was steep, mostly rocks with a few low bushes and sparse grass.

Eleanor had gone on to the brink of the canyon. Bradford was twenty feet or so to her left. I was in the process of filling up the magazine of an old pet .270 I had used from northern British Columbia to Botswana and Iran. It is a pre-1964 Winchester Model 70 Featherweight stocked in plain but hard French walnut by Al Biesen of Spokane and fitted with a Leupold 4X scope on the now-obsolete Tilden mount. It has the original Winchester barrel with the original Featherweight contour. The only thing Biesen did to the metal was to put the release lever for the hinged floorplate in the forward portion of the trigger guard and checker the bolt knob.

This is a terrific rifle. I bought it from the Erb Hardware Company of Lewiston, Idaho. Year after year it holds its point of impact. Carry it in a saddle scabbard, jounce it around in a hunting car on safari, ship it a few thousand miles by air, let it get rained on for hours in a Scotch deer forest, shoot it at sea-level or at 10,000 feet, in the crackling heat of the Kalahari Desert or under the glaciers in the sub-arctic Stone sheep country of British Columbia and it always lays them in the same place. It is also one of those rare light sporters that will group into a minute of angle—if I am using good bullets and do my part.

I had just finished slipping the last cartridge into the chamber and putting on the safety when Eleanor, who has eyes like an eagle, said, "Deer . . . two deer. The lower one's a buck."

Two deer were scooting up the far side of the canyon about 225 to 250 yards away. Both were waving big white tails. I could dimly make out antlers on the lower one.

The sight of those flaunting flags across the canyon made me shed twenty-five years. Once again I was back in my favorite Calelo Hills along the Mexican border of southern Arizona, where I had some small reputation among the local yeomanry of being a fair hand on running whitetails. I sat down quickly, put the intersection of the crosswires just to the left of the buck's head for lead, and squeezed the trigger. So far as results went, it was almost as spectacular as a brain shot on an elephant. The buck fell, started rolling, and tumbled clear out of sight into the brush and timber at the bottom of the canyon.

"Some shot!" said Bradford.

The buck was a big one. It had long brow points and four points on each beam—a four-pointer Western count, a 10-pointer Eastern count. He had been hit rather far back through the lungs. Down there in that narrow canyon it was so dark that the exposure meter said half a second at f/2 would be about right. Since we had no flash, good pictures under those conditions were impossible. Later someone would come out from the ranch with a packhorse and get him.

By now the sun was up and bright, and while the others went along around the head of the canyon where I had shot the buck and to the head of the next, I stayed behind admiring the scenery. Far below, the little creek glistened through the timber along its banks and as it twisted through the meadows. The meadows were still green, the pines dark and somber, but along the creek cotton-woods and willows were shimmering gold, and patches of crimson sumac blazed on the hillsides.

Up in the high country at the head of the creek, ridges where the Salmon River elk ran, an early storm had frosted the dark timber with snow. Far below against the green of a pasture I saw some moving black dots. The glasses showed me I was looking at a feeding flock of wild turkeys.

Clear down in the bottom of the main canyon I heard a fusillade of shots. I made a mental note that they were probably fired by the Californians who were going to try for deer before they went in to Moose Creek for elk. I hurried to catch up with the other O'Connors, who were out of sight over a ridge.

I heard two quick shots. Then I saw Eleanor and Bradford, rifles in hand, sitting on the hillside looking down.

"Get anything?" I asked.

"Buck mule deer, sort of a collaboration," Bradford said.

"The heck it was," Eleanor said. "I shot behind it and then Bradford dumped it. See? It's lying down there on the road."

The glasses showed me a young buck mule deer close to 300 yards away.

When we returned to the ranchhouse we found that the Californians had taken three whitetail bucks out of a herd of eight. The largest had heavy antlers with three points and a brow tine on each side. Though their measurements were the same as those of my deer, this buck appeared to be heavier. The next buck was somewhat smaller than mine and the third was a youngster.

Soon a packhorse came in with my buck. He and the largest buck shot by the Californians measured 18 inches in a straight line from the top of the shoulder to the bottom of the brisket. Both were fat and in fine condition. We had no means of weighing them, but I have weighed many mule deer with the same measurements and they have weighed between 185 and 195 pounds. These two whitetail bucks in weight and measurements were every bit as large as typical large four-point mule-deer bucks.

I was interested in comparing them to Arizona whitetails I had

] 445 [

hunted so long. They were just about twice as large, since an average large, mature Arizona whitetail will weigh from 90 to 110 pounds. As is true among Arizona whitetails, the top of the tails of the old bucks is a grizzled brown whereas the upper portion of the tails of the young bucks is bright orange. Oddly, the tails of these big bucks looked to be the same size as those of their Southern cousins.

The beams of my buck's antlers were a bit over 23 inches long, and the inside spread was 18 inches. I have never shot an Arizona whitetail with beams anything like that long, but I did take one once that had a 20-inch spread. Though the Northwestern whitetail is twice as heavy as his Southwestern cousin, his antlers aren't twice as large.

The coats of the big deer were a bit more brownish and less grayish than those of Coues as I remember them. The young Northwest whitetails have much more grizzled coats than those worn by young Arizona whitetails. These are quite blueish.

Sad to say, my underprivileged wife didn't get another shot. We drove up a precarious ranch road late that afternoon and early next morning when the deer should have been moving. We hunted the heads of several canyons and glassed the points and ridges, but all we saw were does and fawns. The bucks had got the message.

THAT CHRISTMAS BUCK

Archibald Rutledge

In his second appearance in The Deer Book, *Mr. Rutledge takes us back down South for a very special time and a very special hunt. The piece originally appeared in* Plantation Game Trails *(Doubleday).*

WHEN I AM AT LARGE in deer country there is no need for friends to try to lure me off the fascinating following of the white-tail by promises of more abundant sport with smaller game. Quail and ducks and woodcock and the like do not look very good when a man feels that an old buck with majestic antlers is waiting in the woods for some one to talk business to him. I admit that the game of deer-hunting is sometimes tedious and the shooting of the occasional variety; yet my experience has been that the great chance does come to the faithful, and that to make good on it is to drink one of Life's rarest juleps, the memory of whose flavor is a delight for years.

It may be that this love of deer-hunting was not only born in me—the men of my family always having been sportsmen—but was made ingrowing by a curious happening that occurred when I was not a year old. One day I was left alone in a large room in the plantation house where first I saw the light of day. Lying thus in my crib, what should come roaming in but a pet buck that we had. My mother, in the greatest dismay, found him bending over me, while, if we may believe the account, I had hold of the old boy's horns and was crowing with delight. I have always felt sure that the old stag (since he knew that his own hide was safe) passed me the mystic word concerning the rarest sport on earth. He put it across to me, all right; and I am going to do my best here to hand on the glad tidings. I want to tell about a deer-hunt we had one Christmas not long past.

Things on the plantation had been going badly with me. There were plenty of deer about, and a most unusual number of very large bucks; but our hunting-party had achieved nothing of a nature worth recording. We had been at the business nearly a week, and we were still eating pork instead of venison. That's humiliating; indeed, in a sense, degrading. On a certain Wednesday (we had begun to hunt on the Thursday previous) I took our Negro driver aside. It was just after we had made three unsuccessful drives, and just after some of the hunters had given me a look that, interpreted, seemed to mean that I could easily be sold to a sideshow as the only real fakir in captivity. In the lee of a great pine I addressed my partner in crime.

"Prince," I said, drawing a flask from my pocket, "as deer-hunters you and I aren't worth a Continental damn." (This term, as my readers know, is a good one, sound and true, having been the name of a coin minted before the Revolution.)

"Dat's so, sah, suttinly so," Prince admitted, his eyes glued to the flask, his tongue moistening his lips.

"Now," I went on, "we are going to drive this Little Horseshoe. Tell me where to stand so that we can quit this fooling."

The flask sobered Prince marvelously, as I knew it would. To a Negro there is no tragedy like seeing a drink without getting it; and the possibility of such a disaster made the good-natured Prince grave.

"Dis summer," he said, "I done see where an able buck done used to navigate regular by the little gum-tree pond. Dat must be he social walk," he further explained; "and dat may be he regular run. You stop there, Cap'n, and if he is home, you will bline he eye."

That sounded good to me. Therefore, the calamity that Prince dreaded might happen did not occur; for we parted in high spirits, and with high spirits in at least one of us. But there must have been a prohibition jinx prowling about, for what happened shortly thereafter appeared like the work of an evil fate.

As I was posting the three standers, the man who had already missed four deer took a fancy to the stand by the gum-tree pond. I tried politely to suggest that there was a far better place, for him, but he remained obdurate. I therefore let him stay at what Prince had described as the critical place. And it was not five minutes later that Prince's far-resounding shout told me that a stag was afoot. Feeling sure that the buck would run for the pond, I stood up on a log, and from that elevation I watched him do it. He was a bright, cherry-red buck, and his horns would have made an armchair for ex-President Taft. He ran as if he had it in his crafty mind to run over the stander by the pond and trample him. He, poor fellow, missed the buck with both barrels. His roaring ten-gauge gun made enough noise to have stunned the buck; but the red-coated monarch serenely continued his march. All this happened near sundown, and it was the end of a perfectly doleful day. Prince laid the blame for the bull on me when he said, in mild rebuke:

"How, Cap'n, make you didn't put a true gunnerman to the critical place?"

The next day—the seventh straight that we had been hunt-

ing—it was an uncle of mine who got the shot. And this thing happened not a quarter of a mile from where the other business had come off. My uncle and I were hardly a hundred yards apart in the open, level, sunshiny pine-woods. Before us was a wide thicket of bays about five feet high. The whole stretch covered about ten acres. Prince was riding through it, whistling on the hounds. Suddenly I heard a great bound in the bays. Prince's voice rang out—but a second shout was stifled by him designedly. A splendid buck had been roused. He made just about three bounds and then stopped. He knew very well that he was cornered, and he was evidently wondering how to cut the corners. The deer was broadside to my uncle and only about fifty yards off. I saw him carefully level his gun. At the shot the buck, tall antlers and all, collapsed under the bay-bushes.

Then the lucky hunter, though he is a good woodsman, did a wrong thing. Leaning his gun against a pine, he began to run forward toward his quarry dragging out his hunting-knife as he ran. When he was within ten yards of the buck the thing happened. The stunned stag (tall horns and all) leaped clear of danger, and away he went rocking through the pine-lands. Believing that the wound might be a fatal one we followed the buck a long way. Finally, meeting a Negro woodsman who declared that the buck had passed him "running like the wind," we abandoned the chase. A buckshot had probably struck the animal on the spine, at the base of the skull, or on a horn. Perhaps the buck simply dodged under cover at the shot; I have known a deer so to sink into tall broom-sedge.

That night our hunting-party broke up. Only Prince and I were left on the plantation. Before we parted that evening I said:

"You and I are going out to-morrow. And we'll take one hound. We'll walk it."

The next day, to our astonishment, we found a light snow on the ground—a rare phenomenon in the Carolina woods. We knew that it would hardly last for the day; but it might help us for a while.

In the first thicket that we walked through a buck fawn came my way. He was a handsome little fellow, dark in color and chunky in build. It is possible to distinguish the sex of a fawn even when the lithe creature is on the fly, for the doe invariably has a longer and sharper head and gives evidences of a slenderer, more delicate build. I told the bucklet that I would revisit him when he had something manly on his head.

Prince and I next circled Fawn Pond, a peculiar pond fringed by bays. Our hound seemed to think that somebody was at home here. And we did see tracks in the snow that entered the thicket; however, on the farther side we discerned them departing. But they looked so big and so fresh that we decided to follow them. Though the snow was melting fast I thought the tracks looked as if two bucks had made them. Deer in our part of Carolina are so unused to snow that its presence makes them very uncomfortable, and they do much wandering about in daylight when it is on the ground.

Distant from Fawn Pond a quarter of a mile through the open woods was Black Tongue Branch, a splendid thicket, so named because once there had been found on its borders a great buck that had died of that plague of the deer family—the black tongue, or anthrax. Deciding to stay on the windward side (for a roused deer loves to run up the wind) I sent Prince down to the borders of the branch, telling him to cross it, when together the two of us would flank it out. The tracks of the deer seemed to lead toward Black Tongue, but we lost them before we came to the place itself. While I waited for Prince and the leashed hound to cross the end of the narrow thicket, I sat on a pine-log and wondered whether our luck that day was to change. Suddenly, from the green edges of the bay I was aware of Prince beckoning violently for me to come to him. I sprang up. But we were too slow. From a deep head of bays and myrtles, not twenty steps from where the Negro was standing, out there rocked into the open woods as splendid a buck as it has ever been my fortune to see. He had no sooner cleared the bushes than he was followed by his companion, a creature fit to be his mate. They were two old comrades of many a danger. Their haunches looked as broad as the tops of hogsheads. Their flags were spectacular. They were just about two hundred yards from me, and, of course, out of gunshot. Had I been with Prince at that moment (as I had been up to that fatal time) I should have had a grand chance—a chance such as does not come even to a hardened hunter more than a few times in a hundred years or so. The bucks held a steady course straight away from me; and their pace was a rocking, rhythmic, leisurely one. Speechless I watched them go for half a mile; my heart was pretty nearly broken. As for Prince—when I came up to him, I found him quite miserable and unnerved.

"Oh, Cap'n, if you had only been where I been jest now!" was all he could say.

From the direction that the two great animals had taken the Negro and I thought that we knew just where they were going.

] 451 [

Telling him to hold the hound for about fifteen minutes I took a long circle in the woods, passing several fine thickets where the old boys might well have paused, and came at last to a famous stand on a lonely road. Soon I heard the lone hound open on the track, and you can imagine with what eagerness I awaited the coming of what was before him. The dog came straight for me; but when he broke through the last screen of bays he was alone. The deer had gone on. It was not hard to find where they had crossed the road some ten yards from where I had been standing. Judging from the easy way in which they were running they were not in the least worried. And from that crossing onward they had a perfect right not to be concerned; for beyond the old road lay a wild region of swamp and morass into which the hunter can with no wisdom or profit go.

I did not stop the dog, deciding that by mere chance the bucks might, if run right, dodge back and forth, and so give me the opportunity for which I was looking. The old hound did his best; and the wary antlered creatures, never pushed hard, did some cunning dodging before him. Once again I saw them far away through the woodlands, but a glimpse of their distant beauty was all the comfort afforded me. After a two-hour chase the hound gave them up. Prince and I had to confess that we had been outwitted, and in a crestfallen mood we quitted the hunt for the day.

The next day was my last one at home; and every hunter is surely familiar with the feeling of the man who, up until the last day, has not brought his coveted game to bag. I felt that we should have luck on our side or else be beaten. I told Prince as much, and he promised to be on hand at daybreak.

Before dawn I was awakened by the sound of a steady winter rain softly roaring on the shingle roof of the old plantation house. It was discouraging, to be sure; but I did not forget that the rain ushered in my last day. By the time I was dressed Prince had come up. He was wet and cold. He reported that the wind was blowing from the northeast. Conditions were anything but promising. However, we had hot coffee, corncakes deftly turned by Prince, and a cheering smoke. After such reinforcement, weather can be hanged. By the time that the dim day had broadened we ventured forth into the stormy pine-lands, where the towering trees were rocking continuously, and where the rain seemed able to search us out, however we tried to keep to the leeward of every sheltering object. The two dogs that we had compelled to come with us were wet and discouraged. Their heads, I knew, were full of happy visions of the warm plantation fireside that they had been forced to leave. Besides, it was by no means their last day, and their spirit was utterly lacking in all the elements of enthusiasm.

After about four barren drives, when Prince and I were soaked quite through and were beginning to shiver despite precautions that we took (in Southern deer-hunting a "precaution" means only one thing), I said:

"Now, Hunterman, this next drive is our last. We'll try the Little Corner, and hope for the best."

Two miles through the rainy woods I plodded to take up my stand. All the while I took to do this Prince waited, his back against a pine, and with the sharp, cold rain searching him out. The wind made the great pines rock and sigh. Even if the dogs should break into full chorus I thought I could never hear them coming. At last I reached my stand. A lonely place it was, four miles from home, and in a region of virgin forest. So much of the wide woodland through which I had come looked so identical that it hardly seemed reasonable to believe that a deer, jumped two miles back in a thicket, would run to this particular place. But men who know deer nature know what a deer will do. I backed up against an old sweet-gum tree, waiting in that solitary, almost savage place. I thought that in about a half-hour my good driver, bedraggled and weary, would come into sight, and that then we two disillusioned ones would go home sloshing through the drizzle.

But wonderful things happen to men in the big woods. Their apparently insane faith is not infrequently rewarded. Hardly had I settled myself against the big tree for shelter when, far off, in a momentary lulling of the grieving wind, I heard the voice of a hound. One of the dogs had a deep bass note, and it was this that I heard. Sweet music it was to my ears, you may well believe!

From where I was standing I could see a good half-mile toward
the thickets whence had come the hound's mellow, rain-softened
note. And now, as I looked searchingly in that direction, I saw the
deer, heading my way, and coming at a wild and breakneck pace.
At that distance I took the fugitive for a doe. It was running des-
perately, with head low, and lithe, powerful legs eating up the
pine-land spaces. If it held its course it would pass fifty yards to
the left of me. I turned and ran crouchingly until I thought I had
reached a place directly in the oncoming deer's pathway. I was in
a slight hollow; and the easy rise of ground in front of me hid for a
few moments the approaching racer. I fully expected a big doe to
bound over the rise and to run slightly on my left. I had a slight
suspicion that the deer might be an old buck, with small, poor
horns that on my first and distant view had not been visible. But
it was not so.

Hardly had I reached my new stand when over the gentle swell
of ground, grown in low broomgrass, there came a mighty rack of
horns forty yards away to my right. Then the whole buck came
full into view. There were a good many fallen logs just there, and
these he was maneuvering with a certainty and a grace and a
strength that it was a sight to behold. But I was there for more
than just "for to admire."

As he was clearing a high obstruction I gave him the right barrel. I distinctly saw two buckshot strike him high up—too high.
He never winced or broke his stride. Throwing the gun for his
shoulder, I fired. This brought him down—but by no means
headlong, though, as I afterwards ascertained that twelve buckshot from the choke barrel had gone home. The buck seemed
crouching on the ground, his grand crowned head held high, and
never in wild nature have I seen a more anciently crafty expression than that on his face. I think he had not seen me before I
shot; and even now he turned his head warily from side to side, his
mighty horns rocking with the motion. He was looking for his
enemy. I have had a good many experiences with the behavior of
wounded bucks; therefore I reloaded my gun and with some cir-
cumspection approached the fallen monarch. But my caution was
needless. The old chieftain's last race was over. By the time I

reached him that proud head was lowered and the fight was done.

Mingled were my feelings as I stood looking down on that perfect specimen of the deer family. He was in his full prime. Though somewhat lean and rangy because this was toward the close of the mating season, his condition was splendid. The hair on his neck and about the back of his haunches was thick and long and dark. His hoofs were very large, but as yet unbroken. His antlers were, considering all points of excellence, very fine. They bore ten points.

My short reverie was interrupted by the clamorous arrival of the two hounds. These I caught and tied up. Looking back toward the drive I saw Prince coming, running full speed. The dogs had not had much on him in the race. When he came up and saw what had happened, wide was the happy smile that broke like dawn on his dusky face.

"Did you see him in the drive, Prince?" I asked. "He surely is a beauty."

"See him?" the Negro ejaculated in joyous excitement. "Cap'n, dat ole thing been lyin' so close that when he done jump up he throw sand in my eye! I done reach for he big tail to ketch him! But I done know," he ended, "dat somebody else been waitin' to ketch him."

I sent Prince home for a horse on which we could get the buck out of the woods. While he was gone I had a good chance to look over the prone monarch. He satisfied me. And the chief element in that satisfaction was the feeling that, after weary days, mayhap, and after adverse experiences, the great chance will come. For my part that Christmas hunt taught me that it is worth while to spend some empty days for a day brimmed with sport. And one of the lasting memories of my life is the recollection of that cold, rainy day in the Southern pine-lands—my last day for that hunting trip—and my best.

GREAT MORNING

Gene Hill

"Hilly," as all his buddies call him, is a close personal friend, but that fact doesn't make me check my praise for his work.

I once called him, in print, "the best outdoor writer since Robert Ruark." Perhaps I was wrong; perhaps he's even better.

Anyway, there's nobody I would rather read; nobody I'd rather be in the field with; and nobody I'd rather hoist a couple with after we've turned the hunt back to camp and slumped in front of the fire.

And I can't think of a better way to close this one down than by inviting him to sit with you and me while the log burns on down and we turn on toward other hunts, other memories to build.—Your obedient Servant, Lamar Underwood.

I GUESS I'VE BEEN deer hunting for something over thirty years, and I suppose I've killed my fair share of deer. I can look back on many moments when everything seemed to come alive at the fleeting footfall of a buck—his very awareness made the forest ring with silence. These times are everlasting in the memory—but even more memorable are the times when I've been really warm.

Deer hunting and subzero weather seem to go hand in hand in my part of the East. And I doubt it has ever been colder on an opening day than the year I got my very first buck.

I woke up that morning about four and crept downstairs to start the fire in the kitchen stove. About the time the fire got going good, the men began to drift in from early-morning chores. The kitchen smelled wonderful once all the men had gotten warm. The air was heavy with woodsmoke, tobacco, odors of dog and barnyard. And the not-so-secret source of most of these damp smells was the long-lost and wonderfully warm felt boots. Felt boots were a standard item in every farmer's wardrobe. If you remember, they were made in two parts. A long, thick, felt, socklike affair that came to the knee was covered by a separate heavy rubber shoe that came just above the ankle and fastened by two or three metal buckles. They were heavy as hell—but they were warm! Naturally I had a pair. I also had on a heavy woolen union suit (over a pair of regular underwear), two pair of heavy bib overalls, I forget how many shirts, and topping all this was a blanket-lined denim coat we called an "overall jacket."

My grandfather put me in the first stand, behind a giant fallen chestnut log. I was told to stay put.

"What if I shoot a deer?" I asked, positive that I would.

"Stay put," was the answer.

And stay put I did. I really didn't have too much choice. Wrapped all around me was a giant horse blanket, the kind with a raft of buckles and straps on it. Nestled between my legs was a kerosene hand lantern. I sat there like a human tent with my own personal furnace going. In those days we didn't worry too much about a deer smelling any of us. I guess because we all smelled like so many horses and cows ourselves. If I didn't smell like a horse, it wasn't the fault of the blanket and the kerosene lamp forcing the odor out for a couple of country miles. I probably would have smelled like a horse anyway—and the outfit was plenty of insurance. The real point of all this is the absolute fact that I was deliciously warm. I was more than warm—I was downright cozy. By the time the sun had risen completely over the horizon I had, of course, eaten all my lunch.

Grandpa came by about ten o'clock and asked me how I was. I was just fine and told him so, adding that I was getting a little hungry. He gave me a couple of sandwiches and a handful of cookies that must have weighed a quarter of a pound apiece, and told me again to stay put. I don't think I could have gotten out of that rig if I'd wanted to, but I promised him, and off he went again.

Under the blanket I held my most cherished possession—an old 1897 Winchester pump gun. It wasn't really mine. Pop had borrowed it for me to use. The thirty-inch full-choke barrel stuck up out of the blanket like a chimney, and I kept swiveling it around as best I could without disturbing the oven arrangement. I can tell you, I was mighty eager to use it.

Along about noon I was about half asleep from so much food and the warmth from the old lantern when a sharp crack of a broken twig brought my eyes open. Against the snow, about a quarter-mile off through the woods, I could see the four legs of a deer cautiously working its way down toward my stand. Buck or doe, I couldn't be sure because of the hazel and birch thickets between us. As slowly as I could I eased the old '97 up out of the blanket and across the chestnut log and began following the legs of that deer closer toward me through the woods.

About fifty yards directly in front of me was a tiny brook with a clearing or two on the other side, along the bank. With absolute certainty, the deer—whatever it was—was heading down toward one of those clearings. I eased the hammer back on the Winchester with a very shaky thumb; buck fever was coming on a little faster than the deer. But if I had seen this sight once in my dreams and my imagination, I'd seen it a thousand times.

I couldn't take my eyes off those four legs . . . three or four more steps, and he'd be in the clearing by the brook. And suddenly there he was! A buck—a big curving Y. Somehow as the barrel swung back and forth over the clearing I managed to shoot. Just one shot. I don't believe I could have pumped that gun if my life depended on it. At the shot the buck twitched, stepped carefully back from the brook and just as cautiously as he had come down began to walk away as I helplessly watched him. I really never thought of the second shell (I was only allowed to have two buck-

shot). With a feeling of abject shame, I saw him disappear into the woods. I had missed him. How would I ever tell Grandpa and Pop?

Well, I sat there feeling lower than a cricket's knee. If I hadn't been eleven, I might have cried. Sooner or later, I knew, the hard part had to come—in the form of my father, and it wasn't fifteen minutes until he showed up. He was kind of smiling, as I remember it.

"You shoot?" he asked.

I nodded.

"Where's the dead deer?"

I said there wasn't any dead deer; that he had just walked away.

"Which way did he walk?"

"Around behind that big beech tree was the last I saw," I told him, fearful that I'd be dealt with pretty harshly for wasting a shell.

"Well, you'd better come along and show me." Pop said, and uncovered me, blew out the lantern and started off toward the beech tree. He made me unload the gun, and I felt pretty small as I shucked out the empty shell that had sat in the chamber, forgotten. I put the other shell in my pocket and trudged along behind him.

I should have suspected something when he quickened his pace as we passed the spot where I had last seen the buck, but deep in misery and head down I just tried to walk in his tracks and keep up. I almost fell over the deer.

"This is him, isn't it?" he said, standing by a fallen fork horn, about fifty yards beyond the big beech.

"Yep," I said, trying to indicate by my tone of voice that I wasn't the most surprised person in the world.

"Well, boy, you'd better drag him down by the brook so's we can clean him out."

I guess I could have dragged a bull moose right then, and drag I did, right into the flowing water where we cleaned and washed him out.

By the time the other men had gathered, and I told how I had shot my first deer, the carcass had frozen solid. Grandpa had come along and gathered up my blanket and lantern and asked me if I'd been warm enough. I said I had, but that I was getting mighty cold again.

"Here, boy," he said, handing me a two-foot loop of rope, "warmest thing in the world."

"How's that going to keep me warm?" I asked.

"Simple," he said, "just wrap one end around the deer's neck and the other around your hand and start walking toward the wagon."

Well, I miss the old felt boots, and I still think the blanket—provided it smells like a dapple-gray—and the lantern are pretty comforting. But to really keep a deer hunter warm, there's nothing like a two-foot rope around a man's hand, with a sleek December buck on the other end.